A Practitioner's Guide to Individual Conduct and Accountability in Financial Services Firms

A Practitioner's Guide to Individual Conduct and Accountability in Financial Services Firms

SWEET & MAXWELL

THOMSON REUTERS

First Edition   2016

Published in 2016 by Thomson Reuters (Professional) UK Limited trading as Sweet & Maxwell, Friars House, 160 Blackfriars Road, London, SE1 8EZ (Registered in England & Wales, Company No.1679046. Registered Office and address for service: 2nd floor, 1 Mark Square, Leonard Street, London, EC2A 4EG).

For further information on our products and services, visit *www.sweetandmaxwell.co.uk*

Typeset by Letterpart Limited, Caterham on the Hill, Surrey, CR3 5XL.

Printed and bound in Great Britain by CPI Group (UK) Ltd, Croydon, CR0 4YY

No natural forests were destroyed to make this product: only farmed timber was used and re-planted.

A CIP catalogue record of this book is available from the British Library.

ISBN: 978-0-414-05073-0

Preface

In July 2007 the world began facing the most serious and disruptive financial crisis since 1929. Significant global economic damage occurred forcing Governments and Central Banks to take a variety of measures to try and improve the economic situation and reduce systemic danger. In the UK following the failure of the Northern Rock Bank in September 2007, the UK financial regulatory authorities took a long hard look at themselves.

New legislation in the form of the Financial Services Act 2012 was passed which established a new UK regulatory framework for the financial services industry. In parallel with the passage of that legislation was the publication of the Report of the Independent Commission on Banking headed by Sir John Vickers. Vickers looked at solutions to the 'too big to fail' banking conundrum, as well as at issues connected with competition in banking. However, a wider course of action was chartered by the Government following Vickers due to revelations concerning serious irregularities by certain banking organisations in connection with LIBOR and related indexes. The Government established a Parliamentary Commission on Banking Standards that would look at banking in its broadest economic, regulatory, cultural and social context and make recommendations.

The Parliamentary Commission concluded that a stronger framework for holding individuals to account than that offered by the FCA's Approved Persons' Regime was needed so that senior individuals could not hide behind ignorance nor collective decision making. The Government introduced changes to the, as then, Financial Services (Banking Reform)

Bill which would implement a new individual accountability framework for banks, building societies and credit unions.

The new regime, however, is not confined to banks with aspects of it being extended to insurers. However, further extension of the regime to all UK financial services firms is now on the cards with HM Treasury consulting on an extended regime coming into operation during 2018.

Creating the new regulatory rules and guidance for the new individual accountability regime in banks and insurers has not been an easy task for the UK regulators nor are they completely straightforward to understand. This practical guide has been created to help all in banks, PRA regulated investment firms and insurers and their advisors, to navigate the new regime with confidence. The overarching policy intention behind the requirements is a laudable one; that of raising standards of conduct across financial services to the benefit of firms, consumers and ultimately the UK as a whole. Banks and insurers (and subsequently all UK financial services firms) need to embrace these aims, and work to demonstrate that they operate with a culture that puts the consumer or client at the heart of their business, as evidenced through the behaviour and approach of their staff.

The new regime for banks and PRA-regulated investment firms became operational on 7 March 2016 (also the effective date for insurers). However, providing a full set of finalised rules and guidance before this date has proved difficult. There have been some notable late policy u-turns most notably being the Government's dropping of the 'reverse burden of proof' in favour of a statutory duty of responsibility. At the time of going to press papers from the regulators on the statutory duty of responsibility were outstanding as were final FCA and PRA rules on statutory references.

Another notable point at the time of going to press was the FCA's announcement that it was jettisoning its planned review into culture in UK banks. It is suggested that this should not be viewed as a watering down of the FCA's focus on culture and individual behaviour. In response to a freedom of information request asking for details of the rationale behind the decision to drop the thematic work, the FCA made clear that it did not mark an end to scrutiny of culture, and explained how the new accountability regime would support cultural change. They said:

> "The cultures in financial institutions only exist as a result of the collective actions of individual employees, so driving cultural change is really about influencing individuals to act in certain ways. Professional integrity, accountability and appropriate remuneration are therefore key foundations for this cultural change.
>
> The new regime will ensure that individuals, their employers and regulators know who is responsible for what, and when things go wrong the right people will be held to account. A map showing individuals' and firms' responsibilities will cover the Senior Managers with overall responsibility in a firm, ensuring that the regulators can focus on the individuals whom firms genuinely see as accountable."

This book aims to help firms execute their regulatory responsibility, and to meet stakeholder expectations, around the behaviour and conduct of their staff. The manuscript for this book was generally completed on 12 February 2016 and, unless otherwise stated, is based on the regulatory papers available at that time.

Biographies

Jane Walshe

is a barrister and fellow of the Chartered Institute of Securities and Investment. She has experience working for the regulator as well as for regulated firms. Jane is currently a consultant in the Financial Services team at Simmons & Simmons. She has also been working with Moody's Analytics on the development of their Compliance Curriculum and is the co-founder of Enforcd, a regulatory intelligence service.

Peter Snowdon

is a partner in the financial services group of Norton Rose Fulbright LLP. He is a highly regarded practitioner on UK and European financial services regulatory matters. He specialises in financial services regulatory law having originally joined the firm from General Counsel's Division of the FSA. Peter covers a wide range of topics but has a particular focus on banking regulation, governance and senior management, conduct of business rules, consumer credit, and regulatory advice in connection with the purchase and sale of regulated businesses. Peter sits on the regulatory and legal Committee of the Association of Foreign Banks. Peter is also the author of the Money laundering chapter of Financial Services Law (Oxford University Press) and the Conflicts and Confidential Information Chapter of the Practitioner's Guide to the Regulation of Investment Banking.

Simon Lovegrove

is head of financial services knowledge—global at Norton Rose Fulbright LLP. He is a specialist in both knowledge management and financial services and markets regulation. He has a degree in law and a master's degree in business law. Before joining Norton Rose Fulbright LLP in January 2006, Simon worked for several years in the funds and financial services team of another city practice. In addition to creating various financial services knowledge products Simon has helped design and implement regulatory training programs both internally and externally to clients and also for a regulator. Since 2007 Simon has had a fortnightly regulatory column in the Financial Times' Financial Adviser Magazine. Recently, Simon has helped edit *A Practitioners Guide to MiFID II.*

Alan Bainbridge

is a corporate lawyer based in London. He focuses on strategic M&A and corporate advisory and has a particular focus on financial institutions. Alan regularly advises on bank specific legislation and is co-author of the Banking Reform Act chapter of Thomson Reuters' Compliance Officer publication, which provides an in-depth analysis of key areas of the Act, including PLAC requirements, bail-in, electrification of the ring-fence and corporate governance for ring-fenced banks. Alan has also written articles on the Act for other publications including the *Journal of International Banking and Financial Law* and the *Proprietary Trading Global Comparison.* Alan is also a member of the BBA's working group on ring-fencing.

Jo Chattle

is a senior knowledge lawyer, having previously worked as a transactional Corporate lawyer for ten years. Jo's particular focus is on corporate governance, directors' duties, annual reporting, shareholder meetings and general corporate advisory work. Jo edits a number of regular publications and organises client training to help clients keep up to date with legal and regulatory developments in these areas. She also produces annual AGM guides for Official List and AIM companies as well as client briefings and articles on topical issues and developments.

Cynthia Cheng

is a corporate lawyer based in London. She focuses on mergers and acquisitions, joint ventures and corporate advisory work and has a particular focus on financial institutions and banking regulation.

Paul Griffin

is Head of the Norton Rose Fulbright Employment Team in London. He specialises in all areas of employment law in both a domestic and international setting. Paul is a highly rated practitioner in both Chambers and Legal 500, the UK's leading legal directories, which describe him as "highly reactive to fast moving situations". Paul is a member of the Employment Lawyers Association, the International Employment Lawyers Association, the Association of Cross Border HR Experts and the Senior City HR Committee. In addition, Paul also sits on the prestigious City of London Law Society Employment Law Committee.

Amanda Sanders

is a Senior Knowledge Lawyer in the Norton Rose Fulbright Employment and Labour team in London where she is involved in all areas of employment law. As a knowledge lawyer she provides legal training for both lawyers and clients, assists lawyers with queries and research and drafts and maintains employment precedents. She has written articles and contributed to a number of texts on various aspects of employment law. Having practiced at another city law firm, Amanda joined the firm in 1995, moving to employment knowledge in 2000.

Catrina Smith

is a partner in the Norton Rose Fulbright Employment and Labour team in London. She focuses on all aspects of employment law, including corporate transactions, discrimination issues and the full spectrum of contentious and non-contentious work. She also advises on corporate governance, remuneration issues and executive appointments and terminations. Much of her work has an international angle. She has particular experience in handling highly sensitive and confidential matters affecting employers. Catrina is a member of the Employment Lawyers Association. She has participated in a number of ELA sub-committees responding to government consultations.

Elisabeth Bremner

is a Partner in the Norton Rose Fulbright LLP financial services regulation and investigations team. She has represented clients in matters involving both UK and overseas regulators and has significant experience in investigations and enforcement actions relating to insider dealing, market abuse, mis-marking, widespread mis-selling and complaints mishandling. She has spent time in-house at a major bank where she managed the global retail investigations team, and has acted as a Skilled Person for the FCA on a significant appointment.

Katie Stephen

is a partner in the financial services group of Norton Rose Fulbright, representing clients in a wide range of contentious regulatory matters including FCA and PRA investigations and disciplinary proceedings relating to issues such as market abuse, mis-selling and systems and controls. She also advises on the conduct of internal investigations and related regulatory issues. She has acted for financial institutions, corporates and high profile individuals. Her experience also includes advising the regulator and she has twice been seconded to the FCA, acting as a legal adviser to the Regulatory Decisions Committee. She is co-author of the Financial Services Decisions Digest published by Lexis Nexis.

Laura Hodgson

is a professional support lawyer with over ten years' experience specialising in insurance and reinsurance law. Laura has
written widely on insurance law, particularly looking at how
developing regulation will impact the UK insurance market.
Laura regularly advises insurance clients on the impact of both
UK and EU regulatory law. Laura has written numerous
articles on the impact of regulation on insurers and reinsurers
and has contributed to a number of leading practitioner and
academic texts on insurance law. Laura holds a post-graduate
certificate in insurance law from University College London.
She also holds a masters' degree in Theology from the
University of Durham.

Contents

1 Setting the scene

Peter Snowdon
Partner
Norton Rose Fulbright

Simon Lovegrove
Head of Financial Services Knowledge—Global
Norton Rose Fulbright

2   Directors' Duties under UK Company Law

Alan Bainbridge
Partner

Johanna Chattle
Senior Knowledge
Lawyer
Norton Rose Fulbright

3   The Regulatory Environment

Jane Walshe
Barrister

4   The Senior Managers and Certified Persons Regime: Conduct Rules for Those Working in Banks and PRA Regulated Proprietary Trading Firms

Jane Walshe
Barrister

5   Non-executive directors

Peter Snowdon
Partner
Norton Rose Fulbright

Simon Lovegrove
Head of Financial Services Knowledge—Global
Norton Rose Fulbright

6 UK branches of foreign banks

Peter Snowdon
Partner
Norton Rose Fulbright

Simon Lovegrove
Head of Financial Services Knowledge—Global
Norton Rose Fulbright

7   Ring-fencing

Alan Bainbridge
Partner
Norton Rose Fulbright

Cynthia Cheng
Associate
Norton Rose Fulbright

8   Employment Issues

Catrina Smith
Partner
Norton Rose Fulbright

Amanda Sanders
Senior Knowledge Lawyer
Norton Rose Fulbright

9 Whistleblowing

Paul Griffin
Partner
Norton Rose Fulbright

Amanda Sanders
Senior Knowledge Lawyer
Norton Rose Fulbright

10 Individual Accountability and Enforcement

Katie Stephen
Partner
Norton Rose Fulbright

Elisabeth Bremner
Partner
Norton Rose Fulbright

Chapter 1

Setting the scene

Peter Snowdon
Partner
Norton Rose Fulbright

Simon Lovegrove
Head of Financial Services Knowledge—Global
Norton Rose Fulbright

1.1   Introduction

Regulation within the UK banking sector has undergone unprecedented change with the introduction of a new regime which has at its core the intention of making individuals more accountable to the UK regulators, the Prudential Regulation Authority (PRA) and Financial Conduct Authority (FCA).

The catalyst for the new regime was the failure of Northern Rock bank in September 2007 and the financial crisis that followed in 2008 and 2009. Alongside the decision to introduce proposals which would reform the supervisory regime of the UK financial services sector (which led to the Financial Services Authority (FSA) being replaced by the PRA and FCA), the Chancellor announced in his June 2010 Mansion House speech a review of the UK banking industry:

> "the new Government is establishing an independent commission on the banking industry. It will look at the structure of banking in the UK, the state of competition in the industry and how customers and taxpayers can be sure of the best deal. The Commission will come to a view. And the Government will decide on the right course of action. Sir John Vickers has agreed to chair the Commission."

In September 2010 the Independent Commission on Banking (otherwise known as the Vickers' Commission) published an issues paper which outlined its preliminary thinking. In April 2011, it published an interim report which primarily focussed on proposals surrounding the ring-fencing of UK retail banks. In September 2011, the Vickers' Commission published its final report entitled "Changing banking for good". The final report included a summary of the responses to its interim report. In general, there was complete disagreement between parties on virtually all of the issues.

1.2 Changing banking for good

The Vickers' Commission final report makes interesting reading noting that the:

> "UK banking sector's ability both to perform its crucial role in support of the real economy and to maintain international pre-eminence has been eroded by a profound loss of trust born of profound lapses in banking standards."

To restore trust in the UK banking industry the final report of the Vickers' Commission set out a number of proposals which were centred around five themes:

- making individual responsibility in banking a reality, especially at the most senior levels;
- reforming governance within banks to reinforce each bank's responsibility for its own safety and soundness and for the maintenance of standards;
- creating better functioning and more diverse banking markets in order to empower consumers and provide greater discipline on banks to raise standards;
- reinforcing the responsibilities of regulators in the exercise of judgment in deploying their current and proposed new powers; and
- specifying the responsibilities of the Government and of future Governments and Parliaments.

However, the Vickers' Commission noted that "no single change, however dramatic, will address the problems of banking standards." It added that "reform across several fronts is badly needed, and in ways that will endure when memories of recent crises and scandals fade."

The Vickers' Commission noted that the principal purpose and effect of the post-financial crisis measures being implemented was to make it less likely that banks would fail. However, it stated that whilst this was all well and good the measures could not guarantee that there would never be a major bank failure and that it was important to make clear that should such a failure occur, the bank should be allowed to fail. Whilst both the payments system and insured depositors would be protected, there would be no bail out for the bank. Until the implicit taxpayer guarantee was explicitly removed, "the task of improving banking standards and culture [would] be immeasurably harder."

1.3 Parliamentary Commission on Banking Standards

1.3.1 *The catalyst for the creation of the Commission*

The birth of the Parliamentary Commission on Banking Standards (the Parliamentary Commission) can be traced back to the revelations about a high-street bank's (and as it would emerge later, a number of other institutions) attempted manipulation of the London Interbank Offered Rate (LIBOR) interest rate benchmark which became public in June 2012.

As noted by some in the market it was, perhaps, surprising that the attempted manipulation of a fairly obscure city index (to large sections of the public at least), with virtually incalculable effect though likely to be very small and which would have generated random winners and losers, should cause such public uproar. However, such was the case as in the public eye banks and their employees had crossed the line. Arguably, the public feeling was that they no longer appeared to be greedy and/or incompetent but had been exposed as "cheats" and "fixers" in ways that most people could intuitively understand as being wrong. As the Parliamentary Commission later put it, it was by this event that "public confidence in bankers and banking [was] shaken to its roots."

The response was political intervention.

On 2 July 2012, the Chancellor announced a series of steps in response to the LIBOR scandal. One was the setting up of the Wheatley Committee to advise on legal reforms that could be incorporated into the Financial Services Bill which was then currently proceeding through Parliament.

However, there were further calls to do more from both within Parliament and outside it. On 5 July 2012, an opposition debate on professional standards in the UK banking industry called for an independent inquiry. A Government amendment, which was passed, called for a joint committee to examine the issues.

On 16 July 2012, the House of Commons approved the following resolution:

> "That a Committee of this House be established, to be called the Parliamentary Commission on Banking Standards, to consider and report on-
>
> a)   professional standards and culture of the UK banking sector, taking account of regulatory and competition investigations into the LIBOR rate-setting process;
> b)   lessons to be learned about corporate governance, transparency and conflicts of interest, and their implications for regulation and for Government policy;
>
> and to make recommendations for legislative and other action."

The Parliamentary Commission published its first report on 21 December 2012 and much of the report focussed on the bank structural separation issue as proposed by the Vickers' Commission. On 19 June 2013, the Parliamentary Commission published its final report which was also entitled, "Changing banking for good". The report is arguably one of the most important papers published and given the public backlash was particularly damning towards the banking industry. In particular it stated:

> "Too many bankers, especially at the most senior levels, have operated in an environment with insufficient personal responsibility. Top bankers dodged accountability for failings on their watch by claiming ignorance or hiding behind collective decision-making. They then faced little realistic prospect of financial penalties or more serious sanctions commensurate with the severity of the failures with which they were associated. Individual's incentives have not been consistent with high collective standards, often the opposite."

As regards the Approved Persons' Regime that the PRA and FCA inherited from the FSA, the Parliamentary Commission was equally critical stating that the regime had "created a largely illusory impression of regulatory control over individuals, while meaningful responsibilities were not in practice attributed to anyone." The Parliamentary Commission added that as a result, "there was little realistic prospect of effective enforcement action, even in many of the most flagrant cases of failure." In light of these comments the Parliamentary Commission proposed a new framework for individuals with the following elements:

- a Senior Persons' Regime, which would ensure that the key responsibilities within banks are assigned to specific individuals, who are made fully and unambiguously aware of those responsibilities and made to understand that they will be held to account for how they carry them out;

- a licensing regime alongside the Senior Persons' Regime, to apply to other bank staff whose actions or behaviour could seriously harm the bank, its reputation or its customers; and
- the replacement of the Statements of Principles and the associated codes of practice, which were felt to be incomplete and unclear in their application, with a single set of Banking Standards Rules to be drawn up by the regulators. These rules would apply to both Senior Persons and licensed bank staff and a breach would constitute grounds for enforcement action by the regulators.

The Parliamentary Commission also called for a more effective sanctions regime against individuals arguing that it was essential for restoring trust in banking. It stated that the current system was failing as enforcement action against Approved Persons at senior levels was unusual despite multiple banking failures. It was also noted that the regulator had "rarely been able to penetrate an accountability firewall of collective responsibility in forms that prevents actions against individuals. The patchy scope of the Approved Persons' Regime, which has left people, including many involved in the Libor scandal, beyond effective enforcement."

To remedy the perceived sanctions problem the Parliamentary Commission recommended a new approach including that:

- all key responsibilities within a bank had to be assigned to a specific, senior individual. Even when responsibilities were delegated, or subject to collective decision making, that responsibility would remain with the designated individual;
- the attribution of individual responsibility would, for the first time, provide for the full use of the range of civil powers that regulators already had to sanction individuals. These included fines, restrictions on responsibilities and a ban from the industry;

- the scope of the new licensing regime would ensure that all those who could do serious harm were subject to the full range of civil enforcement powers;
- in a case of failure leading to successful enforcement action against a firm, there would be a requirement on relevant Senior Persons to demonstrate that they took all reasonable steps to prevent or mitigate the effect of a specified failing. Those unable to do so would face possible individual enforcement action, switching the burden of proof away from the regulators; and
- a criminal offence would be established applying to Senior Persons carrying out their professional responsibilities in a reckless manner, which might carry a prison sentence. Following a conviction, the remuneration received by an individual during the period of reckless behaviour would be recoverable through separate civil proceedings.

The Parliamentary Commission also called for reforms to corporate governance. In particular it stated that, "potemkin villages were created in firms, giving the appearance of effective control and oversight without the reality. Non-executive directors lacked the capacity or incentives to challenge the executives. Sometimes those executives with the greatest insight into risks being added to balance sheets were cut off from decision-makers at board level or lacked the necessary status to speak up. Poor governance and controls are illustrated by the rarity of whistle-blowing, either within or beyond the firm, even where, such as in the case of LIBOR manipulation, prolonged and blatant misconduct has been evident." In light of these weaknesses the Parliamentary Commission suggested a package of recommendations to remedy these defects, including those around resourcing for non-executives.

1.3.2 *Serious regulatory failure*

The UK regulator at the time of the financial crisis, the FSA, also came under criticism from the Parliamentary Commission which stated that "serious regulatory failure" contributed to the failings in banking standards. So called "tick box" compliance also received attention from the Parliamentary Commission which stated that the "misjudgement of the risks in the pre-crisis period was reinforced by a regulatory approach focused on detailed rules and process which all but guaranteed that the big risks would be missed."

The Parliamentary Commission noted that a successful relationship between banks and regulators would depend on regular, frank discussions between senior regulators and senior bank executives, including at the chief executive level. Such a relationship could also be fostered by periodic attendance by the most senior regulators at the meetings of bank boards. The Parliamentary Commission recommended that the FCA and the PRA kept a summary record of all meetings and substantive conversations held with those at senior executive level in banks, the most senior representative of the FCA or PRA present in each case. The Parliamentary Commission expected those records to be made available on request retrospectively to Parliament, usually to the Treasury Committee.

1.3.3 *Failure of board oversight*

Just as the FSA was criticised for its "tick-box" approach to regulatory oversight, the Parliamentary Commission also noted that there was a failure of bank board oversight and capacity to intervene where necessary to address inappropriate risks.

Boards have a responsibility for ensuring that institutions are well governed, for putting in place appropriate structures to support this, and for setting the values of the institution. There was a broad consensus that stronger corporate governance in financial institutions might have helped mitigate some aspects of the financial crisis. However, it was also recognised that this was not just about process, but about how management exercise judgment, the practicalities of risk management, and the behaviour of the wider organisation.

1.3.4 *Remuneration*

It is worth noting that an important aspect of the individual accountability regime concerns remuneration. In its final report the Parliamentary Commission noted that remuneration had "incentivised misconduct and excessive risk-taking" and had reinforced a culture where "poor standards were often considered normal."

The Parliamentary Commission proposed a radical re-shaping of remuneration for Senior Persons and licensed bank staff, driven by a new Remuneration Code, so that incentives and disincentives would more closely reflect the longer run balance between business risks and rewards. The main features of the redesign were:

- much more remuneration to be deferred and, in many cases, for much longer periods of up to 10 years;
- more of that deferred remuneration to be in forms which favour the long-term performance and soundness of the firm, such as bail-in bonds;
- the avoidance of reliance on narrow measures of bank profitability in calculating remuneration, with particular scepticism reserved for return on equity;
- individual claims on outstanding deferred remuneration to be subject to cancellation in the light of individual or wider misconduct or a downturn in the performance of the bank or a business area; and
- powers to enable deferred remuneration to Senior Persons and licensed individuals, as well as any unvested pension rights and entitlements associated with loss of office, to be cancelled in any case in which a bank requires direct taxpayer support.

A detailed discussion of "what happened next" as regards remuneration is outside the scope of this book. However, it is worth noting albeit briefly that in June 2015, the PRA and FCA jointly published Policy Statement PRA 12/15 FCA 15/16: Strengthening the alignment of risk and reward: new remuneration rules (PS15/16). In PS15/16:

- deferral (the period during which variable remuneration is withheld following the end of the accrual period) was extended to seven years for senior managers, five years for risk managers with senior, managerial or supervisory roles at PRA regulated firms and three to five years for all other staff whose actions could have a material impact on a firm (material risk takers);
- the FCA introduced claw-back rules (where staff members return part or all of variable remuneration that has already been paid) for periods of seven years from award of variable remuneration for all material risk takers, which were already applied by the PRA. Both the PRA and FCA claw-back rules were strengthened by a requirement for a possible three additional years for senior managers at the end of the seven year period (10 years in total) where the firm or regulatory authorities had commenced inquiries into potential material failures;
- variable pay for non-executive directors was prohibited;
- it was made explicit that no variable pay including all discretionary payments should be made to the management of the firm in receipt of taxpayer support; and
- the PRA requirements on dual regulated firms to apply more effective risk adjustment to variable remuneration were strengthened.

The new rules on deferral and claw-back came come into force for performance years starting on or after 1 January 2016. The new rules on non-executive directors, updated guidance on ex-post risk adjustment, and all other new or amended rules came into force from 1 July 2015.

1.4 The Government's response to the Parliamentary Commission

1.4.1 Overall conclusions

The Government agreed with the overall conclusions of the Parliamentary Commission and accepted all of its principal recommendations. Specifically, the Government announced on

8 July 2013 that it would implement the following major recommendations of the final report:

- Strengthening individual accountability by:
  — introducing a new Senior Persons' Regime governing the behaviour of senior bank staff;
  — introducing new banking standard rules to promote higher standards for all bank staff;
  — introducing a new criminal offence for reckless misconduct for senior bankers;
  — reversing the burden of proof so that bank bosses were held accountable for breaches within their areas of responsibility (but see para.1.8.1); and
  — working with the regulators to implement the Parliamentary Commission's proposals on pay. This would allow bonuses to be deferred for up to 10 years and enable 100 per cent clawback of bonuses where banks receive state aid (see para.1.3.4 for discussion on the subsequent PRA and FCA Policy Statement).
- Asking the regulators to implement the Parliamentary Commission's key recommendations on corporate governance to ensure that firms have the correct systems in place to identify risks and maintain standards on ethics and culture.
- Supporting competition in the banking sector by:
  — providing the PRA with a secondary competition objective to strengthen its role in ensuring banking markets are effective and deliver good outcomes for consumers; and
  — asking the new payments regulator, once established, to urgently examine account portability and payments system ownership.

1.4.2 Strengthening individual accountability

The Government agreed with the Parliamentary Commission's analysis that accountability and incentives for bankers needed to be strengthened in a way that supported the long term sustainability of banks. The Government noted that it had already taken action through the Financial Services Act 2012 to strengthen individual accountability by setting up a "focused conduct of business regulator" in the FCA, with a "judgement-led regulatory approach to deal with conduct issues in both an effective and proportionate manner." The Government also argued that it had taken swift action to address the attempted manipulation of LIBOR by establishing the Wheatley Review and implementing its key recommendations of bringing benchmark activities within the scope of regulation under the Financial Services and Markets Act 2000 (FSMA) and creating a new, distinct criminal offence for making false or misleading submissions in connection with the determination of bench-marks.

As regards sanctions for the directors of failed banks the Government referred to its July 2012 consultation paper, "Sanctions for the directors of failed banks", which considered proposals for:

- legislation to amend FSMA in order to put in place a "rebuttable presumption" that a director of a failed bank is not suitable to be approved by the regulator as someone who could hold a position as a senior executive in a bank; and
- the introduction of criminal sanctions for serious miscon-duct in the management of a bank including a strict liability offence, offences for negligence, incompetence or recklessness.

The Government accepted the Parliamentary Commission's conclusion that the Approved Persons' Regime had failed and that it would work with the FCA and PRA to create a new framework for regulating individual standards of conduct in banking based on strengthening accountability. Importantly, the Government also noted that the weaknesses in the Approved Persons' Regime affected not just the banking sector but also other parts of the financial services industry. However, to avoid delay to banking reforms, it stated that the Parliamen-tary Commission's recommendations should initially be put in place for banking only.

The Government confirmed that it would introduce the new Senior Persons' Regime which would replace the Approved Persons' Regime. It would also take forward certain key recommendations made by the Parliamentary Commission including:

- "reversing the burden of proof" to ensure that Senior Persons could be held to account for contraventions of regulatory requirements in their areas of responsibility unless they could demonstrate that they took all reasonable steps to prevent the contravention occurring or continuing in the part of the business for which they have responsibility[1];
- extending the time limit for commencing disciplinary action against Senior Persons; and
- giving regulators the power to make approvals of Senior Persons subject to conditions or time limits.

However, the Government decided not to take forward the introduction of the "rebuttable presumption" that was considered in the July 2012 consultation. The Government accepted the Parliamentary Commission's view that the "rebuttable presumption" could be a blunt instrument and agreed that the measure to reverse the burden of proof would be more effective in ensuring accountability by Senior Persons for contraventions in their area of responsibility.

The Government also accepted the Parliamentary Commission's recommendation to introduce criminal sanctions for reckless misconduct in the management of a bank. As recommended by the Parliamentary Commission this offence would be limited to only those who were Senior Persons. The Government also agreed to take forward the licensing regime which was recommended by the Parliamentary Commission which would replace the Statements of Principle (and codes of practice) for Approved Persons with banking standards rules, which would apply to employees who were not subject to prior regulatory approval. The Government also supported the

---

[1] However, see para.1.8.1.

creation of a professional body funded by the banking industry which would promote higher professional standards.

1.4.3 Corporate governance

In its response the Government confirmed that it was committed to strengthening the UK corporate governance framework. In relation to the role of shareholders the Government referred to the Financial Reporting Council's Stewardship Code (the Stewardship Code) which sets out best practice for institutional investors on the monitoring of, and engaging with, the companies in which they invest. The Government noted that the Stewardship Code had been strengthened by mandatory disclosure requirements for asset managers in the FCA rules. These new rules required UK authorised firms managing assets on behalf of professional clients to disclose the nature of their commitment to the Stewardship Code or to explain why it is not appropriate to their business model. The Government also mentioned the Kay Review which further examined the role of investors in equity markets in shaping long-term performance and governance of UK public companies. As for board level governance the Government referred to the Capital Requirements Directive IV (CRD IV) which introduced a specific, legally binding provision for improving risk oversight and mandating clearer lines of responsibility and accountability from the board level down. The Government stated that it would be updating its regulatory mechanisms in line with this and that it would ask the PRA to consult on "clear principles and standards" to ensure effective oversight by the management body as part of this process.

The Government also said that it would ask the regulators to consider introducing rules to ensure effective monitoring and oversight of the skills of the management board to ensure that they were able to understand the business of the institution, its main risk exposures, and the implications of the business and the risk strategy. This would include committing the management body to approve and periodically review the strategies and policies for taking up, managing, monitoring and mitigating the risks the institution is or might be exposed to, including

14

conflicts of interest. Where changes were needed to the role of the chairman, the Government would ask the PRA and FCA to consider taking these forward as part of the development of the Senior Persons' Regime.

1.4.4 Whistle-blowing

The Parliamentary Commission made a number of recommendations to ensure more effective arrangements for whistle-blowing and better support for whistleblowers. In response the Government noted that the Department for Business, Innovation and Skills (BIS) was publishing a call for evidence so that it could better understand the operation of the whistle-blowing framework and to facilitate the consideration of further changes to employment law. The Government considered that the evidence that would be gathered would allow further consideration to be given to the recommendations relating to the content of codes of conduct, support for regulators to maintain effective oversight of whistle-blowing issues and the role the regulators could play with the whistle-blowing information they had, including the interaction with Employment Tribunals. The Government would consider the Parliamentary Commission's recommendations in the context of this wider review.

1.5 The Financial Services (Banking Reform) Act 2014

The Financial Services (Banking Reform) Bill (the Bill) was a carry-over Bill from the 2012-13 Parliamentary session. It was first introduced into the House of Commons on 4 February 2013, received its second reading on 11 March 2013 and was considered in a Public Bill Committee between 19 March and 16 April 2013 across 16 sittings. It was re-introduced into the House of Commons on 9 May 2013 and was considered on report on 8 and 9 July 2013, receiving its third reading on 9 July. The Bill was introduced into the House of Lords on 10 July 2013 and had its second reading on 24 July 2013.

When the Bill was first introduced it set out the new structure for banking with the central element being the ring-fencing of banks' retail deposit and lending activities from their investment banking operations. However, when the Bill was considered on report on 8 and 9 July 2013 further amendments were moved.

On day one of report, the Financial Secretary to the Treasury, Greg Clark MP, stated that the Government would move amendments in the Lords in response to the final report of the Parliamentary Commission. He stated:

> "I can confirm today that the Government will strengthen individual accountability by introducing a tough new regime that is recommended to cover the behaviour of senior bank staff; introducing new rules to promote higher standards for all bank staff; introducing a criminal offence for reckless misconduct by senior bankers – those found guilty could face a jail sentence; working with the regulators to implement the [Parliamentary] Commission's proposals on pay, specifically to allow bonuses to be deferred for up to 10 years and enable 100 per cent clawback of bonuses where banks receive state aid; and reversing the burden of proof so that senior staff are held accountable for regulatory breaches within their areas of responsibility. We will also ask regulators to implement the [Parliamentary] Commission's key recommendations on corporate governance. That will ensure that firms have to have the correct systems in place to identify risks and maintain standards on ethics and culture."

An in-depth discussion of the subsequent Parliamentary debates is outside the scope of this book as the original Bill practically trebled in size following the introduction of the Government's amendments to implement the recommendations of the Parliamentary Commission. Importantly, during this time the Senior Persons' Regime was re-termed as the Senior Managers' Regime. The licensing regime became known as the Certification Regime. The Bill received Royal Assent on

18 December 2013 and subsequently became the Financial Services (Banking Reform) Act 2014 (the Act).

The Act's specific provisions concerning individual account-ability will be discussed in detail later on in this book. But in terms of the Act's general layout Pt 4 sets out the provisions concerning the conduct of persons working in the financial services sector. These provisions mainly make amendments to FSMA. The table below sets out the relevant sections in Pt 4 of the Act and their impact on FSMA[2].

Section number	Topic	Amendment to FSMA
18	Functions for which approval is required	Section 59 FSMA amended
19	Senior management functions	New section 59ZA FSMA inserted
20	Statements of responsibilities	Section 60 FSMA amended
21	Vetting by relevant authorised persons of candidates for approval	New section 60A FSMA inserted
22	Determination of applications for approval	Section 61 FSMA amended
23	Power to give approval subject to conditions or for limited period	Sections 61 and 62 FSMA amended
24	Changes in responsibilities of senior managers	New section 62A FSMA inserted
25	Duty to notify regulator of grounds for withdrawal of approval	Section 63 FSMA amended
26	Variation of approval	New sections 63ZA, 63ZB and 63ZC FSMA inserted

---

[2] See also paras 1.8.1 and 1.8.2. The Bank of England and Financial Services Bill is intended to make certain changes to the legislation including removing the reverse burden of proof and amending ss.64A and 64B FSMA.

Section number	Topic	Amendment to FSMA
27	Statement of policy	New sections 63ZD and 63ZE FSMA inserted
28	Extension of limitation periods for imposing sanctions	Sections 63A and 66 FSMA amended
29	Certification of employees by relevant authorised persons	New sections 63E and 63F FSMA inserted
30	Rules of conduct	New sections 64A and 64B FSMA inserted
31	Requirement to notify regulator of disciplinary action	New section 64C FSMA inserted
32	Definition of "misconduct"	Section 66 FSMA amended and new sections 66A and 66B FSMA inserted
33	Meaning of "relevant authorised person"	New section 71A FSMA inserted
34	Recording information about senior managers	Section 347 FSMA amended
35	Consequential amendments relating to Part 4	n/a
36	Offence relating to a decision causing a financial institution to fail	No amendment to FSMA – standalone provision
37	Section 36: interpretation	No amendment to FSMA – standalone provision
38	Institution of proceedings	No amendment to FSMA – standalone provision

1.6　The Banking Standards Board

1.6.1　Introduction

On 19 September 2013, Sir Richard Lambert (former Editor of the Financial Times and Director General of the CBI) was asked by the chairmen of Barclays, HSBC, Lloyds Banking Group, Royal Bank of Scotland, Santander, Standard Chartered and Nationwide to come up with proposals for a new organisation to raise standards in UK banking. This built on the earlier mentioned recommendation of the Parliamentary Commission for a professional body to be established by the industry. Sir Richard was asked, among other things, to examine the need for standardised skills and qualifications to be embedded across the UK banking sector, and to consider how best to raise overall standards of behaviour.

In February 2014, the Banking Standards Review published a consultation paper which asked for comments on Sir Richard's initial thoughts. The consultation paper generated nearly 200 responses that shaped the recommendations that were published in a report on 19 May 2014.

1.6.2　Recommendations

The May 2014 report stated that it was "deliberately aspirational in nature" and that it was informed by the belief that "the banking sector must voluntarily raise its game if it is to win back trust, and that there is a vital public interest in it doing so."

The report set out the proposed objectives of a new Banking Standards Review Council (BSRC), and the broad principles by which it would operate. The objectives of the BSRC would be to contribute to a continuous improvement in the behaviour and competence of all banks and building societies doing business in the UK. It would also act as an independent champion of better banking standards in the UK, and be driven

19

by the interests of customers and of the wider group of stakeholders with a concern for the well-being of the British banking system.

The report proposed that the BSRC would do this by:

- requiring participating banks and building societies to commit to a programme of continuous improvement under the headings of culture, competence and customer outcomes, and to report back on their performance to the public every year;
- setting standards of good practice. That would mean identifying activities where voluntary standards would serve the public interest, and working with practitioners and relevant stakeholder groups to come up with agreed procedures. Examples could include whistle-blowing protocols, the approach to retail sales incentives, banks' processes for handling small businesses in distress, or the management of high-frequency trading;
- publishing an annual report that set out where progress was being made both by the sector and by individual banks and building societies, and where more needs to be done;
- having a meeting once a year with non-executive directors or, in their absence, risk or reputation committee chairs of the larger banks and building societies to discuss the institution's progress relative to the previous year and to its peers;
- working with the industry and its stakeholders to develop a single principles-based code of practice in alignment with the high-level principles being considered by the regulators;
- identifying and encouraging good practice in learning, development and leadership, with a particular focus on behaviour and ethics;
- helping the banks meet the obligations being placed on them by new legislation, such as the certified persons regime; and

- working with the professional bodies already active in the banking industry to increase the value placed on professional qualifications.

The nine recommendations of the BSRC are set out below.

BSRC Recommendation Nos.	Comment
1	The BSRC should be established with the aim of contributing to a continuous improvement in the conduct and culture of banks and building societies doing business in the UK, and of supporting high standards in the future.
2	The governance, funding and reporting arrangements of the BSRC should underwrite its independence and credibility. It must be transparent and open in all its activities, and seek widespread support from the industry.
3	The BSRC should seek to engage with all banks, both wholesale and retail, and building societies doing business in the UK. Its approach should be aspirational, and it should aim to make the relevant question not "Why would you support such an organisation" but rather "Why wouldn't you?"
4	The BSRC should engage with banks and building societies, rather than with their individual employees.
5	The BSRC will complement the work of the regulators by focusing its efforts on identifying and championing good practice. It should aim to align its work with theirs, and avoid duplication.

BSRC Recommendation Nos.	Comment
6	Banks and building societies will work with the BRSC to raise standards of conduct over time in the ways described in the report.
7	The BSRC should work with the industry and its wider group of stakeholders to identify specific areas of banking activity where voluntary standard setting would benefit customers and advance the public interest. The standards it develops should be kept under review, to ensure that they remain relevant in changing circumstances.
8	The BSRC should work with its different stakeholders to identify and promote good training practice across a wide range of banking activities. Where possible, it should build on existing foundations.
9	The BSRC should support and not duplicate the activities of the professional bodies, and should work with them and with the banks and building societies to change perceptions of the value of their programmes.

The report noted that the BSRC should aim to publish a full report on the state of banking standards and good practice in the first half of 2015. The full report would set out its priorities for the following twelve months, and provide the starting point for its first annual report, covering the performance of the sector and of individual banks and building societies in 2016. In addition, in 2015 the BSRC would start identifying and publishing examples of good practice in the industry, and begin working on its priority areas for standard setting.[3]

---

[3] At the time of writing this chapter (December 2015), the BSRC had not published

On 1 November 2014, the chairmanship of the BSRC passed from Sir Richard Lambert to Dame Colette Bowe, the former Ofcom chair. Her appointment followed a process involving an independent selection panel chaired by the Bank of England Governor, Mark Carney which included, among others, the Archbishop of Westminster, Cardinal Vincent Nichols. One of her first jobs at the BSRC was to appoint a chief executive. Alison Cottrell, a former HM Treasury Director of Financial Services, took up the chief executive role in April 2015 when the BSRC was launched. The BSRC was subsequently renamed the Banking Standards Board (BSB).

In a City AM interview[4] with Dame Colette Bowe in December 2015 it was mentioned that the BSB's first step was to send letters to the chairmen of ten banks—HSBC, Lloyds, Santander, Barclays, RBS, Standard Chartered, Nationwide, Metrobank, Citigroup and Morgan Stanley—asking them to lay out what they were doing "in the area of culture and behaviour" and what indicators they were using to measure success. All ten chairmen reportedly replied by early October 2015. In addition the BSB had been holding focus groups with employees at each of the banks, asking workers what they thought of the culture in their workplace and whether the "tone from the top" in company mission statements were consistent throughout their organisations. All the information would be compiled into individual audit reports that the BSB would send to the directors of each of the banks. On 29 December 2015, there were press reports that the banks had received their reports from the BSB. It was also reported that the BSB would publish its own annual report in the spring of 2016.

1.6.3 The future?

Interestingly, at the end of the BSRC's May 2014 report there is a section that moves forward by five to ten years and takes an optimistic viewpoint. It notes that the shape of the UK banking

---

its full report nor examples of good industry practice. However, it was subsequently reported in the press that the BSB would publish its annual report in the spring of 2016.

[4] City AM interview with Dame Colette Bowe on 7 December 2015.

industry has changed significantly with retail banking being largely conducted online, but with physical branches still existing to support individual customers and small businesses. A number of innovative newcomers have significantly widened the banking choices available to the public. On the wholesale side, banks are carrying more equity capital than they had grown used to, and have shed their riskiest business. More bankers have professional qualifications of one kind or another. Good practice is seen everywhere as a competitive advantage, and the Government does not place mandates with banks that do not publicly commit to meeting and surpassing the accepted industry standards. The BSRC is seen as an uncontroversial fact of life, like the Takeover Panel. The BSRC's annual report is taken seriously for its views of the industry's performance in the past year, and of the sector's current standing with the public. Its standards, which the banks seek to meet and surpass, are providing seriously useful information about the norms of good practice in sensitive areas. Bankers are no longer embarrassed to say what they do for a living, and politicians have found other footballs to kick.

It will be interesting to see what those who may pick up this book in 2020 think!

1.7 Extending the scope of the individual accountability regime

1.7.1 *Insurance firms*

The decision by the PRA to amend the requirements applied to insurers along the lines of the Senior Managers' Regime for banks was taken on the basis that operating two distinct regimes would be "complex and inefficient". However, given the different business models upon which insurers operate, the regime for banks and that for insurers will not be identical. The different approach to be taken to insurers is also the consequence of distinct legislation at both a UK and European level which constrains the manner in which the PRA and FCA may regulate individuals in firms. Chapter 11 covers insurance firms in more detail.

1.7.2　FICC markets

The Fair and Effective Markets Review (FEMR) was established by the Chancellor in June 2014 to conduct an assessment of the way UK wholesale financial markets operate, help restore trust in those markets in the wake of a number of high profile abuses, and influence the international debate on trading practices. In August 2014, the FEMR made recommendations to HM Treasury to bring a further seven major UK-based fixed income, currencies and commodities (FICC) benchmarks into the scope of the UK benchmark legislation originally put in place to regulate LIBOR. These recommendations were implemented by HM Treasury on 1 April 2015. On 27 October 2014, the FEMR published a consultation document examining what needed to be done to reinforce confidence in the fairness and effectiveness of the FICC markets. A final report was published on 10 June 2015.

The FEMR final report made certain recommendations regarding improving individual accountability in the FICC markets. The reasons behind the recommendations were threefold:

- senior managers had become increasingly remote and unaccountable for the maintenance of standards in day-to-day trading operations;
- senior managers faced few apparent consequences for failing to ensure that their teams upheld appropriate standards of market practice; and
- there was an increasing shift in power within firms and their management teams towards trading staff, reflecting the factors outlined above and the high profitability of trading desks.

The FEMR noted in the final report that the introduction of the individual accountability regime would substantially improve accountability. However, it concluded that the regime could be used to help strengthen standards in the FICC markets further in three ways: first, by using the regime to give stronger "teeth" to voluntary codes; second, by extending its application more widely across FICC markets; and third, by mandating a more specific form for regulatory references to minimise the risk of what it called "rolling bad apples".

In relation to the individual accountability regime giving teeth to voluntary codes the FEMR noted that the regime would allow the FCA and PRA to hold individuals to account for conduct failings and require traders and other individuals to comply with five new conduct rules. Such individuals would be personally accountable for any breach of a conduct rule. Conduct rule 5 covering the requirement to 'observe proper standards of market conduct' would, in particular, provide teeth to non-statutory codes and guidelines including those developed by the FICC Market Standards Board.

After some consideration the FEMR also concluded that there was a case for extending elements of the individual accountability regime to a broader range of regulated FICC market participants. The elements that would be extended would include: regulatory pre-approval and Statements of Responsibility for senior managers; certification of individuals with the potential to pose "significant harm" to a firm or its customers; and enforceable conduct rules for individuals. The reasoning behind the proposed extension was that:

- previous FICC market misconduct was not limited to banks;
- non-banks were becoming increasingly important players in FICC markets;
- extending the new conduct rules to a wider range of regulated firms active in FICC markets would emphasise that traders and other individuals in those firms would be personally responsible for observing proper standards of market conduct; and

- regulatory references required under the individual accountability regime could be an effective tool to mini-mise the risk of "rolling bad apples" and should be a requirement for a wider range of regulated FICC firms.

The FEMR therefore recommended that HM Treasury consult on legislation to extend elements of the Senior Managers and Certification regimes to a wider range of regulated firms, covering at least those active in the FICC wholesale markets. It was also noted by the FEMR that the consultation would need to consider the precise scope of the extension and the exact makeup of the expanded regime. Any extension would apply to authorised firms that were active in FICC markets, but were currently outside the scope of the new regimes. That would include: MiFID investment firms, including asset managers and interdealer brokers; hedge funds under the Alternative Investment Managers Directive; and fund managers under the UCITS Directive.

However, the FEMR did not judge it proportionate to extend beyond its existing scope the presumption of responsibility. Nor did it feel that the case had been made to extend the new criminal offence relating to a decision causing a financial institution to fail to other institutions simply because they were active in the FICC markets. This was on the basis that their failure would not pose a systemic and prudential threat to public funds and the economy.

With the transition from the Approved Persons' Regime to the individual accountability regime, responsibility for the assess-ment of certified individuals passes to the firm. The FEMR noted that with the transition there was potentially a signifi-cant loss of information, materially worsening the incidence where individuals with poor conduct records would be recycled between firms: the so-called "rolling bad apples" problem. In response the FEMR concluded that there was a strong case for the FCA and the PRA to mandate a form setting out in detail the minimum information that firms should include in regulatory references. Such a form would build on the information requirements proposed under the individual accountability regime so as to promote a uniform approach. Firms would not be able to use non-disclosure agreements with departing employees to limit the disclosure of information required in the new forms. The FEMR called on the new reference template to be ready by the time the Senior Managers and Certification regimes came into force (7 March 2016).

In the FEMR final report it was stated that to ensure that momentum was maintained it would provide a full implementation update to the Chancellor and the Governor of the Bank of England by June 2016.

1.7.3 *All other financial services firms*

On 15 October 2015, HM Treasury published a policy paper "Senior Managers and Certification regime: extension to all FSMA authorised persons". In this policy paper HM Treasury stated that the Senior Managers' regime, Certification regime and conduct rules would be applied to all sectors of the financial services industry, including investment firms that are not dual regulated, asset managers, insurance and mortgage brokers and consumer credit firms. The framework would replace the Approved Persons' regime in these firms. The legislative basis for extending the regime would be set out in the Bank of England and Financial Services Bill (the Bill) that was introduced into Parliament on 14 October 2015.

The policy paper described three main effects for the firms being brought into the new regime:

- a substantial reduction in the number of appointments that would be subject to prior regulatory approval, although there might be some increase in costs per application, as firms would be required to prepare certain documentation required by the regime including statements of responsibility;
- most approved persons below senior management level would be expected to become certified persons. There would be some costs for firms in complying with certification requirements but these would not be expected

to be large since the firms would already have systems in place for monitoring and recording information about employees' performance and suitability to meet their own human resources needs; and

- firms might incur some additional costs for putting into place systems that ensure that their employees would be notified about, and receive suitable training in, the conduct rules that will apply to them.

The policy paper stated that the principle of proportionality would be "particularly important" as the individual account-ability regime was being extended to all firms operating in the financial services industry. It added that the extended regime would "appropriately" reflect the diverse business models operating in the UK market and be proportionate to the size and complexity of firms.

At the time of writing this chapter it is unclear exactly how proportionality will operate but it is perhaps worth noting that the regulators have already developed a customised regime for particular parts of the banking industry (UK branches of foreign banks which is discussed in Ch.6 and also for credit unions) and one for the insurance industry (discussed in Ch.11). In both cases the regulators consulted on their proposals and the same will occur when the regime is extended to other financial services firms.

In order to give the regulators sufficient time in which to engage stakeholders and consider key issues like proportional-ity the Government intends that the extended regime should come into operation during 2018.

1.8   Changes to the individual accountability regime

1.8.1   Reversal of the burden of proof

The HM Treasury policy paper mentioned in para.1.7 above also contained several important measures. In particular it announced the Government's intention to remove the so called "reverse burden of proof". The Act provided that enforcement action could be taken against a senior manager if:

- a firm had contravened regulatory requirements and that the breach occurred in the part of the business for which the senior manager was responsible; and
- that the senior manager was liable if he or she could not show the regulator that he or she took the steps that it was reasonable for a person in that position to take to prevent the breach occurring or continuing.

This second limb was known as the reverse burden of proof and was considered by many to be an important part of the new regime and as noted earlier in this chapter its introduction was one of the reasons why the Government decided not to take forward the rebuttable presumption.

In place of the reverse burden of proof the Government stated that it was introducing a "statutory duty of responsibility to be applied consistently to all senior managers across the financial services industry." It explained that provisions in the Act would be amended so that the regulators would only be able to take action if they could show that the senior manager failed to take the steps that it was reasonable for a person in that position to take to prevent a regulatory breach from occurring.

To ensure that the reverse burden of proof and the reporting of all conduct rule breaches (see below) would not come into force on 7 March 2016 the Government amended the appropri-ate Commencement Order — the Financial Services (Banking

Reform) Act 2013 (Commencement No.9) Order 2015. The amendments to FSMA (as amended by the Act) will be made under the Bill.

On the same day as the HM Treasury policy paper was published the FCA issued a statement by Tracey McDermott, its acting chief executive which stated:

> "Extending the Senior Managers' and Certification regime is an important step in embedding a culture of personal responsibility throughout the financial services industry.
>
> While the presumption of responsibility could have been helpful, it was never a panacea. There has been significant industry focus on this one, small element of the reforms, which risked distracting senior management within firms from implementing both the letter and spirit of the regime. The Senior Managers' and certification regime is intended to deliver better decisions to help avoid problems arising. We remain committed to holding individuals to account where they fail to meet our standards."

But why the change in policy? The impact assessment that accompanied the Bill stated the following[5]:

> "Introduction of the statutory 'duty of responsibility' is not expected to result in significant cost increases to firms. One of the unintended consequences of enforcing this obligation using a 'reverse burden of proof' has been that firms will have to incur greater costs than originally envisaged in preparing the documentation required by the regulators setting out the allocation of responsibilities in firms, and in negotiating with senior managers concerned about these documents (which may mean having to take legal advice)."

On 20 October 2015, Andrew Bailey (Chief Executive of the PRA) gave evidence on the Bill to the House of Commons

---

[5] Paragraph 114 of the impact assessment to the Bank of England and Financial Services Bill.

Treasury Committee. Selected parts of the notes of Mr Bailey's oral evidence are set out below and these give further insight.

> "Mark Garnier MP[6]: Mr Bailey, can I turn to the issue of the reversal of the reverse burden of proof, which constitutes an O-turn, really, does it not? Can I start off by asking you what discussions you have had with banks? I refer specifically to the Financial Times talking about banks having 'high-level meetings with the Bank of England about it as recently as last week'. Were you party to those meetings?
>
> Andrew Bailey: There has not been a high-level meeting. I have had quite a lot of discussions with banks about it. I have had even more discussions with lawyers about it, I have to say. I would be very happy, if you like, to give you a perspective on the question, because it is in the Bill. There is no question that if you look across the Senior Managers' and Certification regime the issue that has attracted most attention has been—whether you call it the presumption of responsibility or the reversal of the burden of proof, it is essentially the same thing. That is the one that has attracted most attention.
>
> Mark Garnier MP[7]: What I am trying to get is a sense of, if there has been lobbying that has been going on, where that lobbying has been coming from. You talk about the banks—they have met you once, I think—and lawyers. Presumably lawyers are arguing the legal case of whether or not you can have this reverse burden of proof to start off with and whether it necessarily would work in a court of law. What about the Treasury? Have you had many meetings with the Treasury?

---

[6] See Q127 of the notes of oral evidence on Bank of England Bill, Treasury Committee Tuesday 20 October 2015.

[7] See Q128 of the notes of oral evidence on Bank of England Bill, Treasury Committee Tuesday 20 October 2015.

Andrew Bailey: Yes, because in the creation of the clauses of the Bill we were consulted on those, as we would expect to be.

Mark Garnier MP[8]: You talk about this being a change of process, not one of substance. Can you expand on what you mean by that?

Andrew Bailey: I would love to, yes. The key thing for me in the Parliamentary Commission recommendations in this respect—certification is very important, but I am talking about senior managers for the moment—is that the problem with the existing Approved Persons' Regime is that the test of substance is whether you can point to something for which the individual is personally culpable. Did they sign off on loan agreements that go bad? Did they sign off on provisioning agreements that were bad? As you know because we have had many discussions in this Committee, the problem then turns out that these cases do not stand up at this point.

Andrew Bailey: The substance of the Senior Managers' regime, as I interpret it, which is very important, is that it holds the individual responsible for the outcomes in the area for which they are responsible. It shifts it from having to prove they did something or they deliberately did not do something to responsibility in their stated area, and you are not relying on finding individual actions. That is crucial. If there were any suggestion in this legislation that that was changing, I would be here telling you that I did not support it, but that does not change.

Andrew Bailey: What does change—this goes back to my point about process—is that the presumption established that in respect of one area, the duty, or the responsibility, was placed upon the individual then to prove that they had not strayed from the path of responsibility, not upon the regulator. It is that that has caused all the noise.

---

8 See Q129 of the notes of oral evidence on Bank of England Bill, Treasury Committee Tuesday 20 October 2015.

Andrew Bailey: My judgment on this is that we are at risk of two things happening here. One is we are at risk of the noise—you have probably heard this as well—quickly morphing into 'guilty until proven innocent'. There are a lot of lawyers going around talking about the human rights legislation. The second thing that has led to, in my estimation, as we have gone through this process over the summer and into the autumn, is my worry that, as you know, the test then is one of whether they took reasonable actions and there is a tick-box mentality coming back in here. I am getting a lot of people coming and saying, 'You have to tell us how you will interpret this'. 'If we have a risk appetite statement the board has adopted, that is a tick in that box. If we have a risk committee, that is a tick in that box. If the CRO is alive, that is a tick in that box.' That is not the point. The point is this is judgment, because our regime operates on judgment. If that is the way the presumption ends up, then we are going to end up in the same place we have ended up with the Approved Persons' Regime; it is not going to function.

Andrew Bailey: My view—and I give you this view—is that I support the change, because what the change does is turns the process round and puts the judgment back on to us. I would rather it does that than have us heading down this tick-box regime with legal questions around it over human rights. I do not want to come back or have one of my successors come back to you in the future and have to say, 'I am sorry; we could not use this regime in the way that was intended, because it was always a bit doubtful that we could make it stick'. It is far better we come at this point to you and say, 'I do not think this has a sufficient probability of being effective'.

Andrew Bailey: The other point I would make is that the other change the Bill introduces is that it extends the regime across the whole of the fiscal population. That is effectively the whole of the PRA and FCA population, so it is up to about 70,000 firms. It is better, in my view, that it is done consistently. We would rather have one regime than more than one. I do not think there is a strong case for introducing the presumption across the whole shooting match, so, again, that is a good reason for what is done. The key reason is that I have to say I am worried that this piece of this regime, which is crucial, might not work.

Stephen Hammond MP[9]: The key point you are telling us is that the burden of proof on those executives has not changed.

Andrew Bailey: Does not change, yes. That is key.

Stephen Hammond MP[10]: You said in response to one of Mr Garnier's questions that judgment was back on the PRA. Can I just explore what that really means? To use a CPS analogy, the CPS may make a judgment that it is right to prosecute, but that does not necessarily mean that that judgment will necessarily be upheld later on in terms of enforcement.

Andrew Bailey: No. The same is true for us.

Stephen Hammond MP[11]: Can you explain what the judgment process is going to be?

Andrew Bailey: The judgment process in the first instance would be, 'Is there a case to be brought?' The judgment on whether there is a case to be brought rests with us. You are right that then there is a process—and that process too is in the process of being changed—by which justice has to be done. There are appeal mechanisms and so the decision ultimately is not ours, but the key judgment at the start is by us: 'Is there a case to be brought?'

---

[9] Q153 of the notes of oral evidence on Bank of England Bill, Treasury Committee Tuesday 20 October 2015.
[10] Q154 of the notes of oral evidence on Bank of England Bill, Treasury Committee Tuesday 20 October 2015.
[11] Q155 of the notes of oral evidence on Bank of England Bill, Treasury Committee Tuesday 20 October 2015.

Stephen Hammond MP[12]: So, the key is you will make the case.

Andrew Bailey: Make the case, yes. Absolutely.

Stephen Hammond MP[13]: The only difference between now and previously is that now you will have to not only make that case but prove that case.

Andrew Bailey: Yes.

Stephen Hammond MP[14]: Presumably in your minds you will not be making that case unless you have enough evidence to prove that case.

Andrew Bailey: True."

1.8.2   *Conduct rules and reporting*

It is worth noting that the HM Treasury policy paper and the Bill make two further important changes. First, the PRA and FCA may make conduct rules that apply to non-executive directors (NEDs). The Government's thinking here was that there was a gap that needed to be addressed with certain EU Directives requiring Member States to be able to take action against members of an institution's management body (including NEDs). Also, it was felt that there might also be circumstances in which it would be appropriate to take enforcement action against NEDs, such as where they fail to act with honesty and integrity. Second, the provision in FSMA (as amended by the Act) that required banks to report all known or suspected breaches of conduct rules by any employees subject to those rules has been removed. The HM Treasury policy paper simply added that the "regulators can ensure that

---

[12] Q156 of the notes of oral evidence on Bank of England Bill, Treasury Committee Tuesday 20 October 2015.
[13] Q157 of the notes of oral evidence on Bank of England Bill, Treasury Committee Tuesday 20 October 2015.
[14] Q158 of the notes of oral evidence on Bank of England Bill, Treasury Committee Tuesday 20 October 2015.

they are notified of any information about employee misconduct in a more proportionate way in their rules".

1.9   The PRA and FCA papers

The PRA and FCA have published a number of papers on individual accountability in the banking sector which are discussed throughout this book. Some of the more significant papers are set out in the table below.

Date	Name	Comment
30 July 2014	Consultation Paper FCA CP14/13 PRA CP14/14: Strengthening accountability in banking: a new regulatory framework for individuals	First joint PRA and FCA consultation paper on the senior managers' regime, certification regime and new conduct rules for UK banks, building societies, credit unions and PRA designated investment firms. Consultation closed on 31 October 2014.
19 December 2014	Consultation Paper FCA CP14/31 PRA CP28/14: Strengthening accountability in banking: forms, consequential and transitional aspects	Joint PRA and FCA consultation paper setting out proposed transitional arrangements, forms and consequential changes to the PRA Handbook/ Rulebook and the FCA Handbook. The consultation closed on 27 February 2015.

Date	Name	Comment
23 February 2015	Consultation Paper FCA CP15/4 PRA CP6/15: Whistle-blowing in deposit-takers, PRA-designated investment firms and insurers	Joint FCA and PRA consultation paper setting out a package of measures to formalise firms' whistle-blowing procedures. The consultation closed on 22 May 2015.
23 February 2015	Consultation Paper FCA CP15/5 PRA CP7/15: Approach to non-executive directors in banking and Solvency II firms & Application of the presumption of responsibility to senior managers in banking firms	Joint PRA and FCA consultation paper setting out a revised approach to non-executive directors following the initial proposals contained in the July 2014 consultation paper. The deadline for comments was 27 April 2015.
16 March 2015	FCA Consultation Paper CP15/9: Strengthening accountability in banking: a new regulatory framework for individuals – Feedback on FCA CP14/13 PRA CP14/14 and consultation on additional guidance	FCA consultation paper providing feedback to the July 2014 consultation paper and setting out near final rules. FCA also consults on proposed guidance on the presumption of responsibility. The deadline for comments was 16 June 2015.

Date	Name	Comment
16 March 2015	Consultation Paper FCA 15/10 PRA 9/15: Strengthening accountability in banking: UK branches of foreign banks	Joint PRA and FCA consultation paper on the application of the new regime to UK branches of third country banks. The deadline for comments was 25 May 2015.
23 March 2015	PRA Policy Statement 3/15: Strengthening individual accountability in banking and insurance – responses to CP14/14 and CP26/14	PRA policy statement setting out the first set of final PRA rules to implement the individual accountability regime.
27 May 2015	PRA Policy Statement 10/15: The implementation of ring-fencing: legal structure, governance and the continuity of services and facilities	PRA policy statement covering the legal structure arrangements of banking groups subject to ring-fencing, governance arrangements of ring-fenced bodies and arrangements to ensure continuity of services and facilities to ring-fenced bodies.

Date	Name	Comment
7 July 2015	FCA Consultation Paper 15/22: Strengthening accountability in banking: Final rules (including feedback on CP14/31 and CP15/5) and consultation on extending the certification regime to wholesale market activities.	FCA consultation paper setting out final rules on the individual accountability regime as consulted on in CP14/13, CP14/31 and CP15/5.
7 July 2015	PRA Policy Statement 16/15: Strengthening individual accountability in banking: responses to CP14/14, CP28/14 and CP7/15	PRA policy statement providing feedback on those aspects of CP14/14 that were not dealt with in PS3/15, provides feedback on responses to CP28/14 and the proposals relating to banking in CP7/15.
13 August 2015	FCA Feedback Statement 15/3: Strengthening accountability in banking: UK branches of foreign banks	FCA feedback statement containing near final rules on the application of the individual accountability regime to UK branches of EEA and non-EEA banks.

Date	Name	Comment
13 August 2015	PRA Policy Statement 20/15: Strengthening individual accountability in banking: UK branches of non-EEA banks	PRA policy statement setting out final and near-final rules on the application of the individual accountability regime to UK branches of non-EEA banks.
6 October 2015	FCA Consultation Paper 15/31: Strengthening accountability in banking and insurance: regulatory references	FCA consultation on proposals for regulatory references. The consultation closed on 7 December 2015.
6 October 2015	PRA Consultation Paper 36/15: Strengthening accountability in banking and insurance: regulatory references	PRA consultation on proposals for regulatory references. The consultation closed on 7 December 2015.
6 October 2015	FCA Policy Statement 15/24: Whistle-blowing in deposit-takers, PRA designated investment firms and insurers	FCA policy statement setting out a package of rules on whistle-blowing designed to build-on and formalise examples of good practice already found in the financial services industry.

Date	Name	Comment
6 October 2015	PRA Policy Statement 24/15: Whistle-blowing in deposit-takers, PRA-designated investment firms and insurers	PRA policy statement setting out a package of rules on whistle-blowing.
6 October 2015	PRA Supervisory Statement 39/15: Whistle-blowing in deposit-takers, PRA-designated investment firms and insurers	PRA supervisory statement that sets out the expectations of the PRA on how firms should comply with the PRA's rules on whistle-blowing.
9 December 2015	FCA Policy Statement 15/29: Strengthening accountability in banking: Final amendments to the Decision Procedure and Penalties Manual and the Enforcement Guide	FCA policy statement setting out amendments to the Decision Procedure and Penalties Manual and the Enforcement Guide.
16 December 2015	FCA Policy Statement 15/30: Strengthening accountability in banking: UK branches of foreign banks	FCA policy statement that follows up on FCA Feedback Statement 15/3 and publishes final rules
16 December 2015	PRA Supervisory Statement 28/15: Strengthening accountability in banking	Updated PRA supervisory statement that sets out the PRA's approach to strengthening individual accountability in banking.[15]

---

[15] PRA Supervisory Statement 28/15 was further updated on 6 January 2016.

Date	Name	Comment
16 December 2015	PRA Policy Statement 29/15: Strengthening individual accountability in banking: UK branches of non-EEA banks	PRA policy statement setting out final rules on the application of the Senior Managers' and Certification regimes to UK branches of non-EEA banks and PRA-designated investment firms.
6 January 2016	FCA Consultation Paper 16/1: Consequential changes to the Senior Managers' Regime	FCA consults on how it intends to implement the consequential changes to rules and forms to reflect the removal of the requirement on firms to report known or suspected breaches of the conduct rules to the FCA. The consultation closed on 5 February 2016.

Date	Name	Comment
6 January 2016	PRA Consultation Paper 1/16: Strengthening individual accountability in banking: amendments to notification rules and forms	PRA consults on how it intends to implement the consequential changes to rules and forms to reflect the removal of the requirement on firms to report known or suspected breaches of the conduct rules to the PRA. The consultation closed on 8 February 2016.
4 February 2016	FCA Policy Statement 16/3: Strengthening accountability in banking: Feedback on CP15/22 and CP15/31; final rules on extending the certification regime to wholesale market activities and interim rules on referencing.	FCA policy statement setting out final rules on extending the certification regime to wholesale market activities and interim rules on referencing.

1.10 Speeches from the regulators

Speeches from the regulators can often be a source of useful information and whilst writing this chapter the FCA has published a number of interesting speeches on the individual accountability regime. For example the then chief executive of the FCA, Martin Wheatley, gave two speeches—"Nothing to fear from high standards" (24 March 2015) and "Accountability, from debate to reality" (14 July 2015). Selected text from Mr Wheatley's speech in July 2015:

"These changes are part of a wider agenda of cultural change within firms. This is the real prize. At their heart

44

organisations are simply collections of individuals arranged around a common goal. And the 'culture' of these organisations, the rules both spoken and unspoken, are what dictate in reality the behaviours that are acceptable and those that aren't. That is why it is so important to recognise that corporate accountability has to start with individual accountability. The two go hand in hand.

We expect Executive Committees and Boards to be engaged. To satisfy themselves that their governance structures are compatible with the spirit of the regime and the responsible management of their firm. But this doesn't necessarily mean major process overhauls. Here is a real danger of over-engineering the solution."

There is also another interesting speech from the FCA's then director of supervision, Tracey McDermott on wholesale conduct risk (24 July 2015). In particular the following is mentioned:

"One thing that the introduction of the Senior Managers' regime will do is hard-wire responsibility for good conduct into the firm's governance. It is important to stress that the [Senior Managers' regime] and individual accountability does not replace other forms of governance. It does not mean you cannot delegate. It does not mean you have to be followed around by an army of compliance professionals to tell you what to do. What it does mean is that you must run your business well.

You must take responsibility for understanding and managing the risks in your business, you cannot delegate and forget, and you cannot hide in labyrinthine structures where it is all too easy for everyone to say it was not me.

And it is increasingly evident that culture and conduct are two sides of the same coin. Good conduct – hedging that conduct risk – relies on cultural change, and can't happen without it."

The FCA's chairman, John Griffith Jones, gave a speech at the Trust in Banking Conference on 20 October 2015. On the topic of firm culture he mentioned that: "Either way, size or complexity of the overall business can be no excuse for failure to control conduct in each operation."

Mark Steward, Director of Enforcement and Market Oversight at the FCA, delivered a speech entitled "Culture and governance" on 11 November 2015. In his speech Mr Steward mentioned:

> "[B]ecause senior management cannot be watching every-thing all the time, there need to be effective systems and controls to ensure the business is operating effectively and in accordance with standards of conduct that have been designed and approved by senior management. I remember another institution that created terrific systems and controls – but they were all on paper, not implemented. In yet another case, effective systems and controls had been implemented, but they were not maintained – no upkeep, no training for new staff, no repair, review or reporting. All of these mistakes were fatal ones."

Finally, on 2 December 2015 the FCA's acting chief executive, Tracey McDermott gave a speech entitled "Personal account-ability" in which she discussed some of the practical steps firms need to take to ready themselves for implementation:

> "Most important, firms – even complex groups – need to allocate senior management responsibilities clearly. For a group, this starts with working out which of your entities are caught and how they are linked together.
>
> Next, it involves thinking about what the different entities actually do – what activities they carry out and how significant they are.
>
> From here, firms need to identify the individuals that hold Senior Management Functions; the 'Senior Managers' and the likes of the chief executive, executive directors and so

on. Responsibilities then need to be allocated to these people. Most of which are already well understood, such as responsibilities for countering financial crime and training senior staff.

Importantly, firms also need to continue thinking about any gaps – is there anything missing? Or anyone?

Senior managers who have overall responsibility for a whole area or activity in a firm need to be added to the list, regardless of job title. The regime is not designed to re-invent the way that firms organise themselves – but to reflect – and ensure clarity about how this operates in practice.

Finally, firms must then record the resulting allocation of who is doing what – in the form of short statements for each individual, and an overall map for the firm or group as a whole."

The PRA has also published some useful speeches, perhaps most notably "Governance and the role of Board" given by Andrew Bailey (PRA chief executive) on 3 November 2015.

Further speeches from the regulators are expected over the course of 2016. Speeches by senior regulators are often a source of useful "soft" guidance on regulatory policy and approach. Firms would be advised to keep an "eye out" for them.

1.11   A Practitioner's Guide to Individual Conduct and Accountability in Financial Services Firms: an overview

1.11.1   *Directors duties*

Chapter 2 examines directors' duties under UK company law. It first discusses the seven statutory general duties set out in the Companies Act 2006 and their application. It then examines the liability of directors to shareholders. The remainder of the chapter then describes the provisions of the UK Corporate Governance Code and its accompanying guidance.

1.11.2   *The regulatory environment*

Chapter 3 considers the UK regulatory environment. Before looking at the detailed rules governing the behaviour of senior managers and others in regulated firms in the UK, it is necessary to put the requirements into context. An understanding of the current regulatory environment, and in particular of the way in which the UK regulators seek to achieve their aims, is crucial to being able to effectively interpret the rules relating to individuals, found later in this book. This chapter aims to provide an overview of the key tenets of financial services regulation in the UK, from how firms achieve authorisation at the start of their regulatory journey, through to on-going supervision. The UK position is also placed in its wider European and international context.

1.11.3   *The Senior Managers' and Certified Persons regimes: Conduct rules for those working in banks and PRA regulated proprietary trading firms*

Chapter 4 provides detail on the operation of the Senior Managers' and Certification regimes as they apply to UK deposit takers and PRA-designated investment firms. It also discusses the conduct rules that have been introduced as part of the individual accountability regime.

1.11.4   *Non-executive directors*

Chapter 5 notes that non-executive directors (NEDs) have an extremely important and unique role in being able to influence their firm's behaviour. The chapter first looks back at the FSA NEDs conference and the speeches delivered by Clive Adamson and Nausicaa Delfas. It also covers the FSA guidance consultation on NEDs and, briefly, the Hector Sants speech which discussed the concept of "challenge". The chapter then reviews the individual accountability regime as it applies to NEDs working in UK deposit takers and PRA-designated investment firms.

1.11.5 UK branches of foreign banks

Chapter 6 discusses the individual accountability regime and its application to UK branches of EEA and non-EEA banks and PRA-designated investment firms. A key point made in one of the earlier joint PRA and FCA consultation papers was that both regulators are concerned with the governance of the UK branch itself rather than of the bank as a whole. The new Senior Managers' regime for overseas banks is intended to capture those individuals with responsibility for the day-to-day running of the UK branch.

1.11.6 Ring-fencing

Chapter 7 provides an overview of ring-fencing legislation, the legal structure of ring-fenced banks and their governance. The PRA has proposed that appropriate senior managers of ring-fenced banks have a prescribed responsibility "for ensuring that those aspects of the ring-fenced body's affairs for which a person is responsible for managing are in compliance with any ring-fencing obligation."

1.11.7 Employment issues

Chapter 8 discusses the challenges that the individual accountability regime poses for the Human Resource function. The new regime will impact on every aspect of the employee "life cycle" from recruitment and initial regulatory approval, through ongoing supervision and accountability to the termination of the employment relationship. The chapter is broken down into four substantive sections covering employment issues relating to the Senior Managers' regime (including drafting statements of responsibility and management responsibility maps), the Certification regime, conduct rules and corporate governance — board responsibilities.

1.11.8   Whistle-blowing

Chapter 9 covers whistle-blowing. The Senior Managers' regime includes an increased responsibility on the employee to disclose information both to the regulator and to the employer. This is likely therefore to bring about an increase in the levels of whistle-blowing in the financial services sector. On 6 October 2015, the FCA and the PRA published policy statements containing new rules on whistle-blowing. The rules are intended to build on and formalise examples of good practice already found in the financial services industry. The chapter has four distinctive sections covering: (i) protected disclosures by workers under the Public Interest Disclosure Act 1998; (ii) the new FCA and PRA rules; (iii) prescribed persons disclosure publication; and (iv) practical considerations concerning the introduction of a whistle-blowing policy.

1.11.9   Individual accountability and enforcement

Chapter 10 discusses individual accountability and enforcement. It was, perhaps, one of the most difficult chapters to write given the UK Government's decision late in 2015 to remove the "reverse burden of proof" in favour of a statutory duty of responsibility. The chapter also discusses some of the lessons that can be learnt from previous FCA enforcement cases and the FCA enforcement process itself.

1.11.10   The future regime for managers in insurance companies

Chapter 11 covers the individual accountability regime for managers in insurance companies. The chapter first discusses the Solvency II governance requirements and then the PRA senior insurance managers' regime and the FCA Approved Persons' regime for Solvency II firms. The chapter also covers FCA and PRA conduct rules and the areas of overlap between Solvency II and the senior insurance managers' regime.

1.11.11 Conduct rules for financial services firms not in scope

Many firms will not be subject to the new individual accountability regime until 2018, which is the approximate date by which the Government would like one regime to apply to individual behaviour in financial services firms. Until that time, a number of financial services firms must abide by the existing rules. This final chapter provides an overview of these rules.

Chapter 2

Directors' Duties under UK Company Law

Alan Bainbridge
Partner

Johanna Chattle
Senior Knowledge
Lawyer
Norton Rose Fulbright

2.1 Introduction

In considering the concept of directors' duties under UK company law it is important to determine first who the directors of a company are, as it is to these directors that such duties will apply.

The provisions in the Companies Act 2006 (CA 2006) concerning directors' duties apply to directors of companies registered under the CA 2006 or earlier UK companies legislation and not to those involved in running partnerships, limited partnerships or limited liability partnerships. The CA 2006 does not define the term "director" although all companies registered under the CA 2006 are required to have directors (at least one in the case of private companies and at least two in the case of public companies).[1] However, it includes a general provision which states that the term "director" includes "any person occupying the position of director, by whatever name called".[2] This covers

---

[1] CA 2006 s.154.
[2] CA 2006 s.250.

the position where a company is managed by persons described as, for example, managers or governors rather than directors.

All companies required to publish annual accounts have to state who their directors were during the financial year being reported on[3] and these will be those persons named as the directors of the company in filings made at Companies House. In the main, it will be these persons who have been formally appointed as directors and sit on the board who will be subject to directors' duties and not those who may have the term "director" in their job title but have not been appointed a board director and do not exert the same level of influence over the company's affairs as the formally appointed directors do. However, a person who acts as a director in terms of their involvement in the running of the company without having actually been appointed as such (known as a de facto director) will also be regarded as being subject to the directors' duties described in this chapter, as may a shadow director, a concept considered in more detail below.

Case law in the UK has established that the directors of a company owe their fiduciary duties to the company rather than its shareholders unless a "special factual relationship" between the director and the shareholders in a particular case has been established.[4] This special relationship is something over and above the usual relationship any director has with a company's shareholders—it usually involves a personal relationship or a particular dealing or transaction between the director and a shareholder or shareholders.[5]

When considering directors' duties under company law, the starting point is the statutory statement of directors' duties set out in the CA 2006. Prior to the coming into force of these statutory duties, the general duties directors owed to their company were based on certain common law rules and equitable principles, and they primarily concerned fiduciary

---

[3]   CA 2006 s.416 (1)(a).
[4]   *Peskin v Anderson* [2001] B.C.C. 874; [2001] 1 B.C.L.C. 372.
[5]   *Sharp v Blank* [2015] EWHC 3220 (Ch).

duties of good faith and loyalty and common law duties of skill and care. While the intention behind the CA 2006 was to simplify and modernise company law, rather than be a radical overhaul of companies legislation, the introduction of a statutory statement of directors' duties made significant changes to the language used to frame directors' duties.

2.2   General statement of directors' duties

The statutory statement in the CA 2006[6] sets out seven general duties that are owed to, and are enforceable by, the company. These duties, which are considered in more detail below, are the duties to:

- act within the company's powers;
- promote the success of the company;
- exercise independent judgment;
- exercise reasonable care, skill and diligence;
- avoid conflicts of interest;
- not to accept benefits from third parties; and
- declare any interest in transactions or arrangements with the company.

These general duties are largely a codification of previous case law but with two important exceptions, namely the duty to promote the success of the company and the treatment of conflicts of interest.

2.3   Other duties owed by directors

The statutory statement of general duties does not obviate the need for directors to comply with any other statutory duties contained in the CA 2006. For example, the CA 2006 imposes duties on directors to prepare certain narrative reports such as a strategic report[7] and a directors' report[8] which must be

---

[6]   CA 2006 ss.171–177.
[7]   CA 2006 s.414A.
[8]   CA 2006 s.415.

delivered to the Registrar of Companies with the annual accounts for each financial year,[9] to call a general meeting if requested by shareholders meeting certain conditions,[10] and not to allot further shares unless authorised by the company's articles of association or by shareholders.[11] The CA 2006 also includes statutory rules intended to promote fair dealing by directors with the company. These include rules on substantial property transactions,[12] payments for loss of office,[13] loans and related transactions.[14] The rules provide scope for shareholder approval and exemptions.

The general duties also do not obviate the need to comply with statutory duties imposed on directors under a wide variety of other statutes and regulations, for example, legislation relating to insolvency, environmental and health and safety issues. Additional duties owed by directors to their company include the duty to consider or act in the interests of creditors[15] and the duty of confidentiality, and executive directors who are employees of the company will also owe similar duties to those owed by all employees to their companies.

Directors of companies admitted to the Main Market of the London Stock Exchange will also need to consider any applicable duties in the Financial Conduct Authority's Listing Rules, Disclosure and Transparency Rules and Prospectus Rules, and directors of companies admitted to trading on AIM will need to be aware of their duties under the London Stock Exchange's AIM Rules for Companies. In addition, directors of companies which have adopted codes of practice such as the Lending Code, the BBA Code for Financial Reporting Disclosure and HM Revenue's Code of Practice on Taxation for Banks, need to be aware of the obligations imposed by these codes of practice.

---

[9] CA 2006 s.441.
[10] CA 2006 ss.303 and 304.
[11] CA 2006 s.549.
[12] CA 2006 ss.190-196.
[13] CA 2006 ss.215-222.
[14] CA 2006 ss.197-214.
[15] See CA 2006 s.172(3).

However, this chapter will focus on the duties owed by a director, in his capacity as a director, to the company. The other statutory and regulatory duties mentioned above are outside the scope of this chapter.

2.4 Application of directors' duties

The seven general duties set out in the CA 2006 apply to all directors of a company, so to non-executive as well as executive directors. There has been some uncertainty as to whether the duties also apply to shadow directors, defined in the CA 2006 as persons "in accordance with whose directions or instructions the directors of the company are accustomed to act",[16] as the CA 2006 stated that they did apply to shadow directors, but only to the extent that corresponding common law rules or equitable principles also apply to them.[17]

This uncertainty has now been clarified by amendments to the CA 2006 which came into effect on 26 May 2015. The Small Business, Enterprise and Employment Act 2015 (SBEE Act) includes a number of provisions aimed at enhancing the transparency of UK companies and increasing the accountability of those who control a director, as well as at increasing trust in the UK generally as a place to do business and invest.

The SBEE Act has introduced a provision into the CA 2006 which states that the general duties of a director "apply to a shadow director of a company where and to the extent that they are capable of so applying".[18] The Secretary of State has been given powers to make regulations concerning the application of the general duties to shadow directors, but no such regulations have yet been produced.[19] The definition of a "shadow director" in the CA 2006 has also been extended to make it clear that acting in accordance with directions or guidance given by a person exercising a function conferred by

---

[16] CA 2006 s.251(1).
[17] CA 2006 s.170(5).
[18] CA 2006 s.170(5), as substituted by s.89(1) of the SBEE Act.
[19] SBEE Act s.89(2).

or under legislation does not constitute the person exercising the function as a shadow director and acting on any advice or guidance issued by a Minister of the Crown does not constitute a Minister of the Crown a shadow director.

As well as applying to shadow directors, former directors will continue (following termination of their appointment) to be subject to the general duties to avoid conflicts of interest with the company in relation to opportunities which arose when they were directors of the company and the duty not to accept benefits from third parties in respect of things done or omitted to be done during their directorship.

The CA 2006 makes it clear that the general duties are cumulative, so that more than one duty may apply in a particular case.[20] As a result, the duty to promote the success of the company will not permit the directors to breach their duty to act within their powers, even if they consider that the action will be likely to promote the success of the company. In addition, the statutory general duties do not require or authorise a director to breach any other prohibition or requirement imposed on that director by law.

So far as the relationship between the general duties and a company's constitution is concerned, it is possible for companies, by way of provisions in their articles of association, to go further than the statutory general duties by placing more onerous requirements on their directors. However, the articles cannot dilute the general statutory duties except to the extent permitted by the relevant specific sections in the CA 2006. For example, a director will not be in breach of the duty to exercise independent judgment if he or she has acted in a way that is authorised by the constitution[21] and some conflicts of interests may be authorised by independent directors, subject to the company's constitution.[22]

---

[20] CA 2006 s.179.
[21] CA 2006 s.173(2)(b).
[22] CA 2006 s.175(5).

2.5 The statutory general duties

2.5.1 *The duty to act within powers*

A director is required to act in accordance with the company's constitution and to only exercise powers for the purpose for which they are conferred.[23]

For these purposes, "constitution" is defined widely. It includes:

- the company's articles of association;
- any resolutions and agreements which affect the company's constitution;
- any resolutions or other decisions taken in accordance with the articles; and
- any decisions taken by members or a class of members that can be regarded as equivalent to a decision by the company, for example, a decision taken by informal unanimous consent of all the members.[24]

The CA 2006 does not specify what constitutes a proper purpose and this must be ascertained in the context of the specific situation under consideration. Previous case law will be relevant. Lord Glennie, in the Court of Session, in *West Coast Capital (LIOS) Ltd*,[25] expressed the view that s.171 did little more than set out the pre-existing case law—the test to be applied in determining whether directors were only exercising powers for the purposes for which they were conferred remains a subjective one and essentially one of looking at the purpose or purposes for which the directors were exercising their powers (i.e. their motivation). However, the Privy Council decision in *Howard Smith Ltd v Ampal Petroleum Ltd*[26] makes it clear that an improper motivation can be inferred from an objective assessment of all the surrounding circumstances.

---

[23] CA 2006 s.171.
[24] CA 2006 ss.17 and 257.
[25] [2008] CSOH 72.
[26] [1974] A.C. 821; [1974] 2 W.L.R. 689; 118 S.J.L.B. 330.

The Supreme Court considered the issue in *Eclairs Group Ltd v JKX Oil & Gas Plc* and *Glengary Overseas Ltd v JKX Oil & Gas Plc*.[27] The case concerned the exercise by the board of JKX (a listed company) of a power in its articles to impose restrictions on shares for failure to provide full information about interests in those shares in response to notices served by the company under CA 2006 s.793. The notices were served on shareholders whom the JKX board considered to be corporate raiders and who had made it clear that they opposed resolutions to be proposed by the board at a forthcoming annual general meeting which meant it likely that those resolutions would fail. The Supreme Court confirmed that the principle that directors must exercise their powers for a proper purpose is one of general application and they held, on the facts of the case, that in imposing the restrictions on the shares, the JKX directors had exercised their powers for an improper purpose.

The judge in the High Court had found that while the directors shared a genuine desire to obtain the information which they felt had been withheld, the predominant purpose of a majority of the JKX board in voting to impose the share restrictions was to prevent those shares being voted at the annual general meeting so as to increase the prospects of the relevant resolutions being passed. He held that this was an "improper purpose" and so set the restrictions aside. The Court of Appeal, by a majority, decided that the board's power to impose restrictions permitted by the company's articles was not subject to any significant limitation as to the purposes for which it might be exercised and it allowed JKX's appeal. However, the Supreme Court allowed the shareholders' appeal and held that while the proper purposes for the exercise of the power to impose restrictions on shares might be wider than simply to encourage or coerce the provision of information sought in the s.793 notices, there were still some limits on the use of the power. Proper purposes in this case included encouraging or coercing the provision of information sought in the s.793 notices, protecting the company and its shareholders from making decisions in ignorance of relevant information and also providing a sanction for failure to comply with such notices.

---

[27] [2015] UKSC 71; [2015] Bus. L.R. 1395.

However, its use for the predominant purposes of influencing the outcome of a shareholder meeting was outside any legitimate purpose for which the power may be exercised and was improper. It also offended the constitutional distribution of powers between the different organs of the company as it involved the use of the board's powers to control or influence a decision which JKX's constitution assigned to shareholders.

2.5.2   *The duty to promote the success of the company*

Each director is required "to act in a way he considers, in good faith, would be most likely to promote the success of the company for the benefit of its members as a whole."[28]

In a collection of Ministerial Statements on the duties of directors published in June 2007, it was confirmed that "success" in relation to a commercial company will normally mean a "long-term increase in value", and it is for the directors, by reference to the objectives of the company, to judge and form a good faith judgment about what is to be regarded as success for the members as a whole.

In exercising this duty, directors must have regard, amongst other matters, to six named factors which are not exhaustive.[29] This duty replaced the common law formulation of "bona fide in the interests of the company", otherwise referred to as the "best interests" of the company, although the reference to identified factors goes beyond the common law concept and it requires directors to go through a more distinctive decision-making process to promote the success of the company. In the Ministerial Statements referred to above, it was suggested that "have regard to" means "think about", and the explanatory notes to the CA 2006 state that "it will not be sufficient to pay lip service to the factors, and, in many cases, the directors will need to take action to comply with this aspect of the duty".

As mentioned above, in complying with this duty, directors must have regard to at least the six factors set out in the CA

---

[28]   CA 2006 s.172.
[29]   CA 2006 s.172(1).

2006 which aim to import a strong notion of corporate social responsibility into decision-making. Broadly, these factors are:

- the likely long term consequences of the decision;
- the interests of employees;
- a need to foster relationships with suppliers, customers and others;
- the impact of the company's operations on the community and the environment;
- the desirability of the company maintaining a reputation for high standards of business conduct; and
- the need to act fairly as between the members and the company.

While some factors may not be relevant to a particular decision, since the duty includes an obligation to consider all factors, directors must go through this mental process before dismissing any particular factors as irrelevant. However, the six factors themselves are subsidiary to the overall duty to promote the success of the company. As a result, as the Institute of Chartered Secretaries and Administrators (ICSA), in their "Guidance on Directors' General Duties" published in January 2008,[30] point out, "traditional considerations such as profitability and the financial effects on shareholders are still very important as they are central to this overall duty".

While other stakeholders are referred to in s.172, the duty to promote the success of the company is owed directly to the company and not to these additional stakeholders. Whilst shareholders have a right to bring a derivative claim for loss suffered by the company (see further below), the other stakeholders referred to in the six factors do not have any rights to bring a claim against a director for breach of duty.

Directors should note that the duty imposed by s.172 has effect subject to any enactment or rule of law requiring directors in certain circumstances to consider or act in the interests of creditors of the company.[31] Accordingly the duty is displaced

---

[30] ICSA, Reference No. 080110.
[31] CA 2006 s.172(3).

when the company is insolvent (the Insolvency Act 1986 provides a mechanism under which the liquidator can require directors to contribute towards the funds available to creditors in an insolvent winding up, where they ought to have recognised that the company had no reasonable prospect of avoiding insolvent liquidation and then failed to take all reasonable steps to minimise the loss to creditors). The duty may also be modified by an obligation to have regard to the interests of creditors as the company nears insolvency.

Initially s.172 raised concerns that directors would need to record their consideration of the six named factors to show that they had complied with the duty, leading to increased bureaucracy around the decision-making process of boards and potentially increasing directors' liabilities. However, during the passage of the Companies Bill (as it then was) through Parliament, it was made clear that s.172 was not intended to add to the paperwork of decision-making or require the creation of a paper trail. It was stated that:

> "The clause does not impose a requirement on directors to keep records, as some people have suggested, in any circumstances in which they would not have to do so now".[32]

It was also stated that:

> "There is nothing in this Bill that says there is a need for a paper trail…. I do not agree that the effect of passing this Bill will be that directors will be subject to a breach if they cannot demonstrate that they have considered every element. It will be for the person who is asserting breach of duty to make that case good".[33]

In addition, the Association of General Counsel and Company Secretaries of the FTSE 100 (the GC100), in a paper providing guidance on directors' duties under the CA 2006 prepared in

---

[32] Margaret Hodge, Minister of State for Industry and the Regions, Commons Committee, 11 July 2006.
[33] Attorney General, Lord Goldsmith, Lords Grand Committee, 9 May 2006.

early 2007, expressed the view that directors "are not currently, and should not be, as a result of this legislative codification, forced to evidence their thought processes whether that is with regard to the stated factors or any other matter influencing their thinking. Apart from the unnecessary process and paper work this would introduce into the boardroom, it would inevitably expose directors to a greater and unacceptable risk of litigation, especially in light of the new derivative action also being brought in by the Companies Act 2006".[34]

In practice, this duty has not required a significant change in the way directors make decisions and it has not extensively changed the way companies document their decision-making process. A 2008 case suggests that s.172 has simply codified the previous common law obligation in this area.[35] In that case the court compared the wording of s.172 with the previous formulation of "bona fide in the interests of the company" and concluded that they came to the same thing, with the modern formulation giving a more readily understood definition of the scope of the duties. The court also confirmed that the test is a subjective one. The question is whether a director honestly believed that his or her act or omission was in the interests of the company and the court will not consider that there has been a breach of the duty simply because, in the court's opinion, the particular exercise of the power was not to promote the success of the company. However, the court also noted that a breach will have occurred if it is established that the relevant exercise of the power is one which could not be considered by any reasonable director to be in the interests of the company.

In 2013, when the Parliamentary Commission on Banking Standards (PCBS) published its report on reforms which it believed were necessary to improve standards in the banking industry,[36] it recommended that the Government consult on amending s.172 to remove shareholder primacy in respect of banks, requiring directors of banks to ensure the financial

---

[34] GC100, Companies Act (2006)—Directors' Duties (February 2007).
[35] *Southern Counties Fresh Foods Ltd, Re* (2008) EWHC 2810.
[36] PCBS, Final Report—Changing banking for good (June 2013).

safety and soundness of the company ahead of the interests of its members. The PCBS was concerned that, in the banking sector, shareholder interests appeared to prevail over the other duties and it felt that if directors' duties were changed for specific sectors, such as the directors of large banks, this would make it clear that the pursuit of shareholder value should not be at the expense of financial stability.

The Government, in its consultation on proposals to enhance the transparency of UK company ownership and increase trust in the UK as a place to do business, sought views on this proposal[37] but subsequently reported that most respondents to the consultation felt that the statutory duties of banks should not be changed specifically for bank directors. Given the duty to promote the success of the company explicitly requires directors to have regard to a range of matters in the long-term (and does not override obligations to comply with sector-specific requirements), and the introduction of the Senior Managers regime, the Government decided that the directors' general statutory duties should continue to apply economy-wide and remain unchanged.

2.5.3 Duty to exercise independent judgment

This duty codifies the legal principle that directors must exercise their powers independently and should not fetter their discretion unless properly authorised to do so. Accordingly, directors must not fetter the future exercise of their discretion unless they are acting in accordance with an agreement which has been duly entered into by the company or in a way authorised by or under the company's constitution.[38]

The duty is for directors to exercise independent judgment and the Ministerial Statements on Duties of Directors published in June 2007 make it clear that "the exercise of the judgement of a director must be independent in the sense of it being his own judgement ... the duty does not prevent a director from relying

---

[37] BIS, Transparency and Trust: Enhancing the transparency of UK company ownership and increasing trust in UK business—Discussion Paper (July 2013).
[38] CA 2006 s.173.

on the advice or work of others, but the final judgement must be his responsibility".[39] As a result, directors are not prevented from delegating matters as permitted by the company's articles, for example to board committees, provided they exercise their own judgment in deciding whether to do so, nor does the duty preclude directors from taking professional advice.

2.5.4 Duty to exercise reasonable care, skill and diligence

A director is required to exercise reasonable care, skill and diligence.[40] This must be the care, skill and diligence which will be exercised by a reasonably diligent person with both:

- the general knowledge, skill and experience that may reasonably be expected of the person carrying out the functions carried out by the director in relation to the company (an objective test); and
- the general knowledge, skill and experience that the director has (a subjective test).

As a result, a director needs to display the knowledge, skill and experience set out in the objective test, but, if he or she has specialist knowledge, then the higher subjective test will also need to be met.

In a 2008 case, *Lexi Holdings Plc (In Administration) v Luqman*,[41] the High Court commented that a director is expected to apply to the management and custodianship of the company's property that same degree of care as he might reasonably be expected to apply to the management and custodianship of his own property.

The practical consequences of the objective and subjective limbs of this duty include the following:

---

[39] Attorney General, Lord Goldsmith, Lords Grand Committee, 6 February 2006.
[40] CA 2006 s.174.
[41] [2009] EWCA CIV 117; [2009] B.C.C. 716; [2009] 2 B.C.L.C. 1.

- a member of the audit committee would be expected to exercise greater diligence in relation to the audited accounts;
- the CEO and finance director of a company are likely to be held to a higher standard than a non-executive director; and
- a director who is a qualified accountant would be expected, where this superior knowledge and skill is applicable, to show a higher standard of skill, care and diligence than a director without such qualifications.

2.5.5 Duty to avoid conflicts of interest

The CA 2006 distinguishes between:

- interests in transactions and arrangements with the company (which must be disclosed but need not be approved—see further below); and
- all other conflicts, which will normally require approval.

Directors must avoid all situations in which they have, or could have, a direct or indirect interest that conflicts, or may conflict, with the interests of the company.[42] However, the CA 2006 provisions impose a positive duty on directors to avoid conflicts and potential conflicts. This applies, in particular, to the exploitation of property, information or opportunity, and whether or not the company could take advantage of the property, information or opportunity.[43]

The common law imposed a "disability" on directors in a conflict situation rather than a duty to avoid the conflict situation. However, there is no breach of the statutory duty if:

- the situation cannot reasonably be regarded as likely to give rise to a conflict of interest; or
- if the matter is authorised by independent directors (i.e. those who have no direct or indirect interest in the transaction). In the case of a private company formed on

---

[42] CA 2006 s.175.
[43] CA 2006 s.175(2).

or after 1 October 2008, authorisation can be given unless the company's constitution prevents such authorisation. In the case of private companies formed before 1 October 2008, authorisation can only be given by the independent directors if the constitution contains nothing to the contrary and the shareholders have passed an ordinary resolution permitting such authorisation. For public companies, authorisation by the independent directors can only be given if the company's constitution specifically permits this.

Board authorisation will only be effective if the required quorum is met without counting the director in question or any other interested director and if the conflicted directors have not participated in the taking of the decision or if the decision would have been valid without the participation of the conflicted directors.[44]

The main practical implication of this authorisation process is that public companies need to ensure that their articles of association include the ability to permit any authorisations deemed relevant (as without such a provision, the default position is that the matter is not capable of being approved by the directors and so can only be approved by shareholders), and for private companies, that their articles do not prevent authorisation being given (and, for companies formed before 1 October 2008, that their shareholders have passed the necessary ordinary resolution).

The provision requiring directors to avoid conflict or potential conflict situations tends to cause the greatest difficulty for directors who sit on more than one board, as is the case with the majority of non-executive directors. For example, even if a director of one company obtains approval from that company to sit on the board of a second company, it is unlikely that such authorisation will, of itself, cover future conflicts arising from the second directorship.

---

[44] CA 2006 s.175(6).

In its "Guidance on Directors' General Duties", ICSA points out that a director who has the opportunity to take on another directorship outside the company must consider whether he or she would have a problem in relation to this duty. While multiple directorships would not necessarily need formal authorisation from the board, the question is whether having such directorships is likely to give rise to a conflict of interest.

A GC100 paper published in January 2008 includes a non-exhaustive list of possible situations that could fall within s.175(1) and this list includes situations where a director of the company is also a director of another company that is a competitor of, major shareholder in, or potential customer of or supplier to the company.[45] Directors need to ensure that the company secretary (or other appointed representative) has at all times up to date details (including both the nature and extent of the interest) of other positions (including director-ships) and other conflict situations that the director thinks need authorising, and the board will then have to consider each director's situation.

In deciding whether to authorise a conflict of interest, directors need to remember that they have to consider whether their action is most likely to promote the success of the company in accordance with s.172. Consideration should also be given by each director as to whether he or she has a conflict of interest though a connected person (see further below) or some other indirect interest, for example, an interest of another company of which the director is a minority shareholder or of which he may be a director.

2.5.6 Duty not to accept benefits from third parties

Directors must not accept any benefit from a third party which is conferred because of his or her being a director or his or her doing or not doing anything as a director.[46] Directors should not accept benefits unless such benefits cannot reasonably be regarded as likely to give rise to a conflict of interest or unless

---

[45] GC100, Companies Act 2006—Directors' conflicts of interest (January 2008).
[46] CA 2006 s.176.

the acceptance is authorised by shareholders. The restrictions do not apply to benefits received from the company itself, from any associated company, or from any person acting on behalf of any of those companies and benefits received from a person who provides the director's services to the company are also excluded.[47]

The ICSA Guidance on Directors' General Duties recommends that a company's policy or guidelines as to the acceptance of gifts or other benefits (including any updates) should be approved by the board, possibly on a recommendation from the audit committee. It also suggests that all relevant employees and contractors are informed of the policy or guidelines and any updates and, for the company's protection, they should be required to sign a receipt and acknowledgment to study and comply with the terms of the policy/guidance and any updates. ICSA also believes that it is good practice to set up a register of benefits offered and received above whatever level is decided on by the board and it suggests that the company secretary should report annually to the audit committee (if applicable) on compliance and issues arising.

As mentioned above, the duty not to accept benefits from third parties will continue to apply after a person ceases to be a director in relation to things done or omitted by him before he ceased to be a director.

2.5.7 Duty to declare interest in proposed transaction or arrangement with the company

Directors are not under an obligation to avoid transactions with the company of which they are a director, but if such a transaction is proposed and a director is interested in it (or reasonably ought to be aware that he is interested in it), the director concerned must declare the nature and extent of his interest.[48] In addition, if a declaration is made which then proves to be or becomes inaccurate or incomplete, there is an obligation to update that declaration. A director's interest in an

---

[47] CA 2006 ss.176(2) and (3).
[48] CA 2006 s.177.

existing transaction or arrangement with the company must also be declared, unless previously declared as a proposed interest.[49]

The obligation to declare an interest does not have a materiality threshold so the obligation can involve disclosures of both the smallest change in a director's shareholding and a company entering into a material contract with the director's spouse or with a company in which the director has an indirect interest. There is, however, no breach of this duty if:

- the situation cannot reasonably be regarded as likely to give rise to a conflict;
- the other directors are already aware of the interest or should reasonably have been aware of it;
- the issue concerns the director's interest in his own service contract; or
- the director concerned is the sole director of the company, and the company is entitled to have a single director.

The actual disclosure may be made by a director by one of three methods:

- at a board meeting;
- by notice in writing to the other directors; or
- by general notice.

The obligation to disclose relates to disclosing both the nature and the extent of the interest and so requires some detail in the disclosure as to the "value" of the director's prospective interest in the transaction. The ICSA Guidance on Directors' Duties recommends that when a director does declare his or her interest before a transaction or arrangement is entered into by the company, it is then good practice for the board to take decisions on related matters without the director present. In any event, any requirements of the company's articles of association with regard to conflicts and declarations of interest will need to be complied with.

---

[49] CA 2006 s.182.

2.5.8 *Obligations of connected persons*

The definition of "connected person" in the CA 2006 includes the director's spouse or civil partner, any other person with whom the director lives as partner in an enduring family relationship, the director's children or step-children, any children or step-children of a person with whom the director lives who are under 18 and the director's parents.[50] The definition also extends to any company with which a director is connected (being, broadly, any company in which the director and his connected persons hold more than 20 per cent of the equity share capital or control more than 20 per cent of the voting rights)[51] and to certain trust and partnership arrangements. Since directors must avoid a situation in which they have, or can have, a direct or indirect interest that conflicts or may conflict with the interests of the company, the interest of any of these connected persons must be taken into account in considering whether a director is conflicted under the "conflicts of interest with third parties" provisions of the CA 2006. In addition, since the "conflicts of interest in relation to transactions or arrangements with the company" provisions include the obligation to disclose interests of which the director ought reasonably to be aware, it is likely that connected persons' interests would be taken into account when considering a breach of this duty.

2.6 Liability of directors to shareholders

As referred to above, a director's statutory duties are owed to the company and only the company can enforce them. However, the CA 2006 introduced a new procedure under which a shareholder may bring proceedings on behalf of the company (a derivative claim) which potentially makes it easier for shareholders to sue directors in the name of the company for a broader range of conduct than was previously possible under common law.[52] Shareholders may sue in respect of an act

---

[50] CA 2006 ss.252 and 253.
[51] CA 2006 ss.254 and 255.
[52] CA 2006 ss.260–264.

or proposed act or omission involving negligence, default, breach of duty (which includes the duty to promote the success of the company and a duty to exercise reasonable care, skill and diligence) or breach of trust by a director of the company. Directors can be sued for negligence even where they have not personally profited and there is no need to show wrongdoer control or fraud on the minority.

Although there is now more scope for a shareholder to bring a claim, shareholders need the court's permission to continue with a claim. A court must refuse permission for a claimant to bring a derivative claim where it is satisfied that:

- a person acting in accordance with the general duty to promote the success of the company under s.172 CA 2006 would not seek to continue the claim; or
- a cause of action arises from an act or omission that has not yet occurred and that act or omission has been authorised by the company; or
- the act or omission giving rise to the cause of action has already occurred and has been authorised or ratified by the company.[53]

A number of factors are prescribed that the court must take into account, in particular, when considering whether to give permission for a claimant to continue with a claim. These include:

- whether the shareholder is acting in good faith in seeking to continue the claim;
- the importance that a person acting in accordance with the duty to promote the success of the company would attach to continuing the claim;
- whether the act or omission giving rise to the cause of action could be (and in the circumstances would be likely to be) authorised or ratified by the company;
- whether the company has decided not to pursue the claim;

---

[53] CA 2006 s.263(2).

- whether the act or omission in respect of which the claim was brought gives rise to a cause of action that the shareholder could pursue in his own right rather than on behalf of the company; and
- any evidence before the court as to the views of shareholders of the company who have no personal interest, direct or indirect, in the matter.[54]

Other constraints on bringing a derivative claim include the following:

- the court has discretion to grant permission to continue a derivative claim and it generally awards costs against the claimant if it refuses leave to proceed;
- as a derivative claim is a claim brought for and on behalf of the company in respect of a wrong done to the company, any damages awarded belong to the company and not to the claimant.

2.7 Relief from liability

The majority of breaches of authority by directors may be "cured" by shareholder ratification, either by ordinary resolution or by unanimous shareholder approval. The ability for shareholders to ratify conduct by a director amounting to negligence, default, breach of duty or breach of trust in relation to the company is set out in s.239 CA 2006. Any decision by a company to ratify conduct of a director amounting to negligence, default, breach of duty or breach of trust in relation to the company must be taken by the shareholders without reliance on any votes in favour by the director or any connected person (and a shareholder connected with a director will include certain family members and could include fellow directors).[55] In addition, where proceedings for negligence, default, breach of duty or breach of trust are brought against a director, the court may relieve that director from liability if it considers both that:

---

[54] CA 2006 ss.263(3) and (4).
[55] CA 2006 ss.239(4) and (5).

- the director has acted honestly and reasonably; and
- considering all the circumstances of the case, the director ought fairly to be excused.[56]

Directors can also be protected from liability through the use of indemnities and insurance.

While a company cannot exempt a director from any liability for negligence, default, breach of duty or breach of trust in relation to the company, it can indemnify the director against defence costs, or costs incurred by him or her in a court application for relief, provided that the director repays the costs if he or she is unsuccessful.[57]

In addition, a company is permitted to purchase insurance for its directors and those of an associated company against any liability attaching to them in connection with any negligence, default, breach of duties or breach of trust by them in relation to the company of which they are a director.[58]

2.8 Further guidance on the role of the board and particular directors

Although the general law does not impose specific duties on non-executive directors (or any specific exemptions from liability), nevertheless, the role of a non-executive director is in practice being defined in the UK and elsewhere with increasing precision. Generally, it is now expected that non-executive directors will play a supervisory and monitoring role. It follows that when management fails to perform adequately, or when a company is affected by crisis or scandal, the non-executive director or directors should, and increasingly do, take the lead in identifying and resolving the problem. There is also an increasing expectation and obligation for non-executive directors to provide constructive challenge and help develop proposals on strategy, in the context of a unitary board. In

---

[56] CA 2006 s.1157.
[57] CA 2006 s.232.
[58] CA 2006 s.233.

addition, chairmen of boards are expected to provide leadership and to be responsible for ensuring that the board operates in an effective manner.

Many of these expectations and obligations are set out in the FRC's UK Corporate Governance Code and accompanying guidance, which are considered further below. The UK Corporate Governance Code requirements will be of particular relevance to directors holding senior manager functions in banks and investment firms in light of the specific responsibilities it assigns to the board, its committees, the chairman and the CEO of a listed company. Such requirements should also be considered alongside the governance arrangements for ring-fenced bodies specified by the PRA which are considered in detail in Chapter 7.

2.9   UK Corporate Governance Code

The UK Corporate Governance Code (Code) contains detailed provisions on the role of non-executive directors as well as provisions on the role of the board and board committees, the role of the chairman and the role of the senior independent director of a company. The Code was last published in September 2014 and it applies to companies, wherever incorporated, with a premium listing of equity shares on the Official List of the London Stock Exchange.[59] A corporate governance code for small and mid-size quoted companies, including AIM companies, which adopts key elements of the Code and applies these to the needs and particular circumstances of smaller companies, has been prepared by the Quoted Companies Alliance.[60]

Companies with a premium listing on the Official List have to "comply or explain" against the requirements of the Code in

---

[59] In April 2016 the FRC published the final draft of a new version of the Code which will apply to accounting periods beginning on or after 17 June 2016. The few changes will be to Section C, Accountability.

[60] QCA Corporate Governance Code for Small and Mid-size Quoted Companies 2013.

their annual corporate governance statement in the annual report and the different sections of the Code provide useful guidance which directors of all companies should be aware of.

The preface to the Code points out that boards need to think comprehensively about their overall tasks and the implications of these for the roles of their individual members. Key to this is the leadership of the board chairman, the support given to and by the CEO and the frankness and openness of mind with which issues are discussed and tackled by all directors. It is stressed that it is important to avoid "group think" by ensuring debate is constructive and challenging, and having sufficient diversity on the board should encourage this. The preface also notes that a key role of the board is to establish the culture, values and ethics of the company. The board should set the correct "tone from the top", since if the directors lead by example, good standards of behaviour should permeate throughout all levels of the organisation and this will help prevent misconduct, unethical practices and support the delivery of long-term success.

The remainder of the Code sets out principles of corporate governance, together with a detailed set of provisions providing practical guidance on how these principles should be applied. There are sections of the Code dealing with leadership, the effectiveness of boards and their committees, accountability, remuneration and relations with shareholders and the key recommendations in each area are summarised below.

2.9.1 Leadership

The Code states that the role of the chairman should be separate from that of the CEO and that the division of responsibilities between the chairman and the CEO should be clearly established, set out in writing and agreed by the board.

The Code requires that (except in the case of smaller companies) at least half the members of the board, excluding the chairman, should be independent non-executive directors. Smaller companies (defined as those "below the FTSE 350 throughout the year immediately prior to the reporting year") should have at least two independent non-executive directors and criteria for determining independence are set out in the Code. One of the independent non-executive directors should also be appointed as the senior independent director who should be available to shareholders if they have concerns that have not been resolved through contact with the chairman, CEO or finance director or for which such contact is inappropriate. The senior independent director should also act as a sounding board for the chairman and serve as an intermediary for the other directors where necessary.

The Code makes it clear that the chairman is responsible for leadership of the board and for ensuring its effectiveness and the non-executive directors should constructively challenge and help develop proposals on strategy. As a result, they should scrutinise the performance of management in meeting agreed goals and objectives and monitor the reporting of performance. They should also satisfy themselves as to the integrity of the financial information provided and that the company's financial controls and systems of risk management are robust and defensible. In addition, they are responsible for determining appropriate levels of remuneration for executive directors, and have a key role in appointing and removing executive directors and in succession planning.

The Code stresses the value of the board meeting sufficiently regularly to discharge its duties effectively and it recommends that the non-executive directors should meet as a group at least once a year without the chairman present to appraise the chairman's performance and on such other occasions as are deemed appropriate. In instances where directors have concerns which cannot be resolved and relate to the running of the company or a proposed action, the Code states that they should ensure that their concerns are recorded in the board minutes.

2.9.2 *Effectiveness*

The Code requires the board and its committees to have the appropriate balance of skills, experience, independence and knowledge of the company to enable them to discharge their respective duties and responsibilities effectively. Appointments to the board should be made on merit, against objective criteria and "with due regard for the benefits of diversity on the board, including gender" and boards should have in place plans to ensure "progressive refreshing of the board". All directors are required to be able to allocate sufficient time to discharge their responsibilities effectively.

The Code recommends that there should be a nomination committee (comprising a majority of independent non-executive directors) which should lead the process for board appointments and make recommendations to the board. It should describe the board's diversity policy (including gender) in its report which is included each year in the annual report, together with the measurable objectives it has set for implementing that policy and progress on achieving the objectives.

The Code also recommends that all directors of FTSE 350 companies should be subject to annual election by shareholders. Directors of companies outside the FTSE 350 should be subject to election by shareholders at the first annual general meeting after their appointment and to re-election thereafter at intervals of no more than three years, and the Code recommends that there should be a formal, rigorous and transparent procedure for the appointment of new directors. Non-executive directors should usually be expected to serve two three-year terms but the Code notes that any term beyond six years for a non-executive director should be subject to particularly rigorous review. In addition, the board should undertake a formal and rigorous annual evaluation of its own performance and that of its committees and directors, and board evaluation of FTSE 350 companies should be externally facilitated at least every three years in order to ensure a greater degree of objectivity.

In support of the need for an effective board, the Code requires the chairman to ensure that new directors receive full, formal and tailored induction on joining the board. As part of this, the company should offer major shareholders the opportunity to meet a new non-executive director. The Code also requires the chairman to regularly review and agree training and development needs with each director.

2.9.3 Remuneration

The Code recommends the establishment of a remuneration committee comprising at least three members of the board (two for smaller companies), all of whom should be independent non-executive directors. Executive directors' pay should be subject to the recommendations of the remuneration committee and guidance is given in the Code as to the elements and design of remuneration packages.

2.9.4 Accountability

The Code makes it clear that the board should ensure that the annual report and accounts, taken as a whole constitute a fair, balanced and understandable assessment of the company's position and performance, business model and strategy and it is the board which is responsible for determining the nature and extent of the principal risks it is willing to take in achieving its strategic objectives. The board is required to maintain sound risk management and internal control systems and it should monitor these and, at least annually, conduct a review of the effectiveness of the company's risk management and internal control systems and report on that review in the annual report. The review should cover all material controls, including financial, operational and compliance controls. An explanation of the company's business model and the strategy for delivering the company's objectives should also be included in the annual report each year. In addition, in annual and half-yearly statements, the directors must state whether they consider it appropriate to adopt the going concern basis of accounting and identify any material uncertainties to their ability to continue to do so over a period of at least 12 months from the date of approval of those financial statements. They must also make a statement about longer-term viability, and state whether they believe the company will be able to continue in operation and meet its liabilities as they fall due, taking account of the company's current position and principal risks. The period covered by the statement must be specified and the directors must state why they consider it appropriate, with the expectation being that the period assessed will be significantly longer than 12 months.

The Code also recommends that the board establishes an audit committee comprising at least three directors (two for smaller companies), who should all be independent non-executive directors. Its main role and responsibilities should include:

- monitoring the integrity of the company's financial statements and any formal announcements relating to its financial performance, as well as reviewing any significant financial reporting judgements contained in them;
- reviewing the company's internal financial controls and its internal control and risk management systems unless these are reviewed by a separate risk committee or the board;
- monitoring and reviewing the effectiveness of the internal audit function and the internal audit activities;
- making recommendations to the board on the appointment, re-appointment or removal of the external auditor and approving its remuneration and terms of engagement (FTSE 350 companies are now required to put the external audit contract out to tender at least every 10 years);
- reviewing and monitoring the independence and objectivity of the external auditor and the effectiveness of the audit process; and
- developing and implementing policy on the engagement of the external auditor to supply non-audit services and reporting to the board, identifying any matters in respect of which action or improvement is needed and making recommendations as to the steps to be taken.

2.9.5   *Relations with shareholders*

The Code provides several mechanisms to facilitate greater contact between a company and its shareholders. These provisions include the building up of relations with institutional shareholders with dialogue existing between the parties to enable mutual understanding of objectives. The Code also recommends that the chairman should ensure that the views of shareholders are communicated to the board as a whole, that the chairman should discuss governance and strategy with major shareholders, and that non-executive directors should be offered the opportunity to attend meetings with major shareholders.

2.10   Guidance accompanying the UK Corporate Governance Code

The FRC has published a series of guidance notes designed to assist companies in addressing specific aspects of governance and accountability.[61] These include the following:

2.10.1   *FRC Guidance on Audit Committees*

The FRC Guidance on Audit Committees, published in September 2012, is designed to assist boards in making suitable arrangements for their audit committees, and to assist directors serving on audit committees in carrying out their role.[62]

Although the FRC Guidance on Audit Committees stresses that all directors have a duty to act in the interests of the company

---

[61] The Quoted Companies Alliance has also produced separate guides for remuneration and audit committees of small and mid-size quoted companies (including AIM companies).

[62] In April 2016 the FRC published a final draft of revised Guidance on Audit Committees which will be effective for accounting periods beginning on or after 17 June 2016. The Guidance has been updated to align it with the new requirements for audit committees being introduced by, among other things, implementation of the EU Statutory Audit Regulation (EU/537/2014) and the EU Statutory Audit Directive (2014/56/EU) and changes to the ethical standards for auditors.

and all remain equally responsible for the company's affairs as a matter of law, it points out that the particular role of the audit committee is, acting independently from the executive, to ensure that shareholders' interests are properly protected in relation to financial reporting and internal control. It contains recommendations about the conduct of the audit committee's relationship with the board, with the executive management and with the internal and external auditors.

2.10.2 FRC's Guidance on Risk Management, Internal Control and Related Financial and Business Reporting

The FRC's Risk Management Guidance was published in September 2014 and it aims to help boards and audit committees with their compliance with the accountability section of the Code by bringing together elements of best practice for risk management.[63] It also aims to prompt boards to consider how to discharge their responsibilities in relation to the existing and emerging principal risks faced by the company, reflect sound business practice whereby risk management and internal control are embedded in the business process by which a company pursues its objectives, and highlight related reporting responsibilities.

2.10.3 FRC's Guidance for Directors of Banks on Solvency and Liquidity Risk Management and the Going Concern Basis of Accounting

This Guidance was published at the same time as the FRC's Risk Management Guidance and it addresses supplementary considerations for the banking sector. It explains the context of solvency and liquidity risk assessments for banks, as well as providing supplementary guidance in relation to the identification and reporting of going concern material uncertainties in

---

[63] The FRC has also published a version of its Risk Management Guidance for companies that do not apply the UK Corporate Governance Code.

the financial statements and in relation to wider business reporting about solvency and liquidity risks and viability in the case of a bank.

2.10.4   Guidance on Board Effectiveness

In March 2011, the FRC published its Board Effectiveness Guidance. The Board Effectiveness Guidance is not intended to be prescriptive but its aim is to make boards think about how they can carry out their role most effectively.

2.10.4.1   The role of the board and directors

2.10.4.1.1   An effective board

The Board Effectiveness Guidance makes it clear that the role of the board is to provide entrepreneurial leadership within a framework of prudent and effective controls which enables risk to be assessed and managed. It sets out certain characteristics of an effective board (including providing direction for management and making well-informed and high quality decisions) and it points out that an effective board should not necessarily be a comfortable place. Challenge and teamwork are essential features. Board diversity is seen as an important driver of a board's effectiveness as it creates a breadth of perspective among the directors and breaks down a tendency towards "group think".

2.10.4.1.2   Role of the chairman

The Board Effectiveness Guidance looks at the role of the chairman and sets out a number of responsibilities the chairman should assume. These include ensuring that there are no "no go" areas which prevent directors from operating effective oversight of the nature and extent of the significant risks the company is willing to embrace in implementing its strategy, making sure that, as part of its decision-making, the board applies sufficient challenge to major proposals and fostering relationships between the non-executive directors and the executive team. The Board Effectiveness Guidance also points out that all board committee chairmen have an important leadership role similar to that of the chairman, particularly in creating the conditions for overall committee and individual director effectiveness.

2.10.4.1.3   Role of the Senior Independent Director (SID)

The Board Effectiveness Guidance points out that normally the SID should act as a sounding board for the chairman, and lead the evaluation of the chairman on behalf of the other directors, but his or her role is critically important if the board undergoes a period of stress. Boards are advised to ensure that they have a clear understanding of when the SID might intervene to maintain board and company stability. The examples given include when there is a dispute between the chairman and the CEO or when the strategy being followed by the chairman and the CEO is not supported by the entire board.

2.10.4.1.4   Role of executive directors

The Board Effectiveness Guidance looks at the role and duties of the executive directors. Executive directors are encouraged not just to see themselves as members of the CEO's executive team when engaged in board business but to take a wider view. It is the responsibility of the chairman to ensure the executive directors receive appropriate induction and regular training to enable them to fulfil their role.

The Board Effectiveness Guidance also looks at the role of the CEO and it points out that the relationship between the CEO and the chairman is a key one that can help increase the board's effectiveness. Both are responsible for ensuring that appropriate standards of governance permeate throughout the organisation and the CEO must ensure that he/she makes the board aware, when appropriate, of the views of employees on issues of relevance to the business. The CEO must also make sure the board knows the views of the executive directors on business issues so that the standard of discussion in the

boardroom is improved and any divergence of views held by
the executive team is explained in a balanced manner before a
final decision is taken.

2.10.4.1.5   Role of non-executive directors

The Board Effectiveness Guidance recommends that non-
executive directors, when appointed, should have a comprehensive, formal and tailored induction that extends beyond the
boardroom. It is suggested that partnering a non-executive
director with an executive director could speed up the process
of familiarising the non-executive director with the company's
main areas of business activity, especially areas involving
significant risk. Non-executive directors should spend time
learning about the company and the issues it faces as this will
help them make a positive contribution to the board and
generate the respect of the other directors.

Letters of appointment of non-executive directors should state
the minimum time the non-executive director will be required
to spend on the company's business and make it clear that
more time may have to be spent when the company is, for
example, making an acquisition or disposal or is having
difficulties with an operation.

2.10.4.2   *Decision-making*

The Board Effectiveness Guidance states that well-informed
and high-quality decision-making is critical if a board is to be
effective. It looks at means of facilitating good decision-making
(for example, by having high quality board documents,
obtaining expert opinions when necessary and allowing time
for debate and challenge) and provides examples of factors that
can limit effective decision-making. One of the examples given
is inattention to risk, and treating risk as a compliance issue
rather than as part of the decision-making, especially where the
level of risk involved in a project could endanger the stability
and sustainability of the business itself. Other factors include a
dominant personality or group of directors on the board which
can inhibit other directors from contributing, a reluctance to

involve non-executive directors, matters being brought to the board for sign-off rather than debate, or a weak organisational culture.

The Board Effectiveness Guidance suggests extra steps boards may wish to take in relation to significant decisions. Examples given are as follows:

- describing in board papers the process that has been used to arrive at and challenge the proposal prior to presenting it to the board, thus allowing directors not involved in the project to assess the appropriateness of the process as a precursor to assessing the merits of the project itself; or
- where appropriate, putting in place additional safeguards to reduce the risk of distorted judgments by, for example, commissioning an independent report, seeking advice from an expert, introducing a devil's advocate to provide challenge, establishing a sole purpose sub-committee, or convening additional meetings. The Board Effectiveness Guidance also points out that some chairmen favour separate discussions for important decisions. Examples are the concept, the proposal for discussion and the proposal for decision. This gives executive directors more opportunity to put the case at the earlier stages, and all directors have the opportunity to share concerns or challenge assumptions well in advance of the point of decision.

2.10.4.3 Board composition and succession planning

The Board Effectiveness Guidance states that a key element of board effectiveness is appointing directors who can make a positive contribution. The presence of the right skills set in the boardroom will also maximise the opportunities for the company's success in the longer term. In leading recruitment, the nomination committee should consider a diversity of personal attributes among board candidates and a diversity of psychological type, background and gender.

In view of the importance of board committees, it urges that non-executive directors with the necessary technical skills and knowledge relating to the subject matter of those board committees should be recruited. In relation to executive directors, while they may be recruited externally, companies are urged to develop internal talent and capability, for example, through middle management development programmes, partnering and mentoring schemes.

2.10.4.4 *Evaluating the performance of the board and directors*

The Board Effectiveness Guidance states that board evaluations, which should be objective and rigorous, are an excellent mechanism for providing valuable and powerful feedback for improving board effectiveness. It notes that the chairman should have overall responsibility for the process, the SID should lead the process that evaluates the chairman's performance and board committee chairmen should be responsible for evaluating their committees. The outcome of a board evaluation should be shared with the whole board and it is suggested that a review loop to consider how effective the board evaluation process has been could be useful. The Board Effectiveness Guidance also sets out areas which could be considered as part of the board evaluation process.

Chapter 3

The Regulatory Environment

Jane Walshe
Barrister

Chapter aims

Before looking at the detailed rules governing the behavior of senior managers and others in regulated firms in the UK, it is necessary to put the requirements into context. An understanding of the current regulatory environment, and in particular of the way in which the UK regulators seek to achieve their aims, is crucial to being able to effectively interpret the rules relating to individuals, found later in this book. This Chapter aims to provide an overview of the key tenets of financial services regulation in the UK, from how firms achieve authorisation to on-going supervision. The UK position is also placed in the wider European and international context.

3.1 The Financial Conduct Authority and the Prudential Regulation Authority

In April 2013 the Financial Services Authority was replaced as the sole regulator of the UK financial services industry by two new bodies, the Financial Conduct Authority and the Prudential Regulation Authority.[1]

The Financial Conduct Authority (FCA) has an overarching objective of ensuring that relevant markets function well. This is supported by three operational objectives relating to consumer protection, integrity and competition. The FCA must

---

[1] Financial Services Act 2012, Financial Services & Markets Act 2000 s.1B.

89

seek to carry out its general functions in a way that advances the consumer protection and integrity objectives, and whilst doing so should seek to promote effective competition in the interests of consumers (the competition objective). The FCA's general functions are: making rules, issuing codes and general guidance and determining general policy and principles.

The FCA is responsible for the prudential and conduct regulation of single-regulated firms, i.e. those firms who are not also regulated by the PRA. Dual regulated firms are so called because they are regulated by both the FCA, for conduct issues, and the PRA, for prudential issues.

In its 2015/16 Business Plan, the FCA stated that it regulates a total of 73,000 firms, 50,000 of which are consumer credit firms. It is based in Canary Wharf.

The Prudential Regulation Authority is a subsidiary of the Bank of England, although the Government has recommended that it become a committee of the Bank, rather than a subsidiary, in "The Bank of England and Financial Services Bill 2015-16".[2]

The PRA has a general objective to promote the safety and soundness of the firms it regulates, which are banks, building societies, credit unions, insurers and major investment firms (around 1700 in total).[3] It has an insurance objective, which is to contribute to the securing of an appropriate degree of protection for policyholders, and a secondary objective to facilitate effective competition.[4]

---

[2] Financial Services & Markets Act 2000 ss.2B and 2C (inserted by the Financial Services Act 2012).
[3] Figure taken from the PRA website April 2016.
[4] Financial Services and Markets Act 2000, s.2H(1) (inserted by the Financial Services Act 2012).

The FCA's Operational Objectives

The Consumer protection objective

The consumer protection objective is the objective of securing an appropriate degree of protection for consumers. When considering the degree of protection required, the FCA must have regard to a variety of matters, outlined in the legislation, including:

(a) the differing degrees of risk involved in different kinds of investment or other transaction;

(b) the differing degrees of experience and expertise that different consumers may have;

(c) the needs that consumers may have for the timely provision of information and advice that is accurate and fit for purpose;

(d) the general principle that consumers should take responsibility for their decisions.

The Integrity Objective

The integrity objective is protecting and enhancing the integrity of the UK financial system.

The "integrity" of the UK financial system includes:

(a) its soundness, stability and resilience;

(b) its not being used for a purpose connected with financial crime;

(c) its not being affected by behaviour that amounts to market abuse;

(d) the orderly operation of the financial markets, and

(e) the transparency of the price formation process in those markets.

The Competition Objective

The competition objective is: promoting effective competition in the interests of consumers in the markets for:

(a) regulated financial services, or

(b) services provided by a recognised investment exchange in carrying on regulated activities in respect of which it is by virtue of s.285(2) exempt from the general prohibition.

The FCA's Operational Objectives

The matters to which the FCA may have regard in considering the effectiveness of competition in the market for any services mentioned in subs.(1) include:
(a) the needs of different consumers who use or may use those services, including their need for information that enables them to make informed choices;
(b) the ease with which consumers who may wish to use those services, including consumers in areas affected by social or economic deprivation, can access them;
(c) the ease with which consumers who obtain those services can change the person from whom they obtain them;
(d) the ease with which new entrants can enter the market, and
(e) how far competition is encouraging innovation.

The PRA's Operational Objectives

The PRA's General Objective
The PRA's general objective is promoting the safety and soundness of PRA-authorised persons
That objective is to be advanced primarily by:
(a) seeking to ensure that the business of PRA-authorised persons is carried on in a way which avoids any adverse effect on the stability of the UK financial system, and
(b) seeking to minimise the adverse effect that the failure of a PRA-authorised person could be expected to have on the stability of the UK financial system.
The adverse effects mentioned may, in particular, result from the disruption of the continuity of financial services.

The PRA's Insurance Objective
The PRA's insurance objective is contributing to the securing of an appropriate degree of protection for those who are or may become policyholders.
It only applies if the effecting or carrying out of contracts of insurance as principal is to any extent a PRA-regulated activity.

The PRA's Operational Objectives
The PRA's Competition Objective   In discharging its general functions, the PRA must also have regard to the need to minimise any adverse effect on competition in the relevant markets that may result from the manner in which the PRA discharges those functions.

3.2 The Threshold Conditions

The Threshold Conditions are the standards all firms must meet in order to become, and to remain, authorised by the FCA and/or the PRA. They are found in the Financial Services and Markets Act 2000 (Threshold Conditions) Order 2013. They operate as both the initial standards firms must reach, and also create an ongoing obligation to ensure that the business operates in a way that is in full compliance with them. Breach of a threshold condition by a firm must be immediately notified to the relevant regulator and could lead to the revocation of a firm's permission, depending on its duration and extent. Both the FCA and the PRA expect adherence not just to the letter of the threshold conditions, but also to the overarching objectives as explained above.[5]

There are four sets of Threshold Conditions, for the following populations:

- A: FCA conditions for firms authorised and regulated by the FCA only;
- B: FCA-specific conditions for firms authorised by the PRA and subject to dual-regulation;
- C: PRA-specific conditions for insurance firms; and
- D: PRA-specific conditions for banks and dual-regulated investment firms.

---

[5] See Executive Summary of PRA Approach to Banking Supervision, p.5. Available at http://www.bankofengland.co.uk/publications/Documents/praapproach/bankingappr1406.pdf [Accessed 24 February 2016].

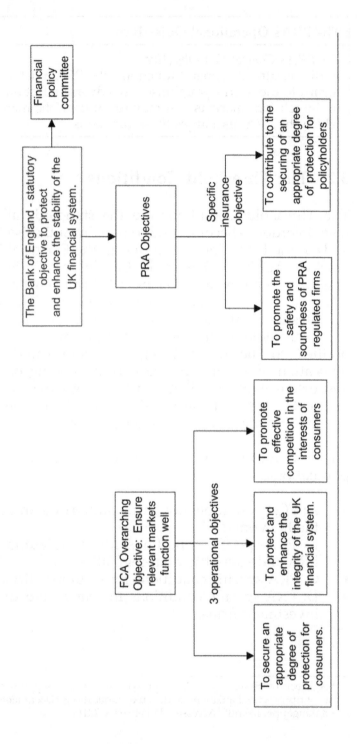

Singly regulated firms will only have to comply with the conditions in A. Dual regulated firms will have to meet the conditions in B, and either C or D.

3.2.1 A summary of TCs regulated firms

A: Summary of TCs for FCA regulated firms (only)[6]	
LOCATION OF OFFICES	Head office or registered office must be in the UK if firm is a body corporate. If it is not a corporate and its head office is in the UK, it must carry on business in the UK.[7]
EFFECTIVE SUPERVISION	Firm must be capable of being effectively supervised by the FCA having regard to all the circumstances including: • nature, scale, complexity; • organisation of business; • whether the firm is subject to consolidated supervision; • product complexity; • close links; • group membership.
APPROPRIATE RESOURCES (financial and non financial)	The FCA must be satisfied that the firm's resources are appropriate, and will consider: • nature and scale of the business to be carried on; • risks to continuity of services; • group membership (relevant to financial resources); • skills and expertise of management (relevant to non-financial resources); • whether its non-financial resources are sufficient to enable compliance with any FCA requirements that may be imposed.

---

6   Financial Services and Markets Act 2000 (Threshold Conditions) Order 2013 Pt 1B.
7   Additional provisions apply to firms carrying on investment services which have no registered office but a head office in the UK, and those seeking to carry on insurance mediation activity. See s.2B of the Order.

A: Summary of TCs for FCA regulated firms (only)[6]	
SUITABILITY	The FCA needs to be satisfied that the firm is a fit and proper person having regard to all the circumstances, including: • the firm's connection with any person; • nature and complexity of the proposed regulated activities; • the need to ensure that the firm can be run appropriately, considering consumer interests and integrity of UK financial system; • the FCA will also consider the level of compliance with FCA requirements and requests for information the firm may have exhibited; • the FCA will also want to ensure that those who manage affairs of firm to have adequate skills and experience to act with probity; • it will also consider whether business conducted soundly and prudently, and the need to minimise financial crime risk.
BUSINESS MODEL	The FCA will need to be satisfied that the Business model is: • suitable for the business; • in interests of consumers and integrity of the system; and • compatible with affairs being conducted in a sound and prudent manner.

B: Summary of FCA conditions for dual regulated firms[8]	
EFFECTIVE SUPERVISION	Firm must be capable of being effectively supervised by the FCA having regard to all the circumstances including: • nature, scale, complexity; • organisation of business; • whether the firm is subject to consolidated supervision; • product complexity; • close links; • group membership.
APPROPRIATE NON FINANCIAL RESOURCES	The FCA only considers non financial resources in the case of dual regulated firms because financial (prudential) matters are reserved for the consideration of the PRA. It will consider resources in the light of: • nature and scale of the businesses proposed or carried on; • risks to continuity of services; • group membership; • skills and expertise of management; • whether sufficient to enable compliance with any FCA requirements that may be imposed.

---

[8] Financial Services and Markets Act 2000 (Threshold Conditions) Order 2013 Pt 1C.

B: Summary of FCA conditions for dual regulated firms[8]	
SUITABILITY	The firm must be a fit and proper person, having regard to the operational objectives of the FCA (a more restricted perspective than that for singly regulated firms, where the FCA will have regard to "all the circumstances"). FCA will consider: • firm's connection with any person; • nature and complexity of the regulated activities proposed or conducted; • the need to ensure firm run appropriately, considering consumer interests and integrity of UK financial system; • level of compliance with FCA requirements and requests for information; • those who manage affairs of firm to have adequate skills and experience to act with probity; • need to minimise financial crime risk. *(NOTE: NOT whether business conducted soundly and prudently as this is a PRA duty)*
BUSINESS MODEL	Firm's business strategy is suitable for the firm having regard to FCA operational objectives.

C: Summary of PRA conditions for insurers, managing agents & Lloyd's[9]	
LEGAL STATUS	Firm must be a body corporate, registered friendly society, member of Lloyd's.

⁹ Financial Services and Markets Act 2000 (Threshold Conditions) Order 2013 Pt1D.

C: Summary of PRA conditions for insurers, managing agents & Lloyd's[9]	
LOCATION OF OFFICES	If firm is a UK body corporate its head office must be in the UK, as must its registered office (if it has one). If it is not a body corporate but has a head office in the UK, it must also carry on business in the UK.
BUSINESS TO BE CONDUCTED IN A PRUDENT MANNER	Firm must have appropriate financial and non financial resources considering: • assets versus liabilities; • appropriate valuation methods; • must remove/reduce risks to safety and soundness, & reduce risks to accuracy of asset and liability valuation; • must be sufficient to comply with PRA requirement that may be imposed; • the effect that the carrying on of the business of effecting or carrying out contracts of insurance by the firm might be expected to have on the stability of the UK financial system or on those who are or may become policyholders of the firm; • the effect that the firm's failure or being closed to new business might be expected to have on the stability of the UK financial system or on those who are or may become policyholders of the firm.

C: Summary of PRA conditions for insurers, managing agents & Lloyd's[9]	
SUITABILITY	The firm must be a fit and proper person, having regard to the PRA's objectives. Relevant considerations: • level of compliance with PRA requirements and requests for information; • those who manage affairs of firm to have adequate skills and experience to act with probity.
EFFECTIVE SUPERVISION	Considerations include: • nature, scale, complexity; • organisation of business; • product complexity; • close links; • group membership.

D: Summary of PRA conditions for deposit takers & other dual regulated firms[10]	
LEGAL STATUS	Body corporate or partnership
LOCATION OF OFFICES	If firm is a UK body corporate its head office must be in the UK, as must its registered office (if it has one). If it is not a body corporate but has a head office in the UK, it must also carry on business in the UK.

---

[10] Financial Services and Markets Act 2000 (Threshold Conditions) Order 2013 Pt 1E.

D: Summary of PRA conditions for deposit takers & other dual regulated firms[10]	
BUSINESS TO BE CONDUCTED IN A PRUDENT MANNER	Firm must have appropriate financial and non financial resources considering: • assets versus liabilities (relevant to financial resources); • appropriate valuation methods (relevant to non-financial resources); • must have resources to identify, monitor, measure and take action to remove/reduce risks to safety and soundness, and reduce risks to accuracy of asset and liability valuation; • non financial resources must be sufficient to comply with PRA requirement that may be imposed.
BUSINESS TO BE CONDUCTED IN A PRUDENT MANNER	Firm must have appropriate financial and non financial resources considering: • assets versus liabilities (relevant to financial resources); • appropriate valuation methods (relevant to non-financial resources); • must have resources to identify, monitor, measure and take action to remove/reduce risks to safety and soundness, and reduce risks to accuracy of asset and liability valuation; • non financial resources must be sufficient to comply with PRA requirement that may be imposed.

D: *Summary of PRA conditions for deposit takers & other dual regulated firms*[10]	
SUITABILITY	The firm must be a fit and proper person, having regard to the PRA's objectives. Relevant considerations: • level of compliance with PRA requirements and requests for information • those who manage affairs of firm to have adequate skills and experience to act with probity.
EFFECTIVE SUPERVISION	Considerations include: • nature, scale, complexity; • organisation of business; • product complexity; • close links; • group membership.

3.2.2 Appropriate resources/appropriate non-financial resources/Business to be conducted in a prudent manner

This condition takes four forms, depending on the firm to whom it applies:

(a) for firms only regulated by the FCA: appropriate resources;
(b) FCA condition for dual regulated firms: appropriate non-financial resources;
(c) PRA conditions for insurers, managing agents and Lloyd's members: business to be conducted in a prudent manner;
(d) PRA conditions for deposit takers and other dual regulated firms (not insurers etc): business to be conducted in a prudent manner.

The FCA conditions above ((a) and (b)) require analysis of quality as well as quantity of resource. In particular, both conditions provide that the FCA will look at appropriateness of resources in the light of risks to the continuity of the firm's services (in line with the FCA's operational objective of consumer protection), and will also consider the skills and expertise of the firm's management. For firms only regulated by the FCA, the regulator will consider their financial as well as their non-financial resources. For dual regulated firms, the FCA threshold condition only requires a firm to have adequate *non-financial* resources—because all matters financial will be dealt with by the PRA—under the "business to be conducted in a prudent manner" TC.

The PRA TCs ((c) and (d) above) "business to be conducted in a prudent manner" are drafted almost identically, apart from the matters that the PRA regards as relevant to consideration of compliance with this objective for insurers versus deposit takers. This TC states that a firm, in order to satisfy this condition, must "in particular have appropriate financial and non-financial resources". This looks at first glance to be a duplication of the FCA condition that will also apply to such firms, of "adequate non-financial resources", but there are important differences. The PRA condition is highly prescriptive, and states that to have appropriate financial resources, the firm *must* have:

- assets that are appropriate given its liabilities;
- adequate liquidity to meet liabilities, taking into account when they fall due or may fall due; and
- the firm must be willing and able to value its assets and liabilities appropriately.

In order to satisfy the non-financial resources condition, the legislation states that the firm *must* have:

- resources to identify, monitor, measure and take action to remove or reduce risks to its:
  — safety and soundness;
  — accuracy of its valuation of assets and liabilities;
- the business carried on by the firm must be, to a material extent, managed effectively; and
- the non-financial resources must also be sufficient to enable the firm to comply with:

—   requirements imposed or likely to be imposed on the firm by the PRA in the course of the exercise of its functions; and any other requirement in relation to which the PRA is required to maintain arrangements.

For both firm populations (insurers and deposit takers) the PRA will consider the following when assessing fulfilment of this TC:

*   continuity of services;
*   group membership;
*   nature, scale and complexity ;
*   consideration of the effect that the carrying on of the business might be expected to have on the stability of the UK financial system;
*   the effect that the firm's failure might be expected to have on the stability of the UK financial system. This introduces the concept of "resolvability" into the threshold conditions.

For insurers only, the PRA will consider the effects of the firm's business on those who are or may become policyholders; and the effect that the firm's failure or the firm being in run-off might be expected to have on those who are or may become policyholders. These factors are in line with the PRA's insurance specific objective of contributing to the securing of an appropriate degree of protection for policyholders, and to ensure that policyholders have an appropriate degree of continuity of cover for the risks they are insured against.

Firms need to continuously think about how they evidence to their regulator(s) that these TCs are met.

3.2.3   *Suitability*

The suitability TC applies to all firms (both FCA and dual regulated), and the regulators will consider the following when assessing fulfilment:

*   whether the firm is fit and proper;

- the need to ensure the firm runs appropriately—considering consumer interests and the integrity of UK financial system;
- level of compliance with FCA/PRA requirements and requests for information;
- whether managers have adequate skills and experience and act with probity;
- whether business is conducted soundly and prudently (this requirement is reserved for PRA consideration in the case of dual regulated firms);
- the need to minimise financial crime risk.

These provisions require a firm to consider the impact of its actions on consumers and on the integrity of the system as a whole. Since the mid 2000's the FSA has been urging firms to "treat customers fairly" and the requirement is one of the Principles for Businesses.

It is also important for dual regulated firms to note that both the PRA and the FCA will assess the probity, skills and experience of those who manage the affairs of the firm when deciding on compliance with the suitability TC. The PRA and the FCA will consider matters through the prism of their own objectives.

Compliance and HR teams can help support senior managers in their firm to comply with both the FCA and the PRA suitability requirement—and to bear in mind the on-going obligation to meet it. Training, competence, continuing professional development and evidencing of all of these things will be critical, as well as making sure that managers themselves fully appreciate what is expected of them.

3.2.4 *Effective supervision*

The "effective supervision" TC is drafted identically in each of the four sections and the regulators will assess whether a firm can be effectively supervised by looking at close links, group membership, product complexity, organisation of the business and its nature, scale and complexity.

3.2.5 Business Model

There are two different versions of the Business Model TC, which is an FCA TC, applicable to all firms, as follows:

- business model TC for firms only regulated by the FCA—which requires that the model is:
  — suitable for the business;
  — in the interests of consumers and integrity of the financial system;
  — compatible with affairs being conducted in a sound and prudent manner.
- business model TC for dual regulated firms, which states that the business strategy of the firm must be suitable having regard to the FCA's operational objectives.

Firms will have to carefully explain their business model and the rationale behind it in order to satisfy this condition.

3.3 Principles for Businesses and Fundamental Rules

Once a firm has satisfied the Threshold Conditions it will become authorised, under Pt 4A of the Financial Services & Markets Act 2000 (sometimes known as receiving "Part 4A Permission"). Firms will be authorised to conduct various regulated activities in relation to certain categories of client, and product, depending on what they have applied for.

Once authorised, a firm must comply with all elements of the FCA Handbook and PRA Rulebook that apply to their business. All firms must comply with the high level FCA Principles for Businesses. In addition, dual regulated firms must also comply with the PRA's Fundamental Rules. Firms need to comply both with the letter and the spirit of the rules and principles.

3.3.1   *The FCA's Principles for Businesses*

The Principles for Businesses (the Principles) sit at the apex of the regulatory framework governing the behaviour of UK regulated firms. They are wide ranging, far reaching and enable the FCA to take action against a firm in an extensive range of circumstances, even when a specific rule breach cannot be proven. They exist to ensure that firms behave in ways that adhere to the regulator's statutory and operational objectives.

The Principles are closely linked to the Statements of Principle and Conduct Rules that apply to approved persons. Individuals who are approved have direct personal responsibility to adhere to the principles applying to them, as well as ensuring that their firms meet the standards given in the Principles for Businesses. There is a significant amount of overlap between the Principles that apply to firms and the conduct standards that apply to approved persons, and with the Threshold Conditions and Statutory Objectives. The same themes run through each set of aims and standards. Familiarity with these themes and what they mean for the way in which a firm is run and managed is essential for leaders, senior managers, managers and those who advise them, as well as other groups, working within regulated firms.

The FCA has jurisdiction over all the Principles for Businesses (which have the status of rules) and can take action against any firm for breaching them. They are:

1. Integrity	A firm must conduct its business with integrity.
2. Skill, care and diligence	A firm must conduct its business with due skill, care and diligence.
3. Management and control	A firm must take reasonable care to organise and control its affairs responsibly and effectively, with adequate risk management systems.

4. Financial prudence	A firm must maintain adequate financial resources.
5. Market conduct	A firm must observe proper standards of market conduct.
6. Customers' interests	A firm must pay due regard to the interests of its customers and treat them fairly.
7. Communications with clients	A firm must pay due regard to the information needs of its clients, and communicate information to them in a way which is clear, fair and not misleading.
8. Conflicts of interest	A firm must manage conflicts of interest fairly, both between itself and its customers and between a customer and another client.
9. Customers: relationships of trust	A firm must take reasonable care to ensure the suitability of its advice and discretionary decisions for any customer who is entitled to rely upon its judgment.
10. Clients' assets	A firm must arrange adequate protection for clients' assets when it is responsible for them.
11. Relations with regulators	A *firm* must deal with its regulators in an open and cooperative way, and must disclose to the *appropriate regulator* appropriately anything relating to the *firm* of which that regulator would reasonably expect notice.

3.3.2 The relationship between the Principles and the Threshold Conditions

A commitment to following the Principles is required from all firms when they are first applying authorisation. A willingness and ability to comply with them is an essential component of the satisfaction of the threshold conditions. Specifically, the "Suitability" TC is reflected in the Principles. When assessing suitability the FCA will look at a firm holistically, and will consider, amongst other things:

- The firm's relationships and connections with other firms/persons. At the stage where a firm is seeking authorisation, its relationship with other entities in a group structure is of great interest to the FCA, due to the impact this may have on the firm's ability to do business in a range of circumstances, its resolvability and complexity. Also, the FCA needs to be satisfied that the firm is not engaged in any way with another entity that would impede the regulator's ability to regulate it. At an individual level, the FCA will want to know who is behind the firm, and whether there are controlling minds beyond the Directors named on the application form. These considerations are given effect by a number of the Principles, most notably Principle 1: Integrity, Principle 2: Skill, care and diligence and Principle 3: Management and control. Firms seeking authorisation, or a variation of permission that would enable them to conduct more business, need to consider their adherence to the Principles as well as the Threshold Conditions.

- The nature (including the complexity) of any regulated activity that the applicant firm carries on or seeks to carry on. The regulators will need to be satisfied that a firm has the right strategy, structure and management in place, as well as the prudential strength, to be allowed to conduct the business it is proposing. A number of the Principles overlap with this, most notably Principle 2: Skill, care and diligence, and Principle 3: Management & Control.

- The need to ensure that the applicant firm's affairs are conducted in an appropriate manner, having regard in particular to the interests of consumers and the integrity of the UK financial system. Consumer interests are specifically referred to in three Principles. These are Principle 6: Customers' interest, Principle 7: Communications with clients and Principle 9: Customers relationships of trust, and so there ought to be no doubt in the mind of the regulated community as to the significance of the customer experience in financial services regulation. The concept of integrity as it applies to the behaviour of firms (which encompasses all firm behaviours) is found in Principle 1: Integrity. Market Conduct is specifically covered by Principle 5: Market conduct. The protection of the consumer and ensuring integrity of the UK financial system are two of the FCA's operational objectives, that support the overarching objective of ensuring relevant markets function well.

- Whether the firm has complied and is complying with requirements imposed by the regulators in the exercise of its functions, or requests made by the FCA, relating to the provision of information to the FCA and, where the firm has so complied or is so complying, the manner of that compliance. The need for a firm to behave in an open and co-operative way with the regulator is essential if it is to be effectively supervised. The duty is reflected in Principle 11: Relations with regulators. The manner in which a firm engages with the regulator can have a significant impact on how it experiences regulation, and on how the regulator perceives it. These matters are also considered under the Threshold Condition of "effective supervision".

- Whether those who manage the applicant firm's affairs have adequate skills and experience and act with probity. The character and skills of those who manage a firm are subject to a great deal of scrutiny from the regulator, who seeks to ensure that only those with the right experience and approach be allowed to run regulated firms. This is directly reflected in Principle 3: Management and control, as well as in the Statements of Principle for Approved Persons.

- Whether the applicant firm's business is being, or is to be, managed in such a way as to ensure that its affairs will be conducted in a sound and prudent manner. Principle 3: Management and control relates to these matters, as does Principle 4: Financial prudence. Matters of prudence and sound management are also considered under the Threshold Condition of "Adequate resources". The concepts of careful financial stewardship and prudence have always been a key component but have assumed even greater importance since the crash, with law makers keen to ensure that tax payer bailouts of financial institutions and related instability are events not easily repeated.

- The need to minimise the extent to which it is possible for the business carried on by the firm to be used for a purpose connected with financial crime. Principle 1: Integrity and Principle 5: Market Conduct relate most directly to considerations under this heading, although other Principles are also relevant.

3.3.3 Status of the Principles

The Principles are "made rules" under s.137 of the Financial Services and Markets Act 2000, which means that enforcement action can be taken when any of them are breached by a firm. They give the FCA a substantial amount of power to take action against firms in a vast array of circumstances, and where it may not be possible to pin point a specific rule breach. In many enforcement cases, however, the Principles are cited alongside other rules that have been breached (for example the client assets rules found in the Client Assets section of the FCA Handbook (CASS), in a client money case, in addition to Principle 10: Client Assets).

3.3.4 Breaches of the Principles

The whole range of sanctions can be invoked against a firm that is found to have breached one or more of the Principles, including fine, prohibition, public censure, injunction, or the use of product intervention or financial promotion powers. Criminal action may also be taken by the FCA in cases of criminal market abuse (insider dealing for example), and for money laundering or terrorist financing offences, amongst other things.

3.3.5 The PRA's Fundamental Rules

In common with the Principles, the Fundamental Rules (FRs) are high-level rules. They collectively act as an expression of the PRA's general objective of promoting the safety and soundness of regulated firms and insurance objective of contributing to securing an appropriate degree of protection for those who are or may become policyholders. The FRs apply to all PRA regulated firms irrespective of size and business carried on.

The FRs themselves state that:

"Firms must ensure they are compliant with all applicable PRA rules and directly applicable EU regulations, including the Fundamental Rules, as set out in the PRA Rulebook. The Fundamental Rules require firms to act in accordance with 'safety and soundness' by setting specific high-level requirements on them, namely:"

Fundamental Rule 1	A firm must conduct its business with integrity
Fundamental Rule 2	A firm must conduct its business with due skill, care and diligence
Fundamental Rule 3	A firm must act in a prudent manner
Fundamental Rule 4	A firm must at all times maintain adequate financial resources
Fundamental Rule 5	A firm must have in place effective risk strategies and risk management systems.
Fundamental Rule 6	A firm must organise and control its affairs responsibly and effectively
Fundamental Rule 7	A firm must deal with its regulators in an open and co-operative way, and must disclose to the PRA appropriately anything relating to the firm of which the PRA would reasonably expect notice.
Fundamental Rule 8	A firm must prepare for resolution so, if the need arises, it can be resolved in an orderly manner with a minimum disruption of critical services.

In its Approach to Banking/Insurance Supervision documents, updated in March 2016 and found on the PRA website,[11] the PRA states that:

> "as with the Threshold Conditions, it is vital that boards and senior management understand the Fundamental Rules, the more detailed rules in the PRA Rulebook and the directly applicable EU regulations, and establish within their firms a culture that supports adherence to the spirit and the letter of the requirements."

This strong and unequivocal language creates an obligation within firms to ensure that their senior staff familiarize themselves with these FRs, and actively consider their application to all areas of the firm's activities, and embed the philosophy they encapsulate (behaving with integrity and prudence etc) in to the firm's culture.

The PRA encourages firms to exercise judgment, and take responsibility for what the FRs mean in relation to their business. As they are high level, within their broad scope, compliance can be achieved in different ways.

3.4 Conduct and culture

The global financial crisis prompted domestic and international regulatory bodies to reassess the way in which they sought to control markets, firms and individuals. There was widespread recognition of the notion that a rules-based approach to regulation had proved insufficient in ensuring well functioning markets and fair treatment of consumers, and although the UK had tried to move to a more principles based approach prior to the crisis, this too proved ineffective. In addition to the Statutory Objectives, Threshold Conditions, Principles for Businesses and Fundamental Rules discussed thus far, the regulatory agenda has widened to include

---

[11] *http://www.bankofengland.co.uk/pra/Pages/policy/handbook.aspx, http://www. bankofengland.co.uk/publications/Documents/praapproach/bankingappr1406.pdf,* p.85 [both accessed April 2016].

concepts of how a firm conducts itself, and by extension mitigates its "conduct risk", and the culture within which it operates.

Central to these themes is the drive to ensure that senior managers in firms not only ensure that the letter of the rules is complied with, but also their "spirit". Senior managers themselves are expected to take full responsibility for their decisions, and give due consideration to all relevant matters, by, for example, considering the impact of a strategy on a firm's customer base rather than just on its balance sheet. An additional motivation on the part of regulators in tightening up the controls around individual behaviour is to ensure that the right people can be held to account should mistakes or misconduct occur.

In the view of the supra-national standard setting body the Financial Stability Board, senior leaders in firms are responsible for setting the tone, and by extension the culture, of their organisation. In the UK, the FCA has also spoken of the need for the right tone from the top, and has made it clear that having the right "culture", i.e., one which puts customers and market integrity at the heart of the firm's business, is an important component of conduct risk. In fact, the FCA's predecessor, the Financial Services Authority, was also interested in how a firm conducted its business, particularly in relation to retail clients, and initiated the "treating customers' fairly" (TCF) project as far back as 2006. Although ideas of the importance of conduct and culture in financial services firms and markets are not in themselves new, they have been given an increased emphasis due to the crisis.

The FCA has not specifically defined culture, or conduct risk, but has said that it will assess culture by looking at areas of a firm's business and behaviours and drawing conclusions; "joining the dots", to use the FCA's own phrase.[12]

---

[12] Clive Adamson Speech, "The Importance of Culture in Driving Behaviours of Firms and how the FCA will Assess This", available at *http://www.fca.org.uk/news/ regulation-professionalism* [Accessed February 24, 2016].

Clive Adamson, former Director of Supervision at the FCA, has put forward[13] the idea of culture as being like the DNA of a firm, and has said that in the FCA's view an effective culture is one that supports a business model and business practices that have at their core the fair treatment of customers and behaviours that do not harm market integrity.

3.4.1 Drivers of culture at a firm

According to the FCA, the key drivers of culture at a firm, which are heavily inter-linked, are:

- Tone from the top: whereby the CEO and senior managers set out the key company values, and personally demonstrate them through their actions. The values must then be translated into behaviours throughout the organisation.
- Business practices and ways of behaving: the positive culture set from the top must be translated into effective business practices. This is a way to make cultural elements more measurable and "hard edged". Firms need to embed the behaviours that they have identified as being critical to execute their cultural strategy and approach, and to measure these.
- Performance management, employee development and reward programmes: the FCA has identified that in order to embed the right cultural practices a firm needs to deploy a number of different levers, including remuneration, effective recruitment and promotion policies, and measurement and monitoring of employees' performance.

3.4.2 How the FCA assesses culture

The FCA may assess the culture of a firm through a range of different measures such as:

- how a firm responds to, and deals with, regulatory issues;

---

[13] Clive Adamson Speech, "The Importance of Culture in Driving Behaviours of Firms", available at *http://www.fca.org.uk/news/regulation-professionalism* [Accessed February 24, 2016].

- what customers are actually experiencing when they buy a product or service from front-line staff;
- how a firm runs its product approval process and what factors it takes into account;
- the manner in which decisions are made or escalated;
- the behaviour of that firm in certain markets;
- remuneration structures;
- board level engagement with all of the above issues, and more, including whether the board probes high return products or business lines, and whether it understands strategies for cross-selling products, how fast growth is obtained and whether products are being sold to markets they are designed for.

In its 2015/16 Business Plan the FCA announced a plan to conduct a thematic review on

> "whether culture change programmes in retail and wholesale banks were driving the right behaviour, in particular focusing on remuneration, appraisal and promotion decisions of middle management, as well as how concerns are reported and acted on".

However, in late 2015, at the conclusion of the scoping phase of the project, the FCA decided not to continue to subsequent phases. In response to a Freedom of Information Act request,[14] the FCA published it's rationale for the ceasing of the work in January 2016. It said that:

> "As we analysed this information in more detail and considered how we could take forward the second phase of the work it became even clearer that each firm has, and needs to have, its own approach. They need to build a strong culture from the top down, leading by example and setting the right incentives that will work in their firm, and their culture. We therefore concluded that conducting the second phase of the thematic review was not the best way to achieve the cultural change required bank by bank. The

---

[14] *http://www.fca.org.uk/static/documents/foi/foi4350-information-provided.pdf* [Accessed February 24, 2016].

idiosyncratic nature of each individual institution meant that issuing generalised good and poor practice guidance was unlikely to be of sufficient value to justify continuing to focus our resources on the cross-firm work rather than by addressing this firm by firm with individual institutions. Our initial scoping work did include some useful findings about the areas under review which we have fed back to firms and which we will use in our ongoing work. It did not however amount to an analysis of good and poor practice.

Given these factors, we decided that the best way to support and drive on-going efforts to improve culture is to continue to engage individually with firms to encourage their delivery of cultural change as well as supporting other initiatives outside the FCA. We will also continue to focus on the importance of culture and of incentives and reward in the other work we do whether as part of our thematic programme or in our day to day authorisation, supervision and enforcement work."

The FCA also provided additional information on its approach to culture, in this document. They said that the Senior Managers and Certification Regime:

"has accountability at its core. The cultures in financial institutions only exist as a result of the collective actions of individual employees, so driving cultural change is really about influencing individuals to act in certain ways. Professional integrity, accountability and appropriate remuneration are therefore key foundations for this cultural change.

The new regime will ensure that individuals, their employers and regulators know who is responsible for what, and when things go wrong the right people will be held to account. A map showing individuals' and firms' responsibilities will cover the Senior Managers with overall responsibility in a firm, ensuring that the regulators can focus on the individuals whom firms genuinely see as accountable."

The FCA said that it would work on culture through the medium of accountability, incentives, remuneration and performance management, and that it would continue to support and drive culture change in the most effective way, by:

1. focusing on engagement with individual firms through supervision;
2. using its position as the conduct regulator to promote constructive discussions with various stakeholders including industry and consumer groups;
3. offering support to the increasing number of initiatives outside the FCA on banking culture, such as the work being done by the G30 and by the BSB;
4. continuing to demand high standards of conduct, backed by supervision and enforcement action if necessary, such that an appropriate culture remains a top priority for banks' management.

3.4.3   Conduct Risk

The FCA has provided ideas[15] on how a firm might begin to assess conduct risk, which it has identified as having three main causes:

Inherent factors A range of inherent drivers of conduct risk interact to produce poor choices and outcomes in financial markets. These drivers are a combination of supply-side market failures (e.g., information problems) and demand-side weaknesses (e.g., inbuilt biases), which are often exacerbated by low financial capability among consumers.

Structures and behaviours Structures, processes and management (including culture and incentives) that have been

---

[15]   FCA 2014 Risk Outlook.

designed into and become embedded in the financial sector, allowing firms to profit from systematic consumer shortcomings and from market failures.

Environmental factors Long-running and current economic, regulatory and technological trends and changes are important drivers of firm and consumer decisions.

Consideration of conduct risk issues is also central to the FCA's methodology when conducting firm-specific supervision under the Firm Systematic Framework, which is covered in more detail later on in this chapter, as well as when it is doing event-driven work or looking at issues and products. The Firm Systematic Framework has as one of its elements an assessment of governance and culture, which includes an assessment of the effectiveness of a firm's identification, management and reduction of conduct risk.

Further pointers on how to identify and manage conduct risk were provided by Tracy McDermott, then Director of Supervision, investment, wholesale and specialists), in a speech delivered in July 2015. Ms McDermott identified five conduct questions firms should be asking themselves:

1. How are the conduct risks inherent within the business identified?	A firm must ask the right questions of the business, conduct root cause analysis when problems are identified and learn from past mistakes.

2. Who is responsible for managing the conduct of the business?	The FCA expects firms be asking themselves how they are encouraging their employees to be and feel responsible for actually managing the conduct of their business. Essential within this is encouraging the first line of defence, the business itself, to manage conduct risk. McDermott said that they understand their business better than anyone else; they know where the risks are and they should—if correctly incentivized—have the greatest interest in long term, sustainable good business practices. They need to understand that is part of their job and be helped to do it well.
3. What support mechanisms does the business have to enable people to improve the conduct of their business or function?	Examples of effective support mechanisms may be where new product and new business approval committees are robust and appropriately represented by the control functions, or by a firm having training and induction programmes that lay out a its expectations of its staff. Further, management information should be provided to those in supervisory roles that is useful, timely and genuinely helps them supervise their staff. McDermott went on to say: "Ultimately this is also about creating what we sometimes call a culture of appropriate escalation, where people can speak up when they observe poor behaviour or are unsure about what to do. Too often people are unwilling to do this, or are penalised if they do."

4. How do the board and executive committees gain oversight of the conduct of the organisation?	At a basic level, this is about what information the board and executive see, and how they take it into account in their decision-making. McDermott acknowledged that although progress has been made in getting conduct issues onto board agendas, there is still some way to go in getting them to take conduct implications into account in every strategic decision and recognise that *their* decisions can have just as big an impact on the way business is conducted as the behaviour and decisions of those who report to them.
5. Finally, do firms have any perverse incentives or other activities that may undermine any strategies put in place to answer the first four questions.	

Ms McDermott pointed out as an example the fact that most employees of any firm will never—or rarely—see the CEO. Their role models are not board members but might be the top trader or the desk head. If they see a colleague rewarded and promoted, even if their behaviour is not consistent with the values of the firm, this does not send a clear message that such behaviour is not tolerated.

One of the aims behind the rules governing individual behaviour is to ensure that staff work together to create and maintain a positive culture that meets regulatory expectations around customer treatment and market integrity. How a firm achieves its aims in this regard will be a matter primarily for the Board to decide. In the current regulatory environment questions of a firm's culture, and of its conduct, and how it identifies, manages and mitigates "conduct risk", are central to the operation of a successful and compliant business.

3.5   FCA Supervisory Approach

The two regulators supervise firms from the perspective of their own objectives. The PRA, therefore, seeks to ensure that firms operate in a way that does not pose a threat to the safety and soundness of the UK financial system. The FCA seeks to ensure that firms play their part in enabling relevant markets to function well. The PRA supervises dual regulated firms from a prudential perspective, with the FCA focusing on conduct matters. For singly regulated firms, the FCA will supervise them from both a prudential and a conduct perspective.

The FCA supervisory model is judgment led and outcomes focused, and puts both the interests of the consumer and market integrity at its heart. Firms are classified as either "fixed" or "flexible" portfolio. They are supervised using the three pillars model.

3.5.1   *The three pillars of FCA supervision*

The FCA uses a three pronged approach to supervising firms, known as the three pillars of supervision.

3.5.2   *Three pillar supervision model for fixed portfolio firms*

Fixed portfolio firms are a small population of firms out of the total regulated by the FCA, that based on factors such as size, market presence and customer footprint, require the highest level of supervisory attention. They are allocated a named individual supervisor, and are proactively supervised using a continuous assessment approach.

Fixed portfolio firms will be subject to Pillar 1 of the three pillar model of supervision. Pillar 1 proactive supervision generally covers a 12 to 36 month cycle and will involve firm meetings, review of management information, an annual strategy meeting and other proactive firm work. Deep dive(s) assessments that look at how a firm's business operates in practice may also be scheduled as part of the supervision strategy. In relation to business model and strategy analysis (BMSAs) the FCA will

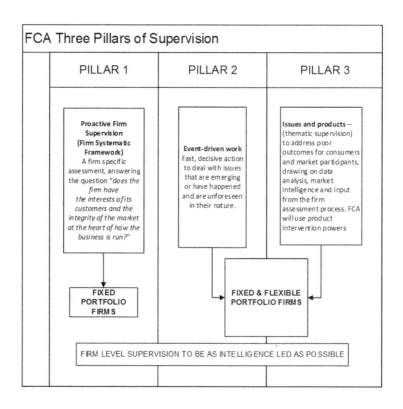

FCA Three Pillars of Supervision

PILLAR 1	PILLAR 2	PILLAR 3

Proactive Firm Supervision (Firm Systematic Framework) A firm specific assessment, answering the question *"does the firm have the interests of its customers and the integrity of the market at the heart of how the business is run?"*

Event-driven work Fast, decisive action to deal with issues that are emerging or have happened and are unforeseen in their nature.

Issues and products – (thematic supervision) to address poor outcomes for consumers and market participants, drawing on data analysis, market intelligence and input from the firm assessment process. FCA will use product intervention powers

FIXED PORTFOLIO FIRMS

FIXED & FLEXIBLE PORTFOLIO FIRMS

FIRM LEVEL SUPERVISION TO BE AS INTELLIGENCE LED AS POSSIBLE

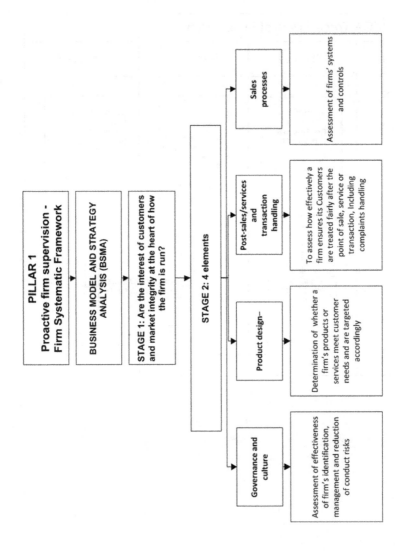

pay particular attention where it sees common indicators of heightened risk such as strategies that depend on cross-selling. For all fixed portfolio firms the FCA will conduct periodic analysis, normally across a peer group of firms sharing similar business models or activity. Peer group BMSAs for wholesale firms focuses primarily on business lines. Also, cross-border services and activities are as relevant to FCA assessments of wholesale firms as individual legal entities.

A firm evaluation (a summary of the FCA's view of a firm or group based on all the information it has about it) is undertaken in a cycle ranging from 1 to 3 years depending on the scale of the firm/group's activities and the FCA's assessment of risk. Key messages from the firm evaluation are given in a letter to the board of directors. The FCA aims to discuss its view with the board and its senior management and will usually attend a board meeting. Interim reviews of the firm evaluation are carried out during the supervisory cycle.

Pillar 2 event-driven, reactive supervision is discussed below as is Pillar 3 issues and product supervision.

3.5.3   *Three pillar supervision model for flexible portfolio firms*

The majority of the firms regulated by the FCA will be flexible portfolio, which means that they do not have a named supervisor and use the FCA Customer Contact Centre to communicate with the FCA, in the first instance.

They are supervised under Pillars 2 and 3 of the 3 Pillar model. Pillar 1 proactive supervision does not apply to flexible portfolio firms.

Pillar 2 event-driven, reactive supervision has a pre-emptive focus, aiming to identify and prevent consumer detriment and threats to market integrity before they happen. Risks and problems can be discovered through a number of sources, including information from the firm as well as data analysis. The FCA's focus is on addressing the most important issues

125

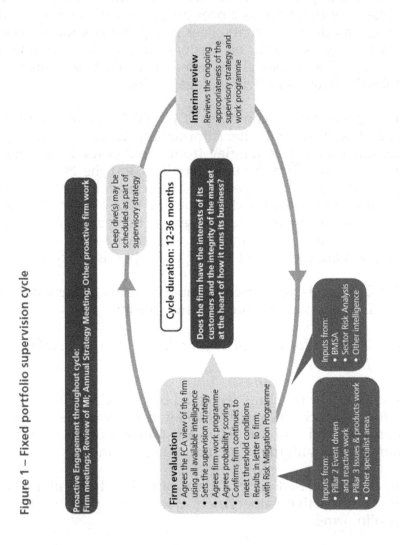

Figure 1 – Fixed portfolio supervision cycle

Interim review
Reviews the ongoing appropriateness of the supervisory strategy and work programme

Deep dive(s) may be scheduled as part of supervisory strategy

Cycle duration: 12-36 months

Does the firm have the interests of its customers and the integrity of the market at the heart of how it runs its business?

Proactive Engagement throughout cycle:
Firm meetings; Review of MI; Annual Strategy Meeting; Other proactive firm work

Firm evaluation
• Agrees the FCA view of the firm using all available intelligence
• Sets the supervision strategy
• Agrees firm work programme
• Agrees probability scoring
• Confirms firm continues to meet threshold conditions
• Results in letter to firm, with Risk Mitigation Programme

Inputs from:
• BMSA
• Sector Risk Analysis
• Other intelligence

Inputs from:
• Pillar 2 Event driven and reactive work
• Pillar 3 Issues & products work
• Other specialist areas

Diagram reproduced from FCA's Approach to Supervision for Fixed Portfolio firms (September 2015).

126

that affect its objectives. It expects firms to fix the root causes of problems as well as the symptoms. It expects firms to have a comprehensive and credible plan of action to mitigate risks.

Pillar 3 issues and products supervision. The FCA's work under this pillar is fundamental to its approach to identifying and mitigating risks across multiple firms or whole sectors. Through sector analysis the FCA identifies common emerging risks, new products and other issues that it examines through a range of activities including thematic reviews. The FCA's findings from this work are communicated to the industry and firms are expected to consider and act as necessary on the findings.

3.5.4 FCA Prudential classifications

All authorised firms have their conduct supervised by the FCA and have a conduct classification. FCA only regulated firms (around 25,000, not including consumer credit firms) will also have their prudential activities supervised by the FCA and will have a prudential classification ranging from P1 to P4. The 1,700 remaining firms, which are dual regulated, have their prudential status regulated by the PRA.

Firms that are prudentially regulated by the FCA fall into four prudential categories: P1, P2, P3 and P4. The prudential categories determine the intensity of the prudential supervision of the firm. The prudential classification is:

- P1 firms and groups are those whose failure could cause significant, lasting damage to the market place, consumers and client assets, due to their size and market impact.
- P2 firms and groups are those whose failure would have less impact than P1 firms, but would nevertheless damage markets or consumers and client assets.
- P3 firms and groups are those whose failure, even if disorderly, is unlikely to have a significant market impact. They have the lowest intensity of prudential supervision.

- P4 firms are those with special circumstances—for example, firms in administration—for which bespoke arrangements may be necessary.

For P1 and P2 firms the FCA carries out a comprehensive capital and liquidity analysis and a risk management capability assessment.

The FCA Handbook sets out minimum financial resources requirements (FRR) for all firms and this is the starting point for any prudential supervisory review. The scope and nature of an FRR is:

- P1 firms have a capital and (if applicable) liquidity assessment every two years.
- P2 firms have a capital and (if applicable) liquidity assessment every three to four years.

The FCA does not usually carry out prudential assessments for P3 firms nor does it proactively review or challenge how these firms calculate and meet their FRR. P3 firms are monitored by the FCA in two ways. First, reactively using an alerts-based system that allows the FCA to identify and deal with firms that have breached their prudential requirements. Secondly, through targeted cross-firm work assessing whether firms in a peer group are meeting the FRR.

3.5.5 *The FCA's Ten Supervision Principles*

The FCA has ten supervision principles, which provide firms with the FCA's perspective, when it is conducting supervisory activity.

1. *Ensuring fair outcomes for consumers and markets.* This is the dual consideration that runs through all of the FCA's work; the FCA will assess issues according to their impact on both consumers and market integrity.
2. Being *forward-looking and pre-emptive,* identifying potential risks and taking action before they have a serious impact.

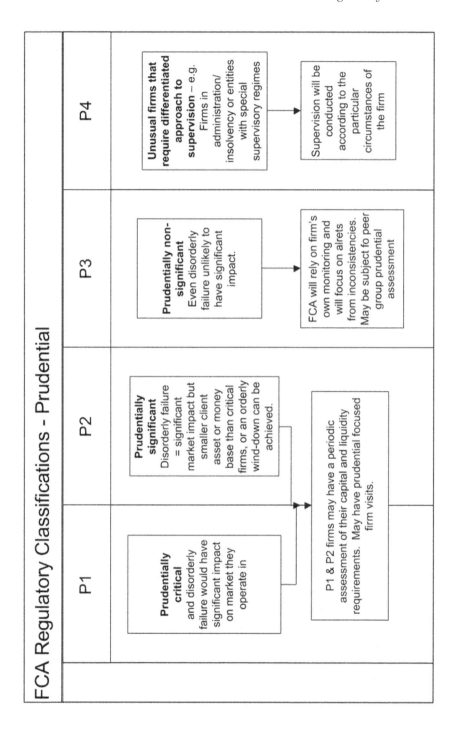

FCA Regulatory Classifications - Prudential

P1	P2	P3	P4
Prudentially critical and disorderly failure would have significant impact on market they operate in	**Prudentially significant** Disorderly failure = significant market impact but smaller client asset or money base than critical firms, or an orderly wind-down can be achieved.	**Prudentially non-significant** Even disorderly failure unlikely to have significant impact.	**Unusual firms that require differentiated approach to supervision** – e.g. Firms in administration/ insolvency or entities with special supervisory regimes
P1 & P2 firms may have a periodic assessment of their capital and liquidity requirements. May have prudential focused firm visits.		FCA will rely on firm's own monitoring and will focus on alrets from inconsistencies. May be subject fo peer group prudential assessment	Supervision will be conducted according to the particular circumstances of the firm

3. Being *focused on the big issues and causes of problems. The FCA states that it will* concentrate its resources on issues that have a significant impact on its objectives.
4. Taking *a judgment-based approach,* with the emphasis on achieving the right outcomes.
5. *Ensuring firms act in the right spirit* which means they consider the impact of their actions on consumers and markets rather than just complying with the letter of the law.
6. Examining *business models and culture,* and the impact they have on consumer and market outcomes. The FCA is interested in how a firm makes its money, as this can drive many potential risks.
7. *An emphasis on individual accountability,* ensuring senior management understand that they are personally responsible for their actions—and that they will be held to account when things go wrong.
8. Being *robust when things go wrong,* making sure that problems are fixed, consumers are protected and compensated, and poor behaviour is rectified along with its root causes.
9. *Communicating openly* with industry, firms and consumers to gain a deeper understanding of the issues they face.
10. *Having a joined-up approach,* making sure firms get consistent messages from the FCA. The FCA will also engage with the PRA to ensure effective independent supervision of dual-regulated firms, and work with other regulatory and advisory bodies including the Financial Ombudsman Service, Financial Services Compensation Scheme, Money Advice Service and international regulators.

3.5.5.1   *Fair outcomes for consumers and markets*

The wording of the first supervision principle to include markets as well as consumers marks a subtle but important difference between many of the FCA's previous pronouncements on "fair outcomes for consumers", and ensures that outcomes are noted as a critical consideration in both the retail and the wholesale markets. The supervision principle ties in with the FCA's overarching objective: to ensure that "relevant markets function well". It is a very broad principle of supervision, and has the potential to encompass all of a firm's activities. The philosophy underpinning it is that the FCA will focus on the end result of a firm's activity or behaviour, and the impact this has on consumers and markets. This is an approach the FCA has been speaking and writing about extensively.

Firms, in whichever sphere they operate, need to make sure that they are assessing the outcomes of their activities, for their customers and the markets in which they operate. For retail firms this will mean monitoring and testing work that encompasses, for example, mystery shopping and risk-based analysis of client files to ensure the suitability requirements have been met. In the wholesale environment, a focus on stamping out conduct that may lead to unfairness in markets will be key; such behaviours are high up on the regulator's agenda due in part to recent scandals involving benchmark fixing. Further, poor behaviour in the wholesale markets can have a knock on effect to retail markets and consumers. Tackling these issues will require firms to get their "culture" right—an issue that is contained in another of the supervision principles.

3.5.5.2   *Complying with the spirit, as well as the letter, of regulation*

The fifth supervision principle, "Ensuring firms act in the right spirit, which means they consider the impact of their actions on consumers and markets rather than just complying with the letter of the law", shows that firms have to adhere to (and to provide evidence of adherence to) high-level principles and codes of behavior, as well the letter of the law. This means that firms, as well as the regulator, need to employ people who can use their judgment in deciding whether customer outcomes are fair, and whether staff are behaving in ways that are supporting, rather than impeding, fair operation of the markets in which they operate.

Again, this principle points to the need for a firm to get its culture right. The FCA continues to bang the drum on this issue, and although some evidence suggests lessons are being learned (the December 2014 thematic work on the provision of retail investment advice—TR14/21—found that most firms understood the requirements and were adhering to them, for example), newspaper headlines continue to highlight poor cultural behaviours in the financial services industry.

The FCA continues to focus on a firm's attitude to the industry in which it operates, as evidenced by its culture. Compliance with the letter of the law remains important, but equally important will be adherence to high ethical standards, and promulgating a market and consumer positive culture.

3.5.6   Enhanced Supervision

In June 2014 the FCA published a document entitled Tackling serious failings in firms: A response to the Special Measures proposal of the Parliamentary Commission on Banking Standards (the PCBS Report).[16] The document provides an overview of the FCA's existing approach to supervision, and contains details of its "Enhanced Supervision Model". The document should be read alongside the PRA Statement of Policy on "The use of PRA powers to address serous failings in the culture of firms", by dual regulated firms.

The Enhanced Supervision Model sits between standard supervision and enforcement action, and will be deployed where the FCA identifies that a firm presents serious risks to its objectives, due to a serious failure of culture, governance or standards, and they do not think that the usual supervisory approach will be sufficient to tackle the issues in a timely way.

It is not a precursor to enforcement action that a firm has first been made subject to enhanced supervision; the FCA says that "it is important that regulators use judgment, rather than a set of consequential processes, to determine what regulatory tools and powers are appropriate. Enforcement investigations may therefore begin without a firm having been placed in Enhanced

---

[16] http://www.fca.org.uk/static/article-type/news/tackling-serious-failings-in-firms.pdf [Accessed 24 February 2016].

Supervision." It is also likely to be the case that firms subject to enhanced supervision may be referred for enforcement action at a later stage, or even concurrently, if the supervision is aimed at remedying problems that have been identified and is not intended to punish firms for misconduct that might already have occurred, which is the role of enforcement.

The FCA provides the following indicators of the kinds of failings that would lead to Enhanced Supervision (or other regulatory action):

- the observation of numerous or especially significant conduct failings or repeated failings that when examined individually might not be considered serious;
- occurrence of failings in several business areas, as this is an indicator of wider cultural issues within the firm;
- a poorly functioning Board, for example failing to challenge executives or take a lead in considering conduct;
- evidence of control areas such as Risk, Compliance and Internal Audit being poorly managed, under-resourced, or unable to make their voices heard at board level;
- evidence of weak risk management (the FCA may consider the PRA's findings in relation to prudential risk management); or
- evidence of other weaknesses in the way in which the board and senior management influence key cultural factors, for example "tone from the top", pay and incentives, and their adherence to the firm's values.

3.5.6.1 *Enhanced supervision model will apply to all firms and not just banks*

Although the Enhanced Supervision model has been created in response to the PCBS report and recommendations, it is not limited in application to banks. The FCA make clear that their supervisory model, including the enhanced supervision element, applies to all regulated firms in whichever sector they operate. Senior individuals and boards in all firms therefore need to actively engage with issues of culture and conduct on a firm-wide basis, if they are not already doing so.

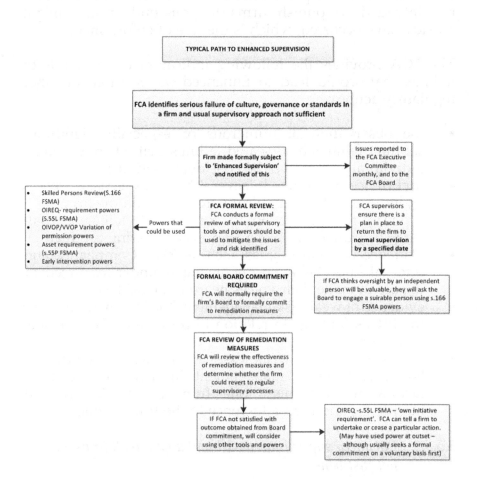

TYPICAL PATH TO ENHANCED SUPERVISION

FCA identifies serious failure of culture, governance or standards In a firm and usual supervisory approach not sufficient

Firm made formally subject to 'Enhanced Supervision' and notified of this

Issues reported to the FCA Executive Committee monthly, and to the FCA Board

- Skilled Persons Review(S.166 FSMA)
- OIREQ- requirement powers (S.55L FSMA)
- OIVOP/VVOP Variation of permission powers
- Asset requirement powers (s.55P FSMA)
- Early intervention powers

Powers that could be used

FCA FORMAL REVIEW: FCA conducts a formal review of what supervisory tools and powers should be used to mitigate the issues and risk identified

FCA supervisors ensure there is a plan in place to return the firm to **normal supervision by a specified date**

FORMAL BOARD COMMITMENT REQUIRED
FCA will normally require the firm's Board to formally commit to remediation measures

If FCA thinks oversight by an independent person will be valuable, they will ask the Board to engage a suitable person using s.166 FSMA powers

FCA REVIEW OF REMEDIATION MEASURES
FCA will review the effectiveness of remediation measures and determine whether the firm could revert to regular supervisory processes

IF FCA not satisfied with outcome obtained from Board commitment, will consider using other tools and powers

OIREQ -s.55L FSMA – 'own initiative requirement'. FCA can tell a firm to undertake or cease a particular action. (May have used power at outset – although usually seeks a formal commitment on a voluntary basis first)

3.5.6.2 Firms likely to be made subject to enhanced supervision for a defined period

When a firm is placed under Enhanced Supervision, and all that this entails, it is likely to be for a set period. The FCA document[17] states that FCA supervisors will ensure there is a plan in place to return the firm to "normal" supervision by a set date. The FCA is not clear on whether this date will be notified to the firm itself but this is likely to be the case as there is nothing to be gained from not providing the firm with this information. Knowing the timeframe in which the FCA expects the firm to remedy the deficiencies identified is likely to help firms meet the FCA's expectations.

3.5.6.3 The buck stops at the top

Enhanced Supervision is intended to tackle "the most serious failings in standards, governance or culture within a firm", and the underlying failings at a senior level in firms. The indicators of when the FCA might deploy Enhanced Supervision make clear that it will be used as a direct method of holding a board responsible for the tone they set within their firm.

Those working in the risk, compliance and internal audit functions (the control functions) might wish to draw to their board's attention one particular indicator as to when the Enhanced Supervision may be used, i.e. when there is evidence of control areas such as Risk, Compliance and Internal Audit being poorly managed, under-resourced, or unable to make their voices heard at board level. Boards who wish to avoid coming under intense regulatory scrutiny therefore need to ensure that their control functions have a "seat at the table", and are properly resourced, managed and can be heard.

Enhanced Supervision has at its centre the requirement that the board undertake to make certain changes. It is likely that the FCA will seek to achieve undertakings via voluntary methods initially, but will not hesitate to deploy statutory powers where

---

[17] https://www.fca.org.uk/static/article-type/news/tackling-serious-failings-in-firms.pdf [Accessed 24 February 2016].

the voluntary route is ineffective. Where the FCA is of the view that it has no option but to use statutory powers to compel a firm to behave in a certain way, this will reflect poorly on the firm and may even impact upon its compliance with the threshold conditions, in particular the "Suitability" TC.

3.6 How the FCA supervises individuals

3.6.1 *Controlled functions*

The FSMA gives the PRA and the FCA certain powers and responsibilities over individuals that carry on certain roles within the UK financial services industry. These roles are known as "controlled functions" and the individuals performing them are described as "approved persons". An approved person must obtain regulatory approval before performing a controlled function.

A UK bank is dual regulated in the sense that conduct of business supervision is carried out by the FCA and prudential supervision by the PRA. Unsurprisingly, when a financial institution is dual regulated the PRA and FCA have divided responsibility for approving individuals carrying on controlled functions.

The different types of controlled function can be grouped under the following headings: governing functions, required functions, systems and controls function, significant management function and customer dealing function. The first four of these controlled functions are referred to as "significant influence functions" and individuals performing them are subject to intensive supervision by the regulators as such persons often occupy a senior management position within their firm and can influence matters such as business strategy, culture and compliance with regulatory requirements.

The controlled functions that the PRA has designated responsibility for in a dual regulated firm like a bank focus on the roles that it considers are particularly important for ensuring that a financial institution's business is run in a safe and sound manner. All of the governing functions (covering directors, non-executive directors and the chief executive), some of the required functions and the systems and controls function are specified by the PRA. The FCA takes responsibility for certain required functions and the customer dealing function.

3.6.2 *Application for approval*

The application for approved person status is a detailed process.

Making the application involves completing and providing the necessary paperwork and further guidance on the process can be found on each regulator's website. Applications need only be submitted to one regulator: applications for a PRA controlled function will need to be sent to the PRA, and those for an FCA controlled function to the FCA. An application from a dual regulated firm for an individual to carry out both a PRA and FCA controlled function should be submitted to the PRA only which will then pass on the relevant information to the FCA.

For dual regulated firms like a UK bank, the PRA leads the assessment of applications for approval of PRA designated controlled functions. However, the approval of the individual will not be given unless both the PRA and FCA are satisfied that it should be.

How long the PRA will need to determine an application varies depending on the circumstances and in particular whether there is evidence of non-disclosure and/or adverse information on the applicant. In these cases further information may be requested which will mean that the statutory clock on determining the application is stopped until that information has been received. Nevertheless, the PRA has a statutory obligation to determine the application within three months of receipt.

The PRA will take a proportionate approach in its assessment of applications, taking into account all matters relating to an individual's fitness and propriety. Where appropriate, the PRA may also interview candidates as part of its assessment. This is particularly the case for the most senior roles at the largest firms although, at its discretion, the PRA may also choose to interview other candidates.

The interview can be a daunting process for applicants and the questions that will be asked by the regulator will depend to a large extent upon the facts of the application. It is worth noting, however, that executive director positions can often expect to undergo the most intensive interview experience and will be expected to have a very detailed knowledge of the business of their prospective firm, the markets in which it operates and the key risks arising from the business model. Candidates for non-executive director positions can also expect to face difficult questions particularly concerning the scope and responsibilities of their prospective role and their ability and willingness to challenge executives.

If a decision is made to approve the application, the PRA will inform the firm by issuing an approval notice. If the application is not successful and the PRA and/or the FCA propose to refuse the application, the PRA will inform the applicant by issuing a Warning Notice which will include details of an appeals process.

The regulators also have the power to issue conditional or time limited approvals. The rules on this can be found in SUP 10C.11.[18]

---

[18] CP15/9, FCA near final rules SUP10C.11.

3.6.3   On-going requirements

Once approved, the approved person must comply with and meet on an on-going basis:

- the requirements set out in the Statements of Principle and Code of Practice for Approved Persons (APER) which can be found in the PRA and FCA Handbooks; and
- the fit and proper test for approved persons set out in section 61 FSMA (within both the PRA and FCA Handbooks there is a sourcebook called the "Fit and Proper Test for Approved Persons" which provides further guidance on this test).

Under FSMA, both regulators are given a range of powers to take action against approved persons who fail to satisfy the expected standards of conduct or who cease to be fit and proper. The main powers include withdrawing an approved person's approved status, granting a prohibition order and taking disciplinary action for misconduct which includes levying a fine on the individual concerned.

Despite the requirements the regulators have sometimes found it difficult to bring enforcement action against senior managers. The reasons are partly to do with the problems of complexity in firms' structures and a lack of clarity in structures about which senior management are directly responsible for individual decisions. Also, within large organisations a number of decisions are, quite properly, made by committees, so attributing individual responsibility for those decisions can be difficult.

3.6.4   Attestations

The UK financial services industry has seen more and more instances where CEOs, chairmen, boards and other senior managers have been required to provide a written attestation confirming their firm's compliance with particular regulatory requirements. Both the PRA and the FCA can use the self-attestation tool but it appears that the FCA is more willing to use it.

The requirement for senior management to self-attest has caused concern in the market and it is worth noting that in the summer of 2014 there was any exchange of letters between the FCA and the FCA Practitioner Panel on the use of attestations. In particular, the FCA said that it would be issuing revised internal guidance which would emphasise the importance of clarity and transparency when using attestations.

Self-attestation cannot simply be ignored by a firm and its senior management. Principle 11 of the FCA Principles for Businesses provides that a firm must deal with its regulators in an open and co-operative way and disclose anything relating to the firm of which that regulator would reasonably expect notice. The same requirement can be found in the PRA's Fundamental r.7. Part XI of the FSMA adds a further layer in that it gives the regulators extensive information gathering powers including the power to require information (s.165) and reports by skilled persons (s.166).

The dilemma that self-attestation brings to senior management is that by signing the attestation without complete certainty that your firm complies with the applicable requirements potentially opens them up to enforcement action. However, on the other hand seeking to negotiate caveats to put into the attestation may frustrate the regulator and ultimately lead to enforcement action.

It appears that there may be few options when dealing with self-attestation but it might be worth keeping in mind the following points:

• an attestation request will usually accompany the results of a regulatory review or consultation so it is important to pay close attention to the specific findings of the regulator's study;

- consider carefully current procedures, systems and controls as to whether they would be open to criticism by the regulator;
- do not under estimate how much time and effort is involved in conducting a thorough self-assessment;
- bear in mind that the regulators are in a strong position to compare and contrast good and poor practice between regulated forms so consider conducting a gap analysis from an external perspective; and
- consider how individual exposure might be mitigated.

3.7 PRA Approach to Supervision

The PRA supervises, from a prudential perspective only, around 1,700 firms, which are insurers, systemically important investment firms (designated investment firms) and deposit takers. The PRA Approach to Supervision is set out in two documents, one for insurers, one for banks and investment firms, first published in April 2013, and most recently updated in March 2016.

The PRA has a general objective to promote the safety and soundness of the firms it regulates, and within this it focuses primarily on the harm that they can cause to the stability of the UK financial system.

The key elements of the PRA's approach[19] are:

- It relies significantly on judgment. The PRA supervises firms to judge whether they are safe and sound, and whether they meet, and are likely to continue to meet, the Threshold Conditions.
- The PRA's approach is forward looking; it assesses firms not just against current risks, but also against those that could plausibly arise in the future.

---

[19] Material taken from PRA approach to banking supervision (March 2016). See *http://www.bankofengland.co.uk/publications/Documents/praapproach/bankingappr1603.pdf* [Accessed 22 March 2016].

- The PRA focuses on those issues and those firms that pose the greatest risk to the stability of the UK financial system.

3.7.1 *PRA Categories of impact for deposit takers, investment firms and insurers*

The PRA divides all deposit-takers, designated investment firms and insurers into the five categories of impact below:

Category 1

- The most significant deposit-takers, designated investment firms or insurers whose size, interconnectedness, complexity and business type give them the capacity to cause very significant disruption to the UK financial system (and through that to economic activity more widely) by failing or by carrying on their business in an unsafe manner.
- Insurers whose size (including number of policyholders) and type of business mean that there is very significant capacity to cause disruption to the interests of a substantial number of policyholders.

Category 2

- Significant deposit-takers, designated investment firms or insurers whose size, interconnectedness, complexity and business type give them the capacity to cause some disruption to the UK financial system (and through that to economic activity more widely) by failing or by carrying on their business in an unsafe manner.
- Insurers whose size (including number of policyholders) and type of business mean that there is significant capacity to cause disruption to the interests of a substantial number of policyholders.

Category 3

- Deposit-takers, designated investment firms or insurers whose size, interconnectedness, complexity and business type give them the capacity to cause minor disruption to the UK financial system by failing or by carrying on their business in an unsafe manner, and where difficulties across a whole sector or subsector have the potential to generate disruption.
- Insurers whose size (including number of policyholders) and type of business mean that there is minor capacity to cause disruption to the interests of a substantial number of policyholders.

Category 4

- Deposit-takers, designated investment firms or insurers whose size, interconnectedness, complexity and business type give them very little capacity individually to cause disruption to the UK financial system by failing or by carrying on their business in an unsafe manner, but where difficulties across a whole sector or subsector have the potential to generate disruption.
- Insurers whose size (including number of policyholders) and type of business mean that there is very little capacity to cause disruption to the interests of a substantial number of policyholders.

Category 5

- Deposit-takers, designated investment firms or insurers whose size, interconnectedness, complexity and business type give them almost no capacity individually to cause disruption to the UK financial system by failing or by carrying on their business in an unsafe manner, but where difficulties across a whole sector or subsector may have the potential to generate some disruption.
- Insurers whose size (including number of policyholders) and type of business mean that there is no

143

capacity to cause disruption to the interests of a substantial number of policyholders.

The PRA uses quantitative and qualitative analysis to allocate firms to categories. Numerical scoring based on firms' regulatory reporting provides a suggested categorisation, which supervisors review in light of qualitative analysis to confirm that it presents a full picture of a firm's potential impact. It also considers the external context in which firms operate, uses peer group analysis and assesses whether the PRA can effectively supervise the activities that a firm carries out.

In addition to being given an impact category, insurance firms are assigned a place in the Proactive intervention framework, more of which is discussed below.

3.7.2   *Management and Governance*

The PRA makes clear to firms that the responsibility for ensuring compliance with the letter and spirit of regulatory requirements sits with the firm's board and management.

> "it is the responsibility of each firm's board and management to manage the firm prudently, consistent with its safety and soundness, thereby contributing to the continued stability of the financial system. This goes beyond complying with the letter of the PRA's detailed requirements, for example, on adequate capital and liquidity and risk management and controls, and it often means firms acting more prudently than they would otherwise choose. It also goes beyond core responsibilities for all boards and management, such as ensuring that individuals appointed to senior management positions are competent to fill such roles, setting the firm's strategy and policies clearly, and ensuring that these are applied throughout the organisation, with responsibilities clearly apportioned."[20]

---

[20] PRA approach to banking supervision, para.71, *http://www.bankofengland.co.uk/publications/Documents/praapproach/bankingappr1603.pdf* [Accessed 22 March 2016].

3.8   PRA Approach to Insurance Supervision

In addition to the PRA's overarching objective of promoting the safety and soundness of the firms it regulates, it has a specific insurance objective which is to contribute to the securing of an appropriate degree of protection for policyholders, and specifically to ensure that policyholders have an appropriate degree of continuity of cover for the risks they are insured against. As with all PRA-regulated firms, insurers will be subject to FCA regulation for conduct of business issues, and it is the FCA that will be responsible for ensuring that customers are treated fairly.

The PRA will not be concerned with guarding against the failure of all insurance firms, but with seeing that failure, when it does occur, is managed in an orderly way, that minimises market disruption and adverse effects on policyholders.

The PRA's decision making is intended to be judgement led, and based on evidence and analysis. It is also forward looking and will seek to prevent risks from crystallising.

The PRA's risk framework as it will apply to insurers contains three elements:

1.   the potential impact that an insurer could have on financial stability and policyholders, both by the way it carries on its business and in the event of failure;
2.   how the external context in which an insurer operates and the business risks it faces (together, its risk context) might affect the viability of the firm; and
3.   mitigating factors, including:
     a.   its management and governance and its risk management and controls (operational mitigation);
     b.   financial strength, specifically capital and liquidity (financial mitigation);
     c.   its resolvability (structural mitigation).

The PRA conducts a risk assessment of a firm both by looking at the firm, and by comparing it to other firms in its peer group. The use of peer analysis is a feature of PRA supervision.

As mentioned previously, all PRA-regulated firms will be assigned to one of five impact categories and assigned a place in the Proactive intervention framework, the stages of which are:

- Stage 1: Low risk to viability of firm—normal level of supervisory monitoring and actions.
- Stage 2: Moderate risk to viability of firm—deficiencies in risk or governance practices identified. Increased supervision, more reporting, risk profile review.
- Stage 3: Material risk to viability of firm—significant threats to a firm's financial safety or soundness may have been identified. Would be required to submit a realistic recovery plan designed to address specific current problems and to initiate recovery actions. May include: capital raising; asset disposal; business transfer or sale of the firm; and reduction of contracts.
- Stage 4: Imminent risk to viability of firm—real risk the firm will fail to meet requirements for ongoing authorisation. Likely to lose authorisation to write new business. Firm to accelerate and complete recovery actions in short-order, showing PRA that these have mitigated the imminent risk to the viability of the firm. PRA to work with FSCS in planning liquidation.
- Stage 5: Resolution/winding-up under way—PRA would trigger the appropriate insolvency process and the insolvency practitioner would work with the FSCS and PRA to effect continuity of cover and/or compensation to eligible claimants.

The PRA writes annually to each insurer's Board, outlining the small number of key risks that are of greatest concern and on which it requires action. The PRA will expect root cause analysis to be conducted in firms to see if it is exposed on any of the areas highlighted.

More can be read on the PRA's approach to insurance supervision in the March 2016 document, found on the PRA website.[21]

3.9   International regulatory environment

The regulatory spotlight on individuals is not a UK centric theme.

Since the onset of the 2008 financial crisis, sweeping international reforms have been introduced which have transformed the global financial services sector. The changes that have been introduced have sought not only to improve the economic governance of nations but also to strengthen the supervisory and regulatory oversight of financial markets and institutions themselves. These changes have been based largely on the ambitious G20 commitments set by international partners in Pittsburgh in 2009. These commitments have been turned into international standards by bodies such as the Financial Stability Board (FBS), the International Organization of Securities Commissions and the Basel Committee on Banking Supervision (BCBS). Such international standards have then be transposed into EU law through Directives and Regulations like the Capital Requirements Directive IV (CRD IV), the Capital Requirements Regulation and the Markets in Financial Instruments Directive (recast) (MiFID II).

In this section we briefly look at two important international papers:

- the FSB Guidance on Supervisory Interaction with Financial Institutions on Risk Culture;
- the BCBS revised Guidelines on Corporate Governance Principles for Banks.

We then briefly turn to the CRD IV and MiFID II governance requirements.

---

[21]   http://www.bankofengland.co.uk/publications/Documents/praapproach/insuranceappr1603.pdf.

3.9.1 FSB indicators of a sound risk culture

In April 2014 The Financial Stability Board (FSB) published finalized Guidance on Supervisory Interaction with Financial Institutions on Risk Culture,[22] subtitled "A Framework for Assessing Risk Culture" (the FSB Guidance).

The FSB Guidance is intended to help firms (particularly those that are systemically important financial institutions—SIFIs), and their supervisors, to effectively assess risk culture. It is not intended to be used as a check list or to encourage a tick box approach on the part of supervisors, or firms, but rather provides ideas on the sorts of indicators that may illustrate effective and ineffective management of risk.

Key ideas in the FSB Guidance chime closely with the regulatory agenda of the PRA and FCA. UK bodies. This illustrates that regulatory reform, and the emphasis on good customer outcomes, stems from a global regulatory agenda.

The overarching thrust of the FSB Guidance is to help firms ensure that

> "employees in all parts of the institution conduct business in a legal and ethical manner. An environment that promotes integrity should be created across the institution as a whole, including focusing on fair outcomes for customers."

It is clear from a reading of the FSB Guidance that the concept of conduct risk is incorporated within risk culture as described by the FSB, which empahsises the importance of tone from the top and incentives, among other things.

The FSB states that a sound risk culture should emphasise throughout the firm the importance of ensuring that:

---

[22] *http://www.financialstabilityboard.org/publications/140407.htm* [Accessed 24 February 2016].

(i)   an appropriate risk-reward balance consistent with the firm's risk appetite is achieved when taking on risks;

(ii)   an effective system of controls commensurate with the scale and complexity of the firm is properly put in place;

(iii) the quality of risk models, data accuracy, capability of available tools to accurately measure risks, and justifications for risk taking can be challenged; and

(iv)   all limit breaches, deviations from established policies, and operational incidents are thoroughly followed up with proportionate disciplinary actions when necessary.

These overarching considerations illustrate that the purpose of a sound risk culture is to enable a firm to take calculated risks, in a controlled way, and not to mitigate all risks, which would be contrary to the effective functioning of the business. In fact, the stronger a firm's risk culture is, the more risks it ought to be able to take, and the more freedom from regulatory intervention it might have because regulators will trust its risk culture and controls.

3.9.1.1   *Indicators of a sound risk culture*

Four indicators, which must be looked at collectively and viewed as mutually reinforcing, are identified by the FSB, which also states that they do not represent an exhaustive picture, or checklist.

Firms, whilst being aware that the above indicators are non-exhaustive, can nonetheless use them as a starting point against which to assess their own risk culture and the way in which they are measuring, monitoring and mitigating various aspects of conduct risk. They are:

- Tone from the top: A firm's leadership should promote, monitor and assess risk culture, consider its impact on safety and soundness and make changes where necessary. A key value that the board and senior management should espouse is the expectation that staff act with integrity; non-compliance within or outside the organisation should be promptly escalated.

- Accountability: Relevant employees at all levels understand the core values of the institution and its approach to risk, are capable of performing their prescribed roles, and are aware that they are held accountable for their actions in relation to the firm's risk-taking behaviour. Staff acceptance of risk-related goals and related values is essential.
- Effective communication and challenge: A sound risk culture promotes an environment of open communication and effective challenge in which decision-making processes encourage a range of views; allow for testing of current practices; stimulate a positive, critical attitude among employees; and promote an environment of open and constructive engagement.
- Incentives: Performance and talent management encourage and reinforce maintenance of the financial institution's desired risk management behaviour. Financial and non-financial incentives support the core values and risk culture at all levels of the firm.

3.9.1.2   General supervisory guidance

The FSB Guidance points out that there are risks inherent in a proactive and invasive supervisory approach, and that the challenge for supervisors is to strike the right balance between taking a more intensive, proactive approach and not unduly influencing strategic decisions of the firm's management. They also say that supervisors should be mindful of unintended consequences in trying to influence risk culture. These points are not expanded upon further, but may reassure firms that this supra-national standard setting body is alive to the risks of unwise supervisory intervention. The points also illustrate that supervisors must stay on the right side of the fine line that separates their work from the strategy of the firm.

However, supervisors will still actively engage with a firm's business model; it will be for firms themselves to prove to their supervisor that their business model and strategy are customer focused, that the firm behaves with integrity and has a positive and embedded risk culture.

The FSB Guidance also says as part of its general supervisory guidance, that supervisors should gather evidence from the full range of supervisory activities so as to avoid the assessment of risk culture being perceived and managed as a compliance-driven exercise.

3.9.2 Basel Committee on Banking Supervision

The Basel Committee on Banking Supervision (BCBS) published[23] revised Guidelines on Corporate Governance Principles for Banks in July 2015 (the BCBS Guidelines). The original Guidelines were published in 2010, and this proposed revision is intended to update them to increase the emphasis on risk governance.

The Guidelines are:

Principle 1: Board's overall responsibilities:	The board has overall responsibility for the bank, including approving and overseeing the implementation of the bank's strategic objectives, governance framework and corporate culture.
Principle 2: Board qualifications and composition	Board members should be and remain qualified, individually and collectively, for their positions. They should understand their oversight and corporate governance role and be able to exercise sound, objective judgment about the affairs of the bank.
Principle 3: Board's own structure and practices	The board should define appropriate governance structures and practices for its own work, and put in place the means for such practices to be followed and periodically reviewed for ongoing effectiveness.

---

[23] http://www.bis.org/bcbs/publ/d328.htm [Accessed 24 February 2016].

Principle 4: Senior management	Under the direction and oversight of the board, senior management should carry out and manage the bank's activities in a manner consistent with the business strategy, risk appetite, incentive compensation and other policies approved by the board.
Principle 5: Governance of group structures	In a group structure, the board of the parent company has the overall responsibility for the group and for ensuring that there is a clear governance framework appropriate to the structure, business and risks of the group and its entities. The board and senior management should know and understand the bank's operational structure and the risks that it poses.
Principle 6: Risk management	Banks should have an effective independent risk management function, under the direction of a Chief Risk Officer (CRO), with sufficient stature, independence, resources and access to the board.
Principle 7: Risk identification, monitoring and controlling	Risks should be identified, monitored and controlled on an ongoing bank-wide and individual entity basis. The sophistication of the bank's risk management and internal control infrastructure should keep pace with changes to the bank's risk profile, to the external risk landscape and in industry practice.
Principle 8: Risk communication	An effective risk governance framework requires robust communication within the bank about risk, both across the organisation and through reporting to the board and senior management.
Principle 9: Compliance	The bank's board of directors is responsible for overseeing the management of the bank's compliance risk. The board should establish a compliance function and approve the bank's policies and processes for identifying, assessing, monitoring and reporting and advising on compliance risk.

Principle 10: Internal audit	The internal audit function provides independent assurance to the board and supports board and senior management in promoting an effective governance process and the long-term soundness of the bank.
Principle 11: Compensation	The bank's remuneration structure should support sound corporate governance and risk management.
Principle 12: Disclosure and transparency	The governance of the bank should be adequately transparent to its shareholders, depositors, other relevant stakeholders and market participants.
Principle 13: The role of supervisors	Supervisors should provide guidance for and supervise corporate governance at banks, including through comprehensive evaluations and regular interaction with boards and senior management, should require improvement and remedial action as necessary, and should share information on corporate governance with other supervisors.

The revised Principles and guidance:

- expand the guidance on the role of the board in overseeing the implementation of effective risk management systems;
- emphasise the importance of the board's collective competence as well as the obligation on individual board members to dedicate sufficient time to their mandates and to remain current on developments in banking;
- strengthen the guidance on risk governance, including the risk management roles played by business units, risk management teams, and internal audit and control functions (the three lines of defence), as well as underline the importance of a sound risk culture to drive risk management within a bank;
- provide guidance for bank supervisors in evaluating the processes used by banks to select board members and senior management; and
- recognise that compensation systems form a key component of the governance and incentive structure through

which the board and senior management of a bank convey acceptable risk-taking behaviour and reinforce the bank's operating and risk culture.

3.9.2.1   The Role of the Board and Senior Management

In the introduction to the BCBS Guidelines the BCBS says that one of the primary objectives of the revision is to explicitly reinforce the collective oversight and risk governance responsibilities of the board. Another important objective is to emphasise key components of risk governance such as risk culture, risk appetite and their relationship to a bank's risk capacity. Risk culture is defined as "a bank's norms, attitudes and behaviours related to risk awareness, risk taking and risk management and controls that shape decisions on risks. Risk culture influences the decisions of management and employees during the day-to-day activities and has an impact on the risks they assume".

The BCBS recognises, as the FSB did, the critical role played by the board and board risk committees in strengthening a bank's risk governance; they are responsible for evaluating and promoting a strong risk culture as well as for establishing and communicating the risk appetite.

Principles 1 to 3 of the BCBS Guidelines deal with the board, and are supported by detailed guidance. The themes are familiar, and echo the views of the FCA and the PRA as to the role and remit of the board, particularly around culture. In addition to setting strategy and business objectives, the BCBS says that the board should establish the bank's corporate culture and values, oversee the implementation of an appropriate governance framework, and develop and monitor the bank's risk appetite statement. The board also has responsibility for overseeing the design and implementation of the bank's compensation system, and ensuring that it is aligned with the desired risk culture and risk appetite.

The BCBS Guidelines provide a greater level of detail on what constitutes a good corporate culture and values. They state that "a fundamental component of good governance is a demonstrated corporate culture of reinforcing appropriate norms for responsible and ethical behavior". "Tone from the Top" needs to be established by:

- the board setting and adhering to corporate values for the itself, senior management and other employees that create expectations that all business should be conducted in a legal and ethical manner;
- promoting risk awareness within a strong risk culture, conveying the board's expectation that it does not support excessive risk-taking and that all employees are responsible for helping ensure that the bank operates within the agreed risk appetite and risk limits;
- ensuring that appropriate steps are taken to communicate throughout the bank the corporate values, professional standards or codes of conduct it sets, together with supporting policies; and
- ensuring that employees, including senior management, are aware that appropriate disciplinary or other actions will follow unacceptable behaviours and transgressions.

Furthermore, the BCBS Guidelines add that a code of conduct or code of ethics, or comparable policy, should define acceptable and unacceptable behaviours, and should explicitly disallow behaviour that could lead to any reputation risks or improper or illegal activity, such as financial misreporting, money laundering, fraud, anti-competitive practices, bribery and corruption, or the violation of consumer rights. In addition, it should make clear that employees are expected to conduct themselves ethically in addition to complying with laws, regulations and company policies.

A bank also needs a culture which enables timely and frank discussion and escalation of problems further up the chain. Such a culture can be supported by a comprehensive whistle-blowing policy.

3.9.2.2 Risk Appetite Statement

The BCBS Guidelines state that a bank's risk appetite statement should:

- include both quantitative and qualitative considerations;
- establish the individual and aggregate level and types of risk that the bank is willing to assume in advance of and in order to achieve its business activities within its risk capacity;
- define the boundaries and business considerations in accordance with which the bank is expected to operate when pursuing the business strategy; and
- communicate the board's risk appetite effectively throughout the bank, linking it to daily operational decision-making and establishing the means to raise risk issues and strategic concerns across the bank.

3.9.2.3 Training and competence of board members

Principle 2 of the BCBS Guidelines has been enhanced with the insertion of the words "individually and collectively", which empahsises that members of the board have to be, and remain, qualified for their positions on an individual basis and as a group. The board should be comprised of people with a "balance of skills, diversity and expertise, who collectively possess the necessary qualifications commensurate with the size, complexity and risk profile of the bank".

Although the notion of collective skill is intended to allow for diversity on the board, (i.e. not everyone is expected to be a financial whizz), in the current climate fairly high standards of financial, risk and regulatory literacy are expected from every board member. This is made clear by a paragraph in the BCBS Guidelines which speaks about the need to induct and offer continued training and support to board members. It says, "more extensive efforts should be made to train and keep updated those members with more limited financial, regulatory or risk-related experience". This indicates that the expectation is that all members of a bank board should be able to understand key regulatory and risk concepts, and will not be excluded from this obligation merely because their remit is, for example, human resources, rather than the financials.

The BCBS Guidelines state that, as a group, a board should come from varied backgrounds so that a diversity of views is promoted. However, this must be balanced with the need to ensure that board members are sufficiently skilled. The requirement to offer extra training and support to those who may have a weaker grasp of risk and regulation (perhaps because they do not come from a traditional banking background), is a clear sign that whilst diversity is welcomed, it carries with it a responsibility to ensure that all board members know enough about banking and the risks inherent in it to effectively exercise their duties.

In the UK, banks subject to the BCBS Guidelines will also be subject to the Senior Managers and Certified Persons regime. Individual competence, responsibility and accountability are key tenets of the UK regime; those recruited to a board as a "diverse" voice—perhaps because their experience is in insurance, or in another corporation, rather than banking, need to be vigilant in ensuring that they know everything the regulator would expect them to know, to adequately perform as a board member. A good understanding of risk and regulation will be essential.

3.9.2.4   Senior Management

Revised Principle 4, of the BCBS Guidelines, and its accompanying guidelines, covers senior management, and echoes points made by the UK regulators around personal accountability and conduct. It makes clear that as well as directing senior managers, the board must also oversee their work. Further, senior managers no longer have to merely *ensure* that the bank's activities are consistent with its risk profile and strategy, but actively *carry out and manage* the bank's activities. They are also obliged to ensure activities are carried out consistently with policies around incentive compensation.

Senior management "should recognise and respect the independent duties of the risk management, compliance and internal audit functions and should not interfere in their exercise of such duties".

Senior managers have a general reporting duty to the board and should also keep the board "regularly and adequately informed of material matters", including:

- changes in business strategy, risk strategy/risk appetite;
- bank performance and condition;
- breaches of risk limits or compliance rules;
- internal control failures; and
- legal or regulatory concerns.

3.9.2.5 *Governance of Group Structures and overlap with UK Ring-Fencing provisions*

Principles 5: Governance of Group Structures, has been extended in the BCBS Guidelines by the insertion of a duty on the parent company board not just to ensure "adequate corporate governance across the group", but for ensuring that there is a "clear governance framework". Additionally, the board and senior management are now required to "know and understand the bank's operational structure and the risks that it poses".

The guidelines that accompany the Principle are more detailed than the 2010 version, and include a new section on complex or opaque structures. It outlines challenges inherent in running a business via complex legal entities created for legal, regulatory or tax purposes. Senior management and the board as appropriate are required to be mindful of the challenges, and to take appropriate action to avoid or mitigate them by:

- avoiding setting up unnecessarily complicated structures or an inordinate number of legal entities;
- continually maintaining and reviewing appropriate policies, procedures and processes governing the approval

and maintenance of those structures or activities; including fully vetting the purpose, the associated risks and the bank's ability to manage those risks prior to setting up new structures and initiating associated activities;

- having a centralised process for approving the creation of new legal entities based on established criteria, including the ability to monitor and fulfil each entity's regulatory, tax, financial reporting, governance and other requirements;

- establishing adequate procedures and processes to identify and manage all material risks arising from these structures, including lack of management transparency, operational risks introduced by interconnected and complex funding structures, intragroup exposures, trapped collateral and counterparty risk. The bank should only approve structures if the material risks can be properly identified, assessed and managed;

- ensuring that the activities and structure are subject to regular internal and external audit reviews.

The BCBS Guidelines on group governance and structure are consistent with the PRA's ring-fencing proposals, part of the aim of which is to make banks simplify group structures by more closely aligning business lines with legal entities. The PRA will focus on ensuring that ring-fenced bodies are protected from shocks that originate in the rest of the group (or the global financial system), and that continuity of core services for retail clients is protected.

The new BCBS Guidelines delineate, for the first time, the functions of compliance, risk and internal audit, emphasising their importance and the need for them to have strong lines of communication with the board.

3.9.2.6 Compliance

The 2010 Principles made no specific mention of compliance. Principle 9 of BCBS Guidelines rectifies this. Guidelines that accompany Principle 9 confirm that an independent compliance function is a key component of the bank's second line of defence, that bears responsibility for promoting and monitoring that the bank operates with integrity, and in compliance with applicable laws, regulations and internal policies.

The fact that the BCBS has named the promoting and monitoring of integrity as the first duty of compliance is arguably indicative of the global recognition of the failure of rules alone to prevent things going wrong. Firms may still adhere to rules, but be behaving without integrity.

The guidelines go on to remind banks that compliance starts at the top, and says that it will be most effective in a corporate culture that empahsises standards of honesty and integrity and in which the board and senior management lead by example. Importantly, they also say that compliance concerns everyone within the bank and should be viewed as an integral part of the bank's business activities.

These ideas have been emphasised in the UK by the FCA and the PRA, and elsewhere, by the Financial Stability Board (for example) since the financial crisis. However, these guidelines are of note because they provide a reasonable amount of detail on what the relationship between the compliance function and the board should be like.

The guidelines state that the board and management are accountable for the bank's compliance. It is of note here that *management* has not been restricted to only *senior management*, as is seen elsewhere in the BCBS Guidelines. Therefore all those to whom senior managers delegate duties, and who perform a managerial role, are accountable for compliance within their area. The UK Senior Managers and Certified Persons regime, goes a little further than this, and makes nearly all staff in banks bear some responsibility and accountability for complying with conduct rules (integrity etc).

The BCBS Guidelines say that it is the bank's senior management who are responsible for establishing a written compliance approach and policies that contain the basic principles to be followed by the board, management and staff, and explains the main processes by which compliance risks are to be identified and managed through all levels of the organisation. They further provide that clarity and transparency may be promoted by making a distinction between general standards for all staff members and rules that only apply to specific groups of staff.

- They also elucidate what the role of compliance ought to be, as follows:
- Promoting and monitoring: the compliance function should promote and monitor that the bank operates with integrity and in compliance with laws, rules etc.
- Provision of advice: the compliance function should advise the board and senior management on compliance laws, rules and standards, including keeping them informed of developments in the area.
- Education and training: the compliance function should help educate staff about compliance issues.
- Central point of contact for relevant matters: the compliance function should act as a contact point within the bank for compliance queries from staff members.
- Production of Guidance in the form of manuals, procedures etc: the compliance function should provide guidance to staff on the appropriate implementation of compliance laws, rules and standards in the form of policies and procedures and other documents such as compliance manuals, internal codes of conduct and practice guidelines.

In summary, compliance's role is supportive and advisory. This corresponds with the Senior Management Arrangements, Systems and Controls rules on compliance, which provide that the role of the compliance function is threefold: to monitor, and to advise and assist staff within the firm. Additionally the BCBS Guidelines remind banks that the compliance function must have sufficient authority, stature, independence, resources and access to the board, and management should respect the independent duties of the compliance function and not interfere with them.

The spotlight put on the role of the compliance function, and the role of the board in ensuring compliance with rules and standards, including behavioural standards, brings the thinking of this body into line with that of domestic and international regulators. The BCBS Guidelines illustrate how complicated and multi-faceted the role of the compliance function is, in the current climate, bearing as it does a duty to monitor not just adherence to rules, but also behaviours that may be unethical, or go against a bank's promotion of integrity as a fundamental principle.

3.9.2.7   Internal Audit

Principle 10 of the BCBS Guidelines covers internal audit. The accompanying guidance states that the board and senior management can enhance the effectiveness of the internal audit function by:

- providing the function with full and unconditional access to any records, file data and physical properties of the bank, including access to management information systems and records and the minutes of all consultative and decision-making bodies;
- requiring the function to independently assess the effectiveness and efficiency of the internal control, risk management and governance systems and processes;
- requiring internal auditors to adhere to national and international professional standards, such as those established by the Institute of Internal Auditors;
- requiring that audit staff collectively have or can access knowledge, skills and resources commensurate with the business activities and risks of the bank;
- requiring timely and effective correction of audit issues by senior management; and
- requiring the function to perform a periodic assessment of the bank's overall risk governance framework, including but not limited to an assessment of:
  — the effectiveness of the risk management and compliance functions;

- — the quality of risk reporting to the board and senior management; and
- the effectiveness of the bank's system of internal controls.

Examples are provided as to how the board and senior management can respect and promote the independence of the internal audit function, by:

- ensuring that internal audit reports are provided to the board without management filtering and that the internal auditors have direct access to the board or the board's audit committee;
- the head of the internal audit function's primary reporting line is to the board (or its audit committee), which is also responsible for the selection, oversight of the performance and, if necessary, dismissal of the head of this function;
- if the chief audit executive is removed from his or her position, this should be disclosed publicly. The bank should also discuss the reasons for such removal with its supervisor.

The role of the internal auditor has been subject to domestic debate and comment in recent years. In June 2013 the UK Chartered Institute of Internal Auditors issued final recommendations for internal auditors in financial services.

3.9.2.8   Risk

Three of the Principles in the BCBS Guidelines deal with Risk:

Principle 6: Risk management Banks should have an effective independent risk management function, under the direction of a Chief Risk Officer (CRO), with sufficient stature, independence, resources and access to the board.

Principle 7: Risk identification monitoring and controlling Risks should be identified, monitored and controlled on an ongoing bank-wide and individual entity basis. The sophistication of the bank's risk management and internal control infrastructure should keep pace with changes to the bank's risk profile, to the external risk landscape and in industry practice.

Principle 8: Risk communication An effective risk governance framework requires robust communication within the bank about risk, both across the organisation and through reporting to the board and senior management.

The accompanying guidelines to Principle 6 contain more detail on the duties and obligations of the risk management function. They provide that the key activities of the risk management function should include:

- identifying material individual, aggregate and emerging risks;
- assessing these risks and measuring the bank's exposure to them;
- supporting the board in its implementation, review and approval of the enterprise-wide risk governance framework which includes the bank's risk culture, risk appetite, RAS and risk limits;
- ongoing monitoring of the risk-taking activities and risk exposures to ensure they are in line with the board-approved risk appetite, risk limits and corresponding capital or liquidity needs (i.e. capital planning);
- establishing an early warning or trigger system for breaches of the bank's risk appetite or limits;
- influencing and, when necessary, challenging material risk decisions; and
- reporting to senior management and the board or risk committee, as appropriate, on all these items, including but not limited to proposing appropriate risk-mitigating actions.

Under Principle 6 detailed guidance is provided on the role of the CRO, which says that the role holder needs to be independent, have access to any information necessary to perform the duties of the role, and have duties "distinct from other executive functions". In addition to supporting the board in its development of the bank's risk appetite, and for

164

translating this into a risk limits structure, the CRO should manage and participate in key decision-making processes, examples of which include strategic planning, capital and liquidity planning, new products and services, compensation design and operation.

The accompanying guidance under Principles 7 and 8 covers the role of the risk management function in identifying risks at a firm, group and subsidiary level. Such identification and measurement of risk across complex group structures is an essential part of a global drive towards banks being easily recoverable and resolved, in stressed situations.

Principle 8 deals with the communication of risk, and requires banks to have an effective risk governance framework. The guidance says a strong risk culture should promote risk awareness and encourage open communication and challenge about risk-taking across the organisation as well as vertically to and from the board and senior management.

The BCBS has also recently published two papers specifically on the quantification and measurement of operational risk.

3.9.3   CRD IV/MiFID II Governance requirements

The revised Markets in Financial Instruments Directive (MiFID II) introduces a number of new provisions on an investment firm's management body, which are far more detailed and prescriptive than the requirements found in MiFID I, and which apply the requirements imposed on banks by CRD IV to investment firms.

Members of management bodies must be of sufficiently good repute, act with honesty and integrity and devote sufficient time to performing their functions. They are also limited in the number of appointments they take on: they can hold a maximum of one executive directorship with two non-executive directorships; or four non-executive directorships. However, with permission, individuals can hold an additional non-executive directorship (and roles in non-commercial organisations do not count towards the total).

The requirements are numerous, and include, among other things, the need for large investment firms' nomination committees to set gender targets for the composition of the management body (which will need to be made public), and a requirement for firms to devote adequate human and financial resources to the induction and training of the management body, and are summarised in this diagram – the box at the bottom of which shows the existing MiFID I provision, which is far shorter and less detailed.

In addition, under MiFID II firms will need to comply with art.88 of CRD IV, as shown above.

3.9.3.1 EBA and ESMA Guidelines

EBA and ESMA are required to adopt joint guidelines, that will apply to all firms MiFID and CRD IV firms, on art.91(12) of CRD IV, covering:

(a) the notion of sufficient time commitment of a member of the management body to perform his functions, in relation to the individual circumstances and the nature, scale and complexity of activities of the institution;
(b) the notion of adequate collective knowledge, skills and experience of the management body;
(c) the notions of honesty, integrity and independence of mind of a member of the management body;
(d) the notion of adequate human and financial resources devoted to the induction and training of members of the management body;
(e) the notion of diversity to be taken into account for the selection of members of the management body.

ESMA suggests that it will require regulators to receive extensive information on the management body and persons directing the business, including the usual things such as personal details and full CV, details of personal referees,

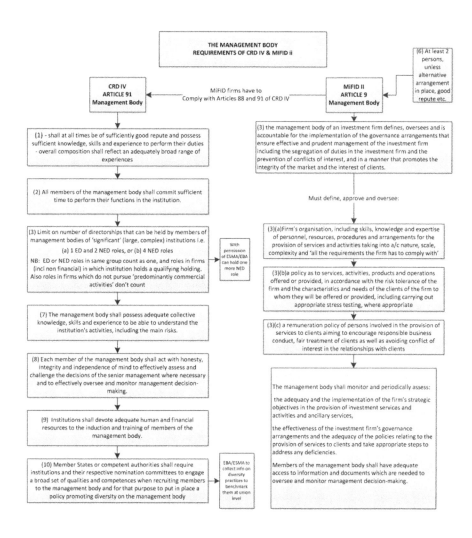

EXISTING MIFID 1 PROVISION: Article 9

Persons who effectively direct the business

1. Member States shall require the persons who effectively direct the business of an investment firm to be of sufficiently good repute and sufficiently experienced as to ensure the sound and prudent management of the investment firm.

2. Member States shall require the investment firm to notify the competent authority of any changes to its management, along with all information needed to assess whether the new staff appointed to manage the firm are of sufficiently good repute and sufficiently experienced.

3. The competent authority shall refuse authorisation if it is not satisfied that the persons who will effectively direct the business of the investment firm are of sufficiently good repute or sufficiently experienced, or if there are objective and demonstrable grounds for believing that proposed changes to the management of the firm pose a threat to its sound and prudent management.

4. at least 2 persons.

criminal records, investigations, information on pervious dismissal from employment. EMSA also suggests that firms be required to provide information on the minimum time that will be devoted to the performance of the person's functions within the firm (annual and monthly indications); the human and financial resources devoted to the induction and training of the members (annual indications); and the number of executive and non-executive directorships currently held by the person. This is a significant level of detail—the requirement to state how many hours per month and per year senior people are expected to work could produce some interesting submissions. It also has the potential to raise important questions of employee rights where indicated hours end up being far exceeded almost from day one, rather than where unforeseen events create an additional workload. This also ties in with the idea of being able to devote sufficient time to the performance of the role.

Chapter 4

The Senior Managers and Certified Persons Regime: Conduct Rules for Those Working in Banks and PRA Regulated Proprietary Trading Firms

Jane Walshe
Barrister

This Chapter provides detail on the operation of the Senior Managers and Certified Persons Regime as it applies to UK deposit takers and PRA regulated designated investment firms. The rules relating to insurers are covered elsewhere in this book.

4.1 Introduction: The Financial Services (Banking Reform) Act 2013

The Financial Services (Banking Reform) Act 2013 received royal assent on December 18th 2013. It implements the recommendations of the Independent Commission on Banking, separating investment banking from retail banking (the ring-fence), and the key recommendations of the Parliamentary Commission on Banking Standards on the conduct of senior persons and others in banking and investment management. The Act creates the statutory framework for the Senior Managers and Certified Persons Regime by amending the Financial Services and Markets Act 2000.

The Act is divided into eight parts, covering ring-fencing of banks, the creation of a payment systems regulator and bail-in stabilisation options, among other things. Part 4 of the Act is entitled "Conduct of Persons working in financial services sector". The legislative provisions have been added to by the Regulators in rules found in their respective handbooks. The PRA rules are found in the following sections of the PRA Rulebook: Senior Management Functions, Allocation of Responsibilities, Certification, Fitness and Propriety, Conduct Rules, Notifications, Senior Managers Regime: Applications and Notifications, Senior Managers Regime: Transitional Provisions. The rules are supplemented by a Supervisory Statement, SS28/15 "Strengthening individual accountability in banking",[1] and a Statement of Policy, "Conditions, time limits and variations of approval".

In March 2016 the PRA published Supervisory Statement SS5/16 "Corporate governance: Board responsibilities", which is also relevant to the duties of board level senior managers.

The FCA rules are found in a new section of the FCA Handbook, entitled the Code of Conduct sourcebook (COCON), in the Senior Management Arrangements, Systems and Controls section of the FCA handbook, sections 4.5–4.9, and section 5.2 and in various other amended sections, in the Fit and Proper Test for Approved Persons (FIT) and in the Supervision Manual Chapter 10C.[2]

4.1.1   Commencement

The Senior Managers and Certification Regime commenced on 7 March 2016. The conduct rules apply to those within the Senior Managers and Certification Regime on 7 March 2016 although firms have an additional year (until 7 March 2017) to

---

[1] The PRA's final rules and statements were published in July 2015, in Policy Statement PS16/15, Strengthening individual accountability in banking: responses to CP14/4, CP28/14 and CP7/15.

[2] The FCA's final rules were published in July 2015, in CP15/22, Strengthening accountability in banking: Final rules (including feedback on CP14/31 and CP15/5) and consultation on extending the Certification Regime to wholesale market activities.

produce certificates for staff in the Certification Regime. There are two exceptions: the Client Dealing and Algorithmic trading significant harm functions in the Certification Regime do not take effect until 7 September 2016, which is the date by which firms must have identified and trained these individuals. This is because the FCA only published final rules in relation to the addition of these functions, in February 2016.[3]

The submission deadline for grandfathering notifications for senior managers was 8 February 2016.

Staff who do not fall within the Senior Managers' Regime or the Certification Regime will be subject to the conduct rules from 7 March 2017 (apart from excluded staff whose jobs are unrelated to the provision of the financial service, e.g. post room staff, receptionists).

4.1.2 Definition of Senior Manager in a Bank or Investment firm

The Act inserts new sections in FSMA 2000 which allow the FCA and the PRA to designate certain functions within UK deposit takers and PRA regulated proprietary trading firms as "senior manager functions".

A senior manager function is one which will require the person performing it to be responsible for managing one or more aspects of the firm's business, relating to a regulated activity, which involve, or might involve *a risk of serious consequence for the firm, or for business or other interests in the United Kingdom* (FSMA s.59ZA).

---

[3] Policy Statement 16/3.

4.2 Senior Managers in Banks, Building Societies, Credit Unions and PRA regulated proprietary trading firms

The Senior Managers and Certified Persons regime (SMR) is aimed at improving accountability, culture and behaviour in the banking industry. The regulators have said that it is intended to create a new framework to encourage individuals to take greater responsibility for their actions, and to make it easier for both firms and regulators to hold individuals to account.

Although the PRA and FCA have published rules, guidance and supervisory statements which may be different in some respects, the intention is that the rules for the SMR operate jointly as a single cohesive regime in practice. A common approach will be deployed by both regulators to the statement of responsibilities, the responsibilities maps and handover arrangements. FCA SUP 10C.9 deals specifically with minimising overlap with the PRA regime. Where an individual proposes to hold both a PRA senior manager function (SMF), and an FCA *governing* function, the FCA governing function is disapplied and the individual need only obtain approval from the PRA. The governing function duties are effectively rolled up into the PRA function. A table at SUP 10C.9.9 provides examples of how this works in practice.

4.2.1 *Scope*

Only those working in "relevant authorised persons" can be designated as senior managers falling within the SMR by the regulators. A "relevant authorised person" is defined in s.71A FSMA. It must be a UK institution which meets either of the two following conditions:

1. it has permission under Pt 4A of FSMA to carry on the regulated activity of accepting deposits, and is not an insurer, or;

2. it is an investment firm, with permission under Pt 4A to carry on the regulated activity of dealing in investments as principal, and when carried on by it this activity is a PRA-regulated activity.

Only a handful of firms fall under category (b) above as most PRA regulated proprietary trading firms will also be deposit takers and hence will fall within category A.

A parallel regime under existing Approved Persons rules will operate for all other financial services firms, apart from insurers, who will operate with a mix of the old and the new and are required to run a more limited version of the SMR, known as the Senior Insurance Managers Regime (SIMR) but not to operate a Certified Persons regime. More about the regime governing Solvency II and non-Solvency II insurance firms can be read in Chapter 6.

The Fair and Effective Markets Review, published in June 2015, has also recommended that elements of the SMR be extended across all those active in the fixed income, currency and commodity markets who are not already within the regime, such as interdealer brokers and asset managers. The Review suggests requiring regulatory pre-approval and "Statements of Responsibility" for senior managers; certification of individuals with the potential to pose "significant harm" to a firm or its customers; and enforceable Conduct Rules for individuals.

In October 2015, the UK Government announced that it plans to extend the regime to all financial services firms, by 2018.

4.2.1.1 *SMR to operate on a legal entity basis*

Each "relevant authorised person", i.e. legal entity, within a group will need to operate its own SMR. Some banking groups may have a number of legal entities; only those that accept deposits will need to comply with the SMR (non deposit taking entities, which do not fall within the PRA regulated proprietary trading definition either, may have to operate under the pre-existing approved persons regime, or, if they are insurance firms, the insurance regimes).

Firms that operate with more than one deposit taking legal entity will need to map out which senior managers will perform which function for each entity. Each entity will need a governance map and each senior manager will need a Statement of Responsibilities relating to the duties they have on an entity basis. These matters are discussed further below.

4.2.2 Senior Management Function

The senior management function (SMF) is a controlled function designated by either regulator, and captures a far smaller population of staff than the previous "significant influence function" categories it replaces. This is intentional, as the SMF holders are expected to be the key decision makers in firms. Individuals requiring approval as senior managers include:

- the board (apart from non-executive directors who do not hold a specific role—"standard" NEDs);
- for larger and more complex firms, executive committee members (the layer below the board);
- heads of key business areas meeting certain quantitative criteria;
- individuals in group or parent companies exercising significant influence on the firms' decision- making; and
- where appropriate, individuals not otherwise approved as Senior Managers but ultimately responsible for important business, control or conduct-focused functions within the firm.

Senior Managers performing these functions will be caught by the SMR whether they are based in the UK or abroad.[4] The key criterion is that their function relates to the carrying out of a regulated activity. An individual based outside the UK can perform an SMF if he is responsible for managing an area

---

[4]   SYSC 4.5.2R, "there is no territorial limitation on the application of this section".

relating to the firm's Part IV Permissions. The PRA Supervisory Statement provides that the individual should be directly responsible for taking decisions about how a UK firm should conduct their UK-regulated activities, rather than for group strategy. A senior manager based abroad would be likely to need approval where they are responsible for the execution of group strategy in the UK, specifically.[5]

Section 59ZA(2) of the Financial Services (Banking Reform) Act 2013 states that a function is a senior management function, in the relation to the carrying on of a regulated activity by the firm, if:

- the function will require the person performing it to be responsible for managing one or more aspects of the firm's affairs, so far as relating to the activity; and
- those aspects involve, or might involve, a risk of serious consequences: (a) for the firm; or (b) for business or other interests in the United Kingdom.

Section 59ZA(3) of the Act says that "managing" includes, for these purposes, taking decisions, or participating in the taking of decisions, about how one or more aspects of the firm's affairs should be carried on.[6]

The PRA and the FCA have designated separate SMFs for which they are responsible. The complete list of SMFs is as follows:

SMF	Description	FCA function	PRA function
SMF1	Chief Executive function		Y
SMF2	Chief Finance function		Y
SMF3	Executive Director function	Y	
SMF4	Chief Risk function		Y
SMF5	Head of Internal Audit function		Y

---

[5]   SS28/15, para 2.14-2.15.
[6]   SUP 10C.3.12 G.

SMF	Description	FCA function	PRA function
SMF6	Head of Key Business Area function		Y
SMF7	Group Entity senior manager function		Y
SMF8	Credit Union SMF (small credit unions only)		Y
SMF9	*Chairman function*		Y
SMF10	*Chair of the Risk Committee function*		Y
SMF11	*Chair of the Audit Committee function*		Y
SMF12	*Chair of the Remuneration Committee function*		Y
SMF13	*Chair of the Nominations Committee function*	Y	
SMF14	*Senior Independent Director function*		Y
SMF15	DOES NOT EXIST[7]		
SMF16	Compliance Oversight function	Y	
SMF17	Money Laundering Reporting function	Y	
SMF18	Other Overall Responsibility function	Y	
SMF19	Head of Overseas Branch (incoming non-EEA branches only)		Y
SMF21	EEA branch senior manager function	Y	
SMF22	Other local responsibility function (incoming non-EEA branches only)	Y	

---

[7] The early proposals included an SMF15 Non Executive director function but it has now been decided that NEDs who do not perform SMF9-14 will not require approval under the SMR, although they will be subject to certain conduct rules. See the NED chapter for more detail on this.

Emphasis indicates SMFs to be held by approved NEDs, rather than executives. PRA functions are those which require pre-approval from the PRA, with FCA consent. FCA functions require FCA pre-approval only.

4.2.3 PRA SMFs

The PRA SMFs[8] are divided up between executive, oversight, group entity and credit union functions, as follows.

Type	SMF	Description of PRA controlled function
PRA Executive Functions	SMF 1	Chief Executive function
	SMF 2	Chief Finance function
	SMF 4	Chief Risk function
	SMF 5	Head of Internal Audit function
	SMF 6	Head of Key Business Area function
	SMF 19	Head of Overseas Branch (incoming non-EEA branch)
PRA Oversight Functions *(to be held by approved NEDs)*	SMF 9	Chairman function
	SMF 10	Chairman of Risk Committee function
	SMF 11	Chairman of Audit Committee function
	SMF 12	Chairman of Remuneration Committee function
	SMF 14	Senior Independent Director function
PRA Group Entity Function	SMF 7	Group Entity Senior Manager function
PRA Credit Union Function	SMF 8	Credit Union Senior Manager Function

---

[8]   PRA Rulebook Senior Management Functions.

4.2.3.1   PRA Executive Functions

The Chief Executive Function (SMF1) is the function of having responsibility, under the immediate authority of the governing body, alone or jointly with others, for carrying out the management of the conduct of the whole of the business (or relevant activities) of a firm.

The Chief Finance function (SMF2) is the function of having responsibility for management of the financial resources of a firm and reporting directly to the governing body of the firm in relation to its financial affairs.

The Chief Risk function (SMF4) is the function of having responsibility for overall management of the risk controls of a firm, including the setting and managing of its risk exposures, and reporting directly to the governing body of the firm in relation to its risk management arrangements.

The Head of Internal Audit function (SMF5) is the function of having responsibility for management of the internal audit function of a firm and for reporting directly to the governing body of the firm on the internal audit function.

The Head of Key Business Area function (SMF6) is the function of having responsibility, for management of a business area or division of a firm, which meets a quantitative test. Rule 3.6 provides that the function applies where the area under management has:

- gross total assets equal to or in excess of £10 billion; and/or
- either:
  — accounts for more than 20 percent of the firm's gross revenue; or
  — where the firm is part of a group, accounts for more than 20 percent of the total gross revenue of the group; and

— the person performing that function does not report to a person performing the Head of Key Business Area function in respect of the same business area or division of the firm.

The idea is to capture those managing an area that is so large in relative terms to the size of the firm (even though the sum could be far below £10 billion) that it could jeopardise its safety and soundness and so substantial in absolute terms (£10 billion even though it may be less than 20 percent of the gross revenue of the firm) that it warrants an SMF, even though the senior manager performing it may report to the chief executive or another SMF.

It will be for firms themselves to identify staff falling within this category. The PRA expects the most senior individual responsible to be put forward.

The application of the Senior Managers' Regime to overseas firms is discussed in detail later in this book.

4.2.3.2   PRA Oversight Functions

The PRA oversight functions are those held by non-executive directors.[9]

The Chairman function (SMF9) is the function of having responsibility for chairing, and overseeing the performance of the role of, the governing body of a firm.

The Chairman of Risk Committee function (SMF10) is the function of having responsibility for chairing, and overseeing the performance of any committee responsible for the over-sight of the risk management systems, policies and procedures of a firm specified in the Risk Control 2 section of the PRA rulebook, including where applicable to the firm, a committee established in accordance with Risk Control 3.1. Risk Control 3.1 provides as follows:

---

[9]   Do not apply to Credit Unions.

"(1) A firm that is significant must establish a risk committee composed of members of the management body who do not perform any executive function in the firm. Members of the risk committee must have appropriate knowledge, skills and expertise to fully understand and monitor the risk strategy and the risk appetite of the firm.

(2) The risk committee must advise the management body on the institution's overall current and future risk appetite and assist the management body in overseeing the implementation of that strategy by senior management.

(3) The risk committee must review whether prices of liabilities and assets offered to clients take fully into account the firm's business model and risk strategy. Where prices do not properly reflect risks in accordance with the business model and risk strategy, the risk committee must present a remedy plan to the management body. "

The Chairman of Audit Committee function (SMF11) is the function of having responsibility for chairing, and overseeing the performance of any committee responsible for the oversight of the internal audit system of a firm specified in the PRA Rulebook, Compliance and Internal Audit, para.3 of which states:

"3.1 A firm must, where appropriate and proportionate in view of the nature, scale and complexity of its business and the nature and range of its financial services and activities, undertaken in the course of that business, establish and maintain an internal audit function which is separate and independent from the other functions and activities of the firm and which has the following responsibilities:

(1) to establish, implement and maintain an audit plan to examine and evaluate the adequacy and effectiveness of the firm's systems, internal control mechanisms and arrangements;

(2) to issue recommendations based on the result of work carried out in accordance with (1);

(3) to verify compliance with those recommendations; and

(4) to report in relation to internal audit matters in accordance with General Organisational Requirements 4.2. "

The Chairman of Remuneration Committee function (SMF12) is the function of having responsibility for chairing, and overseeing the performance of any committee responsible for the oversight of the design and the implementation of the remuneration policies of a firm, including where applicable to the firm, a committee established in accordance with Remuneration 7.4. Remuneration 7.4 provides as follows:

"7.4 A CRR firm that is significant in terms of its size, internal organisation and the nature, scope and complexity of its activities must establish a remuneration committee, and ensure that the committee:

(1) is constituted in a way that enables it to exercise competent and independent judgment on remuneration policies and practices and the incentives created for managing risk, capital and liquidity;

(2) comprises a chairman and members who are members of the management body who do not perform any executive function in the firm;

(3) is responsible for the preparation of decisions regarding remuneration, including those which have implications for the risk and risk management of the firm and which are to be taken by the management body; and

(4) takes into account, when preparing such decisions, the long-term interests of shareholders, investors and other stakeholders in the firm as well as the public interest. "

The Senior Independent Director function (SMF14) is the function of performing the role of a senior independent director, and having particular responsibility for leading the assessment of the performance of the person performing the Chairman function.

Non-executive directors who do not perform any of the above functions will not fall within the SMR. More on non-executives can read in the Non-Executive Directors Chapter.

4.2.3.3 *Group entities*

The Group Entity Senior Manager function (SMF7)[10] is the function of having a significant influence on the management or conduct of one or more aspects of the affairs of a firm in relation to its regulated activities (other than in the course of the performance of another PRA senior management function) and which is performed by a person employed by, or an officer of:

(1) a parent undertaking or holding company of a firm; or
(2) another undertaking which is a member of the firm's group.

In PS3/15, the PRA stated that it does not expect a significant increase in the numbers of individuals required to hold approval, who are based in a parent or other group entity, when compared with the previous position, under the pre-March 2016 regime.

In order to identify who may need approval as an SMF7, a firm should first look at those in a group or parent who were previously approved, because the policy the PRA will apply will be the same. The PRA states that the approach of both regulators to UK subsidiaries and branches of overseas-headquartered groups under the old Approved Persons Regime (APR) has been to not require approval of senior individuals located overseas whose responsibilities in relation to the United Kingdom are linked to the development of the group's overall strategy. Approval is needed where the

---

[10] Does not apply to credit unions.

individual is responsible for implementing the group's strategy in the UK entity (or entities) and has not delegated that responsibility to a senior individual based in the United Kingdom.

The legislation makes this clear, because in order for a function to be capable of being defined as an SMF, it must be linked to the firm's UK-regulated activities (FSMA s.59ZA).

In order to decide whether a senior manager in a parent or other group entity needs to be approved as an SMF7 (or another SMF), a firm should consider the following questions:

- Does the manager have a significant influence over the regulated activities of the UK entity?
- Is the manager responsible for the implementation of global strategy in the UK entity?
- Has the manager delegated responsibility for implementing strategy in the UK to another person?

If the answers to the first two questions are "yes" and the answer to the third is "no", is it more likely than not that the individual will need approval as an SMF. The PRA further states that where an individual is directly involved in the management of a UK branch or subsidiary or takes direct decisions about how these entities conduct their UK-regulated activities, it is highly likely that he or she will require approval as Group Entity Senior Manager or another SMF. A firm will need to work out what "direct involvement" looks like, and to document their rationale. The PRA suggests consulting organizational structure charts and analysing to whom key responsibilities have been allocated.[11]

4.2.3.4 *Credit Union Senior Manager Function*

The Credit Union Senior Manager function (SMF8) is the function of having responsibility for the conduct of, and/or chairing the committee of management of a credit union.

---

[11] PRA SS28/15, para 2.14-2.16.

4.2.3.5 *Temporary cover for a Senior Manager Function*

A firm can allow an individual to perform a PRA senior management function without obtaining approval as long as the appointment is solely to provide cover for a PRA approved person whose absence is temporary or reasonably unforeseen; and the appointment is for less than 12 weeks in a consecutive 12-month period.[12]

4.2.4 *PRA Prescribed responsibilities*

In addition to the definitions of the SMFs above, the PRA has made rules setting out prescribed responsibilities which firms, depending on their size, will be required to allocate among their SMFs, and which will need to be included on their statement of responsibilities. They are found in the Allocation of Responsibilities section of the PRA Rulebook.[13] The PRA has adopted a proportionate approach to the allocation of the responsibilities, with different requirements pertaining to firms depending on their size. The PRA's general expectation is that they will be allocated to the Senior Manager they are most closely linked to. A full list of PRA and FCA prescribed responsibilities is reproduced below.

There are two important rules on the allocation of these responsibilities that must be adhered to:

- Responsibilities (f),(j)(k)(l)(m) in the table below must be allocated to approved Non-Executive Directors (i.e. PRA SMFs 9-12 and 14, and FCA SMF13).[14]
- Individuals who are only approved as SMF18—Other Overall Responsibility function cannot hold any PRA prescribed responsibilities.[15]

---

[12] PRA Rulebook, Senior Management Functions, 2.3.
[13] PRA Rulebook, Allocation of Responsibilities 4.1.
[14] PRA Rulebook, Allocation of Responsibilities, 3.2(1).
[15] PRA Rulebook, Allocation of Responsibilities, 3.6(1).

4.2.4.1 *Small CRR firms (assets of £250mn or less) and Credit Unions[16]*

A small CRR firm means a CRR firm which has gross total assets of £250 million or less, determined on the basis of the annual average amount calculated across a rolling period of five years (calculated by reference to the firm's annual accounting date). Where the firm has been in existence for less than five years, the calculation will be made on the basis of the annual average amount for the period during which the firm has been in existence (calculated by reference to the firm's annual accounting date).

Small CRR firms, and credit unions will only have to allocate the following prescribed responsibilities.

- responsibility for the firm's performance of its obligations under the senior management regime;
- responsibility for the firm's performance of its obligations under the certification rules;
- responsibility for compliance with the firm's obligations in relation to its management responsibilities map;
- responsibility for allocation of all small firm prescribed responsibilities;
- responsibility for implementing and managing the firm's risk management policies and procedures;
- responsibility for managing the systems and controls of the firm;
- responsibility for managing the firm's financial resources; and
- responsibility for ensuring the governing body is informed of its legal and regulatory obligations.

4.2.4.2 *Prescribed Responsibilities for specific types of firm[17]*

In addition to the general list of prescribed responsibilities, certain specific types of firm must also allocate the following responsibilities amongst their senior managers.

---

[16] PRA Rulebook, Allocation of Responsibilities 5.1.
[17] PRA Rulebook, Allocation of Responsibilities 4.2.

- Proprietary Trading: if the firm carries out proprietary trading, responsibility for the firm's proprietary trading activities.
- Risk: if the firm does not have a person who performs the Chief Risk function, responsibility for the compliance of the firm's risk management systems, policies and procedures with the requirements of Risk Control 2.1 to 2.4;
- Outsourced internal audit function: if the firm outsources its internal audit function, responsibility for taking reasonable steps to ensure that every person involved in the performance of that function is independent from the persons who perform external audit, including:
  — supervision and management of the work of outsourced internal auditors; and
  — management of potential conflicts of interest between the provision of external audit and internal audit services;
- Ring Fenced body: if the firm is a ring-fenced body, responsibility for ensuring that those aspects of the firm's affairs for which a person is responsible for managing are in compliance with the ring-fencing obligations. This must be allocated to someone who performs a PRA senior management function or an FCA designated senior management function (but not if that is the Other Overall responsibility function); and that person is responsible for managing any area of the ring-fenced body's business that is subject to a ring-fencing obligation.[18] The PRA's Supervisory Statement provides further guidance on this and states:

> "2.27 The PRA expects ring-fenced banks (RFBs) to allocate the responsibility for ensuring that the areas of the firm which they are responsible for managing comply with the ring-fencing obligations, to the majority, if not all, of their SMFs (except the FCA's SMF18), including those NEDs in scope of the SMR. This is an exception to the expectation that Prescribed Responsibilities should be allocated only to the individual SMFs

---

[18] PRA Rulebook, Allocation of Responsibilities, 3.4.

they are most closely linked to. The reason for the exception is to incentivise key decision-makers in RFBs to ensure compliance with the ring-fencing obligations throughout the key areas of the firm. "[19]

More on ring-fenced bodies can be read in the Ring-Fence Chapter.

4.2.4.3 *Shared Prescribed Responsibilities*

A firm can, and in many cases will need to, allocate a Prescribed Responsibility to more than one Senior Manager. In such cases, each individual will, in principle, be deemed wholly responsible for it. The PRA states that prescribed responsibilities can therefore be shared but not split. However, if a firm breaches a relevant requirement in an area relating to a Prescribed Responsibility which is shared by two or more Senior Managers, each Senior Manager will have an opportunity to explain how the shared Prescribed Responsibility was discharged in practice when trying to demonstrate that he or she took reasonable steps to avoid the breach.[20] The statement of responsibilities should carry identical wording on the prescribed responsibility that is shared in the main body of the form, but firms can to explain in the free text area how that responsibility is functionally split between the senior managers concerned.

---

[19] PRA SS28/15, 2.27.
[20] PRA SS28/15, 2.42.

4.2.5 FCA SMFs

The FCA has designated fewer senior management functions than the PRA. The FCA's SMFs are as follows:

Type	SMF	Description of FCA controlled function[21]
FCA governing functions	SMF 3	Executive Director function
	SMF 13	Chair of the nomination committee function
FCA required functions	SMF 16	Compliance oversight function
	SMF 17	Money laundering reporting function
Other overall responsibility function	SMF 18	Other overall responsibility function

Note: information on the SMFs that apply to incoming EEA branches, and third country firms is found elsewhere in this book.

The provisions relating to the above functions are found in the Supervision section of the FCA Handbook, at Chapter SUP 10C.5 (governing functions) and SUP 10C.6 (required functions).

4.2.5.1 Other overall responsibility function—SMF 18

The FCA has designed a general senior manager function in order to allow firms flexibility in their organisation and governance arrangements—the "Other overall responsibility Senior Manager". This SMF is intended to capture individuals with overall responsibility for a key function or identified risk, who are performing a function which is not otherwise specified as an SMF requiring approval by either regulator.

---

[21] Diagram reproduced from SUP 10C4.3R.

The SMF18 function holder is not permitted to be allocated PRA or FCA prescribed responsibilities, if their only approval is as SMF18.[22] This suggests that the SMF18 role is slightly junior to the other SMF roles, and the function holders should focus on their specific area, rather than being given additional duties. There is one exception to this—and a firm may allocate the client assets (CASS) prescribed responsibility (FCA prescribed responsibility number 10 in the list below) to an SMF manager who is only approved to perform the SMF18 function.[23]

4.2.5.2 FCA list of key functions likely to apply to most relevant firms

The FCA has provided a list of the key functions that it thinks are likely to apply to most relevant firms, in SYSC 4 Annex 1G. The FCA has produced this list to help firms identify their key business activities and to ensure that firms allocate responsibility for these. However, it does not require firms to have SMFs in each of these roles, and it does not expect these functions to apply in all cases. The expectation is that all SMFs will not be below the top two layers of management (although they may be in exceptional cases). Holders of the functions below could be SMF3 (Executive Directors), or SMF18, if they do not hold any other SMFs.

The key functions are:

Payment services	Settlement
Investment management	Financial or investment advice
Mortgage advice	Corporate investments
Wholesale sales	Retail sales
Trading for clients	Market making
Investment research	Origination/syndication and underwriting
Retail lending decisions	Wholesale lending decisions

---

[22] SYSC 4.7.5R(5).
[23] SYSC 4.7.5R(6).

Design and manufacturing of products intended for wholesale customers	Design and manufacture of products intended for retail customers
Production and distribution of marketing materials and communications	Customer service
Customer complaints handling	Collection and recovering amounts owed to a firm by its customers/Dealing with customers in arrears
Middle office	The firm's information technology
Business continuity	Human resources
Incentive schemes for the firm's staff	Providing information in relation to a specified benchmark
Administering a specified benchmark	

4.2.6   FCA Prescribed Senior Management Responsibilities

The FCA prescribed senior management responsibilities are found in SYSC 4.7.7R. Some of the responsibilities mirror those of the PRA. However, the FCA has three FCA specific responsibilities which are

- Overall responsibility for the firm's policies and procedures for countering financial crime (SYSC 4.7.7R(4));
- Overall responsibility for the firm's compliance with CASS (SYSC 4.7.7R(11));
- Acting as the firm's whistleblowers' champion (SYSC 18.4.1).[24]

The FCA expects that a firm will appoint a non-executive director as its whistleblowers' champion, but a firm that does not have a non-executive director would not be expected to appoint one just for this purpose. More on whistleblowing can be read in the Whistleblowing Chapter.

---

[24] Inserted by PS 16/3.

All of the FCA and PRA prescribed responsibilities must be allocated to an SMF holder, apart from someone who is only approved as FCA SMF18—Other overall responsibility senior manager. However, the FCA CASS responsibility is the only one which can be allocated to an SMF18.

The FCA has produced a combined list of FCA and PRA prescribed responsibilities—reproduced below (note: this does not contain the Whistleblowers Champion responsibility as it was inserted after the table was created):

Description of prescribed senior management responsibility (as set out in SYSC, where prescribed by the FCA)		FCA-prescribed?	PRA-prescribed?
Applying to all firms			
a	Responsibility for the firm's performance of its obligations under the senior management regime	SYSC 4.7.7R(1)	4.1(1)
b	Responsibility for the firm's performance of its obligations under the employee certification regime	SYSC 4.7.7R(2)	4.1(2)
c	Responsibility for compliance with the requirements of the regulatory system about the management responsibilities map	SYSC 4.7.7R(3)	4.1(3)
d	Overall responsibility for the firm's policies and procedures for countering the risk that the firm might be used to further financial crime	SYSC 4.7.7R(4)	–
e	Responsibility for the allocation of all prescribed responsibilities in accordance with 3.1	–	4.1(20)
Applying to larger firms			

Description of prescribed senior management responsibility (as set out in SYSC, where prescribed by the FCA)		FCA-prescribed?	PRA-prescribed?
f	Responsibility for: (a) leading the development of; and (b) monitoring the effective implementation of; policies and procedures for the induction, training and professional development of all members of the firm's governing body.	*SYSC 4.7.7R(5)*	*4.1(13)*
g	Responsibility for monitoring the effective implementation of policies and procedures for the induction, training and professional development of all persons performing designated senior management functions on behalf of the firm other than members of the governing body.	SYSC 4.7.7R(6)	4.1(5)
h	Responsibility for overseeing the adoption of the firm's culture in the day-to-day management of the firm.	–	4.1(6)
i	Responsibility for leading the development of the firm's culture by the governing body as a whole.	–	4.1(14)
j	Responsibility for: (a) safeguarding the independence of; and (b) oversight of the performance of; the internal audit function, in accordance with SYSC 6.2 (Internal Audit)	*SYSC 4.7.7R(7)*	4.1(15)
k	Responsibility for: (a) safeguarding the independence of; and (b) oversight of the performance of; the compliance function in accordance with SYSC 6.1(Compliance).	*SYSC 4.7.7R(8)*	4.1(16)

Description of prescribed senior management responsibility (as set out in SYSC, where prescribed by the FCA)		FCA-pre-scribed?	PRA-pre-scribed?
l	Responsibility for: (a) safeguarding the independence of; and (b) oversight of the performance of; the risk function, in accordance with SYSC 7.1.21R and SYSC 7.1.22R (Risk control).	*SYSC 4.7.7R(9)*	4.1(17)
m	Responsibility for overseeing the development of, and implementation of, the firm's remuneration policies and practices in accordance with SYSC 19D (Remuneration Code)	*SYSC 4.7.7R(10)*	4.1(18)
n	Responsibility for the independence, autonomy and effectiveness of the firm's policies and procedures on whistleblowing, including the procedures for protection of staff who raise concerns from detrimental treatment	–	4.1(19)
o	Management of the allocation and maintenance of capital, funding and liquidity	–	4.1(7)
p	The firm's treasury management functions	–	4.1(8)
q	The production and integrity of the firm's financial information and its regulatory reporting in respect of its regulated activities	–	4.1(9)
r	The firm's recovery plan and resolution pack and overseeing the internal processes regarding their governance	–	4.1(10)

Description of prescribed senior management responsibility (as set out in SYSC, where prescribed by the FCA)		FCA-prescribed?	PRA-prescribed?
s	Responsibility for managing the firm's internal stress-tests and ensuring the accuracy and timeliness of information provided to the PRA and other regulatory bodies for the purposes of stress-testing;	–	4.1(11)
t	Responsibility for the development and maintenance of the firm's business model by the governing body;	–	4.1(12)
u	Responsibility for the firm's performance of its obligations under Fitness and Propriety in respect of its notified non-executive directors	–	4.1(4)
Applying in specified circumstances			
v	If the firm carries out proprietary trading, responsibility for the firm's proprietary trading activities;	–	4.2(1)
w	If the firm does not have an individual performing the Chief Risk function, overseeing and demonstrating that the risk management policies and procedures which the firm has adopted in accordance with SYSC 7.1.2 R to SYSC 7.1.5 R satisfy the requirements of those rules and are consistently effective in accordance with SYSC 4.1.1R.		4.2(2)

Description of prescribed senior management responsibility (as set out in SYSC, where prescribed by the FCA)		FCA-pre-scribed?	PRA-pre-scribed?
x	If the firm outsources its internal audit function taking reasonable steps to ensure that every person involved in the performance of the service is independent from the persons who perform external audit, including (a) Supervision and management of the work of outsourced internal auditors and (b) Management of potential conflicts of interest between the provision of external audit and internal audit services		4.2(3)
y	If the firm is a ring-fenced body, responsibility for ensuring that those aspects of the firm's affairs for which a person is responsible for managing are in compliance with the ring-fencing requirements.		4.2(4)
z	Overall responsibility for the firm's compliance with CASS	SYSC 4.7.7R(11)	–
Applying to small firms only			
aa	Responsibility for implementing and management of the firm's risk management policies and procedures		5.2(3)
bb	Responsibility for managing the systems and controls of the firm	–	5.2(4)
cc	Responsibility for managing the firm's financial resources.	–	5.2(5)
dd	Responsibility for ensuring the governing body is informed of its legal and regulatory obligations	–	5.2(6)
Emphasis indicates SMFs to be held by approved NEDs, rather than executives			

4.2.7 *Meaning of overall responsibility*

The FCA defines what having overall responsibility for a function means, in SYSC 4.7.11, which states that it relates to a person who has ultimate responsibility (under the governing body) for managing or supervising that function; and primary and direct responsibility for:

(a) briefing and reporting to the governing body about that function; and
(b) putting matters for decision about that function to the governing body. It does not mean that the person has ultimate authority of the area, because the ultimate decision making body of a firm is its governing body, acting collectively.

The guidance goes on to provide that a person with overall responsibility for a matter will either be a member of the governing body or will report directly to the governing body. Further, having overall responsibility does not mean that the person has day-to-day management control of that function.[25]

The FCA expects that anyone who has overall responsibility for a matter will be sufficiently senior and credible and will have sufficient resources and authority to be able to exercise his management and oversight responsibilities effectively. The FCA expects that a person to whom overall responsibility for an area of a firm is allocated will be the most senior employee or officer responsible for managing that area.[26]

4.2.8 *Multiple approvals and overlaps with PRA SMFs*

The regulators expect firms to put forward to each SMF the most senior individual responsible for managing or overseeing that aspect of the firm's affairs. However, in some cases it may be possible to have more than one person approved to perform the same SMF—perhaps in the case of a job share. In such cases, each individual will be wholly accountable for all the

---

[25] SYSC 4.7.15G.
[26] SYSC 4.7.16G.

responsibilities conferred by that SMF and each may be required to show that they have taken reasonable steps to prevent a breach from occurring or continuing in the management area covered by that SMF. SMFs should only be shared where appropriate or justified.

Individuals are permitted to perform more than one SMF, although they will require separate approvals for each, which may be combined in a single application. However, the PRA does not permit the Chairman and the Chief Executive functions to be held by the same person at the same time. Firms must be aware of various other mandatory SMF requirements, restrictions and independence requirements relating to multiple approvals. These are found in PRA Supervisory Statement: the PRA Senior Managers Regime.

The FCA's Guidance on the sharing of prescribed responsibilities between different people are found in SYSC 4.7.25G to 4.7.27G. The general expectation is that a firm will not normally split an FCA prescribed responsibility between several SMF managers, with each only having responsibility for part. The norm is for a single individual to perform each prescribed responsibility or function. However, where it is appropriate or justified a firm may be able to divide or share a responsibility, for example as part of a job share, or where departing and incoming senior managers work together temporarily as part of a handover.

Where a responsibility is shared, the FCA provides guidance in SUP10C.11.31G about how to prepare the statements of responsibility. In essence each statement should make clear which part of a function the individual is responsible for.

4.2.8.1   *Obligatory SMFs for particular types of firm*

The following table lists the types of firm which the PRA requires to have certain SMFs.

SMF	Firms Covered[27]	Required by
Chief Risk (SMF4)	Banks, building societies and PRA designated investment firms where proportionate	CRD IV, Article 76(5) Risk Control 3.1
Head of Internal Audit (SMF5)	Banks, building societies and PRA designated investment firms where proportionate	MiFID Implementing Directive Article 8. Compliance and Internal Audit 3
Chair of the Risk Committee (SMF10)	Banks, building societies and PRA designated investment firms which are classed as significant CRR firms	CRD IV, Article 76(3) Risk Control 3.1
Chair of the Audit Committee (SMF11)	Banks, building societies and PRA designated investment firms which have their securities admitted to trading on a regulated market who have to appoint a statutory auditor.	Disclosure and Transparency Rules (FCA),Rule 7.1
Chair of the Remuneration Committee (SMF12)	Banks, building societies and PRA designated investment firms which are CRR firms with assets above £15 billion	CRD IV, Article 95(1) Remuneration 7.4
Senior Independent director (SMF14)	Banks, building societies and PRA designated investment firms with a premium listing on the London Stock Exchange	FRC Corporate Governance Code (FRC Code), A4.1 (comply-or-explain)

4.2.8.2 Prohibited combinations of SMF

The PRA allows for a person to perform more than one PRA senior management function, subject to certain prohibitions. A person cannot be the Chairman and the Chief Executive within the same firm at the same time. The head of Internal Audit

---

27 SS28/15, Chapter 2, Table B.

must be separate and independent from the other functions and activities of the firm; the Chairs of the Risk and Remuneration Committees may not perform any executive functions in the firm (marking no change from the previous position); the Chief Risk officer must be an independent senior manager with distinct responsibility for the risk management function; where the firm is too small to have a dedicated Chief Risk officer, the firm can give the responsibilities to another SMF as long as there is not conflict of interest.

The following PRA table shows banned combinations of SMF[28] and their origins.

SMF	Firms Covered	Required by
Chief Executive (SMF1) & Chairman (SMF9)	A firm must ensure that an individual who performs the Chairman Function on its behalf does not simultaneously perform the Chief Executive Function within the same firm.	CRD IV, Article 88(1)(e) Senior Management Functions 7.2
Chief Risk (SMF4)	Must be an independent senior manager with distinct responsibility for the risk management function. Where the nature, scale and complexity of the activities of the CRR firm do not justify a specifically appointed person, another senior person within the firm may fulfil that function, provided there is no conflict of interest.	CRD IV, Article 76(5) Risk Control 3.5
Head of Internal Audit (SMF5)	Must be separate and independent from the other functions and activities of the firm	MiFID Implementing Directive, Article 8 Compliance and Internal Audit 3.1

---

[28] SS28/15, Chapter 2, Table D.

SMF	Firms Covered	Required by
Chair of the Risk Committee (SMF10)	Must not perform any executive function in the firm	CRD IV, Article 76(3) Risk Controls 3.1
Chair of the Remuneration Committee (SMF12)	Must not perform any executive function in the firm	CRD IV, Article 95(2) Remuneration 7.4(2)

In line with the PRA's proposed approach, individuals seeking to perform more than one SMF specified by the FCA will require separate approval for each. The exception to this is the Other overall responsibility SMF, which is only required where the person performing a key function or functions is not already approved as an SMF by the FCA or PRA.

Where an individual is eligible to perform both a PRA SMF and an FCA SMF Governing Function (which are SMF3: Executive Director and SMF 13: Chair of Nomination Committee), the FCA governing function will be rolled up within their PRA function and separate FCA approval will not be required. This will be the case as long as the PRA approval is granted prior to the FCA function being engaged in, and FCA approval was not already held for the FCA function.[29]

If the PRA-approved person stops performing their PRA role, they have three months in which to get FCA approval for the FCA function assuming they are continuing to perform that function; for example if someone ceased to be the Chief Risk Officer (a PRA SMF), but remained a Director of the firm (an FCA governing SMF), they would need to get FCA approval to continue as the FCA SMF within three months.[30]

---

[29] PRA Rulebook, Senior Management Functions paragraph 2.4.
[30] PRA Rulebook, Senior Management Functions paragraph 2.5(2).

However, the roll up provisions only apply in relation to FCA SMF governing functions. This is logical, as it would be highly unlikely (and problematic) if someone were to perform a PRA SMF and another of the FCA SMFs which are not governing functions—e.g. compliance oversight, MLRO, Other overall responsibility senior manager. The point of the SMR is to concentrate responsibility for key areas in the hands of individual senior people, and it may prove difficult for them to hold two roles at the same time. However, this is not technically prohibited, and in some very small banks it may be that the Chief Risk Officer also wishes to perform the Compliance Oversight function; in such a case the person will have to apply for approvals—no roll up will be allowed.

Individuals seeking to perform more than one SMF specified by the FCA will require separate approval for each. The exception to this is the Other overall responsibility SMF, which is only required where the person performing a key function or functions is not already approved as an SMF by the FCA or PRA.

4.3   Statement of responsibilities

Both the PRA and FCA require all applications for a person to perform a SMF to be accompanied by a statement of responsibilities. This is a statutory requirement originating in s 60(2A) FSMA 2000.[31]

The content of the statement is elaborated on by the PRA in PRA Rulebook: Allocation of Responsibilities section and in SS28/15, Chapter 2, paragraph 2.44 onwards, and in FCA SUP10C.11. The FCA and PRA have coordinated their arrangements so that a firm can prepare a single document that will meet the requirements of both regulators about the statement of responsibilities.[32]

---

[31] Inserted by Financial Services (Banking Reform) Act 2013 s.20.
[32] SUP10C.11.14G(4).

The PRA expects the statements of responsibilities of individuals performing these functions of Heads of Key Business Areas and Group Entity Senior Managers to include detailed information of any particular aspects of the firm which they are responsible for managing or overseeing, since their roles may be diverse and they could influence the firm in different ways.

The statement must also contain any prescribed responsibilities that are attached to that person.

The FCA/PRA have produced a joint Statement of Responsibilities.[33] The form itself lists out the various senior management functions and prescribed responsibilities. It contains instructions for its completion at the outset, which provide that:

- It should be drafted to clearly show the responsibilities that the candidate or senior manager is to perform as part of their controlled function and how they fit in with the firm's overall governance and management arrangements.
- It should be consistent with the firm's management responsibilities map.
- It should be drafted in such a way as to be practical and useable by regulators. The FCA and the PRA consider that this would be achieved by succinct, clear statements for each responsibility which would not usually exceed a word limit of 300.
- It must be a self-contained document. There should be one statement per senior manager per firm. Where an individual performs a senior manager function on behalf of more than one firm within a group, one statement of responsibilities is required for each firm.
- A statement of responsibilities must not cross refer to or include other documents, attachments or links.
- A statement of responsibilities should include functions that are included in a PRA controlled function under SUP 10C.11 (Minimising overlap with the PRA approved persons regime).

---

[33] SUP10C Annex 5D.

- If the appropriate regulator considers that the statement of responsibilities is not sufficiently clear to be practical and usable, it could be challenged as part of a candidate's application for approval, or in ongoing supervision.

Any free text that firm may choose to add must not dilute, qualify or undermine the responsibilities prescribed or required by the regulators and should be justified and seek to serve a useful regulatory purpose, namely to clarify the nature and extent of a senior manager's responsibilities.

Where firms add additional responsibilities to those prescribed or required by the regulators, these responsibilities should be presented in a similar format and length to the PRA Prescribed Responsibilities, i.e. each responsibility should be described ideally no more than two sentences with up to approximately 300 words of accompanying explanatory text. The regulators view this as important in order to avoid unnecessary, qualifying or superficial text.

It is apparent from these requirements that the drafting of the Statements of Responsibility is not a straightforward task, especially when one considers the use to which the regulators are likely to put the documents.

4.3.1 *Requirement to submit a revised statement where there has been a significant change*

A firm must submit a revised statement of responsibilities where there has been any significant change in the responsibilities of the SMF manager. Form J is used for this purpose. FCA examples of what may constitute a significant change include[34]:

- Where there has been a variation of the SMF manager's approval, either at the firm's request or at the FCA's or PRA's initiative, resulting in the imposition, variation or removal of a condition or time limit.

---

[34] SUP10C.11.6G.

- Where the SMF has fulfilled or failed to fulfil a condition on approval.
- The addition, re-allocation or removal of any of the following (or part of one):
  — an FCA-prescribed senior management responsibility;
  — a PRA-prescribed senior management responsibility; or
— responsibility for a function under SYSC 4.7.8R (Allocation of overall responsibility for a firm's activities, business areas and management functions).
- The sharing or dividing of a function that was originally performed by one person between two or more persons.
- Ceasing to share a function that was originally shared with another, or others.
- A change is likely to be significant if it reflects a significant change to the job that the person is doing for the firm. Some factors relevant here include:
  — the importance to the firm of the functions being given up or taken on;
  — whether the FCA-approved SMF manager's seniority in the firm's management changes;
  — whether there are changes to the identity, number or seniority of those whom the SMF manager manages; and
  — whether there are changes to the skills, experience or knowledge needed by the SMF manager for the job.

In determining whether a change to a Senior Manager's role and responsibilities is significant, the PRA expects firms to consider all relevant factors, including but not limited to[35]:

- the importance to the firm of the responsibilities being given up or taken on;
- whether the change alters the seniority of the Senior Manager in the firm or group;
- whether there are any changes to the identity, number or seniority of individuals reporting to the Senior Manager; and

---

[35] SS28/15 Chapter 2, 2.55–2.56.

- whether there are any changes to the skills, experience or knowledge required by the Senior Manager.

The PRA further states that whether a significant change has taken place will be determined on a case-by-case basis. Non exhaustive examples of potential significant changes which, in the PRA's view, may require the submission of a revised Statement of Responsibilities, are provided as follows:

- a variation of the individual's approval, either at the firm's, the PRA's or FCA's initiative, resulting in the imposition of a condition or time limit;
- fulfilling or failing to fulfil a condition on approval imposed by the PRA or FCA;
- sharing or ceasing to share an SMF originally performed by one individual among two or more individuals; and
- the addition, re-allocation or removal of any of the following:
  — a PRA or FCA Prescribed Responsibility;
  — responsibility for a function under SYSC 4.7.8R (FCA Overall Responsibility); or
  — any additional responsibility not covered above.

4.3.2 Use of Statement of Responsibilities

The regulators have made clear[36] that they intend for the statement of responsibilities and responsibilities maps to become an important tool for supervising senior managers and assessing the overall corporate governance of firms.

Examples given of the scenarios in which the regulators may refer to the documents include:

- during the initial assessment for PRA approval, where they will be used to highlight the areas which the candidate will be responsible for managing and assess his/her ability to do so.

---

[36] CP 14/13.

- In daily supervision, where the PRA expects to use them to:
  - identify the relevant senior manager to whom specific regulatory queries should be directed;
  - understand changes to the allocation of responsibilities to individuals in response to changes to the firm's business model or as a result of changes in the external environment;
  - clarify which individuals are ultimately responsible for actions which supervisors expect the firm to take; and
- in enforcement cases as evidence of individual responsibility for the area where the breach occurred.

4.4 Responsibilities Map

In addition to Statements, firms will be required to create and maintain firm wide responsibilities maps for each legal entity in a group that is subject to the SMR.

The PRA rules are found in the PRA Rulebook: Allocation of Responsibilities, which provide that the map must be a single, up-to-date document, and should include[37]:

- details of the reporting lines and the lines of responsibility; and
- reasonable details about the persons who are part of these arrangements and their responsibilities.

Specifically, it should contain:

- the names of all the firm's approved persons (including FCA approved persons), notified non-executive directors, credit union non-executive directors and senior management and the responsibilities held by each, including all FCA responsibilities;
- if any PRA senior management functions or FCA designated senior management functions are performed by

---

[37] PRA Rulebook: Allocation of Responsibilities, 7.

more than one person, or any prescribed responsibilities or small firm prescribed responsibilities, as the case may be, are allocated to more than one person, details of how the performance or discharge of the responsibilities is to be carried out by those persons;
- matters reserved to the management body (including the terms of reference of its committees);
- where the firm is a member of a group;
  — how the firm's management and governance arrangements fit together with those of its group and the extent to which the firm's management and governance arrangements are provided by or shared with other members of its group; and
  — details of the reporting lines and the lines of responsibility (if any) to persons who are employees or officers of other group members or to committees or other bodies of the group or of other group members; and
  — details of how these matters fit into the firm's management and governance arrangements as a whole.

The FCA rules on the management responsibilities map are found in SYSC 4.5.[38] The general rule is that a firm must, at all times, have a comprehensive and up-to-date document that describes its management and governance arrangements, including details of the reporting lines and the lines of responsibility and reasonable details about the persons who are part of those arrangements and their responsibilities.

The firm's management responsibilities map must show clearly how any responsibilities covered by a firm's management responsibilities map are shared or divided between different persons. It should be a single document but can be made up of a number of items in one folder. Large firms may have a long and complicated map, but the FCA expects that for small firms, it may be short and simple.[39]

---

[38] CP15/9 Annex C, near final rules.
[39] SYSC 4.5.15R(5).

One purpose of the management responsibilities map is to help the firm and the FCA satisfy themselves that the firm has a clear organisational structure (as required by SYSC). It also helps the FCA to identify to whom it should speak about particular issues and who is accountable if something goes wrong. Specific requirements about what the map should include are found in SYSC 4.5.7R.

The regulators make clear that they intend for the statement of responsibilities and responsibilities maps to become an important tool for supervising senior managers and assessing the overall corporate governance of firms.

In bringing enforcement action against senior managers the FCA will use the individual's statement of responsibilities and the firm's responsibilities map to help inform it of the scope of the senior manager's duties.

The PRA expects these documents to be dynamic as they need to be updated and resubmitted to the PRA when changes occur (which is a statutory requirement).

Retention of the maps is governed by FCA general record keeping requirements found in SYSC 9.1.4. Firms must retain all versions of maps which are subsequently superseded so that the FCA can obtain an accurate picture of where responsibilities vested at a specific point in time.

4.5 Handover arrangements

The FCA's rule relating to handover arrangements is found in SYSC 4.9. A firm must take all reasonable steps to ensure that someone who is becoming an SMF manager, or taking on a new role (and their SMF manager if they have one), has all the information and material that that he could reasonably expect to have to perform the job effectively and in accordance with the requirements of the regulatory system.

A firm must have a policy in place saying how it will comply with this rule, including the systems and controls it uses.

The information that should be made available includes details about unresolved or possible breaches of regulatory requirements, and of any unresolved concerns expressed by regulators. The document should be "practical and helpful" and not just a record, and it should include an assessment of what issues would be prioritised and judgment and opinion, not just facts and figures. A SMF manager who is leaving may prepare a handover certificate, and should contribute to the information and material given to the new role holder.

There is no rule saying that a "handover certificate" must be prepared, just that a firm must take reasonable steps to ensure that an SMF has all the material they need. The production of a handover certificate is suggested as a way of complying with the requirements, in the FCA's guidance (SYSC 4.9.8G), although the FCA accepts that there will be cases in which it will be impractical to ask the predecessor to prepare a handover certificate.

More about handover arrangements can be read in the Chapter on Employment issues.

4.6   The Certification Regime

In addition to the creation of the Senior Manager Functions for relevant authorised firms, such firms must also create and maintain an internal certification regime, for an additional layer of staff.

Those who will need to be certified under the regime will be subject to assessment and approval by the firm itself and will not be given approval by either regulator. The regulators will oversee the way in which firms run their certification regimes, but will not certify staff on an individual basis.

Firms must identify those who will fall within the certification regime at commencement of the SMR, i.e. 7 March 2016, at which point they will be subject to the conduct rules. Firms have been given until 7 March 2017 (an additional year after the effective date of 7 March 2016 for the SMR) to produce certificates for certification employees.

There is a duty is on the firm to take "reasonable care" to ensure that no employee performs any of these functions without having been certified as fit and proper to do so.

The certification must be reviewed on an annual basis, and when a person moves to a new certified function.

4.6.1 PRA certification regime

Given its objective of ensuring the safety and soundness of firms, the PRA has created one Certification Function. It applies where an employee is a "significant risk taker"—as defined in the Material Risk Takers Regulation (related to the Capital Requirements Directive). The definition is different for credit unions.

For firms subject to the Capital Requirements Regulation (CRR firms), a function performed by a significant risk taker will be a certification function, as long as:

- the person is not already approved for a Senior Manager Function;
- their function requires them to be involved in one or more aspects of the firm's affairs so far as relating to a regulated activity carried on by the firm.

The PRA rules are contained in the Certification section of the PRA Rulebook: Certification, and supported by SS28/15, Chapter 3, The PRA's Certification Regime.

The PRA's certification regime is intended to capture individuals to whom the PRA's remuneration rules will also apply, as long as they are not performing another controlled function, and as long as their work has an impact on the UK regulated activity of a firm. An individual employed by an overseas subsidiary of a UK authorised firm falling within the remuneration rules (which capture those at group, parent and subsidiary undertaking levels), will not need to be a certified person where he has no involvement in a regulated activity of the UK firm.

Any function performed by a significant risk taker (subject to the previously mentioned points above) will be a certification function. However, the PRA will not expect firms to issue multiple certificates covering all the different functions a significant risk taker performs. Rather, in a certificate, a firm may describe the function performed by an employee in broad terms, and without listing all the activities that function may involve. The firm must assess whether the employee is fit and proper to perform all aspects of the function as described by the certificate.

When someone moves certified functions during the year, the firm is obliged to assess fitness and propriety before they take up the new function, and not to wait until the annual reassessment.

4.6.2 FCA certification regime

The FCA's certification regime is wider than the PRA's regime.

The FCA requires all those performing an "FCA-specified significant harm function" to be certified, but only if they perform their function from an establishment in the UK or are dealing with a client in the UK (apart from Material Risk Takers).

The FCA's regime captures:

• Those individuals performing functions that would formerly have been Significant Influence Functions that would not fall within the scope of the new SMFs.

- Individuals in customer-facing roles which are subject to qualification requirements (e.g. mortgage and retail investment advisers), as set out in FCA's Training and Competence Sourcebook.
- Individuals in client dealing roles (investment managers, investment advisors, corporate finance advisors).
- Those engaged in algorithmic trading (those responsible for approving or managing the deployment of trading algorithms).
- Anyone who supervises or manages a Certified Person, if they are not an SMF holder.

The FCA regime contains nine categories of staff. 1-7 came into force on 7 March 2016; 8 and 9 come into force on 7 September 2016.[40]

Function	Where defined
(1) CASS oversight	*SYSC* 5.2.32R
(2) Benchmark submission and administration	*SYSC* 5.2.33R
(3) Proprietary trader	*SYSC* 5.2.34R
(4) Significant management	*SYSC* 5.2.35R
(5) Functions requiring qualifications	*SYSC* 5.2.39R
(6) Managers of certification employees	SYSC 5.2.41R
(7) Material risk takers	SYSC 5.2.42R
(8) Client-dealing	SYSC 5.2.44R
(9) Algorithmic trading	SYSC 5.2.49R

4.6.2.1 CASS oversight

In relation to a CASS medium or large firm, the function is that of acting in the capacity of the person allocated the function in CASS 1A.3.1AR (oversight of operational effectiveness). The equivalent function for a CASS large debt management firm is found in CASS 11.3.4R. The role involves:

---

[40] SYSC 5.2.30R.

(1) oversight of the operational effectiveness of that firm's systems and controls that are designed to achieve compliance with CASS;
(2) reporting to the firm's governing body in respect of that oversight; and
(3) completing and submitting a CMAR to the FCA in accordance with SUP 16.14.

The CASS oversight function is only a certification function if the requirements of the role are not already being performed by an SMF holder. Where a senior manager performs the role (under the CASS provisions) there is no requirement to have an additional individual appointed as certified person for CASS oversight.

4.6.2.2 *Benchmark Submission and Administration*

These two certification functions are:

- Benchmark manager under MAR 8.2.3R(1).
- Benchmark administration manager, under MAR 8.3.5R(1).

The detailed rules relating to the conduct of those performing these functions are found in the Code of Market Conduct (MAR), Chapter 8 (Benchmarks), and are supplemented by a very short handbook guide called BENCH, which contains a table showing which other parts of the FCA handbook apply.

The benchmark submission function is the function of acting as benchmark manager with responsibility for the oversight of the firm's compliance with MAR Chapter 8.2. The manager must have the requisite authority and access to resources to enable him to carry out this responsibility.

The duties of the role holder are wide ranging, and cover the close control of submissions and the supervision of employees involved in the submission process.

The benchmark administration manager function is that of acting as benchmark administration manager. The benchmark administration manager must have the requisite level of authority and resources required to enable him to ensure the firm complies with all the requirements contained in MAR 8.3.

The Financial Services Act 2012 s.91 contains an offence of making false or misleading statements, or the creation of false or misleading impressions in relation to specified benchmarks. The offence carries a penalty upon conviction on indictment of seven years imprisonment and an unlimited fine.

4.6.2.3 *Proprietary Trader*

The proprietary trader function is the function of acting as a proprietary trader whose activity involves, or might involve, a risk of significant harm to the firm or any of its customers.

4.6.2.4 *Significant management*

This is the function of acting as a senior manager, with significant responsibility for a significant business unit. The FCA provides that a function holder could, for example, be the head of a unit carrying on the activities of:

- retail banking;
- personal lending;
- corporate lending;
- salvage or loan recovery; or
- proprietary trading.

The function holder could also be a member of a committee (that is, a person who, together with others, has authority to commit the firm) making decisions in the above functions.

When deciding which individuals may need to be appointed to the function, the FCA states that the following additional factors about the firm should be considered:

(1) the size and significance of the firm's business in the United Kingdom. For example, a firm carrying on designated investment business may have a large number of certification employees (for example, in excess of 100 individuals);

(2) the number of regulated activities carried on, or proposed to be carried on, by the firm and (if relevant) other members of the group;

(3) its group structure (if it is a member of a group);

(4) its management structure (for example, matrix management); and

(5) the size and significance of its international operations, if any.

SYSC 5.2.38G states that when considering whether a business unit is significant for the purposes of SYSC 5.2.35 R, the firm should take into account all relevant factors in the light of the firm's current circumstances and its plans for the future, including:

- the risk profile of the unit;
- its use or commitment of the firm's capital;
- its contribution to the profit and loss account;
- the number of employees, certification employees or SMF managers in the unit;
- the number of customers of the unit; and
- any other factor which makes the unit significant to the conduct of the firm's affairs so far as relating to the regulated activity.

The interplay between SMF holders and certification function holders in a firm will need to be carefully worked out. Whether a particular individual ought to be a senior manager and SMF holder, or a certification function holder, will depend on a variety of factors that will be influenced by the size and scope both of their role, and the firm by which they are employed. Firms will need to take a holistic view of their management structures, and the layers within it, in order to decide where the line should be drawn between those who will become SMFs and those who will become certified persons.

4.6.2.5 Functions Requiring Qualifications

Each function involving an activity for which there is a qualification requirement as specified in TC App 1.1.1 (Activities and Products/Sectors to which TC applies) is a certification function. These activities relate to business conducted with retail clients.

4.6.2.6 Managers of Certification Employees

Those who manage certification employees, but who are not themselves SMF managers, must also be certified.

4.6.2.7 Material risk takers

Each function performed by a member of a firm's dual-regulated firms Remuneration Code staff (including any person who meets any of the criteria set out in arts 3 to 5 of Commission delegated regulation (EU) No 604/2014 (criteria to identify categories of staff whose professional activities have a material impact on an institution's risk profile) is a certification function.

4.6.3 Extension of the certification regime to wholesale traders

The FCA extended the certification regime to wholesale traders who would otherwise not be captured, due to not being subject to a qualification requirement, in Policy Statement 16/3 (published in February 2016). This PS has created two additional categories of significant harm function, which apply to individuals that are based in the UK or are dealing with UK clients. The FCA consulted on rules in CP15/22 (July 2015). Firms have until 7 September 2016 to identify staff within these two functions, and to train them in respect of the Conduct Rules, which will also apply from that date.

4.6.3.1   Client Dealing

The first category captures individuals of a similar seniority to those performing the CF30 customer function under the pre 2016 Approved Persons Regime. It covers[41]:

- Advising on investments other than a non-investment insurance contract and performing other functions related to this, such as dealing and arranging.
- Giving advice in connection with corporate finance business or performing other functions in relation to this.
- Dealing, as principal or agent, and arranging (bringing about) deals in investments (other than in a non-investment insurance contract).
- Acting in the capacity of an investment manager and functions connected with this.
- Acting as a bidder's representative.

The function will apply to those dealing not just with retail clients but also professional clients and eligible counterparties, and so differs from the customer function in this regard. In the CP the FCA notes that "dealing with" clients broadly means having contact with clients. Therefore, through capturing those individuals effecting transactions with clients, this function will capture the activity where the investment risk to the firm and client crystallises.

"Clients" will also include corporate finance and venture capital contacts, and any person with whom the firm conducts or intends to conduct business, as such contacts could also pose a risk of significant harm to the firm or any of its customers. The FCA has said that it also proposes to also reflect this meaning of "client" in the scope of the wider Certification Regime and Conduct Rules for UK firms and non-EEA branches, which are limited to individuals that are based in the UK or dealing with a UK client. The rules are found in SYSC 5.2.44R.

---

[41]   SYSC 5.2.45R.

In PS 16/3, the FCA produced this diagram, showing how a firm can identify an employee as a client-dealing significant harm function.

4.6.3.2   *Algorithmic trading*

The FCA's view is that given the extensive use of algorithms in the UK market, it is important that the individuals responsible for the deployment of trading algorithms are fit and proper, for example to ensure that the algorithms are adequately tested through comprehensive testing to assess their potential behaviour, in particular to ensure they are resilient, do not contribute to disorderly markets or breach market abuse or trading venue rules. This category of significant harm will capture individuals with responsibility for[42]:

- Approving the deployment of a trading algorithm or a material part of one.
- Approving the deployment of a material amendment to a trading algorithm or part of one, or the combination of trading algorithms.
- Monitoring or deciding whether or not the use or deployment of a trading algorithm is or remains compliant with the firm's obligations.

The FCA intends for this function to include individuals responsible for all algorithms that are in production and operationally capable of trading, regardless of whether they are actually engaging in trades at any given point, provided that the algorithm is capable of trading. Guidance in SYSC at paragraph 5.2.54 also makes clear that where approval or a decision involves different elements that have been signed-off by different people, all will be deemed to have given approval. However where the same aspects of a decision have been approved up the chain, it will be the most senior decision maker who bears responsibility and will need to be the certified person.

---

[42]   SYSC 5.2.49R.

Figure 1 – Identifying an employee as a client-dealing SHF

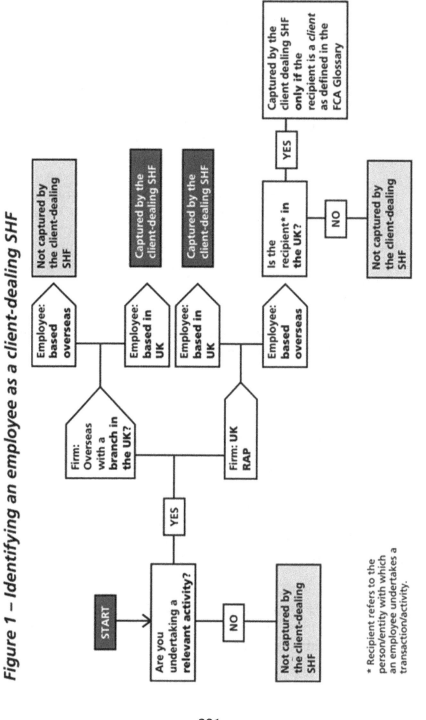

These new functions will only apply in relation to regulated products (as is the case with the rest of the regime), and to UK relevant firms and incoming EEA and non-EEA branches of overseas relevant firms. The rules are found in SYSC 5.2.49R.

4.6.4 *Territorial Limitation of the Certification Regime*

The general rule in relation to the territorial scope of the certification regime is found in SYSC 5.2.19R, and provides that functions only fall within the regime where they are:

- performed by a person from an establishment of the firm (or its appointed representative) in the United Kingdom; or
- the person performing that function is dealing with a client of the firm in the United Kingdom from an establishment of the firm (or its appointed representative) overseas.

A territorial limitation also exists in the Conduct Rules for all relevant staff apart from Senior Managers.

There is one exception for the Material Risk Taker certification function, to the FCA's territorial limitation. An MRT function holder needs to be certified even where they are based abroad and remote book into a UK relevant firm where there is not a UK client. Overseas MRTs will therefore be captured by both the FCA and the PRA function.

Further, no territorial limitation applies in the Conduct Rules for MRTSs. This will mean that where there is a breach of a conduct rule relevant to the FCA's objectives by an MRT, for example in relation to market conduct, the FCA will be able to take action.

Figure 8 below is reproduced from CP15/22, published in July 2015, and provides an overview of the application of the certification regime to different groups.

Figure 8: Application of Certification Regime

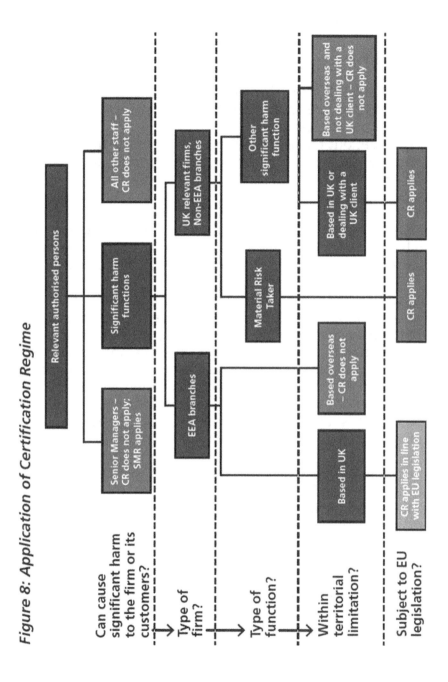

4.6.5 *The certificate*

The certificate:

- must state that the firm is satisfied that the person is a fit and proper person to perform the function(s) to which the certificate relates; and
- must set out the aspects of the affairs of the firm in which the person will be involved in performing the function. (SYSC 5.2.11).

Once a certificate is issued, it is valid for 12 months, for the date of issue. A firm must maintain a record of every employee who has had a valid certificate issued by it. A certificate can be issued for less than, but not for more than, 12 months.[43]

Where a firm fails an individual on the fit and proper test and decides not to issue a certificate, it must issue a written notice to that person, stating what steps (if any) the firm proposes to take in relation to the person as a result of the decision; and the reasons for proposing to take those steps. There are significant employment law overlaps with this provision, and firms may need to amend their employment contracts to make continued employment subject to the maintenance of the standards required by the fit and proper test, for example.

A firm must also consider whether it needs to make a notification to the FCA for breaches of the conduct rules, if the circumstances dictate this, where it refuses to give a certificate to an employee.

Multiple certification functions may be covered by a single certificate, although fitness and propriety for each certification function need to be assessed against the applicable standards. In a certificate, a firm may describe the employee's functions that involve an FCA-specified significant-harm function in broad terms, and without listing all the activities that the function may involve.

---

[43] SYSC 5.2.12.

Where a certification employee switches from one certification function to another during the year, a firm must reassess his fitness and propriety for their new role, before they begin it, and issue a new certificate at that point (if necessary) and not wait until the expiry of the certificate to do so. In some cases a certificate may be drafted broadly enough to enable a new role to be carried out without a new certificate having to be issued.

It is likely that many firms will seek to build the annual certification process into their existing performance management process.

4.6.6   Emergency appointments & 30 day grace period

Where a certification employee has a period of absence that is reasonably unforeseen, a firm can appoint another to fulfil their role for up to four weeks, without that person having to become a certification employee. However, this cannot be done where the absentee held a function requiring a qualification; this is in order to ensure that retail clients are always subject to protection and always dealt with by appropriately qualified individuals.

The FCA has also created a 30 day grace period for a firm's staff based outside the UK, who spend no more than 30 days in the UK performing what would otherwise be a Significant Harm Function. The 30 day grace period does not apply to the Material Risk Taker significant harm function for UK relevant authorised persons, as this function has no territorial limitation. The rule is contingent on the individual being supervised by one of the firm's SMF managers or a certified employee whose certificate covers the significant harm function being undertaken by the individual in question. The FCA says that firms should note that this rule does not impact on the existing "emergency appointments" rule in SYSC 5.2.27R and the two rules continue to operate separately.[44]

---

[44] PS 16/3.

4.7 Fitness and propriety—The FCA

The FCA's Fit and Proper Test, found in the FIT section of the Handbook, contains rules that apply to relevant firms when they are making their own assessment on whether or not to grant a certificate to an individual to perform a function under the certification regime. Such persons will not be subject to any assessment of their fitness and propriety by the regulator.

The same FIT provisions serve as guidance to firms when they submit applications to the regulator for approval, for those wishing to perform an FCA -designated senior management function, or those in firms not affected by the SMR, where all those wishing to hold controlled functions must be subject to approval by the regulator to do so. The regulator itself applies the test.

However, the test remains the same irrespective of whether it is applied by the regulator, by a firm as a rule, or by a firm as guidance.

The test is expected to be used both at the beginning of a firm's engagement with an individual, and in assessing their fitness on an ongoing basis—particularly with a view to assessing whether there may be any grounds on which the regulatory could withdraw approval (in the case of SMF managers).[45] It is closely connected with the "competent employees rule" found in SYSC 5.1 which provides that a firm must employ staff with the skills, knowledge and expertise necessary for the discharge of the responsibilities allocated to them.

Even where the FCA will ultimately decide whether to grant approval to a senior manager within the SMR, a firm must still conduct a fit and proper assessment in relation to the individual, and should have particular regard to whether that person:

1. has obtained a qualification;

---

[45] FIT 1.1.2G(1)(a),(b).

2. has undergone, or is undergoing training;
3. possesses a level of competence; or
4. has the personal characteristics

required by general rules made by the FCA. These rules include SYSC 4.2 (for very senior employees—persons who effectively direct the business), and SYSC 4.3A.3R (management body).[46] The competent employees rule should also be observed, and for those engaged in retail activities, the provisions in the Training and Competence Sourcebook (TC, specifically TC2.1.2R—employees' competence). The FCA will also have regard to these factors.

The main assessment criteria used by the FCA in considering fitness and propriety, and the criteria it also expects firms to apply, to both senior manager (from 7 March 2016) and certification employees (from 7 March 2017), contains three elements, known as the "Fit and Proper Test". This test has not changed since it was first introduced at the turn of the century and regulated firms will be familiar with it. It requires an assessment of the candidate's:

*   honesty, integrity and reputation;
*   competence and capability; and
*   financial soundness.

A firm must also consider the factors outlined in FIT 2.

These factors are the equally applicable and relevant for firms assessing the fitness and propriety of both Senior Managers and those within the certification regime, although firms are not obliged to formally follow the test and issue certificates to certification employees until 7 March 2017. In advance of this date firms will still be bound by the competent employees rule, and can use FIT as guidance.

Firms, when submitting an application for someone who will join the management body of a firm under the SMR are reminded in guidance in FIT to ensure that the management

---

[46] FIT 1.2.1C G.

body as a whole possesses adequate knowledge, skills and experience to understand the firm's activities. Although in such cases the application will be made on the part of the individual, the firm must have a clear understanding of how they complement and fit in with the collective. Statements of responsibly and responsibilities maps will aid this exercise.

For all staff it is considering against the fit and proper test, a firm should consider:

1. the nature, scale and complexity of its business, the nature and range of financial services and activities undertaken in the course of that business; and
2. whether the candidate or person has the knowledge, skills and experience to perform the specific role that the candidate or person is intended to perform.[47]

The individual at the firm tasked with conducting the assessment should ensure they have an up to date job description so that they can accurately apply the skills of the candidate to the requirements of the role.[48]

4.7.1 *Honesty, integrity and reputation*

FIT 2.1.3 G outlines the matters the FCA will have regard to, and that it expects relevant firms to have regard to when assessing a candidate's honesty, integrity and reputation:

- whether the person has been convicted of any criminal offence, whether or not in the United Kingdom.
- whether the person has been the subject of any adverse finding or any settlement in civil proceedings, particularly in connection with investment or other financial business, misconduct, fraud or the formation or management of a body corporate;
- whether the person has been the subject of, or interviewed in the course of, any existing or previous investigation or disciplinary proceedings, by the appropriate regulator, by

---

[47] FIT 1.3.2A G.
[48] FIT 1.3.4B G.

other regulatory authorities (including a previous regulator), clearing houses and exchanges, professional bodies, or government bodies or agencies;

- whether the person is or has been the subject of any proceedings of a disciplinary or criminal nature, or has been notified of any potential proceedings or of any investigation which might lead to those proceedings;
- whether the person has contravened any of the requirements and standards of the regulatory system or the equivalent standards or requirements of other regulatory authorities (including a previous regulator), clearing houses and exchanges, professional bodies, or government bodies or agencies;
- whether the person has been the subject of any justified complaint relating to regulated activities;
- whether the person has been involved with a company, partnership or other organisation that has been refused registration, authorisation, membership or a licence to carry out a trade, business or profession, or has had that registration, authorisation, membership or licence revoked, withdrawn or terminated, or has been expelled by a regulatory or government body;
- whether, as a result of the removal of the relevant licence, registration or other authority, the person has been refused the right to carry on a trade, business or profession requiring a licence, registration or other authority;
- whether the person has been a director, partner, or concerned in the management, of a business that has gone into insolvency, liquidation or administration while the person has been connected with that organisation or within one year of that connection;
- whether the person, or any business with which the person has been involved, has been investigated, disciplined, censured or suspended or criticised by a regulatory or professional body, a court or Tribunal, whether publicly or privately;
- whether the person has been dismissed, or asked to resign and resigned, from employment or from a position of trust, fiduciary appointment or similar;

- whether the person has ever been disqualified from acting as a director or disqualified from acting in any managerial capacity;
- whether, in the past, the person has been candid and truthful in all his dealings with any regulatory body and whether the person demonstrates a readiness and willingness to comply with the requirements and standards of the regulatory system and with other legal, regulatory and professional requirements and standards.

4.7.2 Competence and capability

Fit 2.2.1 G provides that in determining a person's competence and capability, the FCA7 will have regard to all relevant matters including but not limited to:

- whether the person satisfies the relevant FCA7 training and competence requirements in relation to the controlled function the person performs or is intended to perform;
- whether the person has demonstrated by experience and training that they are suitable, or will be suitable if approved, to perform the controlled function;
- whether the person has adequate time to perform the controlled function and meet the responsibilities associated with that function.

For those being considered for an FCA designated senior manager function, the firm should also have regard to:

- whether the person satisfies any applicable training and competence requirements (in relation to the function that the person performs or is intended to perform);
- whether the person has demonstrated by experience and training that they are suitable to perform the function they are intended to perform;
- whether the person has adequate time to perform the function in question and meet the responsibilities associated with that function.

In the case of drug or alcohol abuse related dismissals or convictions, the FCA only considers this in relation to a person's continuing ability to perform the function. In other words, where people are rehabilitated, past indiscretions of this nature may not be held against them.[49]

4.7.3 Financial Soundness

In determining a person's financial soundness, the FCA will have regard, and a relevant authorised person should also have regard, to any factors including, but not limited to:

- whether the person has been the subject of any judgment debt or award, in the United Kingdom or elsewhere, that remains outstanding or was not satisfied within a reasonable period;
- whether, in the United Kingdom or elsewhere, the person has made any arrangements with his creditors, filed for bankruptcy, had a bankruptcy petition served on him, been adjudged bankrupt, been the subject of a bankruptcy restrictions order (including an interim bankruptcy restrictions order), offered a bankruptcy restrictions undertaking, had assets sequestrated, or been involved in proceedings relating to any of these.[50]

Firms should recognise that the list of factors and examples provided by the FCA is not exhaustive, and firms themselves must be satisfied of the fitness and propriety of an individual to perform a certain role, on a case by case basis.

4.8 Fitness and propriety—the PRA

The PRA's rules on fitness and propriety are found in the PRA Rulebook: Fitness and Propriety, supported by a supervisory statement (SS28/15), which apply to the PRA's assessment of whether or not an SMF function applicant is fit and proper, as well as to a firm's own assessment of individuals wishing to

---

[49] FIT 2.2.2 G.
[50] FIT 2.3.1 G.

perform SMFs or PRA certification functions. The provisions are very similar to the FCA's, and the PRA Handbook: Fitness and Propriety states:

In deciding whether a *person* is fit and proper, a *firm* must be satisfied that the *person*:

a.	has the personal characteristics (including being of good repute and integrity);
b.	possesses the level of competence, knowledge and experience;
c.	has the qualifications; and
d.	has undergone or is undergoing all training.

There is no additional "fit and proper test" beyond the above in the rules, although it does appear in SS 28/15, Chapter 4. This provides that the PRA will have regard to the three elements of the fit and proper test, and also that it expects firms to have regard to these.

In addition, the PRA will have regard to the European Banking Authority's Guidelines on the assessment of the suitability of members of the management body and key function holders (the EBA Suitability Guidelines) and in particular to the Assessment Criteria set out in Title II, Chapter IV of those Guidelines[51] (See Annex 1).

## 4.9	Criminal records checks and Regulatory References

Only staff applying for roles under the SMR must have criminal records checks carried out on them, by firms. Those who will perform certification functions do not need to be subject to a criminal records check, although some firms may wish to do this in any event.

---

[51] *http://www.eba.europa.eu/documents/10180/106695/EBA-GL-2012-06–Guidelines-on-the-assessment-of-the-suitability-of-persons-.pdf* [Accessed 24 February 2016].

4.9.1   Regulatory references

The PRA published its rules relating to regulatory references in Policy Statement 16/05.[52] From 7 March 2016, when considering the appointment of an in-scope individual, PRA-regulated firms will be required to:

- Provide a reference to another regulated firm 'as soon as reasonably practicable' upon request containing 'all relevant information' of which it is aware. This requirement already exists under SUP10B of the current PRA Handbook but only applies in respect of Approved Persons. The PRA's first tranche of rules will ensure that it continues to apply to certain functions that will cease to be subject to regulatory pre-approval from 7 March 2016, such as notified NEDs, as well as encompassing all KFHs at insurers, and employees subject to certification under the PRA's Certification rules (ie. a subset of material risk takers ('MRTs')).
- Take reasonable steps to obtain appropriate references covering at least the past 5 years of service from that person's current and previous employers, and from organisations at which that person served as, or is currently, a NED. This is a new requirement which reflects a longstanding supervisory expectation that firms should undertake appropriate due diligence on candidates.

At the time of writing (April 2016) these is no requirement for regulatory references to be provided in a standard template; nor for these references to be updated if subsequent information about the individual's conduct or fitness and propriety subsequently comes to light.

The FCA's final rules are contained in PS 16/03 which inserts SUP10C.16 into the FCA Handbook.

As an interim measure, the FCA has added rules that apply the existing reference requirements to RAPs (i.e. on receipt of a request for a reference in relation to candidates seeking

---

[52] http://www.fca.org.uk/static/fca/documents/policy-statements/ps16-05.pdf.

pre-approved roles, a RAP will be required to provide a reference and include all relevant information). The FCA states in the PS that the interim position ensures that the existing obligation to provide a reference will also apply at commencement of the SM&CR. Under the SM&CR a portion of individuals will no longer be performing a controlled function, and will instead be performing a Significant Harm Function under the CR. The FCA has not extended the interim measure to candidates of these roles. The FCA says that this is a pragmatic solution in the short term, while it considers consultation feedback.

SUP10C.16.1 requires a firm providing the reference to have regard to the purpose of the request, and to give the requesting firm 'all relevant information of which it is aware'. This duty applies also where the firm providing the reference has outsourced the collection of that information to an unregulated third party.

SUP 10C.16.3 provides as follows:

> "A firm supplying a reference in accordance with SUP 10C.16.1R owes a duty to its former employee and the recipient firm to exercise due skill and care in the preparation of the reference. The reference should be accurate and based on documented fact. The firm may give frank and honest views, but only after taking reasonable care both as to factual content, and as to the opinions expressed, and verifying the information upon which they are based."

A full Policy Statement on Regulatory References is due in the Summer of 2016.

4.9.2 Record keeping

Once the regime has commenced, relevant firms will need to keep appropriate records for at least five years to allow them to comply with the conduct rules-focused disclosure requirements.

The conduct rules do not apply retrospectively, so firms will not be required by the proposed rules to give such information relating to a date before the conduct rules come into force.

4.10   Conduct rules

4.10.1   Introduction

The conduct rules (the Conduct Rules) are an important component of the new individual accountability regime and are intended to influence the behaviour of individuals and provide a framework against which both the PRA and the FCA can judge an individual's actions as part of their general supervision of a firm. The Conduct Rules therefore seek to shape the culture, standards and policies of a firm as a whole and promote more positive behaviour that supports the regulators' statutory objectives.

For financial services firms that are within the scope of the new individual accountability regime the Conduct Rules will replace the principles and guidance found within the Statements of Principle and Code of Practice for Approved Persons (APER) which applies to approved persons.

The Conduct Rules
First tier: Individual Conduct Rules
Rule 1: You must act with integrity.
Rule 2: You must act with due skill, care and diligence.
Rule 3: You must be open and cooperative with the FCA, the PRA and other regulators.
Rule 4: You must pay due regard to the interests of customers and treat them fairly.
Rule 5: You must observe proper standards of market conduct.
Second tier: Senior Manager Conduct Rules
SM1: You must take reasonable steps to ensure that the business of the firm for which you are responsible is controlled effectively.

The Conduct Rules
SM2: You must take reasonable steps to ensure that the business of the firm for which you are responsible complies with the relevant requirements and standards of the regulatory system.
SM3: You must take reasonable steps to ensure that any delegation of your responsibilities is to an appropriate person and that you oversee the discharge of the delegated responsibility effectively.
SM4: You must disclose appropriately any information of which the FCA or PRA would reasonably expect notice.
SM5: When exercising your responsibilities, you must pay due regard to the interests of current and potential future policyholders in ensuring the provision by the firm of an appropriate degree of protection for their insured benefits.

4.10.2   *Statutory basis for the new conduct rules*

The statutory basis of the Conduct Rules can be found in the Financial Services (Banking Reform) Act 2013 (the Act). Section 30 of the Act introduced a new s.64A to the Financial Services and Markets Act 2000 (FSMA) which gave both regulators the power to introduce new conduct rules and to apply them to employees of those firms that are within the scope of the new individual accountability regime (rather than just to those individuals subject to regulatory pre-approval).

As amended by the Act s.64A FSMA stated:

> "(1) If it appears to the FCA to be necessary or expedient for the purpose of advancing one or more of its operational objectives, the FCA may make rules about the conduct of the following persons—
>   (a) persons in relation to whom either regulator has given its approval under section 59;
>   (b) persons who are employees of relevant author-ised persons

(2) If it appears to the PRA to be necessary or expedient for the purpose of advancing one or more of its objectives, the PRA may make rules about the conduct of the following persons—

   (a) persons in relation to whom it has given its approval under section 59;

   (b) persons in relation to whom the FCA has given its approval under section 59 in respect of the performance by them of a relevant senior management function in relation to the carrying on by a PRA-authorised person of a regulated activity;

   (c) persons who are employees of relevant PRA-authorised persons.

(3) In subsection (2)—

'relevant PRA-authorised person' means a PRA-authorised person that is a relevant authorised person (see section 71A), and

'relevant senior management function' means a function which the PRA is satisfied is a senior management function as defined in section 59ZA (whether or not the function has been designated as such by the FCA).

(4) Rules made under this section must relate to the conduct of persons in relation to the performance by them of qualifying functions.

(5) In subsection (4) 'qualifying function', in relation to a person, means a function relating to the carrying on of activities (whether or not regulated activities) by—

   (a) in the case of an approved person, the person on whose application approval was given, and

   (b) in any other case, the person's employer

(6) In this section any reference to an employee of a person ("P") includes a reference to a person who—

   (a) personally provides, or is under an obligation personally to provide, services to P under an arrangement made between P and the person providing the services or another person, and

   (b) is subject to (or to the right of) supervision, direction or control by P as to the manner in which those services are provided, and 'employer' is to be read accordingly." "

Section 64A(1) FSMA gives the FCA the power to make rules about the conduct of individuals if it considers it necessary or expedient to advance one or more of its operational objectives. It can make rules about the conduct of persons it has approved to perform a controlled function (whether a designated senior management function in a bank, or another controlled function in any kind of firm). The FCA can also make rules about individuals who do not have approval to perform controlled functions, but are simply employees of a relevant authorised person. Whilst this new power is limited to relevant authorised persons, it is extended to anyone employed in them, at whatever level.

Section 64A(2) FSMA gives the PRA the power to make rules about the conduct of individuals if it considers it necessary or expedient to advance one or more of its statutory objectives. The PRA can make such rules for those individuals it has approved to perform senior management functions in PRA-authorised firms. Given that the FCA can approve individuals to perform controlled functions in relation to PRA-authorised firms s.64A(2)(b) FSMA allows the PRA to make conduct rules that are binding on such individuals, if they are performing a senior management function (whether or not the function has been designated by the FCA as a senior management function). Finally, s.64A(2)(c) allows the PRA to make conduct rules for employees in PRA authorised firms. Again, it extends such power to all such employees.

The rules relate to a relevant authorised person's conduct when performing "qualifying functions".[53] What is a qualifying function is defined in s.64A(5) FSMA and is broad in the sense that it is wider than carrying out regulated activities.

Section 64A(6) FSMA gives further meaning to the term "employee". The provision is intended to ensure that the definition of employee is broad enough to capture someone who, although they are formally self-employed or providing

---

[53] Financial Services and Markets Act 2000 s. 64A(4).

services under a contract for services, are in practice in a position equivalent to an employee. This might in some circumstances include sub-contractors, employees of sub-contractors or employees of a company in the same group as the firm, which is responsible for employing the staff who work for group companies.

As amended by the Act section 64B FSMA stated:

" (1) This section applies where a regulator makes rules under section 64A (conduct rules).
(2) Every relevant authorised person must—
    (a) notify all relevant persons of the conduct rules that apply in relation to them, and
    (b) take all reasonable steps to secure that those persons understand how those rules apply in relation to them.
(3) The steps which a relevant authorised person must take to comply with subsection (2)(b) include, in particular, the provision of suitable training.
(4) In this section 'relevant person', in relation to an authorised person, means—
    (a) any person in relation to whom an approval is given under section 59 on the application of the authorised person, and
    (b) any employee of the authorised person.
(5) If a relevant authorised person knows or suspects that a relevant person has failed to comply with any conduct rules, the authorised person must notify the regulator of that fact.
(6) In this section 'employee', in relation to an authorised person, has the same meaning as in section 64A.
(7) For the meaning of 'relevant authorised person', see section 71A. "

Section 64B FSMA contains a number of important requirements. First, firms within the scope of the new individual accountability regime will have to notify those within the scope of the Conduct Rules that they apply to them. Secondly, such firms must take all reasonable steps to secure that those within the scope of the Conduct Rules understand how the new rules apply in relation to them. Suitable training must be provided.[54]

Section 64C FSMA deals with the requirement where the firm has to notify the regulators of any disciplinary action it has taken against those individuals who are within the scope of the Conduct Rules. Sections 66A and 66B FSMA introduce misconduct offences.

4.10.2.1 *Changes to the statutory basis*

On 15 October 2015, HM Treasury published a consultation paper entitled Senior Managers and Certification Regime: extension to all FSMA authorised persons. Two key proposals in the consultation paper were extending the individual accountability regime beyond the banking sector and introducing a statutory duty of responsibility which would supersede the reverse burden of proof.[55] However, two other important proposals were to apply the Conduct Rules to non-executive directors (NEDs) and remove the requirement on firms to report all known or suspected breaches of the Conduct Rules by employees subject to them to the regulators.

The legislation that would implement the necessary changes, the Bank of England and Financial Services Bill (the Bill), was introduced into the House of Lords on 14 October 2015. At the time of writing this chapter the Bill was continuing its passage through the Lords and had yet to go through the House of Commons.

When introduced to the Lords the Bill sought to amend FSMA (as amended by the Act). Section 21 of the Bill, covering rules of conduct, made amendments to s.64A FSMA by inserting references to "directors of authorised persons" and "directors of PRA authorised persons". It also inserted a new s.64A(7) FSMA which stated that *"In this section "director", in relation to an authorised person, means a member of the board of directors, or if*

---

[54] Financial Services and Markets Act 2000 ss.64B(2) and 64B(3).
[55] The statutory duty of responsibility is discussed in chapter [x] of this book covering enforcement.

there is no such board, the equivalent body responsible for the management of the authorised person concerned". These amendments were intended to bring NEDs into scope as previously s.64A FSMA caught those individuals who were carrying on a controlled function or an employee of an authorised person.

The Government's reasoning for bringing NEDs within the scope of the conduct rules was that certain EU Directives required Member States to be able to take action against members of an institution's management body (including NEDs) and that the gap created had to be addressed. The Government also accepted that it was difficult to justify a position where regulatory enforcement action could be taken against relatively junior employees but not against certain board members.

Section 21 of the Bill also inserted after s.64B(4)(b) FSMA the words *"any person who is a director of the authorised person"*. Importantly, s.21(3)(c) of the Bill also stated that 64B(5) FSMA, which covered the firm reporting obligation, be omitted (deleted).

The Government's reasoning behind removing the reporting obligation in s.64B(5) FSMA was that this would be a very costly obligation for firms, especially the larger firms that employ large numbers of staff, as they would have to put in place detailed systems and controls to ensure compliance. The Government also stated that it would amend the Financial Services (Banking Reform) Act 2013 (Commencement No.9) Order 2015 to ensure that the reporting obligation would not come into force on 7 March 2016.

4.10.3   The FCA and PRA consultations

The FCA and PRA have published a number of papers on the new individual accountability regime. A list of these papers can be found in the introduction to this book. Unsurprisingly in almost all of these papers the Conduct Rules have been mentioned. The following is a summary of some of the key issues that arose in the regulators' papers.

4.10.3.1   The July 2014 consultation

As mentioned elsewhere in this book the joint FCA / PRA Consultation Paper that was published in July 2014[56] was the first substantive paper on the new individual accountability regime. The regulators noted in this Consultation Paper[57] that setting expectations about standards of behaviour through Conduct Rules was an important tool that would influence the behaviour of individuals. Importantly, the Conduct Rules would not only be relevant to the FCA's objectives but also the PRA's. The Conduct Rules would provide a framework against which the regulators would make judgements about an individual's actions as part of their general supervision of a firm. Through their impact on individuals' actions, the Conduct Rules would shape a firm's culture, standards and policies and promote positive behaviours that would support both regulators' statutory objectives. The possibility of enforcement would act as a deterrent against actions or omissions that could damage a firm's prudential position, harm its customers or undermine the integrity of the markets.

The existing rules and guidance in APER, which applied only to approved persons, would be replaced by the Conduct Rules with a far wider application so that they covered all individuals within in-scope firms who were in a position to have an impact on the PRA's and FCA's statutory objectives. The differences in their statutory objectives would reflect the different populations of staff who would be caught by the Conduct Rules. The word "conduct" in the new rules would relate to professional conduct in the ordinary, wider sense, i.e. it would not be limited to conduct of business and would include activities relevant to the PRA as well as the FCA.[58]

The PRA proposed not to retain any of the guidance previously given in the Code of Practice within APER, nor provide as much detailed guidance as the FCA. Instead, the PRA would produce a Supervisory Statement which would reproduce

---

[56]   CP FCA CP14/3 PRA CP14/4.
[57]   Paragraph 5.2 CP FCA CP14/3 PRA CP14/4.
[58]   Fn.3 of CP FCA CP14/3 PRA CP14/4.

some of the more general guidance on the types of conduct that would be likely to comply with (or breach) the Conduct Rules. This approach was not, however, to be taken to indicate that the PRA disagreed with the previous guidance but rather was a reflection as to its general approach to producing policy material.[59] The FCA, on the other hand, proposed to support the Conduct Rules with guidance which would draw on the Code of Practice in APER with additional text added where necessary.

The Conduct Rules would not, however, apply retrospectively.[60]

In the July 2014 Consultation Paper the PRA proposed to apply the Conduct Rules to all individuals who were approved by it or the FCA as senior managers and those who fell within its Certification Regime. The reasoning behind this was that it felt that this population of individuals were able to cause significant prudential harm to a firm and therefore impact the PRA's general objective of promoting the safety and soundness of the firms it regulates. However, the PRA also proposed that certain additional Conduct Rules would apply to senior managers only (see below).

The FCA proposed to apply the Conduct Rules to a much wider population of individuals on the basis that its statutory objectives, particularly in terms of protecting consumers and market integrity, could impact a much broader range of staff. The FCA proposed to apply the Conduct Rules to all individuals approved by it or the PRA as senior managers, all individuals covered by both regulator's Certification Regime and all other employees other than those ancillary staff who performed a role that was not specific to the financial services business of the firm. In light of this final category this essentially meant that only those employees whose role would be fundamentally the same as it would be if they worked in a

---

[59] Paragraph 5.6 CP FCA CP14/3 PRA CP14/4.
[60] Paragraph 4.22 CP FCA CP14/3 PRA CP14/4.

non-financial services firm would be excluded. In the Consultation Paper the FCA gave a list of such people.[61] Like the PRA, the FCA proposed that certain additional Conduct Rules would apply to senior managers only (see below).

A key reason as to why the FCA proposed to include such a wide population of individuals was so that a common understanding of what is acceptable and unacceptable behaviour at all levels of a firm could be achieved and therefore culture change could be effected. Also, the FCA felt that it would mitigate against the risk of firms "gaming" the new rules which might have been the case if the boundary was defined narrowly.[62]

The Consultation Paper noted[63] that in order to be effective, the Conduct Rules had to be:

- a comprehensive description of the fundamental standards the regulators expect from those subject to them;
- clear and accessible so that those subject to the rules can understand what is expected of them; and
- fully enforceable in order to hold those who act in a way that is not compliant with them to account, and to act as an effective deterrent.

The Consultation Paper proposed that the Conduct Rules be split into two tiers. The first tier being individual Conduct Rules that the regulators considered relevant to all those individuals within scope. The second tier would apply only to senior managers and would reflect their management duties for the specific part of the in-scope firm they were responsible for, as well as their responsibility for the effective running of their firm as a whole.

These proposals have since been adopted in full by the Regulators, and the final Conduct Rules are as follows:

---

[61] Paragraph 5.13 CP FCA CP14/3 PRA CP14/4.
[62] Paragraph 5.14 CP FCA CP14/3 PRA CP14/4.
[63] Paragraph 5.16 CP FCA CP14/3 PRA CP14/4.

First tier – Individual Conduct Rules

- Rule 1: You must act with integrity.
- Rule 2: You must act with due skill, care and diligence.
- Rule 3: You must be open and cooperative with the FCA, the PRA and other regulators.
- Rule 4: You must pay due regard to the interests of customers and treat them fairly.
- Rule 5: You must observe proper standards of market conduct.

Second tier: Senior Manager Conduct Rules

- SM1: You must take reasonable steps to ensure that the business of the firm for which you are responsible is controlled effectively.
- SM2: You must take reasonable steps to ensure that the business of the firm for which you are responsible complies with the relevant requirements and standards of the regulatory system.
- SM3: You must take reasonable steps to ensure that any delegation of your responsibilities is to an appropriate person and that you oversee the discharge of the delegated responsibility effectively.
- SM4: You must disclose appropriately any information of which the FCA or PRA would reasonably expect notice.
- SM5: When exercising your responsibilities, you must pay due regard to the interests of current and potential future policyholders in ensuring the provision by the firm of an appropriate degree of protection for their insured benefits.

As regards enforcement it was proposed that the FCA would be able to enforce all the Conduct Rules against all senior managers and individual Conduct Rules 1 to 5 against those individuals who fell within its Certification Regime and all other employees who were in-scope. The PRA would enforce all the Conduct Rules except individual Conduct Rules 4 and 5 against all senior managers and individual Conduct Rules 1 to 3 against those who fell within its Certification Regime.

The Consultation Paper made it clear[64] that the Conduct Rules would not apply to an individual's actions in their private life if their actions were unrelated to the activities they performed for their firm. Behaviour unrelated to these activities could, however, be relevant for assessing an individual's fitness and propriety.

Where a breach or suspected breach of a Conduct Rule[65] was by a senior manager, it was proposed[66] that the firm would be required to notify the regulator within seven business days of the firm becoming aware of the matter. For other individuals within the scope of the Conduct Rules it was proposed that notification to the regulators be made on a quarterly basis, with firms compiling an aggregated list of the actual or suspected individual breaches, the identities of those to whom the notification relates and the disciplinary action that they need to report for that quarter. Importantly such new notification requirements would not change or remove firms' obligations to report concerns regarding an individuals' conduct under existing regulatory rules and principles such as FCA Principle 11[67] or PRA Fundamental Rule 7.[68]

---

[64] Paragraph 5.31 CP FCA CP14/3 PRA CP14/4.

[65] Following the proposed deletion of s.64B(5) FSMA under the Bank of England and Financial Services Bill it was not clear at the time of writing this chapter whether the regulators would delete the notification obligation or amend it in some way. The regulators discussion of the obligation as set out in the CPs that were published before the Bill entered Parliament has remained in this Chapter.

[66] Paragraph 5.35 CP FCA CP14/3 PRA CP14/4.

[67] A firm must deal with its regulators in an open and cooperative way, and must disclose to the appropriate regulator appropriately anything relating to the firm of which that regulator would reasonably expect notice.

[68] A firm must deal with its regulators in an open and cooperative way and must disclose to the PRA appropriately anything relating to the firm of which the PRA would reasonably expect notice.

4.10.3.2   *The December 2014 consultation*

In December 2014, the FCA and PRA published a further joint Consultation Paper[69] which gave further insight into the timing of the commencement of the Conduct Rules and the new forms that would be used.

In this Consultation Paper it was noted that it was expected that the Conduct Rules would apply to senior managers and persons within the Certification Regimes from the same date[70] and that this date would be from the commencement of the senior managers' regime.[71] Before such commencement firms would need to have identified the employees within the Certification Regimes and have trained them, together with senior managers, on the Conduct Rules and how they related to their role. For the population of individuals within the scope of the Conduct Rules but outside the senior managers' regime and Certification Regime the FCA would confirm the date of commencement. Such date would be after the Conduct Rules had applied to senior managers and those within the Certification Regime.

The Consultation Paper also discussed the new forms for the new individual accountability regime.[72] A new Form H would be used for notifications of Conduct Rules breaches[73] and disciplinary action relating to FCA certification employees and other Conduct Rules staff. Crucially, the PRA proposed that on the notification of Conduct Rule breaches the seven business day deadline would also apply to notifications relating to individuals who fell within its Certification Regime. This meant that Form H would be an FCA only form with the PRA creating its own new form (Form L for the notification of suspected or actual breaches of Conduct Rules by a material risk taker (other than a senior manager) and related disciplinary action by the firm). The PRA acknowledged that there

---

[69] CP FCA 14/31 PRA 28/14.
[70] Paragraph 2.3 CP FCA 14/31 PRA 28/14.
[71] Paragraph 2.30 CP FCA 14/31 PRA 28/14.
[72] Chapter 3 and Appendix 3 CP FCA 14/31 PRA 28/14.
[73] See fn.13.

may be occasions where firms would have to provide separate notifications to it and the FCA at different times. However, it felt that the additional costs would be minimal.[74]

4.10.3.3   *The February 2015 consultation*

The joint FCA and PRA Consultation Paper that was published in February 2015[75] focused on the approach to non-executive directors in banking and Solvency II firms and the application of the presumption of responsibility.

The application of the new individual accountability regime (including the Conduct Rules) to non-executive directors can be found in the Non-Executive Directors Chapter.

4.10.3.4   *The March 2015 consultation*

The joint FCA and PRA Consultation Paper that was published in March 2015[76] provided feedback on the responses to the July 2014 consultation. In relation to the Conduct Rules it was noted[77] that respondents focused on the wide population of individuals that would be within scope. Concerns were expressed about the cost implications of training staff and of reporting any breaches of the obligations, which would be magnified by the scope of the new rules. Whilst listening to the concerns raised the FCA did not make changes to its proposals. It stated[78]:

> "We think it is very important that staff at all levels of an organisation are subject to minimum standards of conduct and held accountable for their actions. The importance of conduct issues should be understood throughout an organisation, it should not stop below a certain level of seniority. The conduct rules we propose are standards we would expect firms to be operating to already; they are

---

[74] Paragraph 3.17 CP FCA 14/31 PRA 28/14.
[75] CP FCA 15/5 PRA CP7/15.
[76] CP 15/9.
[77] Paragraph 4.1 CP 15/9.
[78] "Our response", Paragraph 4.3 CP 15/9.

very high level and should be easy to understand and map across to everyday tasks performed by staff throughout the firm. As a result, we have no plans to narrow the range of staff who are subject to the rules on which we consulted."

4.10.3.5   *The July 2015 PRA Policy Statement*

In July 2015 the PRA published a Policy Statement[79] containing the feedback it received to the consultation on the draft Conduct Rules consulted on in its July 2014 Consultation Paper. The PRA stated[80] that it had not made any changes to the content or the scope of the Conduct Rules as proposed in the Consultation Paper. Respondents generally supported the Conduct Rules and the proposed approach of applying them directly to individuals performing a PRA or FCA senior management function and employees performing a certification function specified by the PRA. The PRA also covered its proposals on how firms should notify the regulator of known or suspected breaches of the Conduct Rules.

The PRA confirmed[81] that the Conduct Rules would commence on 7 March 2016.

In relation to reporting breaches of the Conduct Rules[82] the PRA noted[83] that some concerns had been raised at the proposal set out in the December 2014 consultation to reduce the period for notification of a breach or suspected breach of the Conduct Rules by PRA certified employees from quarterly to within seven business days (in line with the deadline for notifying equivalent breaches by senior managers). However, the PRA decided to keep with the seven business day period for notification[84] on the basis that the population of individuals within its Senior Managers and Certification Regime were, by definition, capable of causing significant harm to a firm and

---

[79] Policy Statement 16/15.
[80] Paragraph 2.4 PS 16/15.
[81] Paragraph 3.17 PS 16/15.
[82] See fn.13.
[83] Paragraph 3.23 PS 16/15.
[84] Paragraph 3.24 PS 16/15.

therefore felt it was proportionate to know about potential misconduct within a short timeframe. The PRA did, however, amend its notification rules in order to clarify that the period of seven business days begins to run from the point at which the firm determines that a Conduct Rule has been (or is suspected to have been) breached. In relation to the term "suspecting" the PRA noted[85] that respondents to the consultation asked for further guidance on what the threshold for this could be but refused to do so arguing that the term "suspects" was used in section 64B FSMA and that it did not have the power to define it further in its rules. In short, it would be for firms to decide whether they suspect a breach of the rules.

The PRA reminded firms[86] that the Conduct Rules would apply only in relation to activities that an individual performs in their capacity as an employee or senior manager of a firm. In many cases behaviour outside work would not involve a breach of a Conduct Rule.

The PRA also discussed the position regarding non-executive directors and the Conduct Rules which is discussed further in the Non-Executive Directors Chapter.

4.10.4 The July 2015 FCA consultation and Final Conduct Rules

In its July 2015 Consultation Paper[87] the FCA set out final rules on the new individual accountability regime and consulted on extending the Certification Regime to certain wholesale market activities. The final FCA Handbook text was set out in Appendix 1 of the Consultation Paper in the Individual Accountability Instrument 2015. This Instrument set out the Code of Conduct sourcebook (COCON) which would be inserted into the block of the FCA Handbook titled "High Level Standards" and follow the Senior Management Arrangements, Systems and Controls sourcebook.

---

[85] Paragraph 3.26 PS 16/15.
[86] Paragraph 3.27 PS 16/15.
[87] CP 15/22.

In the introduction to the Consultation Paper[88] the FCA gave an update as to the commencement of the Conduct Rules. As previously stated the FCA confirmed that individuals subject to either the senior managers' regime or Certification Regime would be subject to the Conduct Rules from the commencement of the new regime on 7 March 2016. For other staff within scope, the commencement would be a year later on 7 March 2017. Firms would have to ensure that all relevant individuals were trained in the Conduct Rules and how they related to their role in advance of commencement.

4.10.4.1 *Notification of breaches of Conduct Rules*

The FCA noted in the Consultation Paper that it was conscious of the burden that will fall to firms to report both suspected and actual breaches of the Conduct Rules[89] and that it had given further thought to ensure that such burden was not disproportionate.[90] In light of this the FCA changed the requirements previously consulted on and provided in its final rules for firms to report suspected and actual breaches of the Conduct Rules on an annual basis in many cases, rather than quarterly. The FCA stated that reporting would be required as follows[91]:

- actual or suspected breaches of the Conduct Rules by senior managers under the senior managers' regime to be submitted by a firm within seven business days of the firm becoming aware of the actual or suspected breach;
- actual or suspected breaches of the Conduct Rules by any other staff who are subject to them be reported annually. The annual notification would be made using Form H[92] and would cover the annual period to 1 October, for submission by the end of October. Nil returns would not be required; and

---

[88] Paragraph 1.4 CP 15/22.
[89] See fn.13.
[90] Paragraph 4.5 CP 15/22.
[91] Paragraph 4.6 CP 15/22.
[92] Chapter 15, Annex 7R Supervision Manual.

- the FCA's existing obligations on all authorised firms to notify the regulators of matters of which it would reasonably expect notice and, specifically, to report a significant breach of a rule immediately on becoming aware of it.

In relation to the second bullet point the FCA stated that in addition to reducing the burden on firms, in terms of the need to submit reports, the change would mean that firms would be able to assess, in many more cases, whether or not a suspicion was founded before reporting it. This was because it would not expect firms to report suspicions that had already been investigated and proven to be unfounded—only suspicions that were either proven or that remained open at the time of reporting would need to be included.

The FCA stated that non-executive directors outside the senior managers' regime, known as Notified NEDs, would not be subject to the Conduct Rules.[93] However, as we have seen earlier when discussing the statutory basis the Government subsequently decided to bring all NEDs within the scope of the Conduct Rules.

4.10.5 Final PRA rules and guidance

The Policy Statement that was published in July 2015 contained the PRA Rulebook: CRR Firms Non-CRR Firms: Individual Accountability Instrument (No.2) 2015 (the Instrument). This instrument set out the Conduct Rules. These will be located in the Conduct Rules Part of the PRA Rulebook. Also, the PRA published the final version of Supervisory Statement 28/15: Strengthening individual accountability in banking (SS28/15). SS28/15 was, at the time of writing this chapter, updated on 16 December following the publication of PRA Policy Statement 29/15: Strengthening individual accountability in banking: UK branches of non-EEA banks.[94]

---

[93] Paragraph 4.10 CP 15/22.
[94] References to SS28/15 are to the updated version published on 16 December 2015.

The Conduct Rules are simply repeated in the Instrument with guidance on them being set out in SS28/15. This was to be expected following the PRA's comments in the joint Consultation Paper that was published in July 2014. However, before focussing on SS28/15 it is perhaps worth noting the amendments to the Fitness and Propriety Part of the PRA Handbook which provide the following update to employment contracts:

3.1 A firm must contractually require any PRA approved person, notified non-executive director or credit union non-executive director to:
(a) act with integrity;
(b) act with due skill, care and diligence;
(c) be open and co-operative with the FCA, the PRA and other regulators; and
(d) disclose appropriately any information to the FCA or PRA which they would reasonably expect notice.
3.2 A firm must contractually require any PRA approved person to:
(a) take reasonable steps to ensure that the business of the firm for which they are responsible is controlled effectively;
(b) take reasonable steps to ensure that the business of the firm for which they are responsible complies with relevant requirements and standards of the regulatory system; and
(c) take reasonable steps to ensure that any delegation of their responsibilities is to an appropriate person and that they oversee the discharge of the delegated responsibility effectively.

SS28/15 applies to banks, building societies, credit unions and PRA designated investment firms. Its purpose is to set out the PRA's expectations as to how firms should comply with the new individual accountability framework (including the Conduct Rules). The following is a summary of some of the key points raised in SS28/15.

SS28/15 notes[95] that under sections 66B(2) and (3) FSMA individuals, including senior managers, can be guilty of misconduct if they breach a Conduct Rule or are knowingly concerned in a contravention of a Relevant Requirement (as defined in s.66B(4) FSMA) by the firm. SS28/15 does not explicitly consider these two potential grounds for misconduct but notes that the PRA will consider each situation on its facts and that there may be instances where a senior manager may be guilty of misconduct by virtue of a breach of the Conduct Rules under s.66B(2) FSMA.

4.10.5.1   Complying with the Conduct Rules—PRA Expectations

Chapter 5 of SS28/15 sets out the PRA's expectations of how individuals who are subject to the individual Conduct Rules and the senior manager Conduct Rules should comply with them. However, the information contained in the chapter is not an exhaustive statement.

The first part of chapter 5 of SS28/15 deals with persons and activities to which the Conduct Rules apply. In particular, it notes that[96] an employee performing a certification function specified by the PRA or a senior management function specified by either regulator will still be subject to the Conduct Rules regardless of whether their firm has issued a certificate or the person has been granted regulatory approval. Where an employee is performing a function that would have been a senior management function but for the twelve week grace period which covers temporary or reasonably unforeseen absences the individual Conduct Rules will apply to the employee but not the senior manager Conduct Rules.[97] Where an employee is performing a function which would be a certification function but for the rules that cover reasonably unforeseen absences of less than two weeks, the performance of that function will not cause any of the Conduct Rules to apply to that person.[98] The Conduct Rules do not relate to an

---

[95]   SS28/15, 2.66.
[96]   SS28/15, 5.3.
[97]   SS28/15, 5.4.
[98]   SS28/15, 5.5.

individual's conduct in their private life unless they behave in a way that may be relevant to any assessment as to whether they are or remain fit and proper.[99]

When assessing compliance with or a breach of a Conduct Rule, the PRA will have regard to the context in which the action was taken. This includes the precise circumstances of the individual case, the characteristics of the particular function performed by the individual in question and the behaviour that is expected in that function.[100] The PRA states[101] that an individual will only be in breach of a Conduct Rule where they are personally culpable. This arises where their conduct was deliberate or the person's standard of conduct was below that which would be reasonable in all the circumstances.

There is no guidance in chapter 5 regarding individual Conduct Rule 1 (act with integrity) as the PRA does not believe it is necessary to provide guidance on what it means to act with integrity.[102]

In relation to individual Conduct Rule 2 (act with due skill, care and diligence) the PRA notes[103] that a manager is unlikely to be an expert in all aspects of a complex financial services business. However, the manager should understand and inform himself/herself about the business sufficiently to understand the risks of its trading, credit or other business activities. Where unusually profitable business is undertaken, or where the profits are particularly volatile or the business involves funding requirements on the firm beyond those reasonably anticipated, a manager should require explanations from those who report to him/her. Should those explanations be implausible or unsatisfactory, then the manager should take steps to test the veracity of the explanations.[104]

---

[99] SS28/15, 5.6.
[100] SS28/15, 5.7.
[101] SS28/15, 5.8.
[102] SS28/15, Chapter 3, fn.3.
[103] SS28/15, 5.9.
[104] SS28/15, 5.10.

As for individual Conduct Rule 3 (must be open and co-operative with the FCA, the PRA and other regulators) the PRA states[105] that it would expect a person to normally report information through the firm's mechanisms for reporting information to the regulators. Relevant factors that will be used when assessing compliance with this Conduct Rule includes the way in which a person has responded to requests from a regulator.

General factors that the PRA will take into account when assessing whether a senior manager has complied with any of the senior manager Conduct Rules include[106]:

- whether the person exercised reasonable care when considering the information available;
- whether the person reached a reasonable conclusion upon which to act;
- the nature, scale and complexity of the firm's business;
- the person's role and responsibilities; and
- the knowledge the person had, or should have had, of regulatory concerns, if any.

Significantly, the PRA states[107] that an individual's Statement of Responsibilities will be important evidence of their role and responsibilities. However, it also recognises that there may be instances where a person is responsible for additional matters that have not been included in their Statement of Responsibilities. This could be due to their Statement of Responsibilities not being kept up-to-date. In light of this the PRA states that a Statement of Responsibilities will not always be treated as a complete list of the matters for which it regards the person as being responsible.

In relation to senior manager Conduct Rule 1 (take reasonable steps to ensure that the business of the firm for which you are responsible is controlled effectively) the PRA notes that if the strategy of the business is to enter high-risk areas, then the

---

[105] SS28/15, 5.11.
[106] SS28/15, 5.12.
[107] SS28/15, 5.13.

degree of control and strength of monitoring reasonably required within the business will be higher.[108] Also, the organisation of business and the responsibilities of those within it should be clearly defined and that reporting lines should be clear to all staff. Where there are dual reporting lines there is a greater need to ensure that responsibility and accountability of each line manager is clearly set out and understood.[109]

As for senior manager Conduct Rule 2 (take reasonable steps to ensure that the business of the firm for which you are responsible complies with the relevant requirements and standards of the regulatory system) the PRA notes that depending on his/her role[110] a person performing a senior management function may not personally put in place the systems of control in the business. However, such person should take reasonable steps to ensure that the business has operating procedures and systems that include well defined steps for complying with relevant requirements and standards of the regulatory system and for ensuring that the business is run prudently.

For senior manager Conduct Rule 3 (take reasonable steps to ensure that any delegation of your responsibilities is to an appropriate person and that you oversee the discharge of the delegated responsibility effectively) the PRA recognises[111] that a person performing a senior management function may not always personally manage the business on a day-to-day basis. The larger and more complex the business, the greater the need for clear and effective delegation and reporting lines. Written documentation may be required that sets out the scope of the delegation and the reporting lines. The PRA states that it will look to the senior manager to take reasonable steps to ensure that systems are in place that result in issues being addressed at the appropriate level.

---

[108] SS28/15, 5.14.
[109] SS28/15, 5.15.
[110] SS28/15, 5.17.
[111] SS28/15, 5.18.

Finally, for senior manager Conduct Rule 4 (disclose appropriately any information of which the FCA or PRA would reasonably expect notice) the PRA notes[112] that this Conduct Rule imposes a greater duty on senior managers than that which is set out in individual Conduct Rule 3 on the basis that they are expected to disclose any information an appropriate regulator would reasonably expect. This includes making a disclosure in the absence of any request or enquiry from the appropriate regulator. The PRA expects[113] that when disclosing something appropriately the senior manager will need to disclose:

- sufficient information for the regulators to be able to understand the full implications of the matter being disclosed;
- in a timely manner; and
- to an appropriate contact at the PRA or FCA (or both), which may include the firm's usual supervisory contact.

On notification of Conduct Rule breaches[114] SS28/15 provides that[115] the PRA does not expect firms to report every instance where there is some possibility that a breach has been committed if there are no reasonable grounds on which to believe that a breach has occurred. Where a firm has reported a suspected or actual breach of a Conduct Rule, it should notify the PRA of any different determination it subsequently makes.

4.10.6 *Final FCA rules and guidance*

As mentioned above in the discussion concerning the July 2015 FCA consultation the final FCA rules and guidance concerning the new conduct regime are located in COCON. In the following section we highlight some of COCON's key provisions although readers would be well advised to read it in its entirety.

---

[112] SS28/15, 5.21.
[113] SS28/15, 5.23.
[114] See fn.13.
[115] SS28/15, 5.29.

When the FCA was consulting on the scope of the Conduct Rules in July 2014 it opted to include a wide population of individuals on the basis that its statutory objectives, particularly in terms of protecting consumers and market integrity, could impact a much broader range of staff. COCON 1.1.2 provides that the Conduct Rules apply to senior managers, those individuals within the Certification Regime and those employees who are not the following:

- receptionists;
- switchboard operators;
- post room staff;
- reprographics / print room staff;
- property / facilities management;
- events management;
- security guards;
- invoice processing;
- audio visual technicians;
- vending machine staff;
- medical staff;
- archive records management;
- drivers;
- corporate social responsibility staff;
- data controllers and processors under the Data Protection Act;
- cleaners;
- catering staff;
- personal assistants or secretary;
- information technology support (i.e. helpdesk); and
- human resources administrators / processors.

COCON 1.1.9R to 1.1.12G deals with the territorial extent of the Conduct Rules. It provides that the Conduct Rules apply to the conduct of senior managers wherever such conduct is performed. It applies to individuals within the Certification Regime and other individuals within scope to the extent that such conduct is performed from an establishment that is maintained by the firm in the UK or involves dealing with a client in the UK from an establishment overseas.[116] The FCA

---

[116] At the time of writing this chapter the FCA had not confirmed the territorial

interprets the phrase "dealing with" as having contact with customers and extending beyond "dealing" as used in the phrase "dealing in investments". An individual will not be subject to COCON to the extent that it would be contrary to the UK's obligations under a Single Market Directive or the so-called "auction regulation".[117]

The final individual Conduct Rules and the senior manager Conduct Rules are set out in COCON 2.1 and 2.2 respectively. These have not changed since consultation (see above). The insurance related senior manager Conduct Rule 5 is dealt with in the Chapter in Insurance.

Provisions concerning training and breaches can be found in COCON 2.3 and 3.1. Perhaps one point to pick out is COCON 2.3.2(2) and (3) which provides that suitable training should "always" ensure that those subject to the Conduct Rules have an awareness and broad understanding of all of the rules in COCON, and that they also have a deeper understanding of the practical application of the specific rules which are relevant to their work. Two examples are given for those individuals who trade in the markets and for those who deal directly with customers.

4.10.6.1 Complying with the Conduct Rules—FCA expectations

COCON 3 sets out certain general factors for assessing compliance. In particular, when assessing compliance with, or breach of, a Conduct Rule the FCA will have regard to the context in which the conduct was undertaken including:

1.   the precise circumstances of the individual case;

---

position regarding NEDs following the October 2015 HM Treasury paper which proposed their inclusion within the scope of the Conduct Rules. However, the author suspects that the territorial extent for NEDs will be the same as for those who are not senior managers.

[117] The auction regulation is defined in the FCA Glossary as Commission Regulation (EU) No 1031/2010 of 12 November 2010 on the timing, administration and other aspects of auctioning of greenhouse gas emission allowances pursuant to Directive 2003/87/EC of the European Parliament and of the Council establishing a scheme for greenhouse gas emission allowances trading within the Community.

2.   the characteristics of the particular function performed by the individual in question;
3.   the behaviour expected of that function.[118]

For firms subject to the UK Corporate Governance Code, the FCA will give due credit if they follow corresponding provisions in the UK Corporate Governance Code when forming a view as to whether a senior manager has complied with COCON.

COCON 4.1 and 4.2 add a further layer to the Conduct Rules by setting out a non-exhaustive list of examples of conduct that would be in breach of each of these rules.

In relation to individual Conduct Rule 1 (act with integrity) COCON 4.1.1G sets out a non-exhaustive list of 19 examples of conduct that would breach the rule. Some of these examples are unsurprising, like falsifying documents and misleading a client about the risks of an investment. Others may, to some, be surprising (for example preparing inaccurate training records).

In relation to individual Conduct Rule 2 (acting with due skill, care and diligence) general examples are set out in COCON 4.1.2 to 4.1.3 with further examples for managers appearing in COCON 4.1.4 to 4.1.8. It is, perhaps, worth setting out in full COCON 4.1.4, 4.1.5 and 4.1.7:

COCON 4.1.4: It is important for a manager to understand the business for which they are responsible. A manager is unlikely to be an expert in all aspects of a complex financial business. However, they should understand and inform themselves about the business sufficiently to understand the risks of its trading, credit or other business activities.

COCON 4.1.5: It is important for a manager to understand the risks of expanding the business into new areas and, before approving the expansion, they should investigate and satisfy themselves, on reasonable grounds, about the risks, if any, to the business.

---

[118] COCON 3.1.2G.

COCON 4.1.7: Where a manager is not an expert in a business area, they should consider whether they (or those with whom they work) have the necessary expertise to provide an adequate explanation of issues within that business area. If not, they should seek an independent opinion from elsewhere, within or outside the firm.

In relation to individual Conduct Rule 3 (you must be open and cooperative with the FCA, the PRA and other regulators) the FCA guidance notes at COCON 4.1.10G that there is no duty on an individual to report information directly to a regulator unless they are one of the persons within the firm who have responsibility for reporting matters to the regulator. However, the guidance caveats this by adding that if a person takes steps to influence the decision not to report to the regulator or acts in a way that is intended to obstruct the reporting of information to the regulator then the regulator will view them as being one of those within the firm with responsibility for deciding whether to report matters to the regulator.

The non-exhaustive list of examples of conduct that would breach individual Conduct Rule 4 (pay due regard to the interests of customers and treat them fairly) are set out in COCON 4.1.13 to 4.1.14. Perhaps two important examples are:

- providing a customer with a product which is different to the one applied for by that customer, unless the customer understands the differences and understands the product they have purchased; and
- failing to provide terms and conditions to which a product or service is subject in a way which is clear and easy for the customer to understand.

In relation to individual Conduct Rule 5 (observe proper standards of market conduct) general consideration should be given as to whether the conduct complies with the Code of Market Conduct (COCON 4.1.15). Manipulating or attempting to manipulate a market or benchmark is also given as an example of failing to observe this rule (COCON 4.1.16).

4.10.6.2 Senior Manager Conduct Rules—FCA Guidance on compliance

Guidance on the senior manager Conduct Rules can be found in COCON 4.2.

In relation to senior manager Conduct Rule 1 (take reasonable steps to ensure that the business of the firm for which you are responsible is controlled effectively) the FCA sets out guidance in COCON 4.2.1 to 4.2.9 on the conduct it would expect to see.

The guidance provides[119] that a senior managers' role and responsibilities are set out in their Statement of Responsibilities. It further adds[120] that senior managers might find it helpful to review whether each area of the business for which they are responsible has been clearly assigned to a particular individual or individuals.

Reporting lines should also be clear to staff and where staff has dual reporting lines there is a greater need to ensure that the responsibility and accountability of each line manager is clearly set out and understood.[121] Where staff have particular levels of authorisation, these should be clearly set out and communicated.[122]

Senior managers are also expected to take "reasonable steps" to satisfy themselves on "reasonable grounds" that each area of the business for which they are responsible has "appropriate" policies and procedures for reviewing the competence, knowledge, skills and performance of each individual member of staff.[123]

A senior manager should also ensure that there is an orderly transition when another senior manager under their oversight and responsibility ceases to perform their function which is

---

[119] COCON 4.2.1G.
[120] COCON 4.2.3G.
[121] COCON 4.2.4G.
[122] COCON 4.2.5G.
[123] COCON 4.2.6G.

taken up by someone else.[124] The FCA guidance states that it would be "appropriate" for such individual vacating their position to prepare a "comprehensive set" of handover notes for their successor. Such notes, at a minimum, should specify any matter that is ongoing which the successor would reasonably be expected to be aware of in order to:

(i)   perform their function effectively;
(ii) ensure compliance with the requirements and standards of the regulatory systems; and
(iii) ensure that the individual with overall responsibility for that part of the business of the firm maintains effective control. Senior managers should also pay attention to any temporary vacancies that exist and take reasonable steps to ensure that suitable cover for responsibilities is arranged.[125]

A non-exhaustive list of examples of conduct that would breach this senior manager Conduct Rule is set out in COCON 4.2.10. Among the examples is failure to take reasonable steps to apportion responsibilities clearly among those to whom responsibilities have been delegated which includes establishing confusing or uncertain reporting lines, authorisation levels or job descriptions and responsibilities.[126]

The guidance on senior manager Conduct Rule 2 (take reasonable steps to ensure that the business of the firm for which you are responsible complies with the relevant requirements and standards of the regulatory system) follows the same format with FCA guidance on expected conduct[127] followed by a non-exhaustive list of examples of conduct that would breach the rule.

Senior managers are expected to take reasonable steps to ensure their firm's compliance with relevant regulatory requirements and ensure that all staff are aware for the need

[124] COCON 4.2.8G.
[125] COCON 4.2.9G.
[126] COCON 4.2.10(2)G.
[127] COCON 4.2.11G to 4.2.15G.

for compliance.[128] Whilst not being required to put in place themselves the systems of control for their business (unless it is within their role and responsibilities) senior managers are expected to take reasonable steps to ensure that their business has operating procedures and systems with well-defined steps for complying with the detail of the relevant regulatory requirements and for ensuring that the business is run prudently.[129] Where they become aware of actual or suspected problems involving possible breaches of regulatory require-ments within their area of responsibility, a senior manager should take steps to ensure that they are dealt with in a timely and appropriate manner.[130] Where an independent review recommends improvements to systems and procedures in a business area, the senior manager responsible for that business area should ensure that any reasonable recommendations are implemented in a timely manner unless there are good reasons not to.[131] What will be reasonable will depend on the nature of the issue being addressed and the cost of the improvement. It will be reasonable for a cost benefit analysis to be carried out when assessing whether the recommendations are reasonable.

Among the non-exhaustive list of examples of conduct that would breach this Conduct Rule[132] is failure to take reasonable steps to monitor (either personally or through a compliance department or other departments) compliance with relevant regulatory requirements[133] and failure to take reasonable steps to implement (either personally or through a compliance department) adequate and appropriate systems of control to comply with relevant regulatory requirements.[134] Specific examples of conduct breaches are given for a senior manager who is a proprietary trader[135] or money laundering reporting officer.[136] A further example is given where a senior manager is

---

[128] COCON 4.2.11G.
[129] COCON 4.2.12G.
[130] COCON 4.2.13G.
[131] COCON 4.2.14G.
[132] COCON 4.2.16G.
[133] COCON 4.2.16(2)G.
[134] COCON 4.2.16(1)G.
[135] COCON 4.2.16(6)G.
[136] COCON 4.2.16(7)G.

responsible for the compliance function.[137] A breach of senior manager Conduct Rule 2 will occur where such individual fails to ensure that:

- the compliance function has the necessary authority, resources, expertise and access to all relevant information; or
- a compliance officer is appointed and is responsible for the compliance function and for any reporting as to compliance; or
- the persons involved in the compliance functions are not involved in the performance of services or activities they monitor; or
- the method of determining the remuneration of persons involved in the compliance function does not compromise their objectivity; or
- the method of determining the remuneration complies, where applicable, with the FCA Remuneration Code.

The guidance on senior manager Conduct Rule 3 (take reasonable steps to ensure that any delegation of your responsibilities is to an appropriate person and that you oversee the discharge of the delegated responsibility effectively) is set out in COCON 4.2.17G to 4.2.22G. A non-exhaustive list of conduct that would be in breach of the rule is set out in COCON 4.2.23 and 4.2.24.

Among other things the guidance notes that a senior manager may delegate the investigation, resolution or management of an issue or authority for dealing with a part of the business to individuals who report to them or to others.[138] However, the senior manager should have reasonable grounds for believing that the delegate has the competence, knowledge, skill and time to deal with the issue.[139] The FCA recognises that a senior manager will have to exercise his/her own judgement in deciding how issues are dealt with and that sometimes that judgement will, with the benefit of hindsight, be wrong.

---

[137] COCON 4.2.16(8)G.
[138] COCON 4.2.17G.
[139] COCON 4.2.18G.

The senior manager will not be in breach of this Conduct Rule unless they failed to exercise due and reasonable consideration before they delegated the resolution of the issue or authority for dealing with the part of the business and failed to reach a reasonable conclusion.[140] The FCA also recognises that a senior manager will not always manage the business on a day-to-day basis themselves. However, the larger and more complex the business, the greater the need for clear and effective delegation and reporting lines, which may involve documenting the scope of that delegation and the reporting lines in writing.[141] Importantly, whilst a senior manager may delegate the resolution of an issue, or authority for dealing with a part of the business, they cannot delegate responsibility for it. It is the senior manager's responsibility to ensure that they receive reports on progress and question those reports where appropriate.[142]

In the list of non-exhaustive examples of conduct that would breach the rule is where a senior manager fails to take reasonable steps to maintain an appropriate level of understanding about an issue or part of the business that he/she has delegated to an individual (whether in-house or outside contractor). This includes the senior manager failing to require adequate reports once the issue or management has been delegated and accepting implausible or unsatisfactory explanations from delegates without testing their accuracy.[143]

When determining if the senior manager Conduct Rule has been complied with the factors that the FCA would expect to take into account include[144]:

- the competence, knowledge or seniority of the delegate; and
- the past performance and record of the delegate.

---

[140] COCON 4.2.19G.
[141] COCON 4.2.20G.
[142] COCON 4.2.22G.
[143] COCON 4.2.23G.
[144] COCON 4.2.24G.

The guidance on senior manager Conduct Rule 4 (disclose appropriately any information of which the FCA or PRA would reasonably expect notice) is set out in COCON 4.2.25G to 4.2.29G. Unlike the previous rules there is no non-exhaustive list of conduct that would be in breach of this rule.

The FCA guidance mentions[145] that there may be some overlap with individual Conduct Rule 3. However, the key difference between them is that individual Conduct Rule 3 normally relates to responses from individuals to requests from the regulator, whereas senior manager Conduct Rule 4 imposes a duty on a senior manager to disclose appropriately any information that the regulator would reasonably expect, including making a disclosure in the absence of any request or enquiry.

The FCA guidance also states[146] that for the purposes of this senior manager Conduct Rule, regulators in addition to the FCA and PRA are those that have recognised jurisdiction in relation to the activities to which COCON applies and have the power to call for information from an individual in connection with their function or the business for which they are responsible. This may include an exchange or an overseas regulator.

If a senior manager comes across information that is something in relation to which he/she thinks the FCA or PRA could reasonably expect notice, they should first determine whether that information falls within the scope of their responsibilities. If it does, then he/she should ensure that, if it is otherwise appropriate to do so, it is disclosed to the regulator. When determining whether conduct complies with this senior manager Conduct Rule the factors that the FCA will expect to take into account include[147]:

---

[145] COCON 4.2.26G.
[146] COCON 4.2.25G.
[147] COCON 4.2.29G.

- whether it would be reasonable for the individual to assume that the information would be of material significance to the regulator concerned;
- whether the information related to the individual themselves or to their firm; and
- whether any decision not to report the matter was taken after reasonable enquiry and analysis of the situation.

Annex 1

EBA Guidelines on the assessment of the suitability of members of the management body and key function holders

Title II- Requirements regarding the assessment of the suitability

Chapter I – Responsibilities & general assessment criteria

4. Responsibilities

4.1 Assessing the initial and ongoing suitability of members of the management body and key function holders should primarily be the responsibility of the credit institution.

4.2 If a nomination committee or equivalent exists, it should actively contribute to fulfilling the credit institution's responsibility for adopting appropriate internal policies on the assessment of the suitability of members of the management body and key function holders.

5. General assessment criteria

5.1 The assessment of the experience of members of the management body and key function holders should take into account the nature, scale and complexity of the business of the credit institution as well as the responsibilities of the position concerned. The level and nature of the experience required from a member of the management body in its management function may differ from that required from a member of the management body in its supervisory function.

5.2 Members of the management body and key function holders should in any event be of good repute, regardless of the nature, scale and complexity of the business of the credit institution.

5.3 Where there is a matter which casts doubt on the experience or good repute of a member of the management body and key function holders, an assessment of how this will or might impinge on that person's suitability should be undertaken. All matters relevant to and available for the assessment should be taken into account, regardless of where and when they occurred.

Chapter II – Assessment by credit institutions

6. Credit institutions' suitability assessment

6.1 Credit institutions should assess the suitability of members of the management body on the basis of the criteria set out in paragraphs 13 to 15 and in accordance with the EBA's Guidelines on Internal Governance at Chapter B.2 and record the assessment and the results. Whenever possible the assessment should be done before the member takes up his or her position. If this is not possible the assessment should be completed as soon as practicable, but in any event within six weeks.

6.2 Credit institutions should re-assess the suitability of a member of the management body when events make a re-assessment necessary in order to verify the person's ongoing suitability. This can be limited to examining whether the member remains suitable taking into account the relevant event.

6.3 When assessing the suitability of members of the management body, credit institutions should assess whether the management body is suitable collectively. Weaknesses within the overall composition of the management body or its committees should not necessarily lead to the conclusion that a particular member is not suitable.

6.4 The credit institution should assess the suitability of key function holders before they are appointed, re-assess their suitability as appropriate and record the assessments and their results.

7. Credit institutions' policies on suitability

7.1. Credit institutions should have a policy for selecting and assessing members of the management body which takes into account the nature, scale and complexity of the business of the credit institution and sets out at least:

    a.   the individual or function responsible for performing the suitability assessment;

    b.   the applicable internal procedure for the assessment of the suitability of a member;

    c.   the necessary competencies and skills of a member of the management body needed to assume that the member has sufficient expertise,

    d.   the information and evidence that a member of the management body should provide to the credit institution for an assessment;

    e.   if the member is to be appointed by the shareholders the measures taken to ensure that shareholders are informed about the requirements for the position and the relevant profile of persons before they are appointed; and

    f.   the situations where a re-assessment of the suitability should be performed, together with measures to identify such situations. These should include a requirement that members of the management body should notify any material change to the credit institution and may include annual notifications of any changes affecting their compliance with the relevant requirements.

    g.   ways in which the credit institution will provide training opportunities, in case there are specific learning and development needs of the members of its management body.

7.2. Credit institutions should have a policy in place for assessing the suitability of key function holders, which takes into account the nature scale and complexity of the business of the credit institution and sets out at least:

    a.   the positions for which a suitability assessment is required;

    b.   the individuals or function responsible for performing the suitability assessment; and

    c.   the criteria for reputation and experience to be assessed for the specific position.

7.3. Credit institutions' policies should consider the different experience needed for the specific management body positions, including positions necessary to comply with national laws on employee representatives.

8.   Credit institutions' corrective measures

8.1. If a credit institution's assessment concludes that a person is not suitable to be appointed as a member of the management body that person should not be appointed or if the member has already been appointed, the credit institution should take appropriate measures to replace this member unless the credit institution takes appropriate measures to ensure the suitability of the member in a timely manner. 8.2. If the credit institution's re-assessment concludes that a member of the management body is no longer suitable, the credit institution should take appropriate measures to rectify the situation and inform the competent authority accordingly.

8.2. When a credit institution takes measures it should consider the particular situation and shortcomings of the member; appropriate measures might include, but are not limited to, adjusting responsibilities between members of the management body; replacing certain persons; and training single members or the whole of the management body to ensure that the collective qualification and experience of the management body is sufficient.

8.3. If a credit institution's assessment concludes that a key function holder is not suitable, the credit institution should take appropriate measures.

Chapter III – Assessment by supervisors

9. Application or notification

9.1. Competent authorities should establish an application or notification procedure applicable to appointments and re-appointments of a member of the management body. Competent authorities should impose rules as to when such applications or notifications need to be made.

9.2. At the request of the competent authority credit institutions should provide all written information necessary to assess the suitability of the members of the management body, including the information contained in Annex I. For any re-appointment this information can be limited to relevant changes and additional information.

9.3. The member of the management body concerned should verify that the information provided is accurate. The credit institution should verify that the information provided is accurate to their knowledge.

9.4. Credit institutions should notify the competent authority when the appointment of a member of the management body is terminated, explaining the reasons.

10. Assessment process

10.1. Competent authorities should ensure that the process applicable to the assessment of the suitability of members of the management body is publicly available.

10.2. Competent Authorities may distinguish between the process applicable to members of the management body in its management function and in its supervisory function, as well as between the initial authorisation of a credit institution and subsequent assessments according to national specificities, the size and structure of the banking sector and national laws concerning the governance of companies.

11. Assessment technique

11.1. Competent authorities should evaluate the information provided by the credit institution, require further evidence of reputation or experience as appropriate and assess the suitability of members of the management body on the basis of the criteria set out in paragraphs 13 to 15 of these Guidelines.

11.2. When assessing the suitability of members of the management body after a credit institution's authorisation in the circumstances described in paragraphs 3(4b) and 3(4c) above, competent authorities may use a selection of these criteria and accord them different weight, taking into consideration relevant national law as well as the result of the review of the specific policies and procedures established by the credit institution for the assessment of these persons' suitability. In the case of paragraph 3 (4c) the re-assessment of suitability should in particular be related to the circumstances that prompted the re-assessment.

11.3. In accordance with national law, competent authorities may, on a risk based approach, interview persons when assessing the suitability of members of the management body. Where appropriate, the interview process may also serve to re-assess the suitability of a member of the management body when facts or circumstances raise doubts about the suitability of this member. The interview process may be used to assess a proposed candidate's knowledge, experience and application of skills in previous occupations, as well as how the qualities of the proposed candidate relate to the skills and experience of the existing members of the management body. The skills assessed may include decisiveness, strategic vision, judgment on risks, leadership, independence of mind, persuasive power, and the ability and willingness to engage in continuous learning and development.

11.4. The assessment under paragraph 3 (4b) by the competent authority should be completed as soon as practicable; the competent authority should set a maximum time period for its assessment which should not exceed than six months. The period for assessment should start on receipt of the complete application or notification.

11.5. Where a competent authority has previously assessed a member's suitability, the relevant record should be updated as appropriate.

11.6. A competent authority may take into account suitability assessments from other competent authorities. For this purpose competent authorities should exchange relevant information on the suitability of persons when requested.

11.7. The competent authority should inform the credit institution of the results of the assessment.

11.8. Competent authorities may assess the suitability of key function holders and should ensure that the applicable process is publicly available.

12. Supervisory corrective measures

12.1. Where a member or credit institution fails to provide sufficient information regarding the suitability of a member to the competent authority, the competent authority should object to or not approve the appointment of that person.

12.2. If a member of the management body is not considered to be suitable, the competent authority should require the credit institution either to not appoint the member or if the member is already appointed to take appropriate measures to replace him or her.

12.3. In cases where a credit institution's measures taken according to paragraph 8 are inadequate, competent authorities should themselves adopt appropriate corrective measures.

Chapter IV – Assessment criteria

13. Reputation criteria

13.1. A member of the management body should be considered to be of good repute if there is no evidence to suggest otherwise and no reason to have reasonable doubt about his or her good repute. All relevant information available for the assessment should be taken into account, without prejudice to any limitations imposed by national law and regardless of the state where any relevant events occurred.

13.2. A member of the management body should not be considered to be of good repute if his or her personal or business conduct gives rise to any material doubt about his or her ability to ensure the sound and prudent management of the credit institution.

13.3. Any criminal or relevant administrative records should be taken into account, considering the type of conviction or indictment, the level of appeal, the punishment received, the phase of the judicial process reached and the effect of any rehabilitation measures. The surrounding, including mitigating, circumstances and the seriousness of any relevant offence or administrative or supervisory action, the time period and the member's conduct since the offence and the relevance of the offence or administrative or supervisory action to the proposed role should be considered.

13.4. The cumulative effects of more minor incidents, which individually do not impinge on a member's reputation but may in sum have a material impact, should be considered.

13.5. Particular account should be taken of the following factors, which may cast doubt on a member's good repute:

    a.   conviction or prosecution of a criminal offence, in particular:

        i.   offences under the laws governing banking, financial, securities, insurance activity, or concerning securities markets or securities or payment instruments, including laws on money laundering, market manipulation, or insider dealing and usury;

        ii.   offences of dishonesty, fraud, or financial crime;

        iii.   tax offences;

        iv.   other offences under legislation relating to companies, bankruptcy, insolvency, or consumer protection;

    b.   relevant current or past investigations and/or enforcement actions relating to the member, or the imposition of administrative sanctions for non-compliance with provisions governing banking, financial, securities, or insurance activities or those concerning securities markets, securities or payment instruments, or any financial services legislation;

    c.   relevant current or past investigations and/or enforcement actions by any other regulatory or professional bodies for non-compliance with any relevant provisions.

13.6. Attention should be paid to the following factors regarding the propriety of the member in past business dealings:

    a.   any evidence that the member has not been transparent, open, and cooperative in its dealings with supervisory or regulatory authorities;

    b.   refusal of any registration, authorisation, membership, or license to carry out a trade, business, or profession; or revocation, withdrawal, or termination of such registration, authorisation, membership, or license; or expulsion by a regulatory or government body;

c. the reasons for any dismissal from employment or any position of trust, fiduciary relationship, or similar situation, or having been asked to resign from employment in such a position; and

d. disqualification by competent authority from acting as a person who directs the business.

13.7. The following situations regarding past and present business performance and financial soundness of a member with regard to their potential impact on the member's reputation should be considered:

a. inclusion on the list of unreliable debtors or any negative records on this kind of list conducted by recognised credit bureau if available;

b. financial and business performance of the entities owned or directed by the member or in which the member had or has significant share with special consideration to any rehabilitation, bankruptcy and winding-up proceedings and whether and how the member has contributed to the situation that lead to the proceedings;

c. declaration of personal bankruptcy; and

d. civil lawsuits, administrative or criminal proceedings, large investments or exposures and loans taken out, in so far they can have a significant impact on the financial soundness.

14. Experience criteria

14.1. The assessment of a member's experience should consider both, the theoretical experience attained through education and training and the practical experience gained in previous occupations. Credit institutions should take into account the skills and knowledge acquired and demonstrated by the professional conduct of the member.

14.2. With regard to assessment of a member's theoretical experience, particular consideration should be given to the level and profile of the education and whether

it relates to banking and financial services or other
relevant areas. Education in the areas of banking and
finance, economics, law, administration, financial
regulation and quantitative methods can in general be
considered to be related to banking and financial
services.

14.3. The assessment should not be limited to the educational degree or proof of a certain period of service in
a credit institution or other firm. A more thorough
analysis of the members" practical experience should
be conducted as the knowledge gained from previous
occupations depends on the nature, scale and complexity of the business as well as the function
performed within it.

14.4. When assessing the experience of a member of the
management body particular consideration should be
given to theoretical and practical experience relating
to:

a. financial markets;

b. regulatory framework and requirements;

c. strategic planning, and understanding of a credit
institution's business strategy or business plan
and accomplishment thereof;

d. risk management (identifying, assessing, monitoring, controlling and mitigating the main types
of risk of a credit institution, including the
responsibilities of the member);

e. assessing the effectiveness of a credit institution's
arrangements, creating effective governance,
oversight and controls; and

f. interpreting a credit institution's financial information, identifying key issues based on this
information and appropriate controls and
measures.

14.5. A member of the management body in its management function should have gained sufficient practical
and professional experience from a managerial position over a sufficiently long period. Short term or
temporary positions can be considered in the assessment, but are usually not sufficient to assume

sufficient experience. The practical and professional experience gained from previous positions should be assessed, with particular regard to:

a.   length of service;

b.   nature and complexity of the business where the position was held, including its organisational structure;

c.   scope of competencies, decision making powers, and responsibilities;

d.   technical knowledge gained through the position about the business of a credit institution and understanding of risks credit institutions face

e.   number of subordinates.

14.6.   A member of the management body in its supervisory function should have sufficient experience to enable him or her to provide constructive challenge to the decisions and effective oversight of the management function. The experience may be gained from academic, administrative or other positions and through the management, supervision or control of financial institutions or other firms. Members of the management body in its supervisory function should be able to demonstrate that they have, or will be able to acquire, the technical knowledge necessary to enable them to understand the business of the credit institution and the risks that it faces sufficiently well.

15.   Governance criteria

15.1.   When assessing the suitability of a member also other criteria relevant for the functioning of the management body should be assessed, including potential conflicts of interest, the ability to commit sufficient time, the overall composition of the management body, the collective knowledge and expertise required and members' ability to perform their duties independently without undue influence from other persons.

15.2.   In assessing a member's independence, the following factors should be considered:

a. past and present positions held in the credit institution or other firms;
b. personal, professional or other economic relationships with the members of the management body in their management function, in the same credit institution, in its parent company or subsidiaries; and
c. personal, professional or other economic relationships with the controlling shareholders of the same credit institutions, with its parent institution or subsidiaries.

15.3. The management body in its management function needs collectively to have sufficient practical experience in credit institutions.

Chapter 5

Non-executive directors

Peter Snowdon
Partner
Norton Rose Fulbright

Simon Lovegrove
Head of Financial Services Knowledge—Global
Norton Rose Fulbright

5.1 Introduction

Non-executive directors or "NEDs" have an extremely important and unique role in being able to influence their firm's behaviour. In this chapter we consider the individual accountability regime and its impact on these key individuals. But before doing so we remind ourselves of how the previous regulator, the FSA, approached the regulation of NEDs.

5.2 Approved Persons

Prior to the Senior Managers' regime s.59 of the Financial Services and Markets Act 2000 provided that all regulated firms were required to take reasonable care to ensure that candidates who performed one or more "controlled functions" for, or on their behalf, did not perform these functions unless they had prior approval from the FSA and then, after legal cutover on 1 April 2013, the FCA or the PRA (with the consent of the FCA for dual regulated firms). Once approval was given, the individual concerned would be known as an "Approved Person" and become personally accountable to the regulator in question. In particular an Approved Person was required to comply with the Statements of Principle and Code of Practice for Approved Persons. Each of the FCA and the PRA could discipline an Approved Person of a PRA-authorised firm (e.g. a bank, systemically important investment firm or insurance firm) who had breached a Statement of Principle that it had issued regardless of whether it was responsible for approving them.[1]

The "non-executive director function" was listed by the FSA and then, after legal cutover, the PRA and FCA as a controlled function. It was classified under the list of controlled functions known as "significant influence functions". NEDs were classified as an Approved Person with direct exposure to the regulators.

List of controlled functions

Significant influence functions	CF1 Director function
	CF2 Non-executive director function
	CF3 Chief executive function
	CF4 Partner function
	CF5 Directors of an unincorporated association
	CF6 Small friendly society function
	CF8 Apportionment and oversight functions (Non-MiFID business only)
	CF10 Compliance oversight function
	CF10A CASS Oversight Operation function
	CF11 Money laundering reporting function
	CF12 Actuarial function
	CF12A With-profits actuary function
	CF12B Lloyd's Actuary function
	CF28 System and controls function
	CF29 Significant management function
Customer functions	CF30 Customer function

---

[1] However, only the FCA could take action against individuals approved to perform a customer function.

| LIBOR | CF40 Benchmark submission function |
| functions | CF50 Benchmark administration function |

5.3 FSA NEDs conference

Before reviewing the individual accountability regime as it applies to NEDs it is worth taking a moment to look at some of the key messages that arose from the FSA's NED conference which took place on 6 December 2011. The conference was the FSA's first conference for NEDs and focused specifically on retail conduct issues. From this conference the FSA published speeches given by Clive Adamson (then Director of Supervision, FSA) and Nausicaa Delfas (then Head of Department, Conduct Supervision, FSA). A Guidance Consultation on the regulator's expectations of NEDs was published the day after the conference.[2]

The following section picks out some of the key messages that can be found in the speeches and the Guidance Consultation. Whilst these materials are fairly old they still provide useful insights into the regulators' views and expectations.

5.3.1 *Clive Adamson's speech*

Key points in Clive Adamson's speech[3] included:

- NEDs have an extremely important and unique role in being able to influence firm behaviour;
- the FSA did not expect a NED as one individual on a board to have all the skills and knowledge that the board needs as a whole;
- the FSA would see the board as collectively responsible for delivering the fair treatment of customers and NEDs play a pivotal role in ensuring that this happens;

---

[2] FSA Guidance Consultation—Non Executive Directors Conference: Delivering fair treatment for consumers of financial services (December 2011).
[3] FSA NED Conference: Delivering Fair Treatment for Consumers of Financial Services—speech by Clive Adamson on 6 December 2011.

- boards are expected to ensure that the business model of
the firm results in the fair treatment of customers. That is
not to say that customer strategies are not being considered but that it is more from a marketing and profitability
perspective as opposed to a fairness perspective; and
- deficiencies in firm culture is a potential root cause of poor
outcomes for retail consumers. The FSA would be paying
close attention to the culture of firms and how the board
has oversight and challenges management on how a good
culture is being embedded throughout the firm.

5.3.2 *Nausicaa Delfas' speech*

Key points in the Nausicaa Delfas speech[4] included:

- NEDs should have a good understanding of their firm, its
strategy, its customers and the types of products that it
sells;
- the FSA's expectation would be that NEDs have the right
understanding and experience of the business to allow
them to scrutinise effectively the performance of management and to deliver informed challenge. The criticism that
arose following the financial crisis was that boards did not
sufficiently understand their firms' business models,
strategies or products – and the risks they were running –
and that boards did not sufficiently challenge their
executive. As Nausicaa Delfas said,

> "as NEDs, you might not possess as in-depth know-
> ledge as the executive management, but you should
> have sufficient knowledge to participate actively in
> the decision-making process of the board and to
> exercise appropriate oversight over the agreed
> strategy";

- the FSA would not expect a NED to have detailed
knowledge of their firm's entire product range but there
would be an expectation that they understand the basic

---

[4] FSA NED Conference: Delivering Fair Treatment for Consumers of Financial
Services—speech by Nausicaa Delfas on 6 December 2011.

concepts and what their firm delivers to customers. The argument here was that if NEDs, as senior industry professionals, could not understand what their firm delivered then it would be difficult to see how customers could be expected to do so;

- NEDs have a part to play in identifying potential risks to customers, not just those to shareholders. One of the key roles for NEDs was using their experience and expertise to identify, highlight and challenge developments that could pose a risk to their firm's strategy, profitability or reputation. The role extends to identifying, highlighting and challenging developments that could pose risks to their firm's customers. Whilst firms' senior management might identify the importance of getting it right on the front line and having good sight of everyday activities such as sales and complaints the FSA would also expect senior management to consider and identify emerging risks to customers, such as those which might result from changes in business strategy, or internally from risks arising from its own incentive schemes. As Nausicaa Delfas put it in her speech:

> "NEDs need to have the experience and aptitude to be alert to these sorts of emerging risks, and they also need to have the right information to hand";

- NEDs need to be comfortable with the information that the board receives and that such information is considered to be appropriate to support decision making. If NEDs do not feel comfortable with the information they are receiving then they would be expected to challenge the executive and the board on it;
- NEDs should provide robust and insightful challenge to executive management on all aspects of the business including on culture. Key cultural drivers that NEDs would be expected to consider and challenge were leadership, strategy and decision-making, reward, controls and recruitment, training and competence; and
- certain examples were given in the speech as to where NEDs had taken active steps to understand more of their

firms' business – for example, a NED putting himself on the marketing mailing list to ensure that (s)he received product updates and literature that a potential customer receives, taking floor walks and/or speaking to staff.

At the end of her speech Nausicaa Delfas discussed how the FSA assessed culture, governance and controls. Firms were told that they could expect the FSA to focus on actual events within the firm and how these had been managed in practice. A non-exhaustive list of topics included the following:

- in relation to the effectiveness of the board, is there sufficient evidence that the board / management committee structures and compositions, plans and policies are effective in identifying the firm's retail conduct risk? Does the board and management's leadership and decision-making support the delivery of fair outcomes?
- in terms of organisational structure, is it unduly complex and is it clear as to who is responsible for different areas? Do executives have responsibility for several functions? For example, risk and finance. Is there a clear conflicts of interest policy? Are arrangements in place to manage potential conflicts of interest?
- in relation to setting strategy, the FSA will want to know if the firm has an effective process for setting, implementing and monitoring their key performance indicators to ensure robust management of any associated retail conduct risks. If a firm is seeking to grow its business and cut costs, the FSA would want to know how the firm will ensure that consumer outcomes are not impacted;
- in relation to strategy, the FSA would expect boards to have debated what constituted risks to customers—"conduct risk"—for their firm, and to have expressed a risk tolerance for this. The FSA would expect risk tolerance to be expressed in ways which were measurable and which drive the management information provided to the board about conduct risk;
- in relation to management information, does the information enable the board to make proactive and timely decisions?

- when it comes to human resources issues, performance, pay, recruitment and training and competencies, what oversight is there? Where they give rise to risks to consumers, are these adequately controlled?

5.3.3   *Guidance consultation*

The Guidance Consultation that followed the FSA's NEDs conference[5] was not finalised but provides a useful steer on the expectations of NEDs in delivering the appropriate management of retail conduct risk within a regulated firm. By retail conduct risk, the regulator meant the risk of a firm treating its retail customers unfairly and delivering inappropriate outcomes. The table below sets out the FSA's expectations where NEDs would be expected to provide challenge.

Business proposals are aligned with the firm's strategy and are within its stated retail conduct risk appetite. A NED should:
- challenge whether the firm has an expressed risk tolerance / appetite statement for retail conduct risk;
- be comfortable with how the board decides on its target customer base and how to segment it;
- encourage the board to discuss customer expectations and how the firm delivers against them; and
- challenge the board to consider the products and services it delivers to customers and whether they are appropriate for the target market; and be comfortable with the board's involvement in new product development.

---

[5]   Guidance Consultation—Non Executive Directors Conference: Delivering Fair Treatment for Consumers of Financial Services (December 2011).

The firm's culture is such that it delivers good behaviours and outcomes, both prudentially and for customers. A NED should:
- encourage the board to embed and maintain a culture that supports an appropriate degree of protection for customers, taking into account factors such as the firm's business plan, risk appetite, remuneration mechanisms and identified internal and external risks;
- identify what prompts this particular discussion – e.g. change of management, change of strategy and crystallised risk;
- challenge the board to provide continuing oversight of the firm's culture particularly in times of change; and
- challenge the board to lead the executive on culture and values; and with the board, monitor against the values that it has set.

NEDs have the right information to enable them to make robust decisions and if they feel they do not, then they should ask for it. A NED should:
- challenge the information the board receives on retail conduct risk;
- ensure the information is sufficient to support decision making;
- encourage the board to challenge the information it receives; and
- challenge the board on how the information is used.

The firm has identified risks to customers. A NED should:
- challenge the board to consider proactively the retail conduct risks the firm might be giving rise to;
- be confident in how the board identifies, mitigates and monitors its retail conduct risk; and
- be comfortable with the level of priority the firm gives to retail conduct risk.

Appropriate actions are in place to mitigate and monitor such risks. A NED should:
- be comfortable that management information captures the key retail conduct risks within the firm;
- challenge that actions are put in place, where possible, to prevent the crystallisation of risk; and
- be confident there is clear accountability for mitigating identified risks.

The board supports the identification and escalation of issues when they go wrong and ensures appropriate resolution. A NED should:

- encourage the board to create an open and collaborative working environment;
- challenge the board to focus on seeking solutions rather than attributing blame;
- be comfortable that the board ensures resolution is fair to all affected customers, i.e. not just those who have complained; and
- challenge the board to monitor whether the recommended actions have led to the appropriate outcomes for customers.

The business learns from identified issues and draws out the wider implications. A NED should:

- challenge the board to identify the root causes to help prevent them happening in the future; and
- where things go wrong, challenge the board not to solely focus on the area where the issue originated, but give consideration to whether it may be apparent in other areas of the business.

5.3.4   Hector Sants' speech

Other notable FSA comments on corporate governance and NEDs following the above conference can be found in Hector Sants' (then CEO of the FSA) speech of 24 April 2012, "Delivering effective corporate governance: the financial regulators role". Importantly, the speech discussed the concept of "challenge" which is not often straightforward to execute. In Sants' view the word "challenge" was not a good word and that what was needed from NEDs was a sufficient understanding of the issues and the confidence to speak up so that the debate could be enhanced. In other words, challenge was about thoughtful debate and not confrontation.

5.4   The individual accountability regime and NEDs

Turning now to the individual accountability regime and NEDs, starting with the statutory basis.

Section 59ZA of the Financial Services and Markets Act 2000 (as amended by the Financial Services (Banking Reform) Act 2013) (FSMA) provides that:

1. This section has effect for determining whether a function is for the purposes of section 59(6) or (6A) a senior management function.
2. A function is a "senior management function" in relation to the carrying on of a regulated activity by an authorised person, if –
    a) the function will require the person performing it to be responsible for managing one or more aspects of the authorised person's affairs, so far as relating to the activity; and
    b) those aspects involve, or might involve, a risk of serious consequences – (i) for the authorised person; or (ii) for business or other interests in the United Kingdom
3. In subsection (2)(a) the reference to managing one or more aspects of an authorised person's affairs includes a reference to taking decisions, or participating in the taking of decisions, about how one or more aspects of those affairs should be carried on.

Section 59ZA of FSMA therefore gives the PRA and FCA the power to include within the scope of the Senior Managers' regime (SMR) every member of an in-scope firm's board. In particular, the reference to "participating in the taking of decisions" is interpreted to include those members of the board who participate in collective decision-making, such as NEDs. However, both regulators are given some flexibility by s.59 of FSMA in the sense that they can designate senior management functions. This effectively gives them the ability to carve out certain members of the board from the SMR.

5.5 Revised PRA proposals

When the PRA/FCA first consulted on the individual account-ability regime in July 2014 the PRA proposed to require pre-approval only in relation to a limited number of NEDs with specific responsibilities as senior managers: the chairman, the senior independent director and the chairs of the audit, remuneration and risk committees. The PRA's reasoning for including these categories of NEDs were that their role would involve, or might involve a risk of serious consequences for a firm's safety and soundness. However, the FCA went much further proposing that all members of an in-scope firm's board should be included in its SMR and that all NEDs not otherwise approved as senior managers by the PRA would require FCA pre-approval. This included the chair of the nomination committee and NEDs without specific responsibilities (referred to in the FCA consultation as "Standard NEDs").

The feedback that the regulators received to the consultation led the PRA and FCA to issue a further joint consultation paper setting out a revised approach to NEDs.[6] The revised approach proposed to make the following NEDs subject to pre-approval and inclusion in the SMR:

- Chairman;
- Chair of risk committee;
- Chair of audit committee;
- Chair of remuneration committee;
- Chair of the nomination committee; and
- Senior independent director.

As can be seen from the above the PRA did not propose to change the categories of NED that would fall within the scope of its SMR but it added a further requirement that in-scope firms would have to ensure that all its board members, regardless of whether they were senior managers, "observe" its conduct rules. In-scope firms would also be required to apply

---

[6] Consultation Paper FCA CP15/5 PRA CP7/15: Approach to non-executive directors in banking and Solvency II firms & Application of the presumption of responsibility to senior managers in banking firms.

the same fitness and propriety standards on all NEDs, irrespective of whether or not they fell within the scope of the SMR. Also, in-scope firms would have to comply with certain notification requirements relating to the appointment of those NEDs who were not within the scope of the SMR (see below). The PRA also issued a draft Supervisory Statement which set out the nature of the responsibilities and accountability of those NEDs that would fall within its SMR and the PRA's proposed approach to the application of the presumption of responsibility to senior managers in in-scope firms.[7]

5.6 Revised FCA proposals

Unlike the PRA, the FCA significantly revised its proposals in the consultation paper. It considerably restricted its SMR by proposing to specify only the chair of the nomination committee in addition to the specified PRA non-executive senior manager functions. Noticeably Standard NEDs were not included within its SMR. The FCA stated in the consultation paper[8] that the primary role of all NEDs was independent oversight and challenge of the executive. It also stated that it recognised that within the duties of the non-executive there were a range of roles and responsibilities. The chairman, senior independent director and committee chairman all had a defined mandate and that it was important that these individuals were captured within the SMR. The FCA also proposed guidance which would be separate from the PRA Supervisory Statement and be read alongside it.

---

[7] The presumption of responsibility was subsequently superseded by the statutory duty of responsibility—see Ch.1 and Ch.10.

[8] Paragraph 2.11, Consultation Paper FCA CP15/5 PRA CP7/15: Approach to non-executive directors in banking and Solvency II firms & Application of the presumption of responsibility to senior managers in banking firms.

5.7   Statements of Responsibility

In the consultation paper the FCA stated that its expectation was that Statements of Responsibilities for NEDs within the SMR would generally be less extensive than those of executive senior managers. However, it added that the Statement of Responsibilities would not be limited to the responsibilities and key business functions specified by the regulators and that it was open to in-scope firms to highlight any additional responsibilities that were specific to NEDs that may have been introduced on the firm's own initiative. The FCA gave the example of succession planning.

5.8   Impact on Standard NEDs

As mentioned above the combined effect of the PRA's/FCA's proposals was that Standard NEDs would not be included in the PRA and FCA SMR for banks, designated investment firms and Solvency II firms. Consequently, Standard NEDs would not be subject to:

- prior approval by the PRA or FCA;
- the requirement to provide a Statement of Responsibilities (although the FCA would still expect details of all members of the board to be included in in-scope firms' responsibilities maps as part of its management and governance arrangements and that, as noted above, it was open to the firm to include any additional responsibilities specific to NEDs);
- the certification regime;
- any of the conduct rules[9];
- the presumption of responsibility[10]; and
- the criminal offence in s.36 of the Financial Services (Banking Reform) Act 2013.

---

[9]   However, see the discussion at para.5.17 regarding the Bank of England and Financial Services Bill.

[10]   Although this was subsequently removed from the individual accountability regime by the Government.

At first glance it might perhaps have been surprising that Standard NEDs were, generally, left outside the certification regime and conduct rules. However, a discussion in the consultation paper[11] shed some light on the reasons for this.

For an individual to come within the certification regime they would have to be an employee of the firm and meet the definition contained in s.63E(9) of FSMA.[12] The PRA and FCA would consider that NEDs would "not generally" be an employee although the statement was made in the consultation paper that it was "possible that they may do in certain circumstances—for example if a NED were to have a contract of employment." However, the FCA felt that it would be unacceptable to seek to apply this analysis on a case-by-case basis as this would give rise to uncertainty and inconsistency and therefore stated that it would not require NEDs to be a part of its certification regime. Similar reasoning was given regarding the non-application of the conduct regime.

The PRA proposed a different approach as to how the conduct rules would be applied to Standard NEDs. Whilst they would not be directly bound by them they would nevertheless be required to "observe" Individual Conduct Rules 1 to 3 and Senior Management Conduct Rule 4.[13] The PRA referred to Ch.3 of its Approach Document to Banking Supervision which provides that "independent directors should stand ready to have an open exchange of views with the PRA on the

---

[11] Paragraphs 2.21 and 2.22 Consultation Paper FCA CP15/5 PRA CP7/15: Approach to non-executive directors in banking and Solvency II firms & Application of the presumption of responsibility to senior managers in banking firms.

[12] Section 63E(9) FSMA: In this section any reference to an employee of a person ("A") includes a reference to a person who – (a) personally provides, or is under an obligation personally to provide, services to A under an arrangement made between A and the person providing the services or another person, and (b) is subject to (or to the right of) supervision, direction or control by A as to the manner in which those services are provided.

[13] Rule 1: You must act with integrity. Rule 2: You must act with due skill, care and diligence. Rule 3: You must be open and cooperative with the FCA, the PRA and other regulators. SMCR4: You must disclose appropriately any information of which the FCA or PRA would reasonably.

performance of senior management.[14]" It added that consequently "a requirement to proactively share relevant issues
with the regulator(s) is a pivotal and pervasive responsibility
of all NEDs, irrespective of whether they are senior managers
or not.[15]"

However, it is worth noting that whilst the proposals reduced
Standard NEDs' exposure to the individual accountability
regime they could still come within the regulatory perimeter
via other means. For instance both the PRA and FCA still have
the ability to prohibit Standard NEDs by virtue of s.56 of FSMA
(prohibition orders). Also both regulators have the ability to
take action against firms and their senior managers for
governance failings.

5.9 Origins of the notification regime for Standard NEDs

In relation to notification requirements the Capital Requirements Directive IV (CRD IV) requires member states to ensure
that board members of firms subject to the Directive will "at all
times be of sufficiently good repute and possess sufficient
knowledge, skills and experience to perform their duties".[16]
The European Banking Authority (EBA) Guidelines on the
assessment of the suitability of members of the management
body and key function-holders appointment (the EBA Guidelines) provides that this includes ensuring that the appointment of all board members is subject to a regulatory approval
or notification process. These EBA Guidelines further recognise
that as members of the management body have specific roles,
the assessment process and criteria can differ.

---

[14] Paragraph 81 PRA Approach to Banking Supervision (June 2014). The Approach
document was subsequently updated in March 2016 and the quoted text can be
found in para.84.
[15] Paragraph 4.9 Consultation Paper FCA CP15/5 PRA CP7/15: Approach to
non-executive directors in banking and Solvency II firms & Application of the
presumption of responsibility to senior managers in banking firms.
[16] Article 91 CRD IV.

The consultation paper mentioned that the PRA considered that a notification process identical or similar to the one proposed for Solvency II firms as set out in PRA consultation paper 26/14[17] could be used for Standard NEDs in firms that were subject to the CRD IV and/or MiFID. The notification requirements would not apply to Standard NEDs of credit unions as the EU obligations did not apply to them.

Notification was further covered in a subsequent policy statement and consultation paper from the PRA and FCA respectively (see below). Also a general discussion of the notification requirements for Solvency II firms can be found in Ch.11.

5.10   Final senior management functions for NEDs

In July 2015, the FCA published Consultation Paper 15/22: Strengthening accountability in banking: Final rules (including feedback on CP14/31 and CP15) and consultation on extending the Certification Regime to wholesale market activities (CP15/22). At the same time the PRA published Policy Statement 16/15: Strengthening individual accountability in banking: responses to CP14/14, CP28/14 and CP7/15 (PS16/15). Both papers contain final rules regarding the treatment of NEDs although as mentioned later in this chapter the Government was to change its position on the application of conduct rules to NEDs.

Both papers did not change the range of senior management functions that would apply to NEDs. These remained as per the previous consultation as being:

---

[17] PRA Consultation Paper 26/14: Senior insurance managers regime: a new regulatory approach for individuals.

PRA non-executive senior management functions	FCA non-executive senior management functions
Chairman (SMF 9)	Chair of the Nomination Committee (SMF 13)
Chairman of the Audit Committee (SMF 10)	
Chairman of the Risk Committee (SMF 11)	
Chairman of the Remuneration Committee (SMF 12)	
Senior Independent Director (SMF 14)	

5.11   PRA feedback—Notified NEDs

In PS16/15 the PRA discussed further the position of Standard NEDs which were now referred to as "Notified NEDs".

The PRA noted that feedback to its previous consultation supported the decision to leave NEDs without specific responsibilities outside the scope of the SMR but that it could possibly lead to the emergence of "two-tier boards" comprising those directors who were within the scope of the SMR and those who were Notified NEDs. The PRA stated that all directors, irrespective of whether they were within the scope of the SMR or not still remained accountable under the Companies Act and, in listed firms, subject to the principles in the Financial Reporting Council Code on a comply-or-explain basis. Also the PRA stated that it considered it vital that boards "as a whole" understood the Threshold Conditions, the Fundamental Rules and more detailed rules in the PRA Rulebook, and establish within their firm a culture that supported adherence to "the spirit and letter of the requirements".

In relation to the assessment and notification regime for Notified NEDs the PRA commented that respondents generally welcomed the regime and provided further information concerning the timing and process for the notification. The PRA stated that it did not require advance notification of planned appointments but would instead have to be notified when the appointment was confirmed—for example when the letter of appointment was issued and accepted. In addition, an updated management responsibilities map would also have to be submitted as the PRA saw the appointment of new NEDs as something that would alter the composition of the management body. The PRA also reminded firms that they could have discussions with it in advance of recruiting new board members.

The PRA confirmed that firms would need to have regard to the same high-level criteria in assessing the fitness and propriety of a Notified NED as they would when assessing a senior manager or employee performing a certification function. The expectations of an individual would depend on the nature of their role, the PRA cited the example of the chair of the Audit Committee being expected to have additional knowledge about audit matters which a Notified NED may not require.

The PRA also updated the requirement proposed in its earlier consultation that a firm must require all members of its management body—including Notified NEDs—to observe Individual Conduct Rules 1–3 and Senior Management Conduct Rule 4. This would be a contractual requirement allowing the firm to enforce these standards. The PRA observed that a firm could, for instance, write a requirement into its Staff Handbook or Code or otherwise make it a condition of employment or appointment. The PRA felt that this requirement would not be too onerous for firms on the basis that contracts usually expressly allowed for any amendments necessary to meet regulatory requirements. Also, the standards being imposed were felt to be ones which members of the management body were very familiar with.

Whilst the PRA could not apply the conduct rules to Notified NEDs in the same way as to those individuals performing a senior management function or certification function the PRA would expect firms to consider compliance as part of their assessment of whether such individuals continued to meet the "fit and proper" standard.

For NEDs who were approved under the Approved Persons regime as a CF2 (non-executive director function) immediately before the commencement of the SMR the PRA stated that they would not need to go through the full assessment and notification procedure. Instead, the firm would need to notify the PRA which of their existing CF2s would be a Notified NED once the new regime came into effect.

The PRA also addressed the position where a NED who was within the SMR changed their role and in effect became a Notified NED. The PRA stated that in such circumstances the firm would not be required to submit information on the person's fitness and propriety again as it would have already been assessed. The PRA would, however, need to be notified that the person's role had changed and that he or she had ceased to perform a relevant senior management function.

The PRA noted that the Fair and Effective Markets Review issued certain recommendations about the form and content of regulatory references to be issued by a current or former employer when a new firm was considering appointing a person to a senior manager or certified role. PS16/15 did not contain further substantive rules on this other than to extend the basic requirement to require a reference from former employers to also cover former NED roles.

One concern that respondents raised was what action the PRA would take if it were not satisfied that a Notified NED was fit and proper. The PRA's response was that generally where it had concerns about the membership of the firm's board it would raise those concerns with the firm's chairman. The PRA also had a range of other options from seeking additional information through to the use of the prohibition power set out in s.56 of FSMA.

5.12 The PRA Supervisory Statement

The PRA's rules on the new accountability regime will be contained in its Rulebook.

Certain provisions in the PRA Rulebook are supplemented by Supervisory Statements which are essentially statements of guidance for firms that are authorised by the PRA. Therefore, when reading a provision in the PRA Rulebook the relevant Supervisory Statement should be read in conjunction with it. The position of Supervisory Statements was further described in the PRA's Approach to Banking Supervision[18] where it stated:

> "The PRA does not plan to issue significant amounts of detailed guidance to clarify its policy, whether in the form of general guidance issued publicly or advice given by supervisors to individual firms. Where the PRA judges that general guidance material is required, this is issued in a consistent format as papers entitled Supervisory Statements. Such material is focused on the PRA's expectations, aimed at facilitating firms' judgements in determining whether they meet these expectations, and will not be overly detailed.
>
> Firms are expected to engage directly with policy material, including rules, EU material and Supervisory Statements, and determine – bearing in mind the overarching principle of safety and soundness – whether they meet the PRA's expectations."

Supervisory Statement 28/15: Strengthening individual accountability in banking (SS28/15) was published with PS16/15. The Supervisory Statement sets out the PRA's approach to strengthening individual accountability in banking and in particular seeks to clarify the responsibilities of those NED functions that are within the scope of the SMR – the chairman, senior independent director and the chairs of the

---

[18] Paragraphs 213 and 214 of The PRA's Approach to Banking Supervision (June 2014).

audit, nomination, remuneration and risk committees. A draft of the Supervisory Statement was published for consultation when the PRA and FCA jointly published an earlier consultation paper.[19] Following PS16/15, SS28/15 was updated in December 2015.

SS28/15 (as updated in December 2015) notes, among other things, that:

- NEDs within the scope of the PRA's SMR are neither required nor expected to assume executive responsibilities but are expected to take on certain responsibilities (see the table below) all of which are non-executive in nature and either inherent in or derive from their chairmanship or senior independent director roles;
- the potential accountability of those NEDs within the scope of the SMR is restricted to those activities for which they are responsible. These include (but are not limited to) ensuring that the board and/or the committees which they chair meet with sufficient frequency, foster an open, inclusive discussion which challenges executives where appropriate and devotes sufficient time and attention to matters within their remit which are relevant to the firm's safety and soundness;
- the role of the chairman is integral to firms' safety and soundness. Consequently, the PRA expects chairmen to seek proactively to remain appraised of matters relating to the board and its individual committees and commit a significantly larger proportion of their time to their functions than other NEDs;
- the PRA would expect responsibility for the firm's performance of its obligations under fitness and propriety in respect of its Notified NEDs to be allocated to the chairman;
- where a firm has a senior independent director the PRA would expect his or her assessment of the chairman to consider, among other things, the extent to which the

---

[19] See Appendix 2 of FCA CP15/5 PRA CP7/15: Approach to non-executive directors in banking and Solvency II firms & Application of the presumption of responsibility to senior managers in banking firms.

chairman has fulfilled his or her responsibilities under the SMR and the quality and sufficiency of resources allocated to the chairman's office;

- the PRA would expect firms to discuss succession planning and proposed change to their board with supervisors irrespective of whether the proposed change relates to a function in scope of the SMR or not;

- a firm's culture is a collective matter for the board but the CEO and chairman should assume a leading role in its development and implementation. Large UK-headquartered banking groups comprising multiple relevant firms may wish to allocate prescribed responsibilities relating to culture to the group CEO and group chairman as opposed to the CEOs and chairmen of the individual legal entities where, for instance, culture is a matter reserved for the group board. However, the PRA adds that they are not, however, "required or expected to do so";

- Statements of Responsibilities of NEDs in scope of the SMR to be less extensive than those of executive senior managers;

- NEDs would not fall within the certification regime unless, in addition to their NED function, they were also performing an additional function which would be a certification function which the PRA would not expect to normally be the case;

- NEDs in-scope of the SMR would be subject to the conduct rules including those applicable only to senior managers. Breaches of the conduct rules by NEDs who fall within the scope of the SMR would be directly enforceable against the individual;

- some conduct rules apply to NEDs in respect of their limited duties only. For instance, the chair of the remuneration committee is likely to discharge his or her responsibilities under Senior Management Conduct Rule 2[20] if (s)he takes reasonable steps to ensure that the remuneration committee complies with the requirements

---

[20] SM2: You must take reasonable steps to ensure that the business of the firm for which you are responsible complies with relevant requirements and standards of the regulatory system.

of "Remuneration"[21] and any specific and relevant requirements imposed by s.55M of FSMA[22], and remains free from undue executive interference in its decision making pursuant to SYSC 7.1.22R and "Risk"[23];

- on the other hand, conduct rules such as the duty to act with integrity, apply to those NEDs within the scope of the SMR and executive senior managers in very similar ways;
- the requirement to 'be open and co-operative with the FCA, the PRA and other regulators' (Individual Conduct Rule 3) and 'disclose appropriately any information of which the FCA or PRA would reasonably expect notice' (Senior Manager Conduct Rule 4) are particularly important for NEDs; and
- Notified NEDs are not directly bound by the conduct rules and are exempt from the accompanying notification requirements. However, if a firm become aware of information that would reasonably be material to the assessment of a current or former Notified NED's fitness and propriety, it must inform the PRA in writing as soon as practicable.

The prescribed responsibilities that were non-executive in nature were set out in Table E of SS28/15 and are set out below.

---

[21] The Renumeration Part of the PRA Rulebook.

[22] Section 55M FSMA—Imposition of requirements by PRA.

[23] SYSC 7.1.22R for credit unions and 3.5 of the Risk Committee Part of the PRA Rulebook ("Risk") for banks, buidling societies and PRA designated investments firms.

SMF	Description of responsibilities	Relevant PRA Rulebook material
Chairman (SMF 9)	Chairing and overseeing the performance of the board. Leading the development and overseeing the implementation of the firm's policies and procedures for the induction, training and development of all directors. Overseeing the assessment of fitness and propriety of those NEDs who are not in scope of the SMR and the related notification requirements to the PRA. Leading the development of the firm's culture by the board.	Fitness and Propriety 2.3, 2.4 and 4.
Chair of the Audit Committee (SMF 11)	Chairing and overseeing the performance of the Audit Committee. Ensuring and overseeing the integrity and independence of the firm's internal audit function (including the Head of Internal Audit).	Compliance and Internal Audit 3.1.
Chair of the Risk Committee (SMF 10)	Chairing and overseeing the performance of the Risk Committee. Ensuring and overseeing the integrity and independence of the firm's risk function (including the Chief Risk Officer).	Risk control 3.5.

SMF	Description of responsibilities	Relevant PRA Rulebook material
Chair of the Remuneration Committee (SMF 12)	Chairing and overseeing the performance of the Remuneration Committee. Overseeing the development and implementation of the firm's remuneration policies and practices.	Remuneration 7.2–7.4.
Chair of the Nominations Committee (SMF 13) [FCA]	Chairing and overseeing the performance of the Nomination Committee.	SUP10C.5.2 R (FCA Handbook).
SID (SMF 14)	Performing the role of a Senior Independent Director (in line with the FRC Code) and leading the assessment of the Chairman's performance.	
Either Chairman (SMF 9) or Chair of the Audit Committee (SMF 11)	Ensuring and overseeing the integrity and independence of the compliance function (including the Head of Compliance). Ensuring and overseeing the integrity, independence and effectiveness of the firm's policies and procedures on whistleblowing and ensuring staff that raise concerns are protected from detrimental treatment.	Compliance and Internal Audit 2.4.

5.13 FCA guidance

Coinciding with the introduction of the individual accountability regime on 7 March 2016 a new sourcebook was inserted into the block of the FCA Handbook titled 'High Level Standards'. The sourcebook is called the Code of Conduct sourcebook or *COCON* for short. It is in this sourcebook that the new FCA guidance on NEDs can be found[24]. The final form of the guidance was set out in CP15/22 and is reproduced below. It is followed by an overview of the FCA feedback in CP15/22. The guidance is separate from SS28/15 and should be read alongside it.

Introduction

This annex applies to non-executive directors (NEDs) who are performing a designated senior management function. It only applies where the individual performing that function is also a NED.

This annex covers the role of a NED in performing the roles in (1) to (4), below:
(1) the role of chairman of the board of directors;
(2) the role of chairman of the nomination committee;
(3) the role of chairman of any other committee (irrespective of whether performing that role is itself a designated senior management function); and
(4) the general NED role.

The FCA's view of the role of a NED is consistent with the duties of directors included in UK company law and the description of the role of a NED in the UK Corporate Governance Code.

---

[24] Annex 1 of COCON.

The general role of a NED

The role of a NED performing the general NED role is to:
- provide effective oversight and challenge; and
- help develop proposals on strategy.

To deliver this, their responsibilities include:
- attending and contributing to board and committee meetings and discussions;
- taking part in collective board and committee decisions, including voting and providing input and challenge; and
- ensuring they are sufficiently and appropriately informed of the relevant matters prior to taking part in board or committee discussions and decisions.

Other key roles of a NED include:
- scrutinising the performance of management in meeting agreed goals and objectives;
- monitoring the reporting of performance;
- satisfying themselves on the integrity of financial information;
- satisfying themselves that financial controls and systems of risk management are robust and defensible;
- scrutinising the design and implementation of the remuneration policy;
- providing objective views on resources, appointments and standards of conduct; and
- involvement in succession planning.

Role of a NED as chair of the board or a committee

Subject to any specific governance arrangements, rules or requirements applicable to the board or particular committees, a NED's responsibility as chairman of the board or a committee includes:
- ensuring that the board or committee meets with sufficient frequency;
- fostering an open, inclusive discussion which challenges executives, where appropriate;

- ensuring that the board or committee devotes sufficient time and attention to the matters within its remit;
- helping to ensure that the board or committee and its members have the information necessary to its and their tasks;
- reporting to the main board on the committee's activities;
- facilitating the running of the board or committee to assist it in providing independent oversight of executive decisions; and
- in relation to the nomination committee, safeguarding the independence and overseeing the performance of the nomination committee.

The chair of the nomination committee should take reasonable steps to ensure that the nomination committee complies with:
- the requirements in SYSC 4.3A about the nomination committee (if that part of SYSC applies to the firm); and
- any specific and relevant requirements relating to the committee or to the matters within the committee's responsibilities.

SYSC 4.3.A.8R and SYSC 4.3A.9R deal with the nomination committee for relevant authorised person.

General approach to the role of a NED

The FCA recognises that NEDs individually do not manage a firm's business in the same way as executive directors. Therefore, the responsibilities for which NEDs are accountable are likely to be of more limited scope.

A NED is neither required nor expected to assume executive responsibilities.

Although NEDs who are subject to the senior management regime for SMF managers have individual duties under that regime, the FCA views the regime and its application as consistent with the principle of collective decision-making.

> The standard of care, skill and diligence that the FCA would expect from a NED is the care, skill and diligence that would be exercised by a reasonably diligent person with:
> - the general knowledge, skill and experience that may reasonably be expected of a person carrying out the functions carried out by the NED in relation to the firm, taking into account the standards in the Handbook (especially COCON and the Decision Procedure and Penalties Manual); and
> - the general knowledge, skill and experience that the NED has.

5.14   FCA feedback on the guidance

In CP15/22 the FCA stated[25] that in response to its earlier consultation it had made "some minor amendments" to its guidance on the role and responsibilities of NEDs and clarified its application. In particular, the FCA stated that the guidance on the role of a NED as committee chair had been amended to more accurately reflect the role. Also, an additional point had been inserted in relation to the role of the chair of the nomination committee in safeguarding the independence of the committee, so as to allow consistency with the prescribed responsibilities for PRA-designated committee chairs. Interestingly, the FCA also stated that the guidance was "consistent with Company Law and does not go beyond what is required under it."

In relation to applying the guidance more widely the FCA mentioned in CP15/22 that when the guidance was consulted on it applied only to individuals performing the chair of the nomination committee function. However, it added that as the guidance on the role of a NED as chair of the nomination committee related generally to their role as committee chair,

---

[25] Paragraph 1.19 Consultation Paper 15/22: Strengthening accountability in banking: Final rules (including feedback on CP14/31 and CP15) and consultation on extending the Certification Regime to wholesale market activities.

and to their general role as a NED, it would be relevant to any chair role. Furthermore the FCA stated[26]:

> "As the FCA has the power of consent for PRA-designated NED approvals, and can take action against all approved NEDs, we consider that it is appropriate for us to set out our expectations in this area for all approved NEDs. We have therefore expanded the scope of the guidance on the role of a NED as committee chair in our final Handbook text to apply to all approved NEDs, whether or not they are performing a PRA or FCA-designated senior management function. Similarly, we have extended the guidance on the general role of a NED to apply to all approved NEDs (but, as discussed previously, our regime will not apply to other NEDs – now known as Notified NEDs)."

Continuing with this theme in relation to the conduct rules and their application to NEDs the FCA stated:

> "The Code of Conduct applies to all activities undertaken by a senior manager. Therefore we have amended the guidance in our final Handbook text to clarify that it applies not only in relation to a NED's role as chair of a designated committee (including the role of chair of the board) and their role as a general NED, but also to any other committee chair role not specified by the regulators. We have therefore applied the guidance on the role of a NED as chair to other (non-approved) chair roles, subject to the specific responsibilities of the committee in question."

The FCA also confirmed that it would only expect firms to allocate those prescribed responsibilities that are non-executive in nature to an approved NED; namely those which relate to the designated committee chair senior management function roles or to the induction, training and professional development of the management body. In CP15/22 the FCA set out a

---

[26] Paragraph 2.43 Consultation Paper 15/22: Strengthening accountability in banking: Final rules (including feedback on CP14/31 and CP15) and consultation on extending the Certification Regime to wholesale market activities.

table describing which of the 30 prescribed responsibilities would be held by senior manager NEDs rather than executives. These prescribed responsibilities follow similar lines to those set out by the PRA and would be applicable to larger firms and cover:

- responsibility for: (a) leading the development of; and (b) monitoring the effective implementation of; policies and procedures for the induction, training and professional development of all members of the firm's governing body (SYSC 4.7.7R(5) of FCA Handbook);
- responsibility for monitoring the effective implementation of policies and procedures for the induction, training and professional development of all persons performing designated senior management functions on behalf of the firm other than members of the governing body (SYSC 4.7.7R(6) of FCA Handbook);
- responsibility for: (a) safeguarding the independence of; and (b) oversight of the performance of; the internal audit function, in accordance with SYSC 6.2 (Internal Audit) (SYSC 4.7.7R(7) of FCA Handbook);
- responsibility for: (a) safeguarding the independence of; and (b) oversight of the performance of; the compliance function in accordance with SYSC 6.1(Compliance) (SYSC 4.7.7R(8) of FCA Handbook);
- responsibility for: (a) safeguarding the independence of; and (b) oversight of the performance of; the risk function, in accordance with SYSC 7.1.21R and SYSC 7.1.22R (Risk control) (SYSC 4.7.7R(9) of FCA Handbook); and
- responsibility for overseeing the development of, and implementation of, the firm's remuneration policies and practices in accordance with SYSC 19D (Remuneration Code) (SYSC 4.7.7R(10) of FCA Handbook).

The FCA also confirmed that it would not expect firms to allocate any overall responsibilities to NEDs nor would it expect a NED to perform the overall responsibility function. However, firms were expected to include any other aspects of an approved senior manager NED's role (other than their

313

general NED duties), such as chairing a committee for which approval was not required, in their Statement of Responsibilities.

Finally, the FCA re-confirmed that its certification regime and conduct rules would not apply to Notified NEDs. It also mentioned that individuals who were performing a Notified NED role would not need to be grandfathered from the commencement of the new regime. Instead, if they were approved for the same role, their approval would simply lapse at commencement.

5.15   Enforcement against NEDs

SS28/15 set out[27] a brief range of hypothetical scenarios where the PRA might consider applying sanctions to those NEDs within the SMR and other scenarios where the PRA was more likely to consider applying sanctions to executive senior managers. One of the possible scenarios where a NED within the scope of the SMR could find themselves potentially accountable would be where the chairman and senior manager NEDs have serious concerns about an overly dominant CEO and that these concerns are not addressed, recorded or discussed by the board or with PRA or FCA supervisors.

5.16   The criminal offence

Section 36 of the Financial Services (Banking Reform) Act 2013 provides that senior managers (including NEDs within the scope of the SMR) of banks and building societies may be prosecuted by the PRA or FCA in some cases for taking a decision that causes an institution to fail. It is expected that such prosecutions will be rare. Decisions on whether to prosecute, and which regulator should prosecute, will be made on a case-by-case basis.

---

[27]   Table F at para.2.28 of Supervisory Statement 28/15.

5.17 The Bank of England and Financial Services Bill

The position regarding the application of conduct rules to Notified NEDs appears to be changing.

At the time of writing the FCA stated in CP15/22 that conduct rules would not apply to Notified NEDs. The PRA stated in PS16/15 that all members of a management body, including Notified NEDs, should "observe" Individual Conduct Rules 1 to 3 and Senior Management Conduct Rule 4 and that this would be a contractual requirement which would allow the firm to enforce these standards. The firm could, for instance, write such a requirement into its staff handbook.

On 14 October 2015, the Bank of England and Financial Services Bill (the Bill) entered Parliament. At the same time HM Treasury published a policy paper[28]. The Bill and the HM Treasury paper are important for a number of reasons including the reverse burden of proof being superseded by a statutory duty of responsibility. The Bill also sought to amend section 64A of FSMA extending the power of the PRA and FCA to make conduct rules applying to directors of authorised persons (NEDs), as well as employees and authorised persons. The Bill also amends s.64B of FSMA to ensure that it applies to directors. This section places a duty on an authorised person to ensure that anyone subject to the conduct rules is aware of those rules and how they apply to them.

One possibility is that the Bill signals that we are heading in the direction where Notified NEDs will become directly subject to the conduct rules. However, such a change in approach is surprising given that this would have been considered previously.

---

[28] Senior Managers and Certification Regime: extension to all FSMA authorised persons.

5.17.1 Why the change in approach?

The HM Treasury paper argued that the regulators did not have the ability to take enforcement action for misconduct against NEDs and that such a gap needed to be addressed due to provisions in certain EU Directives (like the CRD IV) that require member states to be able to take action against members of a firm's management body. It was further argued that there could also be circumstances where it would be appropriate to take enforcement action against NEDs, such as where they failed to act with honesty and integrity and that it was difficult to justify a position where enforcement action could be taken against relative junior staff but not against certain board members.

The impact assessment that accompanied the Bill stated[29]:

> "The extension of rules of conduct to non-executive directors who are not senior managers is not expected to result in any significant costs to business. The main costs from the introduction of rules of conduct arise from larger firms having to put in place systems to identify large numbers of employees to whom the rules of conduct will apply, and to notify and train those employees in the rules. Additional system changes will not be necessary for non-executive directors."

5.18 Governance and the role of boards

Before ending this chapter it might be worth spending a few moments on the speech that the PRA chief executive, Andrew Bailey, gave at the Westminster Business Forum in 2015[30]. In his speech Mr Bailey covered the role of boards stating that they

---

[29] Paragraph 115 of the impact assessment to the Bank of England and Financial Services Bill (July 2015).

[30] Governance and the role of boards. Speech given by Andrew Bailey, Deputy Governor, Prudential Regulation and chief executive officer, PRA. Westminster Business Forum. 3 November 2015.

must be able to set a strategy and risk appetite and oversee implementation, but that they were not a substitute for the role of the executive.

In relation to what supervisors expected of boards, Mr Bailey mentioned that three things stood out for him:

- boards are expected to exercise good judgment in overseeing the running of the firm and to do so on a forward-looking basis;
- that judgement is improved by good constructive challenge from non-executives. A firm's culture should promote discussion, debate and honest challenge. Alarm bells ring when the chief executive or other senior executives are very sensitive to challenge; and
- supervisors depend on non-executives, under the leadership of the chair, to challenge the executive in all aspects of the firm's strategy, which includes the viability and sustainability of the business model and the establishment, maintenance and use of the risk appetite and management framework.

Mr Bailey also added:

"In terms of the Senior Managers' regime, this frames the responsibility of boards. But, as many board members have said to me, if only it was that simple, but you have made it so fiendishly complicated. Well, actually we didn't make it fiendishly complicated, finance has become that way itself – we didn't invent exotic derivatives. There are those who think the answer is to make finance less complicated, but in the real world there are benefits to innovation if risk management is effective."

He later added:

"So, let me put forward a proposition for boards. It is the job of the executive to be able to explain in simple and transparent terms these complex matters to non-executives. In doing so, you should understand the

317

uncertainty around judgements, in what circumstances they could be wrong, and how there can reasonably be different ways to measure things like liquidity. Non-executives should not be left to find the answers for themselves, and they should not feel that they have to do so out of a lack of sufficient confidence in what they are being told. In other words, they should not be pointed towards the haystack with warm wishes for the search ahead."

5.19 Conclusion

As noted in the FSA's NEDs Conference, NEDs have an extremely important and unique role in being able to influence their firm's behaviour and it is for this reason why the regulatory spotlight has been on them since the financial crisis.

For those NEDs who come within the scope of the SMR – chairmen, chairs of the risk, audit, remuneration and nomination committees and senior independent director – there is the allocation of prescribed responsibilities and the completion of Statements of Responsibilities whilst bearing in mind the rules and guidance that the regulators have issued.

For Notified NEDs the individual accountability regime removes the direct relationship that they had with the regulators under the Approved Persons regime. In its place is a PRA notification regime and observance of Individual Conduct Rules and a Senior Management Conduct Rule. However, with the introduction of the Bill it appears that a final decision on whether the conduct rules should apply to all NEDs has been made. NEDs will need to keep an eye on development.

Whilst the focus has been on the new rules and guidance that the new individual accountability regime brings it is worth remembering that the prohibition power under s.56 of FSMA is still available to the regulators. Also, NEDs continue to remain accountable under the Companies Act and, in listed firms, subject to the principles in the Financial Reporting Code on a comply-or-explain basis.

Sitting on a bank's board as a NED was once the pinnacle of aspiration in a City career. But whether the individual accountability regime will change aspirations and indeed provoke an exodus of NEDs remains to be seen.

Chapter 6

UK branches of foreign banks

Peter Snowdon
Partner
Norton Rose Fulbright

Simon Lovegrove
Head of Financial Services Knowledge—Global
Norton Rose Fulbright

6.1   Introduction

The financial crisis demonstrated that financial markets are connected globally and the regulation of third country branches in the EU has become a hot topic. Indeed the third country provisions in the Markets in Financial Instruments Directive (recast) and the Markets in Financial Instruments Regulation were the subject of some of the most heated debates as the new legislation passed through the EU institutions. It is therefore perhaps with little surprise that UK branches of third country banks and the regulation of those responsible for them has also come under the spotlight by the UK's individual accountability regime.

Taking a step back for a moment, the basic position is that international headquartered banks can either operate in the UK as subsidiaries or branches. A subsidiary is a separate legal entity from its parent, and as such requires its own governance and risk management, as well as meeting capital and liquidity requirements in the UK. A branch forms part of the same legal entity as its head office, and therefore will not have its own capital base or board as this is covered in the head office, though local governance is required. International branches of banks form an important part of the UK banking sector.

For subsidiaries the regulators have the same legal powers and follow broadly the same supervisory framework as for UK headquartered banks. However, the responsibilities for prudential supervision of branches are more complex and depend on the standing of a bank's home state regulator and the nature of the bank's business in the UK. In practice prudential regulation is sometimes split between the regulator where the bank is headquartered and the PRA. In terms of establishing a branch in the UK, UK branches of non-EEA banks (referred to hereafter as "non-EEA UK branches") need to be authorised by the PRA whereas EEA banks wishing to establish a branch in the UK (referred to hereafter as "EEA UK branches") have EU Treaty rights to passport into the UK and other Member States (or provide their business remotely through cross border services). For EEA banks seeking to passport into the UK under one of the Single Market Directives, the notification procedure involves their Home Member State regulator liaising with the PRA.

The FCA is the conduct regulator for all banks operating in the UK. As mentioned above EEA banks have the right to passport into the UK and should they establish a physical presence through a branch, the branch will be subject to the FCA's conduct of business rules. For subsidiaries and branches of non-EEA banks, both new and existing, the FCA's Threshold Conditions and conduct of business rules apply, including in areas such as anti-money laundering. For new applicants, authorisation can be granted only where the regulators are satisfied that their respective requirements have been met.

In February 2014, the PRA published a consultation paper concerning its approach to branch supervision of overseas banks[1] which was subsequently followed up by a policy statement[2] and supervisory statement[3] both published in September 2014. It is worth noting that these papers tended to

---

[1] PRA Consultation Paper 4/14: Supervising international banks: the PRA's approach to branch supervision
[2] PRA Policy Statement 8/14: Supervising international banks: the PRA's approach to branch supervision
[3] PRA Supervisory Statement 10/14: Supervising international banks: the PRA's approach to branch supervision

focus on the PRA's approach to supervising the branch or subsidiary rather than on the individuals that operated within them (although they implemented a requirement for a SYSC attestation—see para.6.13 below).

There was some speculation as to whether or not the new individual accountability regime would be applied to UK branches of overseas firms. Ultimately a written ministerial statement made by HM Treasury on 3 March 2014 confirmed that the new rules would apply. This was subsequently followed by George Osborne MP announcing in his Chancellor's Mansion House speech on 12 June 2014 that, "I am also extending the senior managers' regime to cover all banks that operate in this country, including the branches of foreign banks."

This chapter tracks the development of the FCA's and PRA's policy towards branches of banks in the UK. This chapter takes a chronological approach to the development of that policy and should be read in its entirety. The discussion on the final rules can be found in paras 6.10 and 6.11.

6.2   Initial PRA and FCA consultation

In its consultation paper on supervising international banks the PRA noted[4] that "the overarching management and governance of a third-country branch is the primary responsibility of the Home State Supervisor." However, the PRA added that it would:

"be responsible for ensuring that branches have individuals responsible for the oversight of the branch and ensuring compliance with UK regulatory standards. Any senior individuals will require approval by the PRA."

---

[4]   Paragraph 48 PRA Consultation Paper 4/14: Supervising international banks: the PRA's approach to branch supervision

In July 2014 a joint PRA and FCA consultation paper was published on the new individual accountability regime[5]. In Ch.1 of this consultation paper the PRA stated that it would not be specifying any senior management functions applying to an EEA UK branch. This was on the basis that the assessment of competence of persons performing a controlled function in an incoming branch of an EEA bank or PRA designated investment firm was reserved to the Home Member State supervisor under the EU Single Market Directives. The FCA stated that it would consider in future consultations the extent to which it would be appropriate to continue to assess and approve individuals performing certain functions in EEA UK branches, to the extent that those functions were not reserved to the Home Member State supervisor.

In Ch.6 of the consultation paper it was stated that, subject to a draft HM Treasury Order being finalised, the PRA would propose to require at least one individual per incoming non-EEA UK branch to be approved as an Overseas Branch Senior Executive Manager. The PRA proposed that this senior management function would be defined as:

> "the function of having responsibility alone or jointly with others, for the conduct of all activities of the UK branch of an overseas firm which are subject to the UK regulatory system".[6]

The individuals approved would typically be performing activities akin to those of a CEO in relation to the UK branch. In certain circumstances the PRA would require the branch to put forward more than one individual for approval. The example given where this could happen was when the individual originally put forward by the firm was not the most senior individual exercising influence in relation to the UK branch.

---

[5] Consultation Paper FCA 14/13 / PRA14/14: Strengthening accountability in banking: a new regulatory framework for individuals
[6] Paragraph 6.5 Consultation Paper FCA 14/13 / PRA 14/14: Strengthening accountability in banking: a new regulatory framework for individuals.

The PRA also stated in this chapter that its certification regime would not apply to EEA UK branches on the basis that the issue of the fitness and propriety of the staff in those branches, insofar as it relates to prudential matters, was reserved to the Home Member State supervisor[7]. However, the PRA would take a different approach to incoming branches of non-EEA banks and PRA designated investment firms and apply its certification regime to them[8]. Also, the PRA's remuneration rules would apply to non-EEA UK branches on the basis of the criteria set out in the Capital Requirements Directive IV and supporting legislation[9] to identify "material risk takers".

In the same consultation paper the FCA took a less robust view on non-EEA UK branches stating that the HM Treasury Order would have to be confirmed before it could consult on how the new regime applied to them[10]. However, the FCA stated that the position relating to conduct issues in UK branches of overseas banks had the potential to be more complicated and could capture a wider range of individuals. In addition, the FCA had more powers over EEA banks than the PRA as conduct of business matters are reserved to the Host Member State regulator rather than the Home Member State regulator.

6.3   HM Treasury consultation

On 17 November 2014, HM Treasury published its consultation document, "Regulating individual conduct in banking: UK branches of foreign banks". This was the first dedicated consultation extending the individual accountability regime to UK branches of overseas banks.

---

[7] Paragraph 6.6 Consultation Paper FCA 14/13 / PRA14/14: Strengthening accountability in banking: a new regulatory framework for individuals.

[8] Paragraph 6.7 Consultation Paper FCA 14/13 / PRA14/14: Strengthening accountability in banking: a new regulatory framework for individuals.

[9] Commission Delegated Regulation (EU) No 604/2014 of 4 March 2014 supplementing Directive 2013/36/EU of the European Parliament and of the Council with regard to regulatory technical standards with respect to qualitative and appropriate quantitative criteria to identify categories of staff whose professional activities have a material impact on an institution's risk profile.

[10] Paragraph 6.9 Consultation Paper FCA 14/13 / PRA/ 14/14: Strengthening accountability in banking: a new regulatory framework for individuals.

The Financial Services (Banking Reform) Act 2013 (the Act) created the legal framework for the individual accountability regime. Non-UK institutions originally including UK branches of overseas firms were not included in the key definition of "Relevant Authorised Person" (the definition that describes which firms are within the scope of the regime) which the Act inserted into the Financial Services and Markets Act 2000. However, the Act gave HM Treasury the power to bring non-UK institutions within the scope of the regime by Order. Before making such an Order, HM Treasury was required to consult with the PRA, the FCA, and any other persons who might be affected by the proposals. This was the purpose of the consultation document that was published on 17 November 2014.

In the consultation document HM Treasury explained that the effect of the draft Order (the Financial Services and Markets Act 2000 (Relevant Authorised Persons) Order 2015) would be to bring within the definition of "Relevant Authorised Person" those overseas financial services firms that have a branch in the UK and are credit institutions or PRA designated investment firms. The explanatory note to the draft Order stated:

> "The first category of non-UK institution which this Order specifies as relevant authorised persons is those non-UK institutions which are credit institutions that have a branch in the UK and are authorised to accept deposits in the UK."

> "The second category is those non-UK institutions which are investment firms that have a branch in the UK and are authorised to deal in investments as principal in the UK, provided that when dealing in investments as principal in the UK such institutions are regulated by the PRA."

However, the draft Order would not make a senior manager in such a branch potentially liable to the new criminal offence relating to a decision causing a financial institution to fail.

In the remainder of this chapter the term "UK Relevant Authorised Person" is used to describe a UK institution that is a Relevant Authorised Person for the purposes of the Order.

6.4 PRA and FCA consultation on transitional issues

In December 2014 the PRA and FCA issued a further joint consultation paper on the new individual accountability regime, this time covering forms, consequential and transitional aspects. However, the consultation paper stated[11] that the proposals contained within it did not apply to UK branches of firms that were headquartered overseas.

6.5 HM Treasury response to its consultation

The HM Treasury consultation which began on 17 November 2014 closed on 30 January 2015. Soon afterwards on 3 March 2015, HM Treasury announced in a written ministerial statement to Parliament that it would apply the individual accountability regime to UK branches of overseas banks. The written ministerial statement added that the regulators' rules would:

> "help ensure that the [senior managers regime and certification regime] is applied in an appropriate and proportionate way to foreign institutions operating through branches in the UK".

On the same date HM Treasury published a response to its consultation.[12]

HM Treasury noted a number of concerns raised by respondents which included the possible application of the individual

---

[11] Paragraph 1.12 Consultation Paper FCA 14/31 / PRA 28/14: Strengthening accountability in banking: forms, consequential and transitional aspects.
[12] HM Treasury response to consultation—Regulating individual conduct in banking: UK branches of foreign banks.

accountability regime to staff based outside the UK, particularly where there were matrix management structures in place or other arrangements under which staff could report to more than one line manager in relation to different activities. Other respondents suggested that non-UK individuals should only come within the scope of the regime if there was a direct link to UK implementation of any decision they take and that the line managers of those individuals should only be in scope if they were based in the UK or there was a similar direct link. Concerns were also raised to ensure that there was recognition that senior management could be based outside the UK and that it was not necessary to change internal structures in order to bring senior managers to the UK.

The response from HM Treasury was that these concerns would be addressed by the rules that the PRA and FCA would make. HM Treasury also noted that the regime would only apply to activities subject to UK regulation stating that it would be "unlikely" if the regime would apply to individuals responsible for setting a group's strategy worldwide but that it would apply to those responsible for implementing the strategy in the UK branch. HM Treasury also stated that whether the regime would apply to an individual based outside the UK would depend on the facts of the individual case. It added that this was most likely to occur where there was no one of appropriate seniority based in the UK branch with responsibility for a key area or activity subject to regulation in the UK, and an overseas senior manager was directly participating in the management of the UK branch or taking decisions with a direct link to the branch's UK regulated activities. In relation to the certification regime, HM Treasury said that the PRA and FCA would expect that certified persons would be based in the UK or have a "substantial" link to UK customers or activities. No further information concerning the meaning of "substantial" was given.

6.6 PRA and FCA consultation on UK branches of overseas banks

6.6.1 *Introduction*

On 16 March 2015, the PRA and FCA issued a joint consultation paper on the individual accountability regime and its application to UK branches of overseas banks.[13]

A key point made in the consultation paper was that both the PRA and FCA were concerned with the governance of the UK branch itself rather than of the bank as a whole.[14] The new Senior Managers' regime for overseas banks was not intended to capture the boards of incoming branches but rather the individuals responsible for the day-to-day running of the UK branch.

On this linkage to the UK it is perhaps worth mentioning s.59ZA of FSMA which provides that in order for a function to be capable of being designated as a senior management function, it must involve the management of one of more aspects of the bank's affairs relating to regulated activities and which might involve a risk of serious consequences for the bank or for business or other interests in the UK.

Arguably a precedent on the above principle could be found in the FCA Handbook guidance on the Approved Persons Regime which provided that, where an individual based overseas had responsibilities in relation to an incoming UK branch that were limited to setting strategy only, such individuals would not generally be captured as approved persons. However, where the individual was responsible for implementing that strategy in the UK, they were likely to be performing a controlled function and would require approval by one or both regulators.

---

[13] Consultation Paper FCA 15/10 / PRA 9/15: Strengthening accountability in banking: UK branches of foreign banks.
[14] Paragraph 2.4 Consultation Paper FCA 15/10 / PRA 9/15: Strengthening accountability in banking: UK branches of foreign banks.

Another important point that was mentioned in the consultation paper was that the individual accountability regime was designed to be proportionate and the regime for UK branches of overseas banks would take this principle into account.

6.6.2   EEA UK branches

For EEA UK branches the PRA repeated the point made in its earlier consultation paper that it would not be applying any elements of the individual accountability regime. It stated[15]:

> "Under EU law, the Home State Supervisor (HSS) of an EEA firm that operates as a branch in another EEA country is responsible for the prudential supervision of the whole firm (including the branch). As a result, where the PRA is the host supervisor of an EEA branch, it is not responsible for its prudential supervision; this is the role of the HSS. Consequently, none of the PRA proposals in this CP apply to incoming EEA branches."

6.6.3   SMFs and non-EEA UK branches

In relation to senior management functions for individuals in non-EEA UK branches the PRA and FCA proposed the following:

PRA senior management functions	
Head of Overseas Branch	SMF 19
Chief Finance function (if applicable – see below)	SMF 2
Chief Risk function (if applicable – see below)	SMF 4
Head of Internal Audit (if applicable – see below)	SMF 5
Group Entity Senior Manager (if applicable – see below)	SMF 7

---

[15] Paragraph 1.29 Consultation Paper FCA 15/10 / PRA 9/15: Strengthening accountability in banking: UK branches of foreign banks.

FCA senior management functions	
Money Laundering Reporting Officer	SMF 17
Compliance Oversight	SMF 16
Overseas Branch Senior Manager	SMF 20

The consultation paper stated that the PRA proposed that it would require all non-EEA UK branches to have at least one individual approved as a Head of Overseas Branch who would typically be performing activities akin to those of a CEO in relation to the branch. The individual would have the highest degree of individual decision-making authority within the branch over activities and areas subject to UK regulation. The PRA proposed to describe this senior management function[16] as:

> "the function of having responsibility, alone or jointly with others, for the conduct of all activities of the UK branch of an overseas [bank] which are subject to the UK regulatory system".

If more than one individual were to be appointed to this senior management function the onus would be placed on the bank to set out clearly the specific responsibilities of each individual in their respective Statements of Responsibilities.

The consultation paper further noted that for non-EEA UK branches additional senior managers would be required to be put forward for approval by the PRA in the following circumstances:

- where another individual had direct management and/or decision-making responsibility over the UK branch's regulated activities i.e. a UK country head or head of Europe, Middle East and Africa. Where this was the case, the PRA would require this individual to be approved as a

---

[16] Paragraph 2.8 Consultation Paper FCA 15/10 / PRA 9/15: Strengthening accountability in banking: UK branches of foreign banks.

> Group Entity Senior Manager of the UK branch in addition to the Head of Overseas Branch; and
>
> - if the UK branch had dedicated individuals performing certain executive senior management functions namely Chief Finance, Chief Risk and Head of Internal Audit functions. It would be common for large overseas banks to have UK or EMEA-wide heads of finance, risk and/or internal audit with responsibility for all UK entities in the UK group, including the UK branch. In these circumstances the PRA would require these individuals to be approved as their relevant senior management functions in relation to the UK branch.

The consultation paper noted that neither the PRA nor the FCA intended to bring any non-executive director (NED) functions into the scope of the Senior Managers' regime for UK branches. However, it also stated that there could be situations where individuals employed by a UK branch's head office or another group company are approved as a NED (CF 2) of the branch under the Approved Persons' Regime. These individuals would commonly be deemed to be performing the Group Entity Senior Manager function in respect of the branch.[17]

The Overseas Branch Senior Manager function was a new function that the FCA proposed to apply to individuals who would have local responsibility for the activities, business areas and management functions of the non-EEA UK branch. The function, which would apply only in relation to the regulated activities of the non-EEA UK branch, would generally apply to those individuals who were members of the non-EEA UK branch's highest decision making body or who reported directly to it. It would be likely that they would either report to the Head of Overseas Branch or to another member of the local governing body of the branch although they might also have separate reporting lines to individuals and bodies outside the branch structure. The FCA stressed that there was no territorial limitation to the scope of its Senior Manager regime for non-EEA UK branches, and that the scope of this new senior

---

[17] Paragraphs 2.13 and 2.14 of Consultation Paper FCA 15/10 / PRA 9/15: Strengthening accountability in banking: UK branches of foreign banks.

management function would not be limited to individuals within the branch management structure. The FCA also acknowledged that in very small branches it might be the case that there would be no individuals approved to the Overseas Branch Senior Management function with responsibility being left to the Head of Overseas Branch function.

The FCA proposed two further senior management functions, the Money Laundering Reporting Officer (SMF 17) and the EEA Branch Senior Manager (SMF 21). The Money Laundering Reporting Officer function would be defined in the same way as for non-EEA UK branches and UK Relevant Authorised Persons. The EEA Branch Senior Manager function would apply to individuals who would have responsibility for the conduct of certain regulated activities of the UK branch. That individual would have to be involved in:

1. designated investment business other than dealing in investments as principal; or
2. processing confirmations, payments, settlements, insurance claims, client money and similar matters, in so far as this relates to designated investment business; and
3. accepting deposits from banking customers and activities substantially connected with that activity, to the extent to which it does not fall within 1 or 2.

The consultation paper contained a series of examples of how the PRA's and FCA's new branch senior management functions could interact in practice.[18]

The consultation paper also set out a list of Prescribed Responsibilities that could be allocated to any PRA or FCA specified senior management function in respect of a non-EEA UK branch. These are set out below:

---

[18] Paragraph 2.40 Consultation Paper FCA 15/10 / PRA 9/15: Strengthening accountability in banking: UK branches of foreign banks

Shared PRA and FCA responsibilities
1. Responsibility for the branch's performance of its obligations under the senior managers' regime, including implementation and oversight.
2. Responsibility for the branch's performance of its obligations under the certification rules.
3. Responsibility for compliance with the branch's obligations in relation to its management responsibilities map.
4. Responsibility for management of the branch's risk management processes in the UK.
5. Responsibility for the branch's compliance with the UK regulatory regime applicable to the branch.
6. Responsibility for the escalation of correspondence from the PRA, FCA and other regulators in respect of the branch to the governing body and/or the management body of the firm or, where appropriate, of the parent undertaking or holding company of the firm's group.
7. Responsibility for the maintenance of the integrity, independence and effectiveness of the branch's policies and procedures on whistleblowing and for ensuring staff who raise concerns are protected from detrimental treatment.

PRA responsibilities
8. Responsibility for management of the branch's systems and controls in the UK.
9. Responsibility for the allocation of all UK branch prescribed responsibilities.
10. Responsibility for management of the branch's liquidity or, where a liquidity waiver is in place, the submission of information to the PRA on the firm's liquidity position.
11. Responsibility for the production and integrity of the branch's financial information and its regulatory reporting in respect of its regulated activities, including the annual attestation of compliance to the PRA of the branch's compliance with its obligations under SYSC.

FCA responsibilities
12. Responsibility for the branch's policies and procedures for countering the risk that the branch might be used to further financial crime.
13. Responsibility for the branch's policies and procedures for compliance with CASS.

It was also proposed that non-EEA UK branches should prepare, submit and, where appropriate, update a management responsibilities map. However, the requirements would be inherently proportionate and the map would be tailored to the characteristics of the branch so that, for instance, it would set out the matters reserved to the governing body of the branch rather than the ultimate overseas governing body. Notwithstanding this there would also be an expectation that the branch would provide a detailed explanation of how management and governance arrangements fitted in with those of its overseas head office and the wider group. However, for non-complex branches (for example those with small business lines or who do not rely on group governance arrangements) the FCA would expect it to be a simple document summarising the allocation of responsibilities within the bank and the bank's governance arrangements.

Given that in the EEA context the allocation of responsibilities is a matter reserved to the Home Member State the FCA stated that its responsibility framework would not apply to EEA UK branches. In addition, the obligation on senior managers to provide handover certificates when leaving their role would also not apply. As for responsibilities maps, the same principles used for non-EEA UK branches would apply with the addition that EEA UK branches would only be required to include in the map the information necessary to identify the responsibilities of the senior managers and how these fitted in with the management and governance arrangements of the branch as a whole.

6.6.4 *Grandfathering*

As with UK Relevant Authorised Persons, the regulators proposed certain grandfathering arrangements for those senior individuals working in a UK branch of an overseas bank. Those individuals who were performing a significant influence function and whose role would not be substantively changing, would be grandfathered into a corresponding senior management role. A table proposing the approvals that could be grandfathered was set out in the consultation paper.[19]

6.6.5 *Certification and non-EEA UK branches*

In the consultation paper the PRA proposed to base its certification regime for non-EEA UK branches on their material risk taker population notwithstanding that "material risk taker" was an EU concept found in the Capital Requirements Directive IV and supporting legislation. The FCA proposed to include a wider population of individuals and to apply its certification regime in broadly the same way as it proposed for UK Relevant Authorised Persons. One important territorial point that was mentioned in the consultation paper was that the certified individual had to be "based in the UK" or "be dealing with a UK client". However, it is submitted that the consultation paper lacked clarity as to what was meant by dealing with UK clients and what types of interaction this would capture.

6.6.6 *Certification and EEA UK branches*

The PRA proposed not to apply its certification regime to EEA UK branches for the reasons mentioned earlier. The FCA proposed to apply a certification regime, which would include material risk takers, to EEA UK branches with certain modifications, for example it proposed that the CASS oversight function should not apply (the CASS rules do not apply to UK branches of EEA banks) and that a territorial limitation would

---

[19] Paragraph 5.3 Consultation Paper FCA 15/10 / PRA 9/15: Strengthening accountability in banking: UK branches of foreign banks.

be used so that the certification regime would only apply to individuals that were based in the UK.

6.6.7 *Conduct rules and non-EEA UK branches*

Both the PRA and FCA felt that the scope of their respective conduct rules for UK Relevant Authorised Persons were equally applicable for non-EEA UK branches and therefore proposed to proceed accordingly. The FCA added a further proposal that for EEA UK branches, its conduct rules would apply but with the existing limitation in APER which restricted their application to the extent that they were compliant with EU legislation. In addition, there would be a territorial limitation as to the application of the conduct rules to individuals who were not senior managers. The conduct rules would only apply to individuals based in the UK. This territorial limitation would, however, not apply to senior managers in EEA UK branches (see paras 6.10 and 6.11 for further discussion and final rules).

The extension of the conduct rules to UK branches of overseas banks and the practicalities that might arise from it caused concern. Some of those who responded to the consultation paper[20] argued that the practical implications of the regulatory notification requirements in relation to breaches of the conduct rules could be considerable in the case of staff based overseas. It was also argued that a significant amount of personal information would need to be acquired and transferred from overseas legal entities domiciled in both the EEA and non-EEA countries to the UK.

---

[20] See for example the joint response to the consultation from the AFME, AFB and BBA.

6.7 Policy statement(s) and near-final rules

6.7.1 Introduction

In August 2015 the PRA and FCA published separate papers containing near-final rules for the application of the individual accountability regime to UK branches of overseas banks.[21] The rules were near final as at the time of their publication Parliament had not approved the draft Financial Services and Markets Act 2000 (Relevant Authorised Persons) Order 2015.

6.7.2 PRA policy statement

In its policy statement the PRA noted that the responses to its earlier consultation paper agreed with the proposed scope of the Senior Managers' regime for non-EEA UK branches and consequently confirmed that it would not be making any changes to its proposals. However, one aspect where respondents asked for further clarity was the Group Entity Senior Manager function. In response the PRA referred to certain paragraphs of a previous policy statement and supervisory statement[22] citing that these clarified its expectations of when an individual based in a parent or group entity, either in the UK or overseas, would require approval as a Group Entity Senior Manager. The PRA summarised the position as follows:[23]:

- the PRA would not require pre-approval of senior individuals located in overseas parent or group entities whose responsibilities in relation to the UK were limited to developing the group's overall strategy. The PRA's focus would be on those individuals who, irrespective of their

---

[21] PRA Policy Statement 20/15: Strengthening individual accountability in banking: UK branches of non-EEA banks and FCA Feedback Statement 15/3: Strengthening accountability in banking: UK branches of foreign banks—Feedback on FCA CP15/10 / PRA CP9/15.

[22] Paragraphs 2.6 to 2.10 PRA Policy Statement 3/15: Strengthening individual accountability in banking and insurance—responses to CP14/14 and CP26/14 and Supervisory Statement 28/15.

[23] Paragraph 2.4 PRA Policy Statement 20/15: Strengthening individual accountability in banking: UK branches of non-EEA banks.

location, were directly responsible for implementing the group's strategy in the firm's UK branch or UK subsidiaries;

- consequently, if an individual located overseas was directly responsible for how a non-EEA UK branch should conduct its UK-regulated activities and had not delegated this responsibility to a senior manager based in the UK, he or she were likely to require pre-approval as a Group Entity Senior Manager;

- the PRA would not aim or expect to pre-approve individuals as a Group Entity Senior Manager for every non-EEA UK branch, only where justified by the firm's, group's and/or relevant individual's circumstances; and

- in the first instance, firms should consider whether there were any individuals in their parent or group companies, either in the UK or overseas, who may be performing a Group Entity Senior Manager function on behalf of their non-EEA UK branch. In doing so, they should take into account:

  — the respective organisational structures of the group and the non-EEA UK branch;

  — the split of responsibilities between group senior management and the non-EEA UK branch's senior management functions based in the UK; and

  — whether the non-EEA UK branch's senior management functions based in the UK had appropriate delegated authority from the parent or group to ensure that the branch complies with its UK regulatory obligations.

The PRA added that[24] whilst it was keen to minimise the risk of individuals being unnecessarily exposed to conflicting or overlapping regulatory regimes where an individual located overseas was directly responsible for managing a non-EEA UK branch's UK regulated activities, he or she would "inevitably" be subject to UK regulatory requirements as well as the requirements of his or her Home state supervisor.

---

[24] Paragraph 2.5 Policy Statement 20/15: Strengthening individual accountability in banking: UK branches of non-EEA banks

The PRA also illustrated the difference between setting strategy and implementing strategy by referring to the Basel Committee on Banking Supervision's revised corporate governance principles for banks. This is replicated below.

Setting versus implementing strategy

As stated in the Basel Committee on Banking Supervision's revised corporate governance principles for banks, the Chief Risk Officer (CRO) of a bank is "responsible for supporting the board in its engagement with and oversight of the development of the bank's risk appetite and [risk appetite statement] (RAS) and for translating the risk appetite into a risk limits structure."

Although a non-UK headquartered non-EEA banking group's risk appetite, RAS and risk limits will be cascaded down and implemented in its overseas entities, including its UK branch, this will not, in itself, bring the group CRO into the scope of the senior managers' regime.

However, before implementing the group's risk appetite, RAS and risk limits in its UK branch, the firm should ensure that it complies with applicable local regulatory requirements and, if not, make or suggest such modifications as may be necessary. This requirement is reflected in the section on Allocation of Responsibilities in the PRA Rulebook, which includes Prescribed Responsibilities for:

- the management of the branch's risk management processes in the UK;
- the branch's compliance with the UK regulatory regime applicable to the branch; and
- management of the branch's systems and controls in the UK

Setting versus implementing strategy
Those responsibilities should typically be allocated to one of the branch's senior management functions based in the UK, such as the Head of Overseas Branch or, where applicable, the Chief Risk functions. However, if the [UK] branch does not have any UK-based senior managers with appropriate authority to discharge these responsibilities, the firm would need to consider whether the group CRO or another individual based in a parent or group entity should be approved as a Group Entity Senior Manager of the [UK] branch.

As mentioned earlier the PRA consulted on a customised list of thirteen Prescribed Responsibilities for senior managers in non-EEA UK branches. Following the consultation certain amendments to the final version of Prescribed Responsibilities were made and a blackline version showing the changes is set out at the end of this chapter.

In relation to the certification regime for non-EEA UK branches the PRA noted that respondents supported its approach and therefore it did not propose to make any changes to it. It also reiterated the position mentioned in its previous consultations that not all material risk takers would be performing a certification function as some of them, including those in non-EEA UK branches, would be senior managers. Likewise it mentioned that individuals whose functions were not related to the UK regulated activities of the branch would not meet the statutory test for a certification function and therefore fall outside the scope of the PRA's certification regime.

In relation to the conduct rules the PRA noted that respondents supported its approach and therefore proposed not to make any changes to it. Both senior managers and employees performing a PRA specified certification function in non-EEA UK branches would be subject to the three individual conduct rules. Senior managers would also be subject to the four senior manager conduct rules (see Ch.4 of this book).

341

6.7.3 FCA feedback

As one would expect the FCA feedback statement[25] covered the four core areas of the individual accountability regime: the Senior Managers' regime, the certification regime, the conduct rules and the forms and transition to the new regime. In relation to the Senior Managers' regime the headline change concerned the removal of the Overseas Branch Senior Management function and its replacement in non-EEA UK branches of:

- the Executive Director (SMF 3) function. This would operate in a similar way to the Director controlled function (CF 1) for non-EEA UK branches. For non-EEA UK branches this function would be limited to individuals performing a senior management function in relation to the branch only, rather than in relation to the whole firm; and
- a new Other Local Responsibility (SMF 22) function. This would broadly operate in a similar way to the Other Overall Responsibility (SMF 18) function. This function would capture any individuals who had local responsibility for any of the activities, business areas or management functions of the branch, but were not approved to perform any other senior management function in relation to that branch.

The FCA confirmed that the two new functions would capture "the same scope" of individuals as the Overseas Branch Senior Management function. The FCA's reasoning behind the change was that by splitting the senior management function into two it was made clearer which individuals would be captured in each function given that they provide a more accurate description of the senior managers' actual role. Also, the FCA's policy of limiting the function to branch activities was also preserved. The Executive Director function would be limited to individuals performing the function in relation to the branch.

---

[25] FCA Feedback Statement 15/3: Strengthening accountability in banking: UK branches of foreign banks—Feedback on FCA CP15/10/PRA CP9/15.

Whether or not the Executive Director function was needed in every case was not clear with the FCA stating[26] that:

"while we expect that most branches will have individuals performing this function, it is not required if it does not apply to any individual in the branch, for example in smaller branches."

The Other Local Responsibility function would apply if a person with local responsibility was not approved to any other senior management function. If a branch had allocated local responsibility for all its activities, business areas and management functions between its other senior managers, it would not have to have any individuals approved to the Other Local Responsibility function.

The FCA stated that the concept of local responsibility was similar to "overall responsibility" and that the underlying policy intention of the two concepts was the same: to ensure that responsibility for all the activities, functions and areas of the branch was allocated to individuals of an appropriate level of seniority. However, the local responsibility rules apply differently depending on whether the activity or function was under the management of the branch's governing body. The purpose of this differentiation of approach was to ensure that local responsibility is allocated to the most senior individual responsible for the area. The differentiation is:

- for activities or functions that come under the management of the branch's governing body, the local responsibility rules generally reflect the overall responsibility framework but with local responsibility defined in relation to the branch's governing body rather than the firm's ultimate board. The FCA would expect, in this scenario, the individual with local responsibility to be the most senior individual responsible subject to the branch's governing body; and

---

[26] "Our response", p.11 FCA Feedback Statement 15/3: Strengthening accountability in banking: UK branches of foreign banks—Feedback on FCA CP15/10 PRA CP9/15.

- for activities or functions that do not come under the management of the branch's governing body the FCA would expect the individual with local responsibility to be the most senior individual responsible for managing the activity or function, although 'managing' would not mean having day-to-day management control.

Local responsibility would only apply to executive responsibilities. An individual performing a non-executive role, with oversight of an area, would not have local responsibility for that area. Also, a firm would not have to assign local responsibility to those areas where prescribed responsibilities existed and were already assigned to senior managers. For example, there would be no need for an individual to have local responsibility for internal audit if the branch already had a senior manager approved to the Head of Internal Audit function.

In the Feedback Statement the FCA referred back to its consultation where it said that it would retain the existing principle in the Approved Persons Regime that, if an individual based overseas is responsible for setting strategy for a UK branch, the individual would not generally require approval by the FCA. However, where they were implementing strategy in a UK branch, wherever they were based, they were likely to require approval as a senior manager. The FCA noted that in the feedback to its consultation respondents asked for examples illustrating the difference between implementing and setting strategy. Whilst specific examples were not provided the FCA did further illustrate the steps a senior manager in a branch should take when implementing a strategy set by the wider firm, for example to enter a new business line or introduce a new product. In these situations the FCA felt that the senior manager(s) in the UK branch should have the necessary authority to decide whether to implement the strategy in the UK or to challenge the proposal. The senior manager(s) would be responsible for deciding how to implement the strategy in a way that complied with the UK regulatory system and ensure that relevant controls were in place.

In relation to the Compliance Oversight function (SMF 16) the FCA confirmed that where a branch already had an individual approved under the Compliance Oversight (CF 10) function, that individual would be able to grandfather across to the new senior management function without needing to be re-approved. If a branch was not required to have an individual approved to the CF 10 then this would not change under the Senior Managers' regime although the branch still had to ensure that the prescribed responsibility on compliance was allocated to an appropriate senior manager of the branch.

On the EEA Branch Senior Manager function (which is based on the Significant Management (CF 29) function for EEA UK branches) the FCA provided further guidance. Individuals performing this role would be a "senior manager with significant responsibility for a significant business unit". An individual may have significant responsibility for an area if they were head of a relevant business unit or were a member of a committee that takes decisions relating to it. However, the scope of the function would not be limited to the most senior individual responsible for an area with the FCA giving the example that heads of sub-business units might also require approval if their role and business area met the 'significance' threshold. In relation to "significance" guidance in the FCA Supervision manual[27] provides that the firm should take into account all relevant factors in light of the firm's current circumstances and its plans for the future, including:

- the risk profile of that unit;
- its use or commitment of the firm's capital;
- its contribution to the profit and loss account;
- the number of employees or approved persons working in the business unit;
- the number of customers; and
- any other factor which makes the unit significant to the conduct of the branch's affairs.

---

[27] See SUP 10C.8.7.

Remote booking was also covered in the Feedback Statement[28] with the FCA stating that its guidance reflected the policy position that a UK branch could not avoid allocating responsibility for activities that take place at the branch, just because those activities were part of wider transactions and other elements take place overseas. The FCA stated[29] that where:

> "a senior manager has local responsibility for transactions that are remote booked into the branch, they will need to be satisfied that there are appropriate systems and controls in place to ensure this is controlled effectively, in line with the senior manager conduct rules."

In relation to the certification regime the FCA noted that respondents had expressed concerns about territorial application. For non-EEA UK branches the regime was set to apply to individuals that were either based in the UK or dealing with a client in the UK (the territorial limitation). For EEA UK branches the regime would only apply to individuals based in the UK. In the Feedback Statement the FCA stated that the primary test of whether an individual would be captured by the certification regime would be whether they were performing a significant harm function as defined by the PRA and/or FCA. If they were not they would not be caught by the regime. However, if they were, the territorial limitation provided an additional override. The FCA also provided further guidance which was intended to clarify how it would interpret the phrase "a client in the UK". A client would be an individual who would be present in the UK at the time the contract took place. If the client was a firm, a "client in the UK" would mean an office or branch in the UK at the time the contract took place. A client did not have to be permanently resident or incorporated in the UK to be a "UK client" for the purposes of the certification regime.

---

[28] Paragraph 2.40 FCA Feedback Statement 15/3: Strengthening accountability in banking: UK branches of foreign banks—Feedback on FCA CP15/10 / PRA CP9/15.

[29] "Our response", p.21 FCA Feedback Statement 15/3: Strengthening accountability in banking: UK branches of foreign banks—Feedback on FCA CP15/10 / PRA CP9/15.

When compared to the PRA, the FCA proposed to include a wider population of individuals in its certification regime. The primary test of whether an individual would be captured in the FCA's certification regime would be whether they were performing a significant harm function. This function, comprises the following categories: significant management, material risk takers, functions requiring qualifications and CASS Oversight. In relation to material risk takers the FCA amended the function to make it clear that it applied only to members of staff who were subject to the Remuneration Code. In the Feedback Statement the FCA stated that this amendment also applied to UK branches.

The FCA highlighted in the Feedback Statement the overarching provision in its Handbook text that for EEA UK branches, its certification regime would not apply where this would be inconsistent with a Single Market Directive. In other words, an individual would not be considered to be performing a certified function where this would be a matter reserved to the Home Member State. However, the FCA stated that the UK had an obligation under the Single Market Directives to supervise the conduct of incoming EEA UK branches in the UK and that most certified persons would be performing roles that were relevant to conduct supervision and therefore come within the scope of its responsibilities as a Host Member State supervisor. However, the FCA acknowledged that there might be a "limited number" of individuals, particularly in the material risk taker category, whose role was not related to UK conduct and would not need to certified. For functions requiring qualifications the FCA reminded firms that this significant harm function applied to individuals that were performing any of the roles set out in its Training and Competence Sourcebook.[30] The FCA added[31]:

> "For EEA [UK] branches, this function applies to individuals that would be performing one of these roles as if they

---

[30] TC APP 1.1.1R.
[31] "Our response", p.28 FCA Feedback Statement 15/3: Strengthening accountability in banking: UK branches of foreign banks—Feedback on FCA CP15/10 / PRA CP9/15.

> were performing it from a UK relevant firm or non-EEA
> [UK] branch. This does not switch on the UK qualification
> requirements in TC for individuals performing these roles
> in EEA [UK] branches. EEA [UK] branches are able to
> consider the relevant Home State qualifications as part of
> the assessment of fitness and propriety for individuals
> performing these roles, in line with the relevant single
> market directives, although they may also use the UK
> qualifications if they wish."

The CASS Oversight function was also amended so that it covered not only UK Relevant Authorised Persons and non-EEA UK branches but also EEA UK branches with a top up permission.

As with the regime for UK Relevant Authorised Persons, the FCA's rules would not require incoming branches to carry out criminal records checks for individuals applying for roles that came under its certification regime. However, it was left open to firms to carry out such checks where they were legally allowed to do so. The FCA noted in its Feedback Statement that under its consultation incoming branches were required to request regulatory references from non-regulated firms in the same way as UK Relevant Authorised Persons. The FCA stated that firms would have complied with this reference rule if they took all reasonable steps to obtain all relevant information from previous employers. The FCA recognised that in some situations firms would not receive all the requested information and that they would need to consider, based on the information they had received, whether the information was sufficient to satisfy them that the individual was fit and proper before issuing a certificate.

In relation to conduct rules the FCA's consultation position was that individuals in EEA UK branches would be subject to them but only in relation to matters that were within the UK's scope of responsibilities. This was referred to as the "single market override" and mirrored an existing provision under the APER which applies to approved persons in EEA UK branches. The FCA noted in its Feedback Statement that respondents to its consultation had asked for examples of matters that would be outside the UK's scope of responsibilities. However, examples were not forthcoming with the FCA stating[32]:

> "The effect of the single market override is that where a particular conduct rule covers a matter reserved to the Home Member State, the conduct rules and the associated requirements to report breaches do not apply. As each case is unique, it is not possible to give clear universal examples of circumstances that would be reserved to the home member state. Whether a conduct rule breach would be a matter reserved to the Home Member State will depend on the particular circumstances of the breach and will have to be determined by firms on a case-by-case basis."

In addition, the FCA noted in its feedback that for non-EEA UK branches the conduct rules would apply to staff that were based in the UK or dealing with a UK client. The FCA rejected feedback arguing that the scope of its conduct rules for non-EEA UK branches should be limited to individuals that were based in the UK, in line with the regime for EEA UK branches.[33]

In relation to reporting conduct rule breaches for senior managers the FCA considered it important that it be notified promptly and considered that seven calendar days was an appropriate timeframe for both UK relevant firms and incoming branches.[34]

---

[32] Paragraph 4.3 FCA Feedback Statement 15/3: Strengthening accountability in banking: UK branches of foreign banks—Feedback on FCA CP15/10 / PRA CP9/15.

[33] But see later section headed FCA policy statement and final rules.

[34] But note the Government's proposals to remove the obligation to report breaches of rules of conduct to the regulators in HM Treasury paper Senior Managers' and Certification Regime: extension to all FSMA authorised persons (October 2015) and the amendments proposed in the Bank of England and Financial Services Bill.

6.8 The HM Treasury Order finalised

The Financial Services and Markets Act 2000 (Relevant Authorised Persons) Order 2015[35] was made on 4 November 2015 and came into force on 9 November 2015. The non-UK institutions that would become Relevant Authorised Persons were the same as when the Order was in draft form. Article 3 of the Order requires HM Treasury to review article 2 covering the categories of non-UK institution every five years and to publish a report, setting out its conclusions, following each review.

6.9 Final rules

6.9.1 PRA Policy Statement and final rules

On 16 December 2015, the PRA published a policy statement[36] that contained final rules, first published in August 2015 as near-final rules, to implement the Senior Managers' and certification regimes in UK branches of non-EEA banks and non-EEA PRA-designated investment firms.

The PRA stated[37] that the final rules included in the policy statement were almost identical to the near-final rules that were published in August 2015. Some small corrective changes to certain rules had been made, in particular the grandfathering table was updated (reproduced later in this chapter).

At the same time as publishing the policy statement the PRA produced an updated version of Supervisory Statement

---

[35] SI 2015/1865.
[36] PRA Policy Statement 29/15: Strengthening individual accountability in banking: UK branches of non-EEA banks.
[37] Paragraph 1.5. of PRA Policy Statement 29/15: Strengthening individual accountability in banking: UK branches of non-EEA banks.

28/15[38] (SS28/15) which included additional paragraphs set-ting out the PRA's expectations of how UK branches of foreign banks should comply with certain aspects of the individual accountability regime.

The additional paragraphs in SS28/15 were found in paras 2.17 to 2.19 (scope for incoming third country branches) and 2.28 (prescribed responsibilities for incoming third-country branches). The points raised in paras 2.17 to 2.19 of SS28/15 were as follows:

- all non-EEA UK branches must have at least one indi-vidual pre-approved as a Head of Overseas Branch;
- the Head of Overseas Branch should have the highest degree of individual decision making authority in the branch over activities and areas subject to UK regulation;
- all non-EEA UK branches can elect to have more than one individual approved as a Head of Overseas Branch. Where this is the case, all such individuals will be accountable for all the responsibilities conferred by that function;
- all non-EEA UK branches should have additional senior management functions pre-approved by the PRA where: (i) the non-EEA UK branch has individuals performing the Chief Finance, Chief Risk and Head of Internal Audit senior management functions[39]; and (ii) an individual based in a parent or group entity has direct management and/or decision-making responsibility over an incoming non-EEA UK branch's UK regulated activities and has not delegated it to the Head of Overseas Branch or another senior manager based in the branch, he or she may require pre-approval as a Group Entity Senior Manager of that branch[40]; and

---

[38] PRA Supervisory Statement 28/15: Strengthening individual accountability in banking (updated) (December 2015).
[39] The PRA stated that this includes individuals performing these senior manage-ment functions across an overseas-headquartered banking group's UK legal entities, such as a UK Chief Risk Officer with responsibility for risk management across the group's UK subsidiaries as well as the incoming non-EEA UK branch.
[40] The PRA gives the example which might be a head of Europe, Middle East and Africa who is formally based in or employed in one of the group's UK subsidiaries but makes decisions affecting how the branch carries out its UK

351

- non-executive directors were outside the scope of the Senior Managers' regime for non-EEA UK branches but that there may be situations where individuals employed by the non-EEA UK branch's parent or group company sit on the branch's local management committee (or equivalent) and were correspondingly, previously pre-approved as a Director (CF 1) or Non-Executive Directive (CF 2) of a branch under the Approved Persons' Regime. These persons are likely to be performing the Group Entity Senior Manager function in respect of the branch and would require pre-approval or grandfathering under the new regime.

Paragraph 2.28 of SS28/15 noted that there was a customised set of PRA and FCA prescribed responsibilities for non-EEA UK branches set out in its Rulebook under Allocation of Responsibilities 6. These prescribed responsibilities could be allocated to any senior manager in the UK branch except to the FCA's Other Local Responsibility function.

6.9.2 FCA policy statement and final rules

On 16 December 2015, the FCA also published a policy statement[41] that contained final rules, first published in its Feedback Statement in August 2015 as near-final rules, to implement the Senior Managers', certification regimes and conduct rules in UK branches of foreign banks.

The FCA reported in the policy statement that respondents had not raised any new issues regarding the Senior Managers' regime for incoming branches and that as a result it had finalised the near final Senior Managers' rules with only minor, technical amendments that were designed to improve clarity.

---

regulated activities. The PRA noted that in practice the Group Entity Senior Manager of an incoming non-EEA UK branch will be based in the UK but they may also be based overseas.

[41] FCA Policy Statement 15/30: Strengthening accountability in banking: UK branches of foreign banks (final rules).

352

The FCA also reported that no feedback had been received on the territorial scope of the certification regime and conduct rules for EEA UK branches. However, questions had been raised regarding the potentially wide territorial scope of these regimes for non-EEA UK branches.

In response the FCA implemented a temporary measure[42] whereby the rules for non-EEA UK branches were amended so that the test of "dealing with a UK client" was removed. The test of "based in the UK" was retained. By doing so the FCA aligned the requirements for non-EEA UK branches to EEA UK branches. The scope of its rules applying to non-EEA UK branches were narrowed by excluding those individuals who were working in the overseas offices of firms with UK branches. However, individuals performing activities from the UK branch would remain within the regimes. As a result of the changes the FCA removed the guidance on "dealing with a UK client" (contained in the near-final rules) on the basis that it was no longer relevant.

Another point that the FCA raised[43] related to its earlier Feedback Statement where it explained that some firms undertaking deposit-taking under a cross-border services passport would be caught by the definition of "Relevant Authorised Person". This would occur if the firm also undertook activities from a UK branch under an establishment passport (irrespective of whether those activities involve deposit taking or PRA regulated activity). Some respondents queried whether the FCA's rules should apply to such firms on the basis that they would only be caught as a result of the non-deposit taking activities.

---

[42] On p.9 of FCA Policy Statement 15/30: Strengthening accountability in banking: UK branches of foreign banks (final rules) the FCA states: "We consider this a pragmatic solution in the short term that allows incoming branches to finalise their plans for commencement in March 2016. However, we plan to revisit territoriality after commencement to ensure that the regime adequately captures those individuals who could affect the FCA's objectives (including whether it is necessary to extend the branches' certification rules to include some individuals based outside the UK)."

[43] See para.2.8 of FCA Policy Statement 15/30: Strengthening accountability in banking: UK branches of foreign banks (final rules).

In response the FCA took a hard line stating that the legislation did not stipulate that the firm must carry out deposit taking / dealing from the branch (i.e. there is no requirement that the passport (for deposit taking / dealing) should be an establishment passport). It stated that[44] an EEA firm which undertakes deposit taking under a services passport and undertakes other (non-deposit taking / dealing) activities from its UK branch would still be caught by the definition of Relevant Authorised Person and come within its regime. Such firms would not, however, be subject to the PRA Senior Managers' and certification regimes as they did not extend to EEA UK branches.

In chapter 3 of its policy statement the FCA explained that it had made certain minor amendments to its final rules. These were technical changes to clarify the definition of the material risk taker significant harm function for incoming branches, and minor changes to certain forms. In particular the FCA referred back to its earlier Feedback Statement where it explained that in its final rules the definition of the material risk taker significant harm function had been amended to make clear that it only applied to members of staff who are subject to the FCA dual-regulated Remuneration Code (SYSC 19D). The technical amendment the FCA made clarified that this amended description applied to both EEA UK branches and non-EEA UK branches.

The FCA also referred to an earlier consultation paper published in July 2015[45] in which it proposed removing the territorial limitation (based in the UK or dealing with a UK client) for material risk takers so that once an individual was identified as such by an incoming branch or UK Relevant Authorised Person they would be covered by the certification regime irrespective of their activities or geographical location. However, the regulator noted that with the changes to its final rules for non-EEA UK branches removing the "dealing with a

---

[44] See "Our response" in para.2.8 of FCA Policy Statement 15/30: Strengthening accountability in banking: UK branches of foreign banks (final rules).
[45] FCA Consultation Paper 15/22: Strengthening accountability in banking: Final rules (including feedback on CP14/31 and CP15/5) and consultation on extending the Certification Regime to wholesale market activities.

UK client" part of the territorial test it had created a disconnect between the two sets of rules. The FCA proposed to address the disconnect in the resulting policy statement to the consultation paper that would be published in early 2016.

6.10   February FCA policy statement

On 4 February 2016, the FCA published a further policy statement[46] that set out its final rules concerning the extension of the certification regime to wholesale market activities[47] for both UK Relevant Authorised Persons and UK branches of overseas firms (which the FCA defined as 'Foreign Branches'). The policy statement also set out final FCA rules for the territorial scope of the certification regime and conduct rules for material risk takers.

In the policy statement the FCA reported[48] that it had received substantial feedback from firms to its July 2015 consultation paper[49] particularly in relation to the territorial scope of its rules in respect of both UK Relevant Authorised Persons and UK branches of overseas firms.

The FCA stated that the territorial scope of its rules as regards UK branches of overseas firms had since been settled by its December 2015 policy statement. It stated that[50]:

---

[46] Policy Statement 16/3: Strengthening accountability in banking: Feedback on CP15/22 (July 2015) and CP15/31 (October 2015); rules on extending the certification regime to wholesale market activities and interim rules on referencing.

[47] See Ch.4 for further discussion of the certification regime.

[48] See para.1.16 of Policy Statement 16/3: Strengthening accountability in banking: Feedback on CP15/22 (July 2015) and CP15/31 (October 2015); rules on extending the certification regime to wholesale market activities and interim rules on referencing.

[49] Consultation Paper 15/22: Strengthening accountability in banking: final rules (including feedback on CP14/31 and CP15/5) and consultation on extending the certification regime to wholesale market activities.

[50] Paragraph 1.16 of Policy Statement 16/3: Strengthening accountability in banking: Feedback on CP15/22 (July 2015) and CP15/31 (October 2015); rules on extending the certification regime to wholesale market activities and interim rules on referencing.

"We received substantial feedback from firms in response to CP15/22, both formally and through round table meetings with firms and trade bodies. In particular, firms commented on the territorial scope of our rules, both in respect of UK RAPs and Foreign Branches. As mentioned previously, the latter has been dealt with in PS15/30, Strengthening accountability in banking: UK branches of foreign banks (final rules), where we introduced our final rules for the regime as it applies to branches."

In relation to the proposal to remove the territorial limitation for material risk takers in the application of the certification regime and the conduct rules the FCA noted that its December 2015 policy statement had changed the scope of the requirements so that only staff in the UK would be captured. To continue with its July 2015 proposal to remove the territorial limitation for material risk takers in Foreign Branches would be inconsistent with this approach. Therefore the FCA opted to implement its proposal to remove the territorial limitation for UK Relevant Authorised Persons only.

The FCA stated[51]:

"We consulted on removing the territorial limitation for material risk takers in the application of the certification regime and the conduct rules. This proposal was to ensure that the regime covers individuals who could affect the FCA's objectives, wherever they are geographically based. It also sought to align the scope of the FCA's rules on material risk takers with the PRA's. The majority of the feedback supported this policy, citing the importance of ensuring consistency between the FCA's approach and the PRA's approach. However, given the feedback on territorial scope of Foreign Branches and the final rules in PS15/30, we have removed the territorial limitation for UK RAPs only. Practically, this means that if a UK RAP

---

[51] Paragraph 1.20 of Policy Statement 16/3: Strengthening accountability in banking: Feedback on CP15/22 (July 2015) and CP15/31 (October 2015); rules on extending the certification regime to wholesale market activities and interim rules on referencing.

identifies a staff member as a material risk taker, then they are subject to the certification regime irrespective of geographical location or interactions with clients."

6.11 Responsibilities maps

Both the PRA and FCA rules provide that a firm must have a comprehensive and up-to-date document that describes the management and governance arrangements of the UK branch (a management responsibilities map). Further details as to the content of this document can be found in FCA rules[52] and the Allocation of Responsibilities part of the PRA Rulebook concerning Individual Accountability.[53]

In its Feedback Statement the FCA decided that it would provide separate and distinct Statement of Responsibilities forms for non-EEA UK and EEA UK branches.

6.12 SYSC attestation

It might be remembered that when the PRA published its final approach to supervising international banks in 2014[54] it set out a new requirement for a senior individual in a non-EEA UK branch to annually attest compliance with the Senior Management Arrangements, Systems and Controls sourcebook (SYSC) of the PRA Handbook. The requirement was further clarified in a PRA Supervisory Statement[55] which stated that the PRA would "review if there is a continued need for this attestation once it is clear if, and how the senior managers' regime will apply to non-EEA branches." In the consultation paper that

---

[52] See 4.5 and 4.6 of the Senior Management Arrangements, Systems and Controls sourcebook.
[53] See Records 7.2. Allocation of Responsibilities, PRA Rulebook.
[54] Policy Statement 8/14: Supervising international banks: the PRA's approach to branch supervision.
[55] Supervisory Statement 10/14: Supervising international banks: the PRA's approach to branch supervision.

was published in March 2015[56] it appeared that the attestation was to remain as a proposed PRA prescribed responsibility was stated to be[57]:

> "Responsibility for the production and integrity of the branch's financial information and its regulatory reporting in respect of its regulated activities, including the annual attestation of compliance to the PRA of the branch's compliance with its obligations under SYSC."

However, the position changed with the publication of the PRA's August 2015 policy statement containing near final rules.[58] In response to feedback the PRA decided that it would not require all non-EEA UK branches to submit the SYSC attestation annually as a matter of course. The reason for this was that the PRA accepted the argument that respondents put forward that the inclusion of prescribed responsibilities relating to regulatory compliance, risk management and systems and controls would render the need for an annual attestation exercise unnecessary. However, the PRA added that it may ask individual firms or senior managers or "any other appropriate individual" to attest compliance with specific regulatory requirements on an ad hoc basis if it considered that doing so would advance its objectives.

6.13   The offence of causing an institution to fail

The criminal offence in s.36 of the Financial Services (Banking Reform) Act 2013 relating to a decision causing a financial institution to fail will not apply to individuals in UK branches of overseas firms. This offence only applies to senior managers of UK Relevant Authorised Persons.

---

[56] Consultation Paper FCA 15/10 PRA 9/15: Strengthening accountability in banking: UK branches of foreign banks.
[57] See item 11 at para.2.24 of Consultation Paper FCA 15/10 PRA 9/15: Strengthening accountability in banking: UK branches of foreign banks.
[58] Policy Statement 20/15: Strengthening individual accountability in banking: UK branches of non-EEA banks.

6.14   Timing

The timing of the individual accountability regime as it applies
to UK branches is the same as that for UK Relevant Authorised
Persons. The regime starts on 7 March 2016 and notification to
the regulators of the approved persons who will be grandfathered in as senior managers must occur by 8 February 2016.
All relevant authorised persons (including non-EEA UK
branches) have until 7 March 2017 to issue certificates
confirming that each employee performing a certification
function is fit and proper to do so.

6.15   At a glance tables

*The senior management functions in UK branches of EEA and
non-EEA banks*

	PRA Senior Management functions	**FCA Senior Management functions**
Non-EEA branches	Chief Finance function (if applicable) (SMF 2)	Executive Director function (SMF 3)
	Chief Risk function (if applicable) (SMF 4)	Compliance Oversight function (SMF 16)
	Head of Internal Audit function (if applicable) (SMF 5)	Money Laundering Reporting function (SMF 17)
	Group Entity Senior Manager function (if applicable) (SMF 7)	Other Local Responsibility function (SMF 22)
	Head of Overseas Branch function (SMF 19)	
EEA branches		Money Laundering Reporting function (SMF 17)

	PRA Senior Management functions	FCA Senior Management functions
		EEA Branch Senior Manager function (SMF 21)

Prescribed responsibilities

Prescribed responsibility	PRA/FCA
Responsibility for the branch's performance of its obligations under the senior management regime	PRA/FCA
Responsibility for the branch's performance of its obligations under the employee certification regime	PRA/FCA
Responsibility for compliance with the requirements of the regulatory system about the management responsibilities map	PRA/FCA
Responsibility for management of the UK branch's risk management processes in the UK	PRA/FCA
Responsibility for the branch's compliance with the UK regulatory regime applicable to the branch	PRA/FCA
Responsibility for the escalation of correspondence from the PRA, FCA and other regulators in respect of the branch to the governing body and/or the management body of the firm, or, where appropriate, of the parent undertaking or holding company of the firm's group	PRA/FCA
Local responsibility for the branch's policies and procedures for countering the risk that the branch might be used to further financial crime	FCA
Local responsibility for the branch's compliance with CASS	FCA
Responsibility for management of the branch's systems and controls in the UK	PRA

Prescribed responsibility	PRA/FCA
Responsibility for the allocation of all UK branch prescribed responsibilities	PRA
Responsibility for the management of the branch's liquidity or, where a liquidity waiver is in place, the submission of information to the PRA on the firm's liquidity position	PRA
Responsibility for the production and integrity of the branch's financial information and its regulatory reporting in respect of its regulated activities	PRA

Grandfathering—UK branches of non-EEA banks

Significant influence function	PRA Senior Management Function(s)	FCA Senior Management Function(s)
Director function (CF 1)	Chief Finance function (SMF 2) Chief Risk function (SMF 4) Head of Internal Audit (SMF 5) Group Entity Senior Manager (SMF 7) Head of Overseas Branch (SMF 19)	Executive director function (SMF 3)
Non-executive director (CF 2)	Group Entity Senior Manager (SMF 7)	-
Chief executive (CF 3)	Head of Overseas Branch (SMF 19)	-
Systems and Controls (CF 28)	Chief finance function (SMF 2) Chief Risk function (SMF 4) Head of Internal Audit (SMF 5) Group Entity Senior Manager (SMF 7)	Other local responsibility function (SMF 22)

361

Significant influence function	PRA Senior Management Function(s)	FCA Senior Management Function(s)
Significant management function (CF 29) *All non-EEA branches to which the function in the first column applies*	Head of Overseas Branch (SMF 19) Group Entity Senior Manager (SMF 7)	Other local responsibility function (SMF 22)
Compliance oversight function (CF 10)	-	Compliance oversight function (SMF 16)
CASS operational oversight function (CF 10A)	-	Other local responsibility function (SMF 22)
Money laundering reporting function (CF 11)	-	Money laundering reporting function (SMF 17)

Grandfathering—UK branches of EEA banks

Significant influence function	PRA Senior Management Function(s)	FCA Senior Management Function(s)
The significant management function (CF 29)	-	EEA Branch Senior Manager function (SMF 21)
Money laundering reporting function (CF 11)	-	Money laundering reporting function (SMF 17)

Proposed and final Prescribed Responsibilities for non-EEA branches

Proposed Prescribed Responsibilities for non-EEA branches	Final Prescribed Responsibilities for non-EEA branches
Combined PRA/FCA Prescribed Responsibilities	Combined PRA/FCA Prescribed Responsibilities
1. Responsibility for the branch's performance of its obligations under the Senior Managers Regime, including implementation and oversight.	1. Responsibility for the branch's performance of its obligations under the Senior Managers Regime, including implementation and oversight.
2. Responsibility for the branch's performance of its obligations under the certification rules.	2. Responsibility for the branch's performance of its obligations under the employee certification regime ~~rules~~.
3. Responsibility for compliance with the branch's obligations in relation to its management responsibilities map.	3 Responsibility for compliance with the ~~branch's~~ requirements of the regulatory system about the ~~obligations in relation to its~~ management responsibilities map.
4. Management of the branch's risk management processes in the UK.	4. Responsibility for management of the branch's risk management processes in the UK
5. Responsibility for the branch's compliance with the UK regulatory regime applicable to the branch.	5. Responsibility for the branch's compliance with the UK regulatory regime applicable to the branch.
6. Responsibility for the escalation of Correspondence from the PRA, FCA and other regulators in respect of the branch to the governing body and/or the management body of the firm or, where appropriate, of the parent undertaking or holding company of the firm's group.	6. Responsibility for the escalation of correspondence from the PRA, FCA and other regulators in respect of the branch to the governing body and/or the management body of the firm or, where appropriate, of the parent undertaking or holding company of the firm's group.
7. Responsibility for the maintenance of the Integrity, independence and effectiveness of the branch's policies and procedures on whistleblowing and for ensuring staff who raise concerns are protected from detrimental treatment.	7. ~~Responsibility for the maintenance of the integrity, independence and effectiveness of the branch's policies and procedures on whistleblowing and for ensuring staff who raise concerns are protected from detrimental treatment.~~

Proposed and final Prescribed Responsibilities for non-EEA branches	
Proposed Prescribed Responsibilities for non-EEA branches	Final Prescribed Responsibilities for non-EEA branches
PRA-specific Prescribed Responsibilities	PRA-specific Prescribed Responsibilities
8. Responsibility for management of the branch's systems and controls in the UK.	8. Responsibility for management of the branch's systems and controls in the UK.
9. Responsibility for the allocation of all UK branch prescribed responsibilities.	9. Responsibility for the allocation of all UK branch Prescribed Responsibilities.
10. Responsibility for management of the branch's liquidity or, where a liquidity waiver is in place, the submission of information to the PRA on the firm's liquidity position.	10. Responsibility for management of the branch's liquidity or, where a liquidity waiver is in place, the submission of information to the PRA on the firm's liquidity position.
11. Responsibility for the production and integrity of the branch's financial information and its regulatory reporting in respect of its regulated activities, including the annual attestation of compliance to the PRA of the branch's compliance with its obligations under SYSC.	11. Responsibility for the production and integrity of the branch's financial information and its regulatory reporting in respect of its regulated activities, ~~including the annual attestation of compliance to the PRA of the branch's compliance with its obligations under SYSC.~~
FCA-specific Prescribed Responsibilities	FCA-specific Prescribed Responsibilities
12. Responsibility for the branch's policies and procedures for countering the risk that the branch might be used to further financial crime.	12. Local responsibility for the branch's policies and procedures for countering the risk that the branch might be used to further financial crime.
13. Responsibility for the branch's policies and procedures for compliance with CASS.	13. Local responsibility for the branch's policies and ~~procedures for~~ compliance with CASS.

Chapter 7

Ring-fencing

Alan Bainbridge
Partner
Norton Rose Fulbright

Cynthia Cheng
Associate
Norton Rose Fulbright

7.1 Introduction

7.1.1 Background to ring-fencing

Ring-fencing certain core banking activities is one of the principal reforms introduced by the Financial Services (Banking Reform) Act 2013 (the 2013 Act) to ensure the continuity of retail banking services in the UK at times of market turbulence without any bank having recourse to its depositors or to the taxpayer. In conjunction with the Senior Managers' Regime (SMR), ring-fencing is intended to improve public confidence both in the resilience and resolvability of the UK banking system and in the regulatory response to irregular behaviour of both institutions and individuals.

Ring-fencing core services is intended to ensure that: (i) a ring-fenced body (RFB) can continue to provide those services to retail customers by separating the RFB's retail business from any of the firm's wholesale and investment activities in order to limit the RFB's exposure to certain risks; and (ii) RFBs, and groups containing RFBs, can be resolved in the event of crisis with minimal disruption to the provision of core services to retail customers.

7.1.2 Overview of ring-fencing legislation

The Independent Commission on Banking (ICB) was set up in 2010 in the wake of the financial crisis to examine structural and related non-structural reforms to the UK banking sector. The ICB issued its final report in September 2011 proposing, amongst other measures, the ring-fencing of vital banking services from risks elsewhere in the financial system. In June 2012, the Government published a White Paper: "Banking reform: delivering stability and supporting a sustainable economy". This White Paper confirmed that the Government was committed to implementing the ICB's recommendations including those relating to ring-fencing.

In late July 2012, public confidence in the UK banking system was further shaken following revelations about serious irregularities by certain banking organisations in connection with the London Interbank Offered Rate and related indexes. The Parliamentary Commission on Banking Standards (PCBS) was established to look at banking in its broadest economic, regulatory, cultural and social context. The PCBS scrutinised the draft Banking Reform Bill (which would become the 2013 Act) and made additional recommendations; amongst them, the need for a senior managers' regime which would replace the approved persons regime in the banking sector and the creation of a new criminal offence of reckless misconduct in the management of a bank.

The 2013 Act is primarily an enabling Act that provides HM Treasury with the requisite powers to implement the policy underlying it through secondary legislation and provides the FCA and PRA (as the "appropriate regulators" under the 2013 Act) with the power to issue "ring-fencing rules". To date, the following comprise the legislation amended/enacted in relation to ring-fencing:

- Financial Services and Markets Act 2000 (as amended by the 2013 Act) (FSMA);

- Financial Services and Markets Act 2000 (Ring-fenced Bodies and Core Activities) Order 2014 (the Core Activities Order);
- Financial Services and Markets Act 2000 (Excluded Activities and Prohibitions) Order 2014 (the Excluded Activities Order);
- Banking Reform (Loss Absorbency Requirements) Order, in draft form at the time of publication (the Draft Loss Absorbency Order); and
- Financial Services and Markets Act 2000 (Pensions Regulations) Order 2015 (the Pensions Regulations).

7.1.3 *Appropriate regulator rules and guidance*

The 2013 Act requires the appropriate regulator to make provision for realising the following group ring-fencing purposes:

- ensuring as far as reasonably practicable that the carrying on of core activities by an RFB is not adversely affected by the acts or omissions of other members of its group;
- ensuring as far as reasonably practicable that in carrying on its business an RFB:
  — is able to take decisions independently of other members of its group; and
  — does not depend on resources which are provided by a member of its group and which would cease to be available to the RFB in the event of the insolvency of the other member; and
- ensuring as far as reasonably practicable that the RFB would be able to continue to carry on core activities in the event of the insolvency of one or more members of its group.[1]

FSMA also requires the appropriate regulator to make rules with respect to board membership, risk, remuneration policy, human resources policy, disclosure by an RFB, restricting an RFB from entering into a contract with group members other

---

[1] Section 142H of FSMA.

than on arm's length terms, restricting an RFB from paying dividends and making other payments to group members and any other rules the appropriate regulator considers necessary.

Rules drafted to date in relation to ring-fencing are set out in the CRR firms and non-authorised persons: Ring-Fenced Bodies Instrument, which was in near-final form at the time of publication.[2] In addition to the requirements set out in their regulatory rules, the PRA and FCA have issued draft supervisory statements and other guidance, including those specifically relating to ring-fencing.[3] Such supervisory statements and guidance do not have the force of law, but do, nevertheless, set out the regulators' expectations as to how a firm should comply with its rules.

It is proposed that an RFB must be able to demonstrate to the PRA its compliance with all ring-fencing obligations,[4] including those which come directly from legislation. It is thought that this is consistent with the PRA's duty to report to Parliament on compliance with all aspects of ring-fencing. The PRA is consulting on the breadth of compliance which an RFB must be able to demonstrate to the PRA.

7.1.4 Senior Managers' Regime

The PRA and FCA's approach to allocation of senior managers' responsibilities has been to set out some specific requirements that must be allocated among senior managers (Prescribed Responsibilities) whilst also requiring pre-approval of any other individuals who have overall responsibility for an area of the firm's business. The PRA has proposed that appropriate senior managers of RFBs have a Prescribed Responsibility "for

---

[2] Near final form attached to Consultation Paper 37/15: The implementation of ring-fencing: prudential requirements, intragroup arrangements and use of financial market infrastructures (CP37/15).

[3] Near final form attached to CP37/15.

[4] A "ring-fencing obligation" is any obligation, prohibition or other requirement imposed on a ring-fenced body by or under FSMA, by virtue of it being a ring-fenced body, including any statutory instrument made under FSMA and any ring-fencing rule, but not including any rule made by the FCA (Ch.1 of the Allocation of Responsibilities Part of the PRA Rulebook for CRR Firms).

ensuring that those aspects of the ring-fenced body's affairs for which a person is responsible for managing are in compliance with any ring-fencing obligation".[5]

In the context of which senior managers should be assigned the Prescribed Responsibility for ring-fencing it is worth noting para.2.27 of Supervisory Statement 28/15[6]:

"The PRA expects ring-fenced banks (RFBs) to allocate the responsibility for ensuring that the areas of the firm which they are responsible for managing comply with the ring-fencing obligations, to the majority, if not all, of their SMFs (except the FCA's SMF 18[7]), including those NEDs in scope of the SMR. This is an exception to the expectation that Prescribed Responsibilities should be allocated only to the individual SMFs they are most closely linked to. The reason for the exception is to incentivise key decision-makers in RFBs to ensure compliance with the ring-fencing obligations throughout the key areas of the firm."

On shared Prescribed Responsibilities, paras 2.40 and 2.41 of Supervisory Statement 28/15 state:

"PRA Prescribed Responsibilities can be allocated to more than one senior manager. However, where a firm allocates a PRA Prescribed Responsibility to more than one senior manager, each of those individuals will be deemed fully

---

[5] Rule 4.2(4) of the Allocation of Responsibilities Part of the PRA Rulebook for CRR Firms.
[6] Supervisory Statement 28/15: Strengthening individual accountability in banking (SS28/15), as updated on 6 January 2016. It may also worth noting para.3.40 of PRA Consultation Paper 19/14: The implementation of ring-fencing: consultation on legal structure, governance and the continuity of services and facilities. It stated: The PRA proposes to require this ring-fencing responsibility to be allocated to any Senior Managers in an RFB including, where relevant, Group Entity Senior Managers that are responsible for managing any area of the RFB's business that is subject to a ring-fencing requirement. Given that the ring-fencing requirements touch on many aspects of an RFB's business and governance, the PRA expects this responsibility to be allocated to all the senior managers on the board of an RFB and to a majority, if not all, of the RFB's other senior managers. This expectation will be set out in the supervisory statement that will accompany the SMR."
[7] FCA SMF 18—Other Overall Responsibility.

accountable for that responsibility. PRA Prescribed Responsibilities can therefore be shared but not split among two or more SMFs.

Where a PRA Prescribed Responsibility is shared among more than one senior manager, the PRA expects the responsibility to be recorded identically in each of the senior manager's statements of responsibilities. However, firms can utilise the free text section in the statements of responsibilities to provide additional details on how a given shared Prescribed Responsibility applies to the different individuals sharing it in practice."

The first question that the RFB will ask is to which senior managers it needs to assign the Prescribed Responsibility for ring-fencing. On this point perhaps the safest course of action would be to assign it to all individuals carrying on a senior management function[8] but then make reference in the free text section in each of their statement of responsibilities as to how the responsibility will be shared in practice. However, the requirement to assign the Prescribed Responsibility to all senior managers[9] is not absolute in the sense that the Supervisory Statement refers to "the majority, if not all". What constitutes "the majority" will be a question that an RFB and their advisers will have to consider in light of the roles each senior manager will have in the ring-fenced bank. But caution will need to be exercised if this route is taken as it is submitted that by using this wording ("the majority, if not all") the regulator seems to be pushing hard that the "majority" will be the exception rather than the norm. However, where the majority route is taken then it is further submitted that those senior managers within scope will be at least those who sit on the board. The position becomes less clear when it comes to senior managers who may not be on the board (say, Compliance Oversight SMF16).[10]

---

[8] Except for FCA SMF 18.
[9] Except for FCA SMF 18.
[10] FCA SMF 18 are also excluded.

In relation to those NEDs that are not carrying on a senior management function, para.2.27 of Supervisory Statement 28/15 confirms that the Prescribed Responsibility for ring-fencing should not be assigned to them. However, for these individuals it might be worth bearing in mind para.2.38 of Supervisory Statement 28/15 which states:

"Moreover, regardless of the fact that some NEDs are subject to limited individual responsibilities and potential accountability under the SMR, the PRA considers it vital that boards as a whole understand the Threshold Conditions, Fundamental Rules and more detailed underlying rules in the PRA Rulebook. Boards should establish within their firms a culture that supports adherence to the spirit and letter of these requirements."

In light of the Prescribed Responsibility, the next few sections of this chapter provide an overview of the key components of ring-fencing obligations (including a summary of the permitted and excluded activities of the ring-fence and governance requirements of the RFB) and the potential effects of non-compliance (such as group restructuring powers available to the regulators) based on FSMA, its secondary legislation and relevant draft PRA rules published to date.

7.2 The ring-fence: Core activities, excluded activities and prohibitions

7.2.1 What is the nature of the ring-fence?

The principle is to separate the wholesale and investment businesses of a bank from its retail activities to prevent the former having a negative impact on the financial condition of the latter. This objective is defined in the 2013 Act by reference to "core activities": retail activities which may only be carried on by RFBs, themselves prohibited from engaging in what are perceived to be the riskier elements of a banking business.

FSMA (when read with the accompanying secondary legislation) operates by splitting banking business into four
different categories:

- "core activities" and "core services" (which only an RFB
  may carry on);
- "excluded activities" and "prohibitions" (which an RFB
  may not carry on and which, therefore, can only be
  provided by a bank which is not subject to the ring-fencing
  obligations (a Non-RFB));
- exceptions and/or exclusions to the excluded activities
  and prohibitions (which may be carried on by an RFB or a
  Non-RFB); and
- activities which do not fall into any of the above categories
  (such as corporate lending) which may be carried on by
  RFBs or Non-RFBs.

7.2.2 *Which institutions are within the scope of the Act?*

7.2.2.1 *Definition of an RFB*

Section 4 of the 2013 Act provides that an RFB is:

- a "UK institution" (i.e. a body incorporated in the UK);
  and
- carrying on one or more core activities (see para.2.3 below)
  in relation to which it has permission granted by the FCA
  or PRA under Pt 4A of FSMA.

Consequently, the ring-fencing provisions of FSMA do not
apply to branches of foreign banks located in the UK. It is
worth noting that this is in contrast to the SMR and the
accompanying certification regime which will be extended to
apply to branches of foreign institutions located in the UK. This
is discussed further in Ch.6.

A building society (within the meaning of the Building
Societies Act 1986) is expressly excluded from the requirement
to ring-fence although the 2013 Act provides that HM Treasury
may amend building society legislation to apply ring-fencing

to building societies.[11] In addition, HM Treasury may by order and having regard to the continuity of the provision of banking services and improving conditions for new entrants, exempt any UK institution of a particular class from the requirement to ring-fence.

The Core Activities Order sets out the classes of UK institutions which HM Treasury has exempted from the ring-fenced requirements of the 2013 Act. The following are exempt:

- insurance firms regulated under Pt 4A of FSMA to carry out the regulated activities or effecting or carrying out contracts of insurance as principal;
- a registered society (as defined in s.1 of the Co-operative and Community Benefit Societies Act 2014), a Northern Ireland industrial and provident society or a Northern Ireland credit union;
- UK deposit-takers that comply with the relevant event condition; and
- UK deposit-takers that comply with the core deposit level condition.[12]

7.2.2.2 *The relevant event condition*

The relevant event condition exempts certain UK deposit-takers who would only fall under the ring-fencing regime as a consequence of the exercise of powers under the Banking Act 2009. A "relevant event" is:

- as a result of a transfer effected by an instrument or order made under or in accordance with any provision of the Banking Act 2009, the UK deposit-taker or a member of its group:
  — acquires property, rights or liabilities from another institution; or
  — acquires securities issued by another institution;

---

[11] Sections 142A of FSMA and s.7 of the 2013 Act.
[12] Article 11 of the Core Activities Order.

- any other power conferred by or as a result of Pt 1 of the Banking Act 2009 is exercised in relation to the UK deposit-taker.[13]

For the "relevant event condition" to be satisfied, both of the following must apply:

- the UK deposit-taker would not be an RFB but for the occurrence of the relevant event; and
- not more than four years have passed since the date of that relevant event.[14]

7.2.2.3 The core deposit level condition

The core deposit level condition is intended to prevent the costs of ring-fencing operating as a barrier to new entrants.[15] The core deposit level condition requires that in order to be exempt, the following conditions must be satisfied at any particular time:

- in the case of a UK deposit-taker which is not a member of a group, its average core deposit total is equal to or less than £25 billion; and
- in the case of a UK deposit-taker which is a member of a group, the sum of the average core deposit totals for each member of the group that is a relevant group member is equal to or less than £25 billion.

The core deposit level is averaged over a three-year period.

7.2.3 Core services and core activities

The 2013 Act amends FSMA so as to create new objectives of both the PRA and the FCA.[16] Each of the PRA and FCA have additional objectives which include ensuring the continuity of

---

[13] Article 11(2) and (3) of the Core Activities Order.
[14] Article 11(2) and (3) of the Core Activities Order.
[15] Article 12 of the Core Activities Order.
[16] Sections 1 to 3 of the 2013 Act.

the provision of "core services" in the UK; effectively the provision of retail banking services. "Core services" are defined as:

- facilities for accepting of deposits or other payments into an account which is provided in the course of carrying on the core activity of accepting deposits;
- facilities for withdrawing money or making payments from such an account; and
- overdraft facilities in connection with such an account.[17]

The ring-fence applies to institutions, with a minimum deposit size, which are carrying on "core activities", in essence, high-street banking.

The 2013 Act defines a "core activity" as being the regulated activity of accepting deposits (whether carried on in the UK or elsewhere).[18] HM Treasury may, subject to certain conditions, exempt certain deposit activities from being core activities and/or provide for regulated activities other than the taking of deposits to be core activities.[19]

The Core Activities Order sets out circumstances in which accepting a deposit is not a core activity. A "core deposit" is a deposit which is:

- held in an account provided by a UK deposit-taker as part of its activity of accepting deposits;
- held in an account opened at a branch of the UK deposit-taker located in an EEA state (and an RFB is prohibited from maintaining a branch *outside* the EEA);
- except where one or more of the account holders is:
  — a qualifying organisation;
  — a qualifying group member;
  — a relevant financial institution (RFI); or
  — an eligible individual.[20]

---

[17] Section 142C of FSMA.
[18] Section 142B of FSMA.
[19] Section 142B of FSMA.
[20] Article 2(2) of the Core Activities Order.

A "qualifying organisation" means an organisation which has provided a statement signed by or on behalf of the organisation (and accompanied either by a copy of the annual accounts or a signed statement of a recognised accountant) confirming that during the relevant financial year:

- if it is a body corporate or a partnership, it has:
  — a turnover of not less than £6.5 million;
  — a balance sheet total of not less than £3.26 million; and/or
  — not less than 50 employees;
- if it is not a body corporate or a partnership, the organisation's gross income was more than £6.5 million.[21]

A "qualifying group member" is an organisation that has provided to the UK deposit-taker a declaration that it is a member of the same group as a qualifying organisation.[22]

The definition of "relevant financial institution" covers a number of different classes of institution: credit institutions, investment firms, structured finance vehicles, global systemically important insurers, UCITS, management companies or alternative investment fund managers and financial holding companies and mixed financial holdings companies. There are some exceptions to the definition, amongst them: RFBs themselves, building societies, bodies corporate whose principal purpose is making loans secured on residential property and which are funded by their members and recognised clearing houses.[23]

An "eligible individual" is a high-net-worth individual who may place deposits in non-RFBs on the basis that such individuals do not require the higher standard of protection from the interruption of core services provided by RFBs. An eligible individual is defined as being someone who has signed a statement (either accompanied by the signed statement of a

---

[21] Articles 3 to 7 of the Core Activities Order.
[22] Article 8 of the Core Activities Order.
[23] Article 2 of the Excluded Activities Order.

recognised accountant or accepted by the deposit-taker without a confirming statement on the basis that the deposit-taker is satisfied that it is true) confirming that on average during a 12 month eligibility calculation period the individual held assets to the value of not less than £250,000 or more.[24]

7.2.4 *Excluded activities*

RFBs are required not to carry on "excluded activities", defined as:

- the regulated activity of dealing in investments as principal (whether in the UK or elsewhere), unless it is carried out in circumstances specified by HM Treasury by order; or
- any other activity, whether regulated or not and wherever undertaken, which HM Treasury by order specifies.[25]

The Excluded Activities Order provides for an additional excluded activity; that of dealing in commodities on the basis that this would expose RFBs to risks associated with volatile global market prices.[26] The Excluded Activities Order does however permit an RFB to trade in a commodity in the context of taking or realising security over that asset or in relation to a title transfer collateral arrangement.

The Excluded Activities Order also sets out specific circumstances in which an RFB may deal in investments as principal as a blanket ban would seriously impair an RFB's ability to run its business prudently.

---

[24] Article 9 and 10 of the Core Activities Order and para.2.6 of Consultation Paper 15/23: Ring-fencing: Disclosures to consumers by non-ring-fenced bodies.
[25] Section 142D of FSMA.
[26] Article 5 of the Excluded Activities Order.

7.2.5 *Prohibitions*

The 2013 Act provides that HM Treasury may by order, where desirable for ensuring the continuity of the provision of core services, specify certain prohibitions for RFBs.[27] The 2013 Act and the Excluded Activities Order prohibit an RFB from:

- entering into any transaction enabling it to use services provided through an inter-bank payment system unless the RFB is a direct participant or certain other conditions are satisfied;
- incurring a financial institution exposure; or
- maintaining or establishing a branch in any country or territory which is not an EEA member state or having a participating interest in any undertaking which is incorporated in or formed under the law of a country or territory which is not an EEA member state.

HM Treasury has stated that the intention behind the prohibition against financial institution exposures (including exposures to Non-RFBs, investment firms, systemic insurance firms and investment funds) is to protect RFBs against intra-financial contagion. The prohibition is subject to exceptions which are intended to permit an RFB to carry on its business and continue to provide basic banking facilities to its customers. An RFB may:

- have exposures to financial institutions for the purpose of managing their own risks;[28]
- enter into certain transactions with other members of the RFB's group on an arm's-length basis;[29]
- have exposures to financial institutions for the purposes of providing trade financing services (including providing finance, making payments, issuing guarantees, and providing security and indemnities);[30]

---

[27] Section 142(E)(1) of FSMA (as inserted by the 2013 Act).
[28] Article 14(2) and (3) of the Excluded Activities Order.
[29] Article 14(4) of the Excluded Activities Order.
[30] Article 15 of the Excluded Activities Order.

- enter into certain structured finance vehicles and holding debentures issued by such vehicles;[31]
- engage in certain conduit lending transactions;[32]
- enter into repo or reverse repo transactions;[33]
- have exposures arising from the provision of payment services to other financial institutions;[34]
- have exposures arising where the RFB is acting as distributor in connection with the distribution of trade finance or other financial products or investments issued by or services provided by the RFI or in respect of which the RFI is acting as distributor (or the RFI is conversely acting as distributor for the RFB);[35]
- have exposures arising as a consequence of warranties, indemnities, guarantees or covenants given for the benefit of an RFI as part of an acquisition or disposal;[36]
- have exposures arising as a result a breach of duty owed by the RFI to the RFB or the appointment of the RFB as the executor of the estate of any person or of services provided by the RFB in that capacity; and[37]
- have exposure to global systemically important insurers where the RFB has purchased insurance.[38]

7.2.6   *Exceptions to excluded activities and prohibitions*

RFBs will be required to put in place policies and procedures with respect to their use of exceptions under the Excluded Activities Order. The PRA expects such exceptions policies to specify all matters relating to the RFB's use of the relevant exceptions in detail, in order to enable the RFB to easily determine whether a transaction meets the requirements for

---

[31] Article 16 of the Excluded Activities Order.
[32] Article 17 of the Excluded Activities Order.
[33] Article 18 of the Excluded Activities Order.
[34] Article 19 of the Excluded Activities Order.
[35] Article 19 of the Excluded Activities Order.
[36] Article 19 of the Excluded Activities Order.
[37] Article 19 of the Excluded Activities Order.
[38] Article 19 of the Excluded Activities Order.

use under the relevant exception. The exceptions policies must, at a minimum, include the following[39]:

- details of the types of transactions that are permitted to be entered into;
- how the RFB determines that the purpose of the relevant transaction meets the requirements for use of the exception;
- a description of how the RFB separately identifies, manages and controls transactions under the exceptions policies from other transactions; and
- how the RFB manages additional or second-order risks introduced by transactions under the exceptions policies.

The RFB will be required to ensure that its exceptions policies and procedures are kept up to date, implemented effectively and subject to appropriate oversight.

7.3   Electrifying the ring-fence

7.3.1   Background

The 2013 Act confers on the FCA and PRA a group restructuring power which permits them to force financial institutions to restructure their operations if certain conditions arise, including, ultimately, the power to force the disposal of the RFB to an outside party. This power to force through a group restructuring is commonly referred to as the "electrification" of the ring-fence. Section 4 of the 2013 Act introduces a new Pt 9B of FSMA which incorporates the new ring-fencing provisions; the group restructuring powers and associated provisions are contained in ss.142K-142V of the new Pt 9B of FSMA.

---

[39] Paragraph 7.11 (and Rule 17 of the draft Ring-Fenced Bodies Instrument) of CP37/15.

7.3.2 *Application*

The group restructuring powers are exercisable, where certain prescribed conditions are satisfied, in relation to:

- a body corporate incorporated in the UK that carries on one or more core activities in relation to which it has a Part 4A permission and which is a member of a group (i.e. an RFB);
- any other member of an RFB's group that is an authorised person; and
- any parent undertaking of an RFB that is incorporated (and has a place of business) in the UK and which is not itself an authorised person (a qualifying parent undertaking).

For the purpose of FSMA's ring-fence provisions, the "appropriate regulator" in the case of an RFB that is a PRA-authorised person will be the PRA and in all other cases will be the FCA.[40] As UK banks will be PRA authorised, the most active regulator for the purposes of ring-fencing will be the PRA. Regardless, the appropriate regulators cannot utilise their general powers under Pt 4A or 12A of FSMA to bring about a result equivalent to the restructuring group powers conferred by the new Pt 9B of FSMA.

7.3.3 *Scope of group restructuring powers*

The limits of the group restructuring powers available to the appropriate regulator are contained in s.142L(2) of FSMA (in the case of the PRA) and s.142L(3) of FSMA (in the case of the FCA). These are very wide and include:

- the power to impose a requirement on the RFB to: (a) dispose of specified rights to an outside person; (b) apply to the court under Pt 7 of FSMA for an order sanctioning a ring-fencing transfer scheme for the transfer of the whole

---

[40] Section 142K(7) of FSMA.

or part of the RFB's business to an outside person; and/or (c) otherwise make arrangements discharging the RFB from specified liabilities[41];

- in relation to any other member of the RFB's group that is authorised by that regulator (or additionally, in the case of the FCA, where an entity is authorised by a body other than the FCA or PRA), the power to require the authorised person to: (a) dispose of any shares or securities in the RFB to an outside person; (b) dispose of any interest in any other member of the RFB's group to an outside person; (c) dispose of any other specified property or rights to an outside person; and/or (d) apply to the court under Pt 7 of FSMA for an order sanctioning a ring-fencing transfer scheme for the transfer of the whole or part of the authorised person's business to an outside person[42];
- in relation to any other member of the RFB's group that is authorised by the other appropriate regulator (which, additionally, will be the FCA where an entity is authorised by a body other than the PRA or FCA), the power to direct the other appropriate regulator to take any of those steps mentioned above[43]; and
- in relation to a qualifying parent undertaking of the RFB, the power to give a direction to the qualifying parent undertaking requiring it to take any of those steps mentioned above.[44]

Although a qualifying parent undertaking will not itself be an authorised person, ss.142(S) to (V) of the new Pt 9B of FSMA grant specific enforcement powers to the appropriate regulators in circumstances where a qualifying parent undertaking fails to comply with a direction to take any of the steps set out in s.142L(6) of FSMA. In particular, the appropriate regulator will have the power either to impose a penalty, or to issue a public censure on the qualifying parent undertaking or any person who was knowingly concerned in the contravention.

---

[41] Sections 142L(2)(a) and (5) and ss.142(L)(3)(a) and (5) of FSMA.
[42] Sections 142L(2)(b) and (6) and ss.142L(3)(b) and (6) of FSMA.
[43] Section 142L(6), ss.142L(2)(c) and (3)(c) of FSMA.
[44] Section 142L(6), ss.142L(2)(d) and (3)(d) of FSMA.

For the above purposes, an "outside person" is a person who will not be a member of the RFB's group following the implementation of the group restructuring power.[45]

7.3.4 Conditions to be satisfied before exercising the group restructuring powers

An appropriate regulator's group restructuring powers become exercisable only if one or more prescribed conditions are satisfied. Under s.142K of FSMA, these conditions are that:

- acts or omissions of other members of an RFB's group are having an adverse effect on the ability of the RFB to carry on core activities;[46]
- in carrying on its business, the RFB is unable to take decisions independently of other members of its group;[47]
- in carrying on its business, the RFB depends on resources that are provided by a member of its group and which would cease to be available if that member became insolvent;[48]
- the RFB would be unable to continue to carry on the core activities carried on by it if one or more other members of its group became insolvent;[49] and/or
- the RFB or another member of its group has (or is) engaged in conduct that is having, or would be likely to have, an adverse effect on the advancement by the appropriate regulator of its new statutory objectives in relation to the provision of core services in the UK.[50]

However, the appropriate regulator may not exercise group restructuring powers in relation to any person if either the PRA or FCA has previously exercised the group restructuring powers in relation to that person and the decision notice in

---

[45] Section 142L(7) of FSMA.
[46] Section 142K(2) of FSMA.
[47] Section 142K(3)(a) of FSMA.
[48] Section 142K(3)(b) of FSMA.
[49] Section 142K(4) of FSMA.
[50] Section 142K(6) of FSMA.

relation to the current exercise is given before the second anniversary of the date of the decision notice in relation to the previous exercise.[51]

7.4 Legal structure of RFBs

7.4.1 *Banking group structures containing an RFB*

The PRA set out its initial proposals on the legal structure of RFBs in CP19/14.[52] Following CP19/14, the PRA issued PS10/15[53] and subsequently CP37/15 which attached a near-final supervisory statement on the legal structure of RFBs. However, the supervisory statement and guidance on the legal structure of RFBs has yet to be finalised and may be subject to change.

The purpose of ring-fencing is not to legally separate an RFB entirely from the rest of its banking group as it is recognised that there may be diversification benefits associated with banking groups. However, the RFB should be protected from risks which originate in the rest of its banking group or in the global financial system (and to which Non-RFBs in the banking group may be more vulnerable given the nature of their activities). It is not intended that ring-fencing or other measures should ensure that RFBs cannot fail; the approach to the legal structure of RFBs and groups containing RFBs is informed by the PRA's focus on resilience and resolvability. The expectation is that the legal structure of RFBs and their groups should be, if necessary, simplified to align business activities with legal entities and to permit measures which support the RFB's resilience (including the application of financial and non-financial resources to be applied to an RFB on an individual or sub-consolidated basis).

---

[51] Section 142K(6) of FSMA.
[52] Consultation Paper 19/14: The implementation of ring-fencing: consultation on legal structure, governance and the continuity of services and facilities (CP19/14).
[53] Policy Statement PS10/15: The implementation of ring-fencing: legal structure, governance and the continuity of services and facilities (PS10/15).

The PRA has stated that the preferred resolution strategy for banking groups is likely to involve bail-in pursuant to the amended Banking Act 2009 at holding company level (the resolution entity). The bail-in option allows the Bank of England to make one or more resolution instruments to force through a recapitalisation of a failing institution by imposing losses directly on its creditors, including by cancelling their investment interest or converting their interests to equity. If resolution is to occur at holding company level, this obviates the need to separate the RFB entirely from the banking group. However, ring-fencing core services and aligning business activities with the banking group's legal entities should simplify any group restructuring which is required post-resolution and provide additional options to the resolution authorities to minimise disruption to the RFB's provision of core services.

7.4.2 Types of entity that an RFB may own

The PRA expects that an RFB (and, where an RFB sub-group is formed, each entity in the RFB sub-group) will not have ownership rights (including, but not limited to, shares, voting rights or other rights to participate in the capital or profits) or hold capital instruments in any entity which carries on any activity which is excluded or prohibited for the purposes of FSMA.[54] This should prevent an RFB circumventing ring-fencing rules by pushing excluded or prohibited activities down into a subsidiary while remaining exposed to excluded or prohibited losses whether because the RFB remains financially dependent on the income or proceeds of such activities (which may be volatile) or because the RFB is at risk of the subsidiary pushing losses resulting from such activities up to the RFB.

The PRA does not object in principle to an RFB owning other entities and it is currently envisaged that an RFB will be allowed to form sub-groups with other group entities which do not carry on excluded or prohibited activities. The PRA has

---

[54] Supervisory statements 2.3 and 2.4 of CP37/15.

not, and does not intend to, set out the types of subsidiaries which an RFB can (or cannot) own as such determinations should be made on a case-by-case basis taking into consideration the risks that a subsidiary might pose to the ring-fencing purposes (see para.1.3 above).[55] The PRA expects that an RFB should not be materially exposed to risks from its subsidiaries which are largely unrelated to its own business (and, therefore, unrelated to the RFB's core activities); this is, however, an expectation which the PRA will apply proportionately to achieve the outcomes set out by the ring-fencing purposes.[56]

7.4.3 *Types of entity that may own an RFB*

The PRA does not expect that an entity which carries on excluded or prohibited activities (or a subsidiary of such entity) should have ownership rights or hold capital instruments in an RFB as this may expose the RFB to the risks associated with such activities and impact upon the RFB's ability to make independent decisions. In assessing whether an entity which does not carry out excluded or prohibited activities should be restricted from owning an RFB (or a member of its sub-group), the PRA will consider the resilience and resolvability of the RFB and risks posed to the continuity of core activities in light of the ring-fencing provisions. The PRA will adopt this approach proportionately to achieve outcomes set out by the group ring-fencing purposes (see para.1.3 above).[57]

The PRA does not, however, intend to prevent an entity which has ownership rights in an RFB from: (i) maintaining or establishing a non-EEA branch; (ii) having a participating interest in a non-EEA undertaking; or (iii) having ownership rights in an entity which undertakes excluded or prohibited activities.[58]

---

[55] Paragraph 2.4 of PS10/15.
[56] Supervisory statement 2.5 of CP37/15.
[57] Supervisory statement 2.7 of CP37/15.
[58] Supervisory statement 2.7 of CP37/15.

The Excluded Activities Order permits an RFB to incur financial institution exposures to other members of the RFB's group as long as such exposures arise as a result of commercial transactions conducted on arm's length terms or a holding of shares or other securities issued by a subsidiary undertaking of the RFB and are not prohibited under rules made by the PRA or FCA.[59] The PRA therefore expects that entities which own RFBs will be free to lend to other group entities on that basis.

The PRA proposes additional rules requiring an RFB and other entities in its sub-group to establish policies and procedures to support their ability to ensure that intragroup transactions are conducted on arm's length terms.[60] These policies and procedures must at least:

- establish robust processes to identify products, services and all other transactions with group members;
- specify how pricing and non-pricing aspects of intragroup transactions will be determined, including standards for timely recording and settlement (including frequency of settlement);
- specify appropriate change management controls surrounding methodologies and application, including processes for approval and reporting of exceptions to policy;
- include dispute resolution procedures;
- be approved by the board of the RFB and reviewed annually; and
- be subject to regular internal audit assessments.

7.4.4 Sibling structure

The PRA expects an RFB and any group entities which can conduct excluded or prohibited activities to form a so-called "sibling structure" as separate clusters of subsidiaries beneath a UK holding company. This is in keeping with the Government's expectation, as expressed in the House of Lords debate on the Financial Services (Banking Reform) Bill, that banking groups adopt a sibling structure. As discussed (see para.4.1

---

[59] Article 14 of the Excluded Activities Order.
[60] Paragraph 4.6 of CP37/15.

above), a sibling structure beneath a UK holding company facilitates resolution of a banking group in the event of the failure of one or more entities, thereby reducing the likelihood of an RFB's core services being disrupted. It also permits a resolution authority to apply different restructuring options to the RFB as opposed to other group entities.

7.4.5 *Pensions*

The Pensions Regulations are designed to ensure that RFBs are not, and cannot become, responsible for the pension liabilities of (with some exceptions) certain other group entities. From 1 January 2026 (or, if later, five years from the date that the firm became an RFB):

- an RFB must not be an employer in respect of a multi-employer scheme unless:
  — the only other employers in respect of that scheme are wholly owned subsidiaries of the RFB, or other group RFBs (and their wholly owned subsidiaries); or
  — the scheme is a segregated scheme and the RFB is the only employer or the only other employers in respect of that section of the scheme are either wholly owned subsidiaries of the RFB, or other group RFBs (and their wholly owned subsidiaries);
- an RFB may not be a party to an arrangement where it is liable for the whole or part of the pension liabilities of a wholly owned subsidiary of another RFB unless the liabilities relate to a multi-employer pension scheme which meets the necessary requirements; and
- an RFB may not be, or become, party to any share liability arrangements, meaning guarantees, indemnities or bonds in respect of the pension liabilities of any other company.

7.5 Continuity of services and facilities

7.5.1 *Operational continuity*

In CP38/15,[61] the PRA set out its views on the principles that the operational arrangements of all deposit-takers (other than credit unions) and PRA-designated investment firms must satisfy in order to facilitate recovery actions, resolution and post-resolution restructuring. The specific proposals in respect of RFBs (see paras 5.2 and 5.3 below) should be read in conjunction with these principles.

7.5.2 *Group service arrangements*

The PRA set out its initial proposals in relation to group service arrangements in CP19/14. CP37/15 attaches near-final supervisory statements on continuity of services and facilities but this may be subject to change.

In order to fulfil the ring-fencing purposes, the PRA considers it necessary to supplement the existing regulatory framework by imposing additional restrictions in respect of any intragroup service arrangements an RFB may have and any external service arrangements that an RFB may have which may be affected by the financial position of other group entities.

A non-exhaustive list of the types of services and facilities caught by the PRA's supervisory statement (as set out in CP37/15) includes the following types of services and facilities that support the business of the RFB: data-processing services; property management services; information technology; data centres; and back office functions. It is not proposed that an RFB should be required to own and manage directly all such services and facilities which they require but an RFB (and its ring-fenced affiliates) may receive shared services and facilities from other group entities only where such entities are "ring-fenced affiliates" or are "group services entities".

---

[61] Consultation Paper 38/15: Ensuring operational continuity in resolution (*CP38/15*).

"Ring-fenced affiliates" is defined as comprising any member of the RFB's sub-consolidation group, which comprises the undertakings included in the scope of consolidation as a result of a requirement imposed on an RFB under art.11(5) of the Capital Requirements Regulation.[62] It is considered proportionate to allow an RFB to receive services and facilities from within its sub-consolidation group as the sub-consolidation group will be subject to supervision and will not be permitted to perform excluded or prohibited activities.

The definition of "group services entity" means any entity within the same group as the RFB whose only business is to provide services or facilities. It should be noted that this would include a group entity which also provides services and facilities to third parties. A group services entity will be permitted to provide services and facilities across the ring-fence as the PRA considers that it would be disproportionate to require banking groups to have duplicate services or service entities on either side of the ring-fence.

However, the PRA has not permitted additional flexibility which would allow a qualifying parent undertaking which may not meet the definition of "group service entity" to provide services to an RFB. A "qualifying parent undertaking" is defined as a parent undertaking which is a UK company (or at least a company with a place of business in the UK) which is also an insurance holding company, a financial holding company, a mixed financial holding company or a financial institution whilst not being an authorised person itself (or a recognised investment exchange or clearing house). However, if the qualifying parent undertaking is also the resolution entity for the purposes of bail-in at holding company level (see para.4.1 above) then permitting that UK holding company to be a service provider to the RFB is likely to complicate the resolution entity's balance sheet and make any bail-in at that level more complex. It was argued that a qualifying parent undertaking should be permitted to act as service provider for

---

[62] Regulation (EU) 575/2013 of the European Parliament and of the Council on prudential requirements for credit institutions and investment firms and amending Regulation (EU) 648/2012.

an RFB if that qualifying parent undertaking is not the resolution entity in respect of the banking group. The PRA decided against this approach on the basis that a qualifying parent undertaking is too vulnerable to the failure of other group entities and an RFB relying on that qualifying parent undertaking for services would therefore be at risk of service disruption.

7.5.3 Group and third party service arrangements

The PRA expects that RFBs should have service arrangements which cannot be disrupted through the acts, omissions or insolvency of other group members. This may impact contractual arrangements both with group services entities and third parties who are, in each case, permitted to provide services to an RFB under the rules (permitted suppliers). For example, a permitted supplier should not have the contractual right to discontinue services to an RFB because another group entity has entered into resolution or insolvency.[63]

This requirement is, however, intended to be limited and applied proportionately insofar as it applies only to those services which are necessary in order for the RFB to conduct its core activities. In considering whether an RFB's service arrangements may be disrupted by the acts, omissions or insolvency of other group members, the PRA will take into consideration any business continuity arrangements in place.

The requirement is drafted so as to explicitly exclude the provision of services and facilities from financial market infrastructures (FMIs) as any such requirement in respect of FMIs would interfere with their ability to exercise default procedures against an RFB as a consequence of the actions of other members of the RFB's group. For the same reason, the access arrangements an RFB and other group members employ when using an FMI should not prevent the FMI from exercising its default arrangements under the proposed rules.[64]

---

[63] Rule 9.2 of the draft Ring-Fenced Bodies Instrument of CP37/15.
[64] Paragraph 4.8 of PS10/15.

The PRA has recognised that RFBs may have a services framework made up of inter-dependent group services entities and does not view such a services framework itself as a risk; however, the PRA will expect sufficient safeguards to be in place to reduce the probability and impact of disruption to core services provided by the RFB. The PRA has also amended the rules to clarify that sub-contractors will be subject to the same restrictions as any permitted supplier.[65]

7.6 Governance of ring-fenced banks

7.6.1 *General rules*

The 2013 Act requires the PRA to make rules in relation to the governance of RFBs. The PRA set out its preliminary views in CP19/14 and provided further guidance in CP37/15 and CP18/15[66]; the rules and guidance are not yet finalised and may be subject to change.

Governance can be broadly divided into four categories: board membership; risk management; remuneration; and accountability. Governance of RFBs is particularly relevant to the ring-fencing objective of ensuring that RFBs are able to take independent decisions, but also consequentially to other ring-fencing purposes such as protecting the RFB from the acts or omissions of other members of its group. An RFB's ability to take decisions independently is in keeping with the Companies Act 2006 requirement that directors exercise independent judgment and promote the success of the company for the benefit of its members.

The PRA has also recognised that, where it is part of a wider banking group, the RFB will be a subsidiary and its parent company will have to exercise appropriate oversight of the RFB in a manner consistent with good governance. There is an acknowledged tension between the independence expected of

---

[65] Paragraphs 4.6 and 4.7 of PS10/15.
[66] Consultation Paper 18/15: Corporate governance: board responsibilities (CP18/15).

an RFB and the accountability and transparency to be expected by shareholders. The PRA has responded to these perceived issues by stating that it has sought to avoid disrupting the usual mechanisms of accountability more than is necessary to achieve the statutory ring-fencing purposes and that an RFB's ability to take independent decisions does not, of itself, mean that an RFB's policies will be at odds with those of its wider group.[67]

The PRA intends to introduce outcome-focused rules stating the ends that the PRA expects firms to achieve. The PRA expects that outcome-focused rules will permit a degree of flexibility in the structures which firms use to meet the requirements. The PRA has proposed that the following outcomes should be set out as rules[68]:

- RFBs are able to take decisions independently of other members of the group;
- RFBs take all reasonable steps to identify and manage conflicts of interest with other group members;
- RFBs take reasonable steps to identify and manage any conflicts between the duties senior management owe to the RFB and other interests they may have; and
- RFBs can demonstrate how they are meeting ring-fencing rules.

Waivers and modifications of the ring-fencing rules may be granted if a firm's compliance with the rules would be unduly burdensome or would not achieve the purposes for which the rules were made and where the granting of a waiver or modification would not adversely affect the advancement of any of the PRA's objectives. An applicant will be required to demonstrate how its proposed governance structure will compensate for any potential weakening of the regime and how they will ensure that the purposes of the regime are still advanced.

---

[67] Paragraphs 3.5, 3.7 and 3.8 of PS10/15.
[68] Rules 3.1 to 3.4 of the draft Ring-Fenced Bodies Instrument of CP37/15.

As part of its governance procedures, an RFB should be able to demonstrate to the PRA compliance with all ring-fencing obligations, including those which come directly from legislation.

7.6.2 Board and board committee composition and responsibilities

7.6.2.1 Board composition

The 2013 Act requires that the PRA shall make rules on board composition and specifies that an RFB's board includes members who are treated by the rules as being independent of other members of the RFB's group, members who are independent from the RFB and non-executive members.[69] The PRA has therefore proposed that:[70]

- at least half of an RFB's board, excluding the chair, must be independent non-executive directors (NEDs);
  — this does not prohibit independent NEDs on the RFB's board from being independent NEDs on other group boards provided that they can be considered independent from both bodies and continue to fulfil the criteria for the RFB;
  — an executive from another part of the group would be permitted to sit on the RFB board as a non-executive but would not be considered an independent NED;
- the chair of an RFB must be independent during his or her tenure as chair and must not hold another chair position in another group entity board;
  — the chair must be independent on appointment and thereafter must comply with the PRA's proposed independence criteria;
  — independence criteria would not prohibit an independent chair from holding independent NED positions elsewhere in the group but the chair should not

---

[69] Section 142(H)(5)(d)of FSMA.
[70] These proposals are contained in Rule 4 of the draft Ring-Fenced Bodies Instrument of CP37/15.

be responsible for chairing the board of another group entity (outside the RFB's subgroup);
- no more than one-third of an RFB's board members may be current employees or directors of another entity in the group;
  — this is intended to ensure that an RFB is able to take decisions independently of other group members;
  — directors who hold positions in multiple group entities will be required to manage inherent conflicts of interest;
  — by limiting the number to one-third, the PRA is trying to balance the RFB's ability to take independent decisions against the RFB's position in the banking group;
  — where a subsidiary of an RFB forms part of an RFB's subgroup, RFB directors who are also employees or directors of such a subsidiary would not count towards the threshold;
- an RFB executive director on the board of an RFB must not hold other executive director positions on the board of another entity in the group that carries out excluded or prohibited activities;
  — executive directors on the boards of both an RFB and an entity that carries out excluded or prohibited activities would be subject to inherent conflicts of interest; a risk made more acute by the executive nature of their duties; and
  — executive directors of the RFB would still be able to hold executive positions in the parent entity and any entities owned by the RFB.

The criteria[71] for independence exclude persons who:

- have been an employee of the RFB or a member of its group within a period of five years;
- have, or have had, either directly or indirectly a material business relationship with the RFB or a member of the RFB's group within a period of three years;

---

[71] Rule 1.3 of the draft Ring-Fenced Bodies Instrument of CP37/15.

- have received remuneration (other than a director's fee) from the RFB within a period of five years;
- have close family ties with advisers, directors or senior management of the RFB or any member of its group;
- hold directorships in common with other directors of the RFB in any other undertaking that is not a member of the RFB's group;
- have significant links with other directors of the RFB through involvement in any other undertaking that is not a member of the RFB's group of the type which might give rise to a conflict of interest;
- represent a significant shareholder of a parent undertaking of the RFB; or
- have served on the governing body of the RFB or a member of its group for more than nine years from the date of first election.

7.6.2.2 Board responsibilities

The PRA has published a draft supervisory statement: "Corporate governance: board responsibilities" which identifies key aspects of good board governance to which the PRA attaches particular importance in its supervision of firms, including RFBs.

7.6.3 Risk management and internal audit

The PRA expects risk management and other control functions to support and challenge a firm's decisions on the level of risk and the adequacy and integrity of the associated governance, risk management and financial and other control arrangements. These control functions should support an RFB's ability to take decisions independently and also ensure that an RFB is not adversely affected by the acts or omissions of other members of its group. The PRA intends to avoid duplicating or overlapping with the 8th EU Audit Directive and has therefore limited additional rules in relation to risk management and internal audit:

- RFBs should have their own Chairman for each of their risk management and internal audit committees (although the Chairman may be the same as the Chairman of the risk management or internal audit committee for a ring-fenced affiliate or (to be confirmed) a member of the RFB's sub-group); and
- RFBs must ensure that their risk management and internal audit functions have sufficient resources to perform their role (including the identification, monitoring and management of risk), that those resources are at all times identifiable as performing that function for the RFB and that such function supports the ability of the RFB to take decisions independently of its group.

The first rule is intended to ensure that RFBs have senior staff who will be senior managers under the SMR with specific responsibility and accountability for risk management and internal audit.

7.6.4 *Remuneration*

The PRA expects that remuneration be allocated in a manner consistent with sound and effective risk management and the long-term interests of the RFB as distinct from any other member of the RFB's group. Whilst the RFB does not necessarily need to have a separate remuneration policy from other members of its group, the PRA would expect the RFB to take responsibility for the implementation of such policies at RFB level and to adjust them if necessary. This does not mean that RFB employees cannot receive a proportion of their remuneration in a form associated with the group—for example, shares in a parent entity. Where an employee provides services both to the RFB and to other group entities, the rules only require the proportion of remuneration attributable to the services provided to the RFB to comply. The PRA does, however, expect that where an employee provides services to multiple group entities that such services will be provided on an arm's-length basis.[72]

---

[72] Paragraph 3.28 of PS10/15.

7.6.5 HR policies

The PRA's existing requirements are considered sufficient to support the group ring-fencing purposes with the addition of two new rules:

- In carrying on its business, the RFB should not depend on personnel that would cease to be available in the event of the insolvency of another member of the group and that this is reflected in its human resources policy[73]:
  - this is not intended to prevent personnel (including staff from group services entities) from providing services to multiple group entities, including those that undertake excluded or prohibited activities;
  - the RFB's "dependency" on personnel will be considered in light of a range of factors, including how substitutable the skills are, how essential the role is and whether there are suitable contingency arrangements in place;
- Vacancies for independent NEDs on RFB boards must be advertised publicly[74]:
  - this is intended to combat a perceived danger that NEDs on the boards of banking entities are *"self-selecting and self-perpetuating"* and to ensure genuine independence, transparency and a more diverse pool of applicants; and
  - there is an exemption for board chairs who resign their directorships before completing their term as the PRA recognises that a board chair may need to be replaced very quickly in an emergency.

7.6.6 Individual accountability—Senior Managers' Regime for RFBs

As discussed above (see para.1.4), the SMR allocates to senior managers of an RFB the Prescribed Responsibility of ensuring that aspects of the RFB's affairs for which a person is

---

[73] Rule 7.3 of the draft Ring-Fenced Bodies Instrument of CP37/15.
[74] Rule 4.5 of the draft Ring-Fenced Bodies Instrument of CP37/15.

responsible for managing are in compliance with the ring-fencing obligations. Unlike other Prescribed Responsibilities which firms may allocate to a single senior manager whose job description is most closely linked with that responsibility, the ring-fencing Prescribed Responsibility should be allocated to all senior managers responsible for areas covered by the ring-fencing obligations. This reflects the PRA's expectation that all relevant senior managers of an RFB must take individual responsibility for ensuring that the RFB adheres to the ring-fencing obligations.

The ring-fencing Prescribed Responsibility (along with all other relevant Prescribed Responsibilities) must be set out in a Statement of Responsibilities which will have to be submitted when applying for approval on behalf of senior managers, together with a Management Responsibilities Map showing how responsibilities are allocated. These documents provide formal evidence of a senior manager's area of responsibility and may be used as evidence in taking enforcement action.

7.7 Looking forward

Ring-fencing legislation is to be implemented from 1 January 2019 and the PRA has stated its intention to publish the PRA's remaining rules and supervisory statements during the course of 2016.

The question of EU regulation in this area also has yet to be resolved and may impact on UK ring-fencing legislation.

Chapter 8

Employment Issues

Catrina Smith
Partner
Norton Rose Fulbright

Amanda Sanders
Senior Knowledge Lawyer
Norton Rose Fulbright

8.1   Identifying the relevant staff

The new senior managers and certification regimes pose substantial challenges for the Human Resource (HR), legal and compliance function within those organisations affected by the new regime. There are effectively three areas which will have an impact on the these functions: the introduction of the new Senior Managers' Regime (SMR) to replace the significant influence function (SIF) element of the approved persons regime; the new certification regime which will apply to both the senior managers and other bank staff whose actions could seriously damage the bank; and new conduct rules. The regimes will impact on every aspect of the employee "life cycle" from recruitment and initial regulatory approval, through ongoing supervision and accountability to the termination of the employment relationship. The new SMR and certification regulatory regime impose different challenges to the extent that banks need to adopt significant cultural and behavioural changes and amendments to their employment procedures.

8.1.1   Transitional arrangements

One of the first key areas that firms were required to consider was the transitional arrangements which applied including identifying the relevant staff. Those covered by the SIF regime who are senior managers under the new rules would be affected by the new rules. Any individual approved to perform a SIF role and who then performs a corresponding senior manager role could be "grandfathered" into that role. This means that as long as the individual is now performing a role which was not substantially different to their SIF role then they did not need to apply for a fresh approval. Relevant firms, were required to identify those to be "grandfathered" and forms had to be submitted to the regulators by 8 February 2016. In these documents, the relevant firms notified the regulators of the individual's existing SIF approval under the approved person's regime and their equivalent SMF. If there was no equivalent senior manager function then the approvals lapsed. If the individual was allocated additional responsibilities under the new regime then, this in itself, did not make them ineligible for grandfathering. Some individuals could take on new responsibilities or become formally responsible for areas which they may already have been responsible for in practice. However, if an individual has new responsibilities that involves them performing a senior manager function which is not equivalent to the function that he or she performed prior to commencement then he or she was not eligible for grandfathering in respect of that new role. Instead, a new application for approval was required. The grandfathering notification form is set out at Form K. This will apply to other financial services firms to whom the new regime is extended in 2018 and firms will need to provide for those who are already approved under the Approved Persons Regime (APR) to be "grandfathered" into the relevant roles under the new regime.

8.1.2   Senior Managers' Regime

8.1.2.1   Allocation of responsibilities

One of the key aspects of the new regime is that banks must allocate specific responsibilities to individual senior managers. It is anticipated that these individuals will generally be at board level or just below. The key test is whether an individual has overall responsibility for a key function and reports to the board in respect of that function. Firms need to think about which functions are required and allocate responsibilities under the new regime clearly and without any of the functions failing to be allocated.

The FCA and the PRA have set out 17 senior management functions[1]. Not all functions exist in all firms, depending on the firm's size, and some will only be relevant for particular firms. An example given is the function of the Chairman of the Nominations Committee which will only be required where a firm has a committee that performs the function of a nominations committee. Initially the FCA proposed that "standard" non-executive directors could hold senior manager roles. However, following concerns that this may discourage individuals from taking non-executive roles, the regulators proposed that only non-executive directors with specific responsibilities will be senior managers. Annex 3 in CP15/22 (Strengthening accountability in banking) indicates which senior manager functions (SMFs) should be held by approved non-executive directors rather than executives and this includes the Chairman function, the Chair of the Risk Committee, the Chair of the Audit Committee, the Chair of the Remuneration Committee, the Chair of the Nominations Committee and the Senior Independent Director function.

The FCA and PRA rules list 30 Prescribed Responsibilities which must be assigned to the individuals who hold SMFs. The list of Prescribed Responsibilities is set out in Annex 4 in CP15/22 (Strengthening accountability in banking). Those individuals who have overall responsibility for activities,

---

[1]   CP15/22 Strengthening accountability in banking – Annex 3 – July 2015

functions or areas of the business will need to be identified and, in most cases, be pre-approved for SMF's.

Generally the regulators consider that it will not be usual for several senior managers to share an FCA prescribed responsibility. However, sharing will be justified in certain limited circumstances. For example, it may be possible if it is done as part of a job share where it is agreed that an incoming senior manager is to work together with a departing senior manager temporarily as part of a handover. It may also be that a particular area of a firm is co-headed by two individuals who split or share a function or responsibility. Both the FCA and the PRA have made it clear that all senior managers sharing the responsibilities must be jointly responsible. The difference in the role must be clearly set out in the Statements of Responsibilities and the firm's responsibilities map. If those entering into a job share are to be jointly responsible then the exact nature of their responsibilities must be clear in their job description. In principle each of the individuals will be deemed wholly responsible for the role, but if a firm does breach a relevant requirement in an area where the responsibility is shared then the PRA and the FCA have indicated that they will adopt a flexible approach in considering how the shared responsibility was discharged in practice when trying to show that reasonable steps were taken to avoid the breach.

Difficulties also arise for the firm where the individual who holds the SMF is employed by a group company, particularly an overseas group company. The senior manager role has no territorial limitation. The fact that an individual is physically located outside the UK does not automatically mean that they cannot perform a SMF. If an individual located overseas is responsible for implementing the group's strategy in the UK and has not delegated that responsibility to an employee within the UK then they are likely to be performing a SMF. Simply because they are overseas does not prevent them requiring approval if they are undertaking responsibility in respect of the UK firm. Again, this can be a challenge for the UK firm who have to ensure that the senior manager is approved and also is aware of the obligations and duties.

Another point of interest in identifying who will fall within the relevant staff is in relation to temporary cover for an employee who is absent. In relation to covering a SMF then the rules allow temporary cover to be maintained for up to 12 weeks without seeking approval. However, such a person will be subject to the conduct rules during that period and so the firm will have to ensure that all rules of conduct have been notified to the individual.

8.1.2.2   *Statutory duty of responsibility*

When the new regime was first introduced in the Financial Services (Banking Reform) Act 2013 the proposal was to introduce a "presumption of responsibility" with the evidential burden on senior managers to demonstrate that they took reasonable steps to prevent, stop or remedy regulatory breaches. This would, in effect, have amounted to a reversal of the burden of proof. However, the UK Government subsequently decided that the presumption of responsibility would not come into effect.[2] Instead a statutory duty of responsibility will be applied to all senior managers.

The new statutory duty of responsibility may not be as fundamental a change as the original proposal, but it will still require a change in the culture for firms covered by the regime. The senior manager's regime places the senior manager in the particular business unit where the failure occurred to be accountable for the breach. This means that the underlying obligation remains on the senior manager to ensure that they have taken all reasonable steps to prevent regulatory breaches in the areas of the firm for which they are responsible.

The Government believes that the SMR provides the regulators with a bigger toolkit than the regime it replaces. Notwithstanding the removal of the presumption of responsibility there is the increased likelihood of sanction from the regulators, whether that is in the form of a financial penalty, withdrawal of approval or a new criminal offence of reckless misconduct.

---

[2]   HM Treasury Senior Managers and Certification Regime (extension to all FSMA authorised persons) October 2015.

This therefore gives rise to concern as to who will want to take on the responsibility of a senior manager role within the regime? The new regime coincides with the introduction of the tough remuneration regime and whilst the categorisation of who is a "senior manager" may not strictly overlap with those individuals whose variable remuneration is controlled by the Remuneration Code, it is likely that most senior managers will be covered by the Code.

8.1.3 Certification regime

The certification regime applies to individuals whose involvement in their firm's activities might involve a risk of significant harm to the firm or its customers (significant harm functions) The rules describe the roles that are subject to the certification regime[3] The certification regime does tie in with the Remuneration Code to the extent that "material risk takers" are subject to the Certification regime and are those staff who are subject to the Remuneration Code. The firm must therefore ensure that they know who is covered by the certification regime. This again may lead to difficulties in relation to staff in different jurisdictions who may nevertheless be covered and for whom different standards may apply.

8.1.4 Conduct

A new set of conduct rules take the form of brief statements of high-level principles setting out the standards of behaviour for employees. They are based on the old Statements of Principle and the Code of Practice for Approved Persons but they are structured in two tiers. One tier relates to senior managers only. The other tier of the new conduct rules applies to a much wider population of employees than those previously caught. The new conduct rules apply to all bank employees except for a short list of "excepted employees" who fulfil specific non-banking auxiliary functions, for example, HR administrators, catering staff, facilities management. The reasons for the change is to ensure that all staff within the relevant firm will be

---

[3] SYSC 5.2 30R.

aware of what amounts to acceptable behaviour. Again, this provides new challenges to the firm to identify which staff are subject to the new conduct rules and to ensure that they are all aware of, and comply with their obligations.

8.1.5   Non Executive Directors

Only certain NEDs with specific responsibilities fall within the SMR and will need to be pre-approved. These are the chairman, a senior independent director, and the chair of the risk, audit, remuneration and nominations categories. Those who do not need approval are referred to as "notified" NEDs. Both approved and notified NEDs are subject to the statutory and fiduciary duties of directors under UK company law.

As notified NEDs do not fall within the SMR, a gap was identified to the extent that regulators would therefore not have the ability to take enforcement actions against NEDs who do not perform a senior management function. The regulators identified that this gap needed to be addressed as there are provisions in certain EU directives that require member states to be able to take action against members of a management body, including NEDs. The Bank of England and Financial Services Bill therefore provides for the PRA and the FCA to be able to make Rules of Conduct applying to NEDs.[4] In addition, the regulators have suggested that NEDs should be contractually obliged to follow codes of conduct.

8.2   Senior Managers' Regime

8.2.1   Statements of Responsibility and management responsibility maps

8.2.1.1   Drafting of the statement of responsibilities

The new regime requires that every senior manager is given a statement of responsibilities (SOR). The SOR sets out the areas

---

[4]   HM – Treasury – Senior Managers and Certification Regime extension to all FSMA authorised persons – October 2015.

for which a senior manager is responsible and accountable. The SOR may or may not be part of the contract of employment but it will be referred to within the contract. It is a dynamic document which will be subject to change depending on the changes to responsibility.

The details of the SOR will depend upon the allocation of responsibility. Clearly certain required roles will inherently attach to certain functions. Both regulators have a list of prescribed responsibilities which must all be covered.

The SOR is an important document as it provides evidence as to the responsibility of the senior manager. As set out above, under the SMR, the PRA and FCA will be able to take action against an individual if:

- the firm has contravened regulatory requirements;
- the breach occurred in the part of the business for which the senior manager was responsible;
- and the regulator can show that the individual failed to take the steps that it is reasonable for a person in that position to take to prevent a regulatory breach occurring.

The SOR shows the areas for which the senior manager is responsible and therefore has the statutory duty of responsibility. An employee will want to clearly define the level of personal responsibility, whilst the management will need to ensure that all areas of responsibility are covered and there are no gaps. In view of the potential conflicts of interest it is likely that employees will want to take legal advice on the SOR. This will be something that each firm will need to consider including the level of advice and who will cover the cost of such advice.

Since the SOR is such an important document, there is some debate as to whether it will be included as part of the contract of employment. In most cases cross reference will be made to the SOR within the employment documentation to clarify that the employment is conditional on the senior manager covering all areas of responsibility as agreed with the employer.

However, as mentioned above the SOR is a dynamic document and will be subject to change. Difficulties will arise if trying to change the terms of an employee's contract of employment. It is generally not possible to unilaterally vary a contract of employment and, any significant change which is not agreed could lead to a claim for breach of contract and/or constructive dismissal.

In addition to assisting with drafting the new SOR, the function responsible for the SMR will need to ensure that there are processes in place for the SOR and responsibilities map to be kept updated and any significant changes notified to the regulator (e.g. if there is a change in responsibilities or a sharing of responsibilities.)

8.2.1.2 *Management Responsibilities maps*

One of the documents which must be submitted by the firm is a management responsibilities map. This will need to be maintained and updated and is a single document which describes a firm's management and governance arrangements. The importance of this document from an HR point of view is that it must include details of reporting lines. It is important to ensure that the reporting lines on the management responsibilities map reflects the actual reporting lines in the employee's contract of employment.

Relevant firms need to set out this organisational structure. Part of the assessment involves considering whether an individual already falls within that role and whether they then fulfil the SMF. The maps are likely to end up as complex documents which can be further complicated by cross-border arrangements and management structures. As set out above, there may be individuals in an overseas entity who take responsibility for the UK branch and UK regulated activities. Each regulated performance activity must fall within the responsibility of a senior manager and therefore these maps will assist in ensuring that there are no gaps in responsibility.

From an employment perspective, any changes in the govern-ance or reporting structure must be dealt with carefully. A change in a line of reporting could be considered to amount to a repudiatory breach of contract which may result in an employee claiming constructive dismissal. Those taking responsibility for the SMF need to ensure that the reporting lines are discussed with the employees in a sensitive manner.

The management responsibility map falls within a SMF and could fall within the responsibility of the CEO or the Group Entity Senior Manager. They will have responsibility for ensuring that the map is kept up to date and any amendments are notified to the regulator. The PRA has suggested that this map should be updated at least quarterly and whenever there is a significant change in the firm's governance or structure or the allocation of responsibilities or the reporting lines. Pro-cesses must be put in place to ensure that such information is fed back to the senior manager with responsibility for the document, and also for how such information should be sent back to the PRA if there is a significant change requiring the information to be given to the regulator.

8.2.2 Recruitment/Appointment

8.2.2.1 Interview process

The imposition of the SMR will have an effect on the recruitment and appointment procedures for senior managers. Although the number of individuals who are covered by the regime is very small the recruitment process for those employees is likely to be more protracted to deal with the negotiations regarding responsibility and the enhanced checks required (see certification process below). This is combined with the complications of a more limited talent pool from which the individual can be recruited. Any interview process will need to be stringent

8.2.2.2   *The offer*

One of the issues for new senior managers is the offer pack which they will be given. In addition to a draft SOR which will be given, the offer pack will include the relevant handover information. The handover information includes details from the departing employee as to the nature of the role and any unresolved or potential regulatory breaches and unresolved concerns expressed by the PRA, FCA or other regulatory bodies. This document is confidential and highly sensitive in nature and as a result it is likely that the firm will require that the candidate and the candidate's adviser sign a confidentiality agreement prior to offering any role or negotiating any terms. An additional issue will arise where legal advice has been sought in relation to any potential breaches. This advice given to the firm will be privileged as being legal advice privilege. However, if it is shared to candidates then such privilege could be lost. There are various options which could apply. One of these is to inform the new senior manager of the existence of a potential breach, but not to provide the details of the breach until the individual has accepted the offer. As such the information could be shared with them, and such appointment could be subject to a probationary period whilst they consider the disclosure. Firms should consider whether legal advice privilege is likely to be lost before disclosing any such information and consider what approach should be adopted: Will an oral summary be sufficient; can the document be redacted?

It may also be relevant to obtain a warranty or confirmation from the incoming employee that they have seen all the relevant information in the offer pack, have taken legal advice should they wish to and raised all the queries they wish to raise. This makes it clear that they are fully aware of the position and responsibilities they are taking on.

Any offer to the new senior manager must be conditional on senior manager approval, thorough investigation into background checks and references being taken. The HR or legal function will need to adopt new processes in relation to checking references and there may be issues in obtaining information from overseas and data protection issues (see certification issues below).

8.2.3 *Service Agreements/ contracts of employment/non-executive letters of appointment*

Service agreements and contracts of employment may need to be amended to reflect the SMR. In addition to drafting documents for new employees it may also be necessary to consider amendments to existing agreements if the employee is already in situ but is being promoted to a senior manager role. In addition to the points listed below for certification and conduct purposes there are specific points in relation to the SMR.

(a) A warranty should be included that the employee has given full disclosure of all relevant matters during the recruitment process. This is particularly relevant for certification purposes, but it will also be important for those individuals who are accepting a senior manager role.

(b) It may be that the individual has commenced employment but that such employment is conditional on regulatory approval being obtained. Obviously in order to hold a SMF the individual must be pre-approved by the regulator. Therefore any conditional approval must make it clear what requirements need to be fulfilled and the timescale within which that must be achieved. It should also be clear what the effect of failing to comply with those requirements will be. For example, will it be a condition of continued employment or will the employee be entitled to continue employment but at a less senior role? The firm must also ensure that flexibility is included in the wording to reflect any variation to the conditions which may be made by the regulator.

(c) It should be clear that the commencement of the employment and its continuation are conditional on the employee accepting the Statement of Responsibility as amended from time to time and the employee's acceptance of any policy relating to the fit and proper procedure.

(d) A provision should be included making the continued status as a senior manager a condition of continued employment. This means that if the employee loses his status as a senior manager then the employer will be entitled to terminate the employment, possibly without notice. It should also be a requirement that the employee will use their best or reasonable endeavours to ensure that senior manager status is maintained e.g. by attending training, not doing anything which would jeopardise their status.

(e) It may be that changes to remuneration or benefits are required to reflect the new responsibilities. The senior manager may seek a higher level of salary to reflect the increased responsibility. As mentioned above a senior manager may want a clause providing for payment of legal fees not only in relation to the negotiation of the SOR but also in complying with the statutory duty of responsibility. Advice would need to be taken as to whether this is covered by any existing Directors & Officers insurance cover in place.

(f) Any changes to reporting lines must be reflected in the contract of employment to tie in with the responsibilities map.

(g) Changes may be required to the duties clause. Historically a clause is included in an executive director's service agreement which allows for flexibility in favour of the employer, for example that the employer can require the employee to act in a different position or to act for a group company. A senior manager may now resist such a clause as clearly this will impact on the SOR. In addition, the employer will not want the employee to act outside of his/her SOR other than in special circumstance(s). The employer may therefore consider including a clause which places a prohibition on the employee acting outside of SOR other than where requested to do so e.g. in an emergency/crisis situation (for example to temporarily cover the role of another senior manager).

(h) A clause is often included in a service agreement which gives the employer the ability to unilaterally appoint someone to act along-side a director. This is particularly useful where an employee has given notice. If such a clause is not included then any request by the employer for the employee to do so could amount to constructive dismissal. Under the SMR, the senior manager may resist such a clause given the implications on liability. The employer will therefore need to consider amending such a clause so that the appointment can only be made with their consent or can only apply in limited circumstances when the employer would want to retain the unilateral right to appoint someone jointly, for example, where the employee goes on long term sickness absence, family leave, holiday, or where the employee is put on part-time or a flexible work arrangement, suspension, or garden leave. Generally a firm can continue with temporary cover for a senior manager for a twelve week period. However, approval will need to be sought for any cover exceeding twelve weeks. Combined with this clause the employer should insert a clause which requires the employee to give as much notice as possible of absence, for example on family leave, so that this gives the employer sufficient time to appoint someone in the employee's place. In those circumstances an employer could seek approval for the temporary replacement and ensure that such approval is time limited.

(i) The duties clause should also include a provision that there is an express duty on the employee to report to the Board his/her own wrongdoing, and the wrongdoing of others, specifically in relation to the Conduct Rules (see conduct below).

(j) Wording should be included to ensure that the agreement complies with the FCA/PRA Remuneration Code including provisions relating to deferral, claw back and malus wording.

(k) There may need to be new requirements in the contract of employment relating to record keeping. There are requirements to keep regulatory records up to date. In addition, the employee should give an acknowledgement that information about them can be shared with the FCA and

PRA and any future employer. Any failure to give that acknowledgment could end in data protection/privacy issues arising.

(l) There are further important provisions on termination. Most service agreements will already have a current requirement to co-operate on a hand over in the event of termination/suspension/garden leave. This will be more necessary now there is the additional requirement to provide handover information on termination. It should be clear the extent to which the senior manager will be required to provide assistance/information post-termination. It is important to note that the senior manager may want the firm to provide documentation to assist with any action brought by the regulator after they have left the firm. On termination most employers will require the employee to hand over and deliver all documentation and property relating to the employment. However, as the senior manager may need such documentation to show that they have complied with their statutory duty of responsibility then they are likely to ask for the ability to retain documents or to require the employer to preserve documents for him/her and allow continued reasonable access to them.

(m) A Service Agreement can include a clause which is a general power of attorney giving power to another director or senior employee to act on behalf of the employee. This may be resisted by a senior manager out of concern that this could result in unilateral changes to the SOR. A senior manager is likely to want any changes to the SOR to be by agreement only.

(n) As senior managers' liability will be much greater under the SMR the importance of any Directors & Officers insurance cover and/or any indemnities requested in a service agreement will be more important. There are limitations on the extent of indemnities which can be given by a company to a director. However, many directors will seek wider guarantees and indemnities whether they are given in the Service Agreement or in a separate Deed of Indemnity. In addition a senior manager is likely to need to take legal advice to assist in any claims and in defending any action taken by the regulator against them. It is in the interests of both the company and the employee for the full extent of the legal cover available to be clear from the outset. An employer is likely to impose a limit on the amount of legal costs or implement a process for covering such costs.

8.2.4 *Training/ongoing*

Much of the SMR may require a behavioural and cultural change. This will be helped by ongoing training as there will need to be a balancing of the corporate position and the executive's personal responsibilities. The increased regulatory burden may deter well-qualified candidates from applying for senior manager roles. To encourage senior managers, ongoing training will be invaluable. Some of the new training which will need to be given will be in relation to decision making and delegating. Where some of the responsible functions have currently been conducted by a committee they will now need to be taken by individuals or show clear delegation. From a senior manager's point of view they will need to have a clear understanding of their responsibilities and also will need an active role in determining the level and the amount of information that they receive from the business to effectively carry out that role. Under the SMR more extensive documentation may be required to provide evidence of decisions taken. The firm will also need to consider its policy regarding record keeping.

8.2.5 *Handover on exit*

When a Senior Manager leaves employment in most circumstances they should be required to provide information to the new employee on the status of the functions for which they were responsible and details of any potential breaches. It was originally thought that such information would be contained in a formal Handover Certificate. However, this may cause difficulties where an individual leaves a firm in circumstances which make it difficult to arrange an effective handover, either through no fault of the employee (illness or death) or because of issues between the employer and employee. The PRA makes it clear that firms must take all reasonable steps to ensure that before a person begins to perform any SMR they are provided with all the relevant information that they might reasonably expect in order to perform their responsibilities effectively.

Primary responsibility for the handover information will therefore rest with the employer. However, what happens if the employee is unable to complete the information e.g. due to death or illness? This again shows the importance of good record keeping and processes so that the employer can access all the relevant information to be provided to the new employee.

The handover information will be a very important document which will assist in showing the regulators the allocation of responsibility in any future disciplinary action. What happens however where an employee leaves under a cloud and is unwilling to cooperate in the giving of information? It is possible for an obligation to be included in the service agreement or contract of employment that an employee will cooperate in relation to any handover required. In addition, if the employee is entering into any settlement agreement tied to any termination payment then the employer can ensure that any payment is linked to a warranty that the employee complies with all requirements to provide necessary information for the employer to satisfy the obligations in relation to handover material.

Another issue which might arise is in relation to future investigations or enquiries. Most settlement agreements on termination of employment will require an employee to confirm that he/she has returned all documentation relating to the company and has not retained copies of any such information. However, the Senior Manager may wish to have continued access to documents after the employment has ceased, particularly if there is a risk of any claim being brought against the employee. Although the burden of proof is on the regulator to show that the individual failed to take the steps to prevent the regulatory breach, the senior manager is personally accountable and will therefore want to have access to the relevant documents. Rather than allowing an employee to retain potentially confidential information an employer may be more willing to agree to an employee having reasonable access to such information as and when requested. Employers will be unwilling to allow employees to keep, or have access to all information, some of which may be privileged. An employee will have to determine whether this undertaking from the employer is sufficient.

As the senior manager has personal responsibility, the outgoing senior manager is likely to want to take legal advice in relation to the handover arrangements as it will be very important to ensure that the extent of their involvement is clearly documented. Whilst an employer may agree to pay for legal advice on a termination arrangement, taxable benefits in relation to payment for the legal advice is limited to those amounts incurred in negotiating the termination of the employment. If the employer is to agree to pay for advice in relation to handover documentation then a limit should be agreed in relation to that advice separately.

Another important aspect on termination of employment is in relation to the writing of references. There will be an obligation on the employer to comply with regulatory obligations to keep references but also ensuring that factual content is correct bearing in mind the legal obligation regarding references. (See more on certification and regulatory references below)

8.3   Certification regime

8.3.1   Recruitment/Appointment

(a) The new certification regime extends beyond those who are senior managers and applies to all individuals whose involvement in the firm's activities might involve a risk of significant harm to the firm or its customers (s.63E FSMA). The rules on the standards of fitness and propriety essentially remain the same but the evidence required to assess and certify that the standard has been met has changed.

(b) Both the PRA and the FCA[5] have made it clear that the scope of the Certification Regime should be aligned as far as possible with the population of "material risk-takers" who will be subject to the Remuneration Code. It is also clear that this may apply to some non-executive directors.

(c) Under the Approved Persons Regime the regulators kept information about employees in determining whether they should be approved to take on a Controlled Function with a different employer. Although this is effectively still available in relation to senior managers, individuals within the Certification Regime who do not fall within the SMR will not be subject to regulatory pre-approval. Therefore new rules will be implemented in relation to regulatory references (see 8.3.4 below) As the certification regime will now rest with the firm, it will be very important that they are seen to take sufficient steps to ensure that the individual complies with the "fit and proper person" test. The certification process applies not only at the point of recruitment but also on an ongoing basis. The firm must consider the personal characteristics of the employee, ensure that the individual possesses the level of competence, knowledge and experience, has the qualifications and has undergone or is undergoing training. This means that any interview process must be sufficiently probing to establish all those matters listed.

(d) There has been a suggestion that firms may want to send out pre-employment questionnaires to candidates which can ask for further information in relation to disciplinary conduct, training record etc. Any such pre-employment questionnaire from the firm must be carefully drafted to ensure that there are no discrimination issues which may arise from the questions asked. If the firm discovers conduct which might be relevant from the responses to the questionnaire then the firm must make further reasonable

---

[5] (CP15/22) Strengthening accountability in banking – July 2015.

enquiries to establish the circumstances of that conduct and its relevance (if any) to the individual's fitness and propriety.

(e) One of the steps that needs to be taken to confirm that the person satisfies the fitness and propriety test is to obtain references in relation to the employee. This applies to senior managers and also to those subject to the certification regime, PRA senior insurance management functions (SIMFs) under the senior insurance managers regime (SIMR), FCA insurance controlled functions, notified non-executive director (NED) roles and credit union NEDs, and key function holders within an insurer. Obtaining references, may, depending on the employee, be difficult. If the individual is coming from a regulated firm then there is an obligation on that firm to provide a reference which complies with the requirements. However, if the individual is coming from a firm which is not subject to the regulatory regime, or is overseas, then the requirement is for the hiring firm to make reasonable efforts to secure a reference as part of their assessment of the fitness and propriety of prospective candidates. There is concern that this may result in firms seeking to recruit from a smaller pool of candidates for whom they can easily acquire the necessary information in the form of a reference.

(f) The difficulty for the firm in relation to overseas employers is ensuring a standard across different jurisdictions as to what amounts to "fit and proper" As mentioned above, some individuals not employed in the UK may still find that they fall within the SMR and will therefore be subject to certification. A firm should ensure that proper enquiries are made across different areas of the firm where it is part of a group. The PRA has said that in determining the fitness of an individual an employer can take into account assessments of the fitness made by other regulators, but the firm must ensure that it is taking steps to consider the interests of the UK firm in reviewing any such certification.

(g) Firms were already required to declare if an Approved Person candidate had a criminal record, including any spent convictions of which the employer has a legal right to be made aware. This requirement continues for senior managers but not for others subject to certification. In addition, if the person has lived or worked outside the UK for a material time in the previous five years then consent must be sought from the employee to request the information under equivalent overseas legislation. Employers generally will not rely on the individual to declare such information which may harm their application. It should also be noted that it is now unlawful to require an applicant to obtain a copy of their criminal record by means of a subject access request as a condition of employment.[6] Many employers will already have in place practices for making such applications but, where they do not, then the firm will need to sign up to the Disclosure and Barring Service (DBS) to run the checks for senior managers in relation to the UK and will need to consider what equivalent checks will be made outside the UK, if these are possible. In some overseas jurisdictions the authorities will not disclose such information and firms will need to consider what steps to take where no such information is forthcoming. Since such information is "sensitive information" within the terms of the Data Protection Act 1998 the firm needs to ensure that they have in place a policy dealing with processing the information from the criminal records check and how such information is filed. Firms may also want to apply for criminal records checks for staff who are not applying for positions under the SMR, if they are legally required to do so, and firms should have a clear policy about when such applications will be made.

(h) As the certification is to be carried out by the individual firm, the difficulty is how to transfer certification. Each firm will have to carry out its own investigation and will not be able to rely on the certification from a previous employer. The firm must complete the Form A to be submitted to the regulator with assistance from the

---

[6] Data Protection Act 1998 s.56, brought into effect by Data Protection Act 1998 (Commencement No.4) Order 2015 (SI2015/312)

candidate. Both the firm and the candidate must declare that the information is complete and accurate.

(i) Any appointment to a position must clearly be conditional on the approval process being completed. However, difficulties arise where a role, in exceptional circumstances, needs to be covered by someone who is not certified. Originally there was a two week "grace period" in order to give firms time to assess the fitness and propriety of individuals who are filling a temporary or unforeseen appointment, including external contractors. The PRA and the FCA have extended this grace period to four weeks to allow for more time for a firm to obtain the relevant information. However, even in those circumstances it may not be possible to obtain references of individuals to fill an unforeseen vacancy and an initial assessment may need to be made without the benefit of references. Under the SMR the firm has twelve weeks during which a temporary senior manager can be in place. However, the PRA does not think that it is necessary to give firms twelve weeks to seek the necessary information for certification. The twelve week period reflects the need to get an approval from the regulator for the senior manager which is to some extent outside the firms' control. In relation to obtaining the information necessary for certification that is within the firms control and therefore the necessary checks should be available within four weeks.[7]

8.3.2 Contracts of Employment

Contracts of employment may need to be amended to reflect the certification regime.

As the obligation is on the employer to be satisfied that the continuing obligation of fitness and propriety has been met, employers must have processes and procedures in place to ensure that the standards are being met. This may mean an extended obligation on employees to "blow the whistle" on

[7] Policy Statement PS3/15 Strengthening individual accountability in banking and insurance (responses to CP14/14 and CP26/14 – March 2015.

their own and others wrongdoing, including out of work, where this could impact on fitness and propriety. The duties clause within the contract of employment could be extended to ensure that such an obligation reaches a wider group of employees than is currently covered.

In most cases there will already be a provision that continued approval by the regulator is a requirement of continued employment. However, as the obligation now rests with the employer, then the contract should clearly make continued status as a fit and proper person under the employer's policy a condition of continued employment and a requirement by the employee to use best endeavours to ensure that the status is maintained, for example, by attending continued training.

8.3.3 *The Appraisal process*

Most HR functions are responsible for regularly vetting fitness and propriety. Whilst most firms already have full appraisals in place which provide the appropriate competencies for determining the assessment of fitness and propriety, appraisal systems may need to be reviewed to ensure that this is effective and that the annual certification process is built into the existing performance management process. It may also be that there will need to be additional checks outside of the annual appraisal system depending upon the individual's level of responsibility. The FCA guidance highlights that a firm may certify a person only if it is satisfied that the person is fit and proper to perform the function to which the certificate relates. Firms therefore need to act in a proportionate manner depending upon the individual's particular role and therefore the different competencies for different responsibilities need to be clear. The firm needs to ensure that ongoing record keeping obligations support the certification process. This is likely to require a closer alignment of the HR and regulatory functions. Guidance and training are also needed to support the rigorous approach to fitness and propriety within the appraisal system. There may also be changes to the HR and compliance process and function in order to cover the increased administrative and evidential burden on the firm rather than the regulators. Each firm will need to document effectively so that they can demonstrate to the regulators that they are effectively policing self-certification.

8.3.4 *Regulatory References*

Part of the certification requirement will be that reasonable steps are taken to obtain references. This means that firms will also be required to give regulatory references in relation to their own employees who apply for jobs involving senior management or certification functions at other firms. On 6 October 2015, the FCA and the PRA issued a joint consultation paper on regulatory references, which set out proposals for the references to be given.[8] On 4 February 2016, the FCA issued a Policy Statement setting out that in light of the complexity of concerns raised in the significant feedback received to the proposals the new referencing regime would be delayed until after commencement of the new regime.[9] The PRA also issued a press release. The October consultation paper followed the recommendations of the Fair and Effective Markets Review (FEMR). FEMR recommended that "the FCA and the PRA should consult on a mandatory form for regulatory references to help firms prevent the "recycling" of individuals with poor conduct records between firms". The rules on references apply to banks, building societies, credit firms and PRA investment firms (known as Relevant Authorised Persons) and also to insurers. The role for which a regulatory reference must be sought include a senior management function under the Certification Regime; PRA senior insurance management function under the Senior Insurance Managers Regime; FCA Insurance controlled functions; Notified NED roles within a Relevant Authorised Person or Solvency II firm; NEDs in credit unions; and key function holders and notified NED roles within an insurer. As an interim measure until the new referencing regime is introduced additional rules have been

---

[8] FCA CP15/31 / PRA CP36/15 Strengthening accountability in banking and insurance: regulatory references.

[9] FCA PS16/3 Strengthening accountability in banking : Feedback on CP15/22 (July 2015) and CP15/31 (October 2015); rules on extending the certification regime to wholesale market activities and interim rules on referencing.

added to apply the existing referencing requirements for pre-approved roles to Relevant Authorised Persons after 7 March 2016. PRA regulated firms will also be required to take reasonable steps to obtain appropriate references covering at least the past 5 years from the current and previous employer and organisations where the person served as a NED.

The October joint consultation paper proposed new draft rules to be inserted into the PRA and FCA rules. These included:

(i) a requirement to request regulatory references going back six years. These references would need to be sought from former employers regardless of whether the employer is regulated or not;

(ii) specific minimum disclosures must be included in the references to improve disclosures between regulated firms (see 3.4(c) below);

(iii) a standard mandatory template based on the proposed specific disclosures. When completing the template the firm must clearly indicate if there is no relevant information to disclose;

(iv) a continuing obligation to revise a regulatory reference they have given in the past six years where they become aware of matters that would cause them to draft that reference differently. This means that if a firm becomes aware of a regulatory breach by someone who has held office or employment in the firm there is obligation to issue a revised reference to any firm which had requested a regulatory reference in respect of that person in the previous six years;

(v) an express prohibition against firms entering into arrangements which conflict with the regulatory reference given (for example in a settlement agreement);

(vi) a requirement for firms to retain records of ex-employees' conduct and fit and proper information for a period of six years following their termination or resignation from a firm together with a requirement to establish and maintain adequate policies and procedures to comply with regulatory reference requirements; and

(vii) the relevant information extends to roles an individual performed under their "employment" and could therefore extend to services provided or functions performed on behalf of more than one regulated firm in a group.

When a regulated firm is asked for a reference, the joint consultation paper proposed that certain minimum information must be given. This included:

(i)   details of any certification function or controlled function or notified NED held and a summary of the role and its responsibilities;
(ii)   details of any other roles performed while an employee of the firm or as an employee of any firms within the same group in the last six years;
(iii) where the firm has concluded that there has been a breach of the rules of conduct and the facts which led the firm to that conclusion;
(iv)   where the firm has concluded in the last six years that the candidate was not a fit and proper person to perform a function and the facts which led the firm to that conclusion; and
(v)   details of the basis for and the outcome of any disciplinary action as a result of the points above. This includes details of formal warnings which were issued, or any adjustments to the individual's remuneration as part of the disciplinary action. (FEMR had suggested that firms should be compelled to disclose any adjustments to an individual's remuneration as part of the reference. The regulators have proposed limiting this to circumstances where it a result of concluded misconduct investigations.)

The proposed rules on regulatory references were also to apply if the firm is recruiting for a role requiring a regulatory reference within their own firm or group company.

The issues raised in the response to the proposals for regulatory references[10] included legal considerations about

---

[10] FCA PS16/3 Strengthening accountability in banking : Feedback on CP15/22

data protection, the practicalities of updating historic references, the rationale of applying the references to intra-group moves and concerns regarding proportionality. As a result the full Policy Statement on Regulatory References will be published in the summer 2016.

Employers must also ensure, in providing any reference even under the interim provision, that they consider the legal framework governing the provision of information relating to individuals, such as the Data Protection Act 1998 and the Human Rights Act 1998 as well as other legal obligations owed to an employee in providing a reference. Care must be taken to ensure that a refusal to provide a reference is not discriminatory under the Equality Act 2010 (EQA 2010). The protection against discrimination extends to employees who are subjected to discriminatory acts which take place after the employment has ended. In addition, if the employee (or ex-employee) has previously brought discrimination proceedings against the employer, or given evidence or information in connection with such proceedings, or made an allegation of unlawful discrimination or done anything else under or by reference to the discrimination legislation, a refusal to provide a reference may result in a separate and additional claim of victimisation, which can apply post-termination.

If the new regulatory references are implemented as set out in the October 2015 proposals, HR and compliance functions will need to update their record keeping and documentation to ensure that the necessary information is retained for at least six years and so that, going forward, references can be amended and updated as required.

The guidance to the new proposed rules establishes that firms should, wherever feasible conclude investigative procedures before employees depart and avoid giving any legal undertakings to surpress or omit relevant information to secure a

---

(July 2015) and CP15/31 (October 2015); rules on extending the certification regime to wholesale market activities and interim rules on referencing.

negotiated increase. This has a practical difficulty where an employee resigns prior to the completion of a disciplinary procedure.

Under employment law there is no legal requirement generally to provide a reference. If a reference is provided the employer owes a duty of care to an employee about whom he writes the reference[11]. The employer therefore has a duty to take reasonable care in the preparation of the reference and any failure to take this reasonable care may result in a successful claim for negligence if he fails to do so. The obligation is to provide a true, accurate and fair reference. Regulated firms are, however, subject to more stringent duties and will need to complete the mandatory template proposed whilst ensuring that they comply with the duty of care. In many settlement agreements on termination, an employer will agree the reference which it is going to give in relation to the employee and that it will not provide any reference outside this agreed form. It is useful to ensure that any clause agreeing to a reference in a settlement agreement includes the ability by the employer to depart from the agreed reference should any information come to light after the agreement has been signed which would change the terms of the reference. Employers must ensure that no one within the firm gives a reference which is outside the scope agreed in the settlement agreement, but also that any settlement agreement reference complies with obligations to the regulator. In addition, as mentioned above the consultation paper includes a new requirement that firms must not enter into arrangements that conflict with the regulatory reference rules. This means, for example, that a firm should not agree in a settlement agreement to omit relevant information from an employee's record in order to secure a negotiated release.

---

[11] *Spring v Guardian Assurance Plc* [1994] I.C.R. 596

8.3.5   *Non-Executive Directors*

As mentioned above not all non-executive directors (NEDs) will fall within the SMR. The PRA and the FCA therefore issued consultation on whether there should be an introduction of an assessment and notification regime for NED's outside the SMR[12]. One issue was whether leaving some NED's outside the scope of the SMR would lead to "two-tier boards". The PRA has made it clear that the SMR operates alongside the statutory and fiduciary duties that govern director's responsibilities including the requirements of the Companies Act 2006. This means that even though some NED's will have additional responsibilities under the SMR, all NED's should be clear as to their firm's culture in relation to requirements of the PRA and FCA.

As part of the requirement to ensure that there is not a two-tier board, the PRA has consulted on the assessment and notification regime for NED's who fall outside the SMR. This regime was considered important as an alternative to including all NEDs in the SMR. This new regime will require additional information:

(i)   the PRA must be notified when the appointment of the NED is confirmed. This may require a change to the management responsibilities map;
(ii)   firms should have the same high level criteria in assessing the fitness and propriety of a notified NED as they would a senior manager;
(iii) in addition to obtaining references from past employers references should also be sought from organisations where the person has held a NED role;
(iv)   a firm must require all members of its management body to observe the conduct rules set out below and also to comply with the Senior Management Conduct Rule 4 (to disclose appropriately any information to the FCA or PRA of which they would reasonably expect notice). Any

---

[12] (CP7/15) – "Approach to non-executive directors in banking and Solvency II firms & Application of the presumption of responsibility to Senior Managers in banking firms", February 2015.

appointment letters for NEDs must therefore make it clear that the NED is complying with the regulatory requirements and they will observe the same standards as other members of the Board; and

(v) in determining whether the NED is a fit and proper person and therefore satisfies the certification regime, the firm must consider whether the NED has complied with the fundamental conduct standards. Although NEDs who do not hold an SMF are not currently subject to the conduct rules the regulators have suggested that firms should contractually require them to adhere to conduct rules.

8.4 Conduct rules

8.4.1 Appointment/Recruitment

The new Conduct Rules come into effect on 7 March 2016. The existing statements of principle and Code of Practice which apply only to Approved Persons are replaced by the new set of conduct rules which cover a far wider number of the workforce[13]. Relevant firms, however, have until 7 March 2017 to prepare for the application of the conduct rules to the wider workforce, including all bank employees, except for those whose role would be "fundamentally the same as it would be if they worked in non-financial services firm". The view by the regulators is that it is important that staff at all levels of an organisation are subject to minimum standards and are accountable. The importance of conduct issues should be understood throughout the organisation and shouldn't stop below a certain level of seniority. The communication of this expected behaviour to the workforce is very important, particularly as the conduct rules now extend to a wider group of employees. The firm therefore needs to ensure that systems are in place to capture the change in those within the conduct rules. Whether this requires redrafting of documentation and posting of the information in a different place may vary from firm to firm.

---

[13] CP14/13 Strengthening accountability in banking: a new regulatory framework for individuals – July 2014

More stringent conduct rules apply to senior managers. It must be made clear to the employees on appointment, which conduct rules apply to them and the expectations of the firm in complying with these rules.

As part of the transition process there needs to be a discussion as to historic disciplinary matters. If individuals have previously not been caught by these conduct rules then what happens to any historical disciplinary issues? There should be full disclosure by the employees as to any previous misdemeanours. In practice many of the conduct rules would be issues that the employees would be expected to comply with in any event. What may be an issue is Conduct Rule 4 issued by the FCA which requires that an employee must pay "due regard to the interests of customers and treat them fairly." This suggests that all individual advisers will be responsible for the products which they sell to customers. In the final amendments to the FCA handbook in CP15/22 an example of a breach of this rule is where an employee recommends an investment to a customer where it does not have reasonable grounds for believing that it is suitable for that customer.[14] This potentially could lead to more "whistleblowing" in the future as employees report any wrongdoing to their employer or regulator in relation to products to protect themselves under this conduct rule.

Any offer of employment should be conditional on the employee passing any background checks as to previous conduct and any training or probationary period including receiving regulatory references (see 8.3.4 above).

8.4.2 Contracts of employment

The PRA has made it clear that the requirements of the conduct rules should be a contractual requirement[15]. A firm should therefore be able to enforce any standards of conduct. It should

---

[14] CP15/22 Strengthening accountability in banking: a new regulatory framework for individuals – Final rules (including feedback on CP14/31 and CP15/5) July 2015
[15] Amendments to PRA Rulebook – Conduct Standards.

therefore be clear in any Staff Handbook or Code of conduct that it is a condition of employment. Most contracts of employment will already allow for obligations on the employees to comply with all regulatory requirements and therefore should not need substantial review. Where this may be slightly different is in relation to NEDs who may not have full appointment letters.

The clause in a contract of employment relating to duties should be reviewed. One of the key conduct rules relating to the senior managers to is disclose appropriately any information of which the FCA or the PRA would reasonably expect notice (conduct rule SC4). Whilst most contracts of employment place a duty on fiduciaries (directors) to disclose information to the firm or on senior managers to provide details of the wrongdoing of others, the requirement in the conduct rules extends the obligation further and arguably amounts to a duty on senior managers to blow the whistle. One area of uncertainty is what about conduct outside work? If it is considered to affect the conduct within the workplace then arguably the senior manager should inform the PRA or FCA. This will require clear guidance and training.

The employee's contract of employment should clearly acknowledge receipt of a copy of the conduct rules and confirmation that the employee understands the rules as they apply to him/her. This will be evidence should there be any breach of the rules, that the employee knew of the obligations that applied.

It should be clear in any contract that a failure to live up to the conduct rules will be a disciplinary matter and that any serious breach may result in disciplinary action up to dismissal, including summary dismissal.

An obligation should be placed on employees to continue to comply with the conduct rules whether this is by attending ongoing training or asking questions of their employer if they are in doubt.

The employee should acknowledge that information about their conduct can be shared with the FCA/PRA. This is to avoid any issues regarding data protection.

8.4.3 *Appraisals/ ongoing training*

Different conduct rules apply to different categories of staff. The FCA set out rules 1-5 which apply to all conduct rules staff and senior manager conduct rules (SC1-SC4) which apply to senior managers. This requires training, policy and management changes. Although most firms have existing training programmes these may need to be extended to cover new staff who are now to be covered by the conduct rules. In addition, the conduct rules are general in their scope, but the regulators require firms to train all staff so that they are able to understand the nature of the conduct required. This means that the regulators will require the training to take account of the particular roles, including staff being given examples of the issues that might arise in areas that are relevant to their work[16]. Staff need to be trained to an appropriate level in respect of these conduct rules and therefore there is likely to be a more tailored training approach.

Firms need to provide benchmarks against which fit and proper assessments and checks against conduct rules apply. This covers an individual's training record, competence, qualifications and personal characteristics required by an individual in that role. Consideration will also need to be given to the sanctions where an employee's behaviour fall short of the required conduct. Firms will therefore need to ensure that staff are regularly appraised and performance processes are followed.

One issue in relation to ongoing training is reporting requirements for breaches of the Rules of Conduct. Originally, the government had imposed a duty on firms to report actual or suspected breaches of conduct rules to the regulators (FSMA

---

[16] CP15/22 Strengthening accountability in banking: a new regulatory framework for individuals – Final rules (including feedback on CP14/31 and CP15/5) July 2015

s64B(5). This was potentially a very costly obligation, particularly for large organisations. The government published the Financial Services (Banking Reform) Act 2014 (Commencement No.9) Order 2015 to ensure that the obligation in s.64B(5) does not come into force. Instead, the regulators should ensure that they are notified of any information about employee misconduct in a more proportionate way in their rules. The FCA and the PRA consulted about proposed amendments to rules and forms as a result of this change to the FSMA.[17] The consultation stresses that the result is "streamlined reporting requirements so that the forms only require firms to inform (the regulator) of disciplinary action taken against staff as a result of a breach of one or more Rules of Conduct". Disciplinary action is defined as the issuing of a formal written warning, suspension or dismissal, or reduction or recovery of remuneration. The PRA has clarified that if a suspension is only to facilitate an investigation then there is no obligation to notify the regulator, but it will be necessary if the employee is suspended whilst the firm considers disciplinary action.[18] The existing obligations on all regulated firms to notify the regulators of matters of which the regulators would reasonably expect notice such as a material breach of the rules will continue. This obligation is separate from the rules being introduced as part of the SMR and certification regime.

It is clear that the conduct rules are limited to the activities which that person performs in their capacity as an employee or senior manager of the firm. Therefore it is unlikely that actions outside of work will require a notification to the PRA or FCA (although employers would need to consider whether this would have any impact on an employee's status as a fit and proper person). Firms therefore need to set up processes to deal with reporting on conduct where circumstances warrant it (e.g. a disciplinary incident).

---

[17] CP16/1 Consequential changes to the Senior Managers Regime – January 2016; CP1/16 Strengthening individual accountability in banking: amendments to notification rules and forms - January 2016.

[18] PS9/16 Strengthening accountability in banking: responses to CP1/16, and the Certification Part of CP29/15 (March 2016).

There are also certain dangers from an employment law perspective in the reporting obligations to the regulator. Potentially notification to the regulators could amount to a breach of the implied term of mutual trust and confidence or potentially to constructive unfair dismissal. This is unlikely where a notification is made in good faith in accordance with regulatory requirements. Employers must ensure that to avoid any such claims there is a consistency of approach on breach of conduct reports across an organisation. Another legal issue is the effect of disclosing information to a regulator where that information is legally privileged. Careful consideration must be put into exactly which information is to be disclosed. A report containing legal advice may be legally privileged and it may only be necessary for either the FCA or the PRA or both to see certain of the information contained in that report, depending on the facts. Therefore it is important to make it clear to the FCA or the PRA the terms on which the document is being shared and prevent further disclosure. Since senior managers will also have additional obligations to blow the whistle under the conduct rules (senior managers conduct rule 4) they must be trained in which information can be disclosed and the limitation on the widespread circulation of privileged documentation.

Senior managers conduct rule 3 is a new rule that requires senior managers to take reasonable steps to ensure that any delegation of their responsibilities is to an appropriate person and that they oversee the discharge of the delegated responsibility effectively. This is likely to lead to senior managers keeping clear records relating to the delegation of their responsibilities.

8.4.4 *Performance Management and Customers*

One of the conduct rules applying to employees is conduct rule 4 "You must pay due regard to the interests of customers and treat them fairly". This is a new rule which may seem straightforward in theory, but training will need to be provided to support employees in exercising their judgment in practice. This rule needs also to be considered in light of the publication of the FCA guidance on performance management and the risks to customers.[19] Whilst there has been some improvement in the treatment of customers following the changes that have been made to firms' financial incentive structures for sales staff, there is still a risk to customers from the performance management and reporting processes which organisations impose. This FCA guidance considers the ways in which firms can manage the risk of mis-selling being driven by those poor performance management practices.

The FCA saw an increasing level of intelligence about poor performance management practices during 2014, taking action on intelligence from whistle-blowers at some firms. This indicated that some of the practices created an undue level of pressure on staff, which is likely to further increase the risk of mis-selling. Although managers may be imposing the correct culture, middle managers are particularly likely to have to manage conflicts of interest to avoid poor performance management practice. The way sales targets are calculated, and the levels that are set for individuals or teams, is also an important factor in how much pressure staff can be placed under to deliver sales results.

The FCA guidance makes it clear that the HR function should play a key role in how firms set the performance management approach. It sets out various good practice guidelines, including among others:

- include more balanced objectives, including how the employee behaved as opposed to just the outcome of the sale. This will require training for staff on how to assess such staff behaviour;
- keep sales targets under constant review;
- ensure that performance management records are clearly documented;
- improve the quality of the exit interviews to ensure important feedback is gathered effectively and make better use of information from whistle-blowers; and

---

[19] Risks to customers from performance management at firms – Thematic review and guidance for firms (FG15/10).

- avoid the use of public circulation of daily sales figures.
- The FCA expects firms, with staff who deal directly with retail customers, to take actions where appropriate to ensure that risks are adequately managed.

8.4.5 Exit

On termination of employment many employees may enter into settlement agreements. If there are ongoing disciplinary investigations then it may be difficult for employers to agree to enter into settlement agreement. Often a term of such a settlement agreement may be that the parties agree to stop any disciplinary proceedings. However, as mentioned above, if the disciplinary proceedings are not concluded this may cause issues for the firm in relation to their notification requirements to the regulators and also in relation to the references which need to be given. Firms need to give clear guidance to managers on negotiating the terms of any exits.

8.5 Corporate Governance – Board Responsibilities

The PRA has also issued a consultation paper proposing a supervisory statement on its expectations for corporate governance following the implementation of the new regime.[20] The proposed supervisory statement identifies the key aspects of good board governance in a well-run business. The PRA's view is that an effective board:

- establishes a sustainable business model and a clear strategy consistent with that model;
- articulates and oversees a clear and measurable statement of risk appetite against which major business options are actively assessed; and
- meets its regulatory obligations, is open with the regulators and sets a culture that supports prudent management.

---

[20] CP18/15 – Corporate Governance: Board Responsibilities

The PRA sets out guidance on its expectations relating to the key issues for boards to consider. The supervisory statement is not intended to be a comprehensive guide to good corporate governance (it is in addition to the general corporate govern- ance guidelines, for example the Financial Reporting Council's UK Corporate Governance Code). However the supervisory statement does indicate the issues which the regulator will pay close attention to in its supervision of firms. The statement covers areas such as setting strategy, culture, risk appetite, board composition and resources, management information and subsidiary boards.

(a) Setting strategy. The PRA will expect to see evidence that the board has established, and takes decisions consistent with a sustainable business model and manages the firm to a clear and prudent strategy and risk appetite. The setting of corporate strategy is core to the responsibilities of the board. Whilst the board as a whole should own the strategy, the SMR indicates that the chairman and the chief executive will have leading individual roles to play in the board's development and maintenance of the firm's business model.

(b) Culture. The board should articulate and maintain a culture of risk awareness and ethical behaviour for the entire organisation. The culture should be encouraged by various incentives, not limited to remuneration. NEDs have a key role to play in holding management to account for embedding and maintaining culture.

(c) Risk appetite and risk management. The business strategy should be supported by a well-articulated and measurable statement of risk appetite. Such a business strategy should be readily understood by the employees and the board will need to determine how best to circulate and express this strategy. The PRA will expect to see evidence of this active oversight of risks according to the risk appetite. The chair of the risk committee (where relevant) will be deemed responsible for safeguarding the independence, and overseeing the performance of, the firm's executive risk function, including the chief risk officer.

(d) Board composition. Good corporate governance applies to all boards, both parent and subsidiary. The board should include a sufficient number and quality of independent NEDs who must be able to hold the management to account. For listed firms, best practice is that at least half of the board (excluding the chairman) is comprised of independent NEDs. Smaller firms are expected to have at least two independent NEDs.

(e) Roles of executive directors and NEDs. All board members, regardless of their specific duties as executive or non-executive directors, share in the wider board duty to promote the success of the firm and to ensure it continues to meet the Threshold Conditions under the Financial Services and Markets Act 2000. NEDs, and the chairman in particular, are expected to play a key role in challenging executive management and holding them to account effectively. The PRA expects boards to be precise over what duties and responsibilities are delegated to the chief executive or executive management and the limitations and accountabilities associated with each matter. Although most boards may already have in place guidance as to what can be delegated, this should be clear and well documented.

(f) Knowledge and experience of NEDs. Between them, NEDs need to have sufficient current and relevant knowledge and experience to understand the key activities and risks involved in their firm's business model. Board responsibility is collective, however, and NEDs should not simply delegate responsibility for major decisions to individuals among them who are considered specialist in the area under consideration. The key is to have a diversity of experience. It must also be clear to the NED's that they can call on professional advice should they require it. In considering this boards should consider any limitations on the cost of such advice.

(g) Board time and resources. NEDs should ensure they have sufficient time to fulfil their duties and boards should set clear expectations when recruiting new NEDs. It should be clear in any letter of appointment the obligations in respect of time requirements. The PRA expects NEDs to be given adequate support and training to enable them to carry out their duties. Under the SMR, the chairman is expected to lead the development and monitoring of effective policies and procedures for the induction, training and ongoing professional development of board members, in particular non-executives.

(h) Management information and transparency. Provision to the board of timely, accurate, complete and relevant information is a fundamental component in supporting the board to fulfil its duties and responsibilities. The chairman and NEDs are expected to manage the nature, specific content and frequency of the information provided to the board. Management should be open and transparent with the board and ensure it is adequately apprised of all significant matters including key business developments, decisions and activities about which the board should be aware, as well as issues outside the board's stated risk appetite that, due to the nature or impact of the issue, warrants disclosure or escalation to the board. The supervisory statement suggests that NEDs should have unrestricted access to a firm's employees and information as needed to enable them to carry out their duties.

(i) Succession planning. Boards should ensure they have robust succession plans that recognise current and future business needs and address the unexpected loss of key individuals, particularly those covered by the SMR.

(j) Remuneration. The PRA expects a board to oversee the design and operation of its firm's remuneration system ensuring that incentives are aligned with prudent risk taking.

(k) Subsidiary boards. In general the principles of good governance should also apply to regulated material subsidiaries. The PRA considers it generally undesirable for some key positions on the subsidiary board, such as chairman, chair of the key sub-committees, chief executive or finance director, to be occupied by executive members of the group or parent company board. This does not prevent group NEDs from chairing or sitting on the subsidiary board as NEDs. The extent to which the PRA

440

believes subsidiary company boards need to be independent will be influenced by a number of factors for example the size and nature of the business, or a substantial difference in the business model or the incentives of the subsidiary.

(l) Board committees. The role of sub-committees is to support the board. Committees are accountable to the board but should not relieve the board of any of its responsibilities.

8.6   Remuneration

Inappropriate remuneration policies were widely identified as a contributory factor to the financial crisis. As a result, the Remuneration Code was introduced. As of 31 December 2015, there are five remuneration codes applying to different sectors within the financial services industry. The new Remuneration Code for dual-regulated firms, i.e. banks, building societies and PRA designated investment firms (SYSC 19D), was introduced in response to recommendations from the PCBS. The new Code followed a consultation carried on in July 2014 (CP14/14), with final rules published in June 2015 (PS15/16)[21] The key principle of all the codes is that all the relevant firms must ensure that their remuneration policies and practices are consistent with and promote sound and effective risk management. Whilst some of the Remuneration Code SYSC 19D (the Remuneration Code) may apply to all staff, the most stringent requirements are currently applied to those termed "Code" staff who do not satisfy the de minimis concession. For performance periods on or after 1 January 2016, senior managers under the new regime will be subject to even more stringent deferral and clawback rules.

(a) Clawback: The Remuneration Code already requires that employers impose clawback on some remuneration already paid to employees where there has been misconduct or a failure of risk management. Firms can require

---

[21] PS15/16 Strengthening the alignment of risk and reward: New remuneration rules – June 2015

repayment back to the firm of remuneration already paid to employees for a period of up to seven years from the date of the award of the remuneration. In relation to senior managers this should be extended by a further three years (i.e. to a period of ten years), where, at the end of the seven-year period, the firm or a regulator has commenced an investigation which could potentially lead to the application of clawback.

(b) Deferral: Under the new rules, senior managers will be subject to a seven-year deferral requirement with no vesting until three years after the award. Code staff (excluding those covered by the new SMR) will be subject to a five-year deferral requirement. In both cases vesting must be no faster than on a pro-rata basis. All other material risk takers will be subject to a minimum three- to five-year deferral period.

(c) Buy outs: In certain situations firms could buy out the variable remuneration lost by employees when they move to a new employment. The difficulty with this is that it effectively works in favour of those who change employment since the individuals are then no longer at risk of malus adjustments in respect of their former employment. The regulators set out four potential regulatory approaches[22]. These are prohibiting buy out bonuses; requiring the former employer to maintain unvested awards even if the staff member leaves to join a competitor; requiring the appropriate regulator to apply malus to the buy-out bonus if it subsequently transpires that the former employer would have had grounds to reduce the original awards; and requiring the new employer to apply clawback.

The new proposals can cause difficulties for the HR function and the drafting of the employment/remuneration policies. Given that firms may often need to clawback amounts which were paid several years previously and are likely to have been converted into cash and spent, it is vital to ensure that the provisions are both enforceable and operable in practice. The

---

[22] PS15/16 Strengthening the alignment of risk and reward: New remuneration rules – June 2015

terms of any clawback provisions should therefore be explicit and agreed with the executive before the entitlement to payment or award arises and agreed in writing before the event giving rise to the clawback occurs (to avoid any issues regarding deductions from wages under s.13 ERA 1996). They should also include the right to deduct the requisite amount from any salary, bonus or other cash amounts due. In circumstances where it may be particularly difficult to enforce recoupment from an individual once they have left, firms may wish to consider whether it would be desirable to require departing executives to place any money or share awards in escrow until the clawback rights fall away.

Chapter 9

Whistleblowing

Paul Griffin
Partner
Norton Rose Fulbright

Amanda Sanders
Senior Knowledge Lawyer
Norton Rose Fulbright

9.1 Introduction

In the Report of the Parliamentary Commission on Banking Standards (PCBS) "Changing Banking for good" in 2013 (PCBS recommendations), the PCBS expressed its shock at the evidence it heard that people turned a blind eye to misbehaviour and failed to report it. It stated that "Institutions must ensure that their staff have a clear understanding of their duty to report an instance of wrongdoing or 'whistleblowing' within the firm". The FCA and the PRA have both taken steps to encourage whistleblowing and both believe that a change is required in attitudes towards whistleblowing in banks and insurers. The Senior Managers' Regime includes an increased responsibility on employees to disclose information both to the regulator and to their employer. This is likely therefore to bring about an increase in the levels of whistleblowing in the financial services sector.

On 6 October 2015, the FCA and the PRA published policy statements containing new rules on whistleblowing. These rules followed on from a consultation in February 2015 on Whistleblowing in deposit takers, PRA designated investment firms and insurers.[1] The rules are intended to build on and formalise examples of good practice already found in the financial services industry.[2]

It is clear that in the financial services sector a whistleblower is more likely to blow the whistle to the regulator than to their own employer. It is therefore very important for employees and employers to understand the protection afforded to employees by the whistleblowing legislation.

9.2   Protected disclosures by workers under PIDA

The UK whistleblowing legislation was introduced by the Public Interest Disclosure Act 1998 (PIDA) which inserted new provisions into the Employment Rights Act 1996 (ERA 1996). The legislation introduced specific rights for those who disclose information about alleged wrongdoings including the right not to suffer a detriment in employment and the right not to be unfairly dismissed for making such disclosures. Any dismissal will be automatically unfair if the reason or the principal reason for the dismissal is that the employee made a protected disclosure. Although the UK legislation seeks to encourage employees to raise concerns, there is currently no legal or regulatory duty requiring an employer to have whistleblowing arrangements in place.

9.2.1   Who is protected?

In order for an individual to be protected by the provisions under PIDA, the disclosure must be made by a "worker". "Worker" is defined in s.230(3) of the ERA 1996 as:

> "an individual who has entered into or works under (or, where the employment has ceased, worked under): (a) a contract of employment, or (b) any other contract . . .

---

[1]   FCA CP15/4. PRA CP6/15 Whistleblowing in deposit-takers, PRA-designated investment firms and insurers, February 2015.

[2]   Whistleblowing in deposit-takers, PRA designated investment firms and insurers supervisory statement SS39/15 and Policy Statements PS15/24.

whereby the individual undertakes to do or perform personally any work or services for another party to the contract whose status is not by virtue of the contract that of a client or customer of any profession or business undertaking carried on by the individual".

Section 43K ERA 1996 extends this definition where the worker is seeking protection against detriment for making a protected disclosure. This amended definition includes contractors acting under the control of the employer, persons on training courses and doctors, dentists, opticians and pharmacists providing services under statutory schemes. In addition, it has been held that a member of a Limited Liability Partnership (LLP) is also a worker for the purposes of s.230(3) and therefore entitled to bring a claim relating to protected disclosures.[3]

In November 2013, Public Concern at Work, the Whistleblowing Charity, published a report of the Whistleblowing Commission on "The effectiveness of existing arrangements for workplace whistleblowing in the UK". As part of the consultation the Whistleblowing Commission asked whether there should be a broader more flexible definition of worker within PIDA to deal with the many different types of worker and working arrangements in the modern workplace. Although the responses suggested that many respondents agreed that the definition of worker should be extended the definition remains as set out in s.43K. The proposals by the FCA and the PRA suggests that more people within the organisation should be able to qualify for protections (see proposals below).

9.2.2 What amounts to a protected disclosure under PIDA?

In order for the disclosure to be a protected disclosure the disclosure must satisfy the following tests:

- there must be a disclosure of information;

---

[3] Bates van Winkelhof v Clyde & Co LLP v [2014] UKSC 32; [2014] 1 W.L.R. 2047; [2014] I.C.R. 730.

447

- the subject matter of the disclosure must fall within the relevant category[4];
- the worker must reasonably believe that the disclosure of the information is in the public interest; and
- the person to whom the disclosure is made must fall within those persons listed in the legislation.[5]

9.2.2.1   Disclosure of Information

In order to qualify as a qualifying disclosure the employee must provide "information". This means that the disclosure must convey facts, be more than merely a communication and more than an allegation or a statement of the position. The information can be disclosed either verbally or in writing. However, a verbal communication which is an informal or generalised statement is unlikely to be sufficient to amount to a disclosure of information. From both the employer and employee's point of view it is best for any disclosure to be made in writing in order to produce evidence of the disclosure.

An employee must be careful that the information they provide goes no further than making a disclosure. For example, if the worker is informing the employer that the IT system is not secure, then such a provision of information could amount to a qualifying disclosure. However, to then prove the point by hacking into the system could then amount to misconduct which would be a separate issue to the disclosure and the individual would not be protected by the whistleblowing legislation in relation to that hacking.[6]

9.2.2.2   Subject matter of the disclosure

Subject to certain exceptions,[7] in order for the disclosure to be a qualifying disclosure the information must, in the reasonable

---

[4]   ERA 1996 s.43B.
[5]   ERA 1996 ss.43C–43H.
[6]   *Bolton School v Evans* [2006] EWCA (Civ) 1653; [2007] I.C.R. 641; [2007] I.R.L.R. 140.
[7]   ERA 1996 ss.43B(3) and 43(B)(4).

belief or the worker making the disclosure, be made in the public interest and tends to show one or more of the following six categories of wrongdoing:

- that a criminal offence has been committed, is being committed or is likely to be committed;
- that a person has failed, is failing or is likely to fail to comply with any legal obligation to which he is subject;
- that a miscarriage of justice has occurred, is occurring or is likely to occur;
- that the health or safety of any individual has been, is being or is likely to be in danger;
- that the environment has been, is being or is likely to be damaged; and
- the information intending to show any matter falling within any of the proceeding paragraphs has been is being or is likely to be deliberately concealed.

The wrongdoing can be past or present or merely alleged. It is also irrelevant whether the conduct occurred within or outside the UK and may consist of a breach of any applicable foreign law. If a worker makes a disclosure of information about any matter that does not fall into one (or more) of the above categories then they will not be entitled to protection under PIDA in respect of that disclosure even if the employee reasonably believed that the disclosure was in the public interest.

9.2.2.3   *Disclosure in the public interest*

Prior to 25 June 2013, there was no public interest test for qualifying disclosures. However, since that date a public interest test has been inserted into s.43B ERA 1996 requiring individuals to have a reasonable belief that the disclosure was made in the public interest. The statutory objective of introducing the public interest requirement was to reverse the decision in *Parkins v Sodexho Ltd* [2002] I.R.L.R. 109 in which the EAT held that a definition of a qualifying disclosure was broad enough to cover a breach of the whistleblower's own contract of employment. This substantially widened the scope of a qualifying disclosure and meant that it could include an individual's own employment contract including implied terms and statutory employment rights.

The public interest test was considered in the case of *Chesterton Global Ltd v Nurmohamed* [UK EAT/0335/14]. In that case, the EAT held that it was not necessary to show that the disclosure was of interest to the public as a whole, as it is inevitable that only a section of the public would be directly affected by any given disclosure. Therefore the disclosure in that particular case, which related to alleged profit manipulation by the employer, passed the public interest test even though the principal motivation for raising the issue was the effect that the manipulation had on the employee's own rates of commission payment. Since the tribunal was satisfied that the employee had in mind other senior managers whose contracts would also be affected then this was sufficient to amount to public interest. This decision was followed in *Underwood v Wincanton Plc* [UK EAT/0163/15] concerning a grievance raised by four HGV drivers on the allocation of overtime, the EAT holding that an employee could be protected under the whistleblowing legislation even where it related to a contractual matter affecting a group of employees.

The disclosure must "in the reasonable belief" of the worker be made in the public interest and tend to show that one of the six relevant failures has occurred, is occurring or is likely to occur. The reasonable belief requirement balances the right of the worker who considers that there has been an act of malpractice with the interests of the employer which could be damaged by unfounded allegations.

9.2.2.4 *Identity of the individual to whom the disclosure is made*

In order to be a "protected disclosure" a qualifying disclosure must be made only to the category of people contemplated in PIDA. The tiered disclosure regime provides different levels of "hurdles" to comply with in order to secure protection. For example, a worker who makes a qualifying disclosure to his or her employer has fewer conditions to satisfy than a worker who makes a disclosure to a third party. The statutory protection is designed to encourage workers to raise concerns about wrongdoing or malpractice within the organisation for which they work. Disclosures can be made to the following:

- An employer: disclosure of information by a worker will be protected if the worker makes the qualifying disclosure to their employer or, to a relevant "responsible person". A responsible person is someone whom the worker reasonably believes that the conduct relates to or a matter which is the legal responsibility of that person and not the employer. A disclosure to an employer is subject to the least stringent conditions as far as the worker is concerned. A disclosure under an authorised procedure (for example to a confidential hotline under a bribery and anti-corruption policy) may fall within s.43C(2) and be treated as being a qualifying disclosure to an employer.
- A legal adviser: disclosure of information by a worker will also be protected if the worker makes a qualifying disclosure to a legal adviser in the course of obtaining legal advice.
- A Minister of the Crown: a worker can make a disclosure to a UK Government minister where he is employed by an individual or body appointed under any enactment, (for example an NHS body).
- A prescribed person: A worker can make a qualifying disclosure to a "prescribed person". The Secretary of State in the Department for Business, Innovation and Skills prescribes the identity of the prescribed person and its remit. Details of those currently listed are set out in the Public Interest Disclosure (Prescribed Persons) Order 1999 (as amended). Prescribed persons includes HM Revenue and Customs, the Audit Commission, the Health and Safety Executive and also the FCA and the PRA. There is an additional hurdle for the worker to overcome where they are making the disclosure to a prescribed person. The qualifying disclosure will only be protected if:
  — the worker reasonably believes that the fault falls within the remit of the prescribed person;

— the worker reasonably believes that the relevant failure falls within any description of matters in respect of which that person is so prescribed; and

— the worker reasonably believes that the information disclosed and any allegation contained in it are substantially true.

This last requirement suggests that the level of investigation required by the employee is higher than would be the case for a disclosure to an employer.

Furthermore, employment tribunals can send details of whistleblowing claims direct to a "prescribed person" where the claimant has given their express consent. Currently, there is no legal obligation on prescribed persons to take any action in relation to the disclosures that they receive. ERA 1996 s.43FA (inserted by the Small Business Enterprise and Employment Act 2015) empowers the Secretary of State in the Department of Business, Innovation and Skills to make regulations requiring prescribed persons to produce an annual report on disclosures of information made to them by workers (see below).

- The wider public: There will be relatively limited situations in which wider disclosure can be made which will retain the protection under PIDA. If the worker wants to make any disclosure to a non-prescribed regulator, or even the media then there are a number of detailed and complex conditions which need to be satisfied and the most stringent rules apply. In order to gain protection under PIDA, the worker must satisfy the following conditions:

  — the worker must believe that the information disclosed and any allegation contained in it are substantially true;

  — the worker must not have made the disclosure for the purposes of any personal gain;

  — the worker must either, at the time of making the disclosure, reasonably believe that they would be subject to a detriment by their employer if they make a disclosure to the employer or prescribed person; or reasonably believe that material evidence will be concealed or destroyed if a disclosure is made to the employer where there is no prescribed person; or have previously disclosed substantially the same information to their employer or to a prescribed person; and

— in all the circumstances of the case it must be reasonable to make the disclosure.

In determining whether it was reasonable for the worker to make the disclosure the employment tribunal must take into account the identity of the person to whom the disclosure is made; the seriousness of the relevant failure; whether the relevant failure is continuing or is likely to recur; whether the disclosure is made in breach of a duty of confidentiality owed by the employer to any other person; in the case of a previous disclosure to the worker's employer or a prescribed person, the response of the employer or a prescribed person; and, in the case of a previous disclosure to the worker's employer, whether the worker complied with an internal procedure authorised by the employer.

- Disclosures of an "exceptionally serious" nature. In order to qualify for protection under this provision:
  — the worker must reasonably believe that the information disclosed and any allegation contained in it are substantially true;
  — the disclosure must not be made for the purposes of personal gain;
  — the relevant failure is of an exceptionally serious nature; and
  — in all the circumstances it must be reasonable for the worker to make the disclosure, having regard, in particular to the identity of the person to whom the disclosure is made.

In the case of disclosure of an "exceptionally serious" nature, it is not necessary for the worker to have raised the issue internally first or to have reasonably believed that they would be subject to a detriment from their employer or reasonably believe that evidence would be concealed or destroyed. Cases falling within this level of disclosures have included those relating concealment of significant damage to public health and humanitarian issues relating to the exploitation and enslavement of women.

9.2.3 What protection will the employee/worker have?

As mentioned above, a worker who is successful in showing that they have made a qualifying disclosure can be protected from both being subjected to a detriment and unfair dismissal.

9.2.3.1 Detriment

Section 47B(1) ERA 1996 provides that a worker has the right not to be subjected to any detriment by any act or deliberate failure to act, by his or her employer on the ground that the worker has made a protected disclosure. In addition, under s.47B(1A) ERA 1996 a worker has the right not to be subjected to any detriment by any act or a deliberate failure to act done, by another worker of the employer in the course of that other worker's employment, or, by an agent acting with the employer's authority, on the ground that the worker has made a protected disclosure.

The term "detriment" is not defined in the ERA 1996. In considering whether a worker has been subjected to a detriment, the employment tribunal will consider the meaning of detriment established by UK discrimination case law. In particular, a worker suffers a detriment if a reasonable worker would, or might take the view that, they would have been disadvantaged in the circumstances in which they had to work. Simply feeling a sense of grievance is not enough. It is also not sufficient for there to be a detriment where an employer has failed to take any action for a short period. The worker has to show that there was a conscious decision by the employer to take no action.[8] The definition of worker also includes a former worker and therefore a worker who is subjected to a detriment by their former employer, for example by being provided with a bad reference after termination of their employment can still bring a claim for suffering a detriment.

---

[8] *Blackboy Ventures Ltd (t/a Chemistree) v Gahir* [2014] I.C.R. 747; [2014] I.R.L.R. 416.

The worker (claimant in the employment tribunal) must show that they have made a protected disclosure and that there was detrimental treatment. The employer must then show that the protected disclosure did not materially influence the detriment.[9] This places an arguably lower burden of proof on a claimant than in a situation where the claimant is dismissed and it is therefore often easier for the claimant to succeed in a detriment case.

9.2.3.2   Dismissal

Section 103A ERA 1996 renders the dismissal of an employee automatically unfair where the reason (or, if more than one reason, the principal reason) for his or her dismissal is that he or she made a protected disclosure. A dismissal on grounds of having made a protected disclosure is automatically unfair and does not require consideration as to whether the dismissal was reasonable in all the circumstances. Moreover, no qualifying period of employment or upper age limit applies. In addition, there will be no limit on the amount of compensation which may be awarded should the employee be successful.

It is important to note however, that the protection from unfair dismissal only applies to "employees" (i.e. individuals who have entered into, or work or worked under, a contract of employment).

The main difficulty for employees is to be able to prove that the fact that they "blew the whistle" was the reason, or the principal reason, for their subsequent dismissal. In particular this is an issue where there has been an act of misconduct by the employee in addition to any whistleblowing. It is for the employee to show that they made a protected disclosure and that they have been dismissed, but where they have the qualifying period of service (currently two years employment), the burden is on the employer to show the reason for the dismissal.

---

[9]   *Fecitt v NHS Manchester* [2011] EWCA Civ 1190; [2012] I.C.R. 372; [2012] I.R.L.R. 64.

9.2.4 *Claims/remedies*

9.2.4.1 *Claims*

An employee who has been dismissed for having made a protected disclosure is entitled to bring an unfair dismissal claim to an employment tribunal under s.111ERA 1996. The complaint must be made to the employment tribunal before the end of three months from the effective date of termination. A worker who has been subjected to a detriment on the ground of making a protected disclosure may bring a complaint to an employment tribunal under s.48(1) ERA. This complaint must be presented to the employment tribunal before the end of the period of three months beginning with the date of the act or failure to act to which the complaint relates, or, if the act was part of a series of similar acts, the last such act or failure to act. Employment tribunals have discretion to extend the time limit if the claimant can show that it was not reasonably practicable to present the claim in time.

9.2.4.2 *Remedies*

Where an employment tribunal finds in favour of a claimant in a detriment complaint it must make a declaration to that effect. In addition, the employment tribunal may make an award of compensation.[10] Any such award will be the amount the employment tribunal considers just and equitable in all the circumstances of the case having regard to the infringement to which the complaint relates and any loss which is attributable to the act or failure to act which infringed the complainant's right not to be subjected to a detriment. The loss suffered can be loss of earnings or benefits as a result of being subjected to a detriment, but also include compensation for injury to feelings and personal injury.

In relation to unfair dismissal claims an employee can seek reinstatement (reinstatement in the previous position with no

---

[10] ERA 1996 ss.49(1)(a) and 49(1)(b).

financial loss), re-engagement (re-employment in a job comparable to the previous position or other suitable employment) or
compensation. Compensation for unfair dismissal is split into a
basic and a compensatory award. The compensatory award in
a whistleblowing claim is not subject to a cap and there is
therefore no limit on the level of compensation. A compensatory award is based on what is thought to be just and equitable
in all the circumstances and could be very high if the view is
taken that a worker may no longer be able to find employment
as a result of blowing the whistle. The employment tribunal
cannot award compensation for injury to feelings in a dismissal
claim.

An employee who is claiming that he or she has been
dismissed by reason of making a protected disclosure can also
apply to an employment tribunal for "interim relief".[11] This is
an order requiring the employer to re-employ the employee
pending final determination of his or her unfair dismissal
claim. The effect of an interim relief order is that the employee
continues in employment until the full hearing and, in practice
means that the employee is likely to be suspended on full pay
until that date.

9.3   Approach by the FCA and PRA

As mentioned above, a disclosure to the FCA or PRA is
protected under s.43F ERA 1996 as being a qualifying
disclosure. To fall within this section the worker must
reasonably believe that the relevant failure falls within the
description and matters in respect of which the FCA and the
PRA are prescribed persons and that the information disclosed
in any allegation contained in it are substantially true. It does
appear in the financial services industry, whistleblowers are
more likely to blow the whistle to the regulator than to their
own employer. This may be for various reasons: first,
employees may believe that an internal approach is less likely
to result in any action being taken to correct the wrongdoing.
There is no obligation on a firm to take any steps as a result of

---

[11]   ERA 1996 s.128.

disclosure, although it may impact on the continued fitness and propriety of the firm. In addition, employees may believe that a disclosure to a regulator may result in some action being taken by the employer as a fear of disciplinary action being commenced by the regulator against the firm.

Following the evidence to the PCBS the FCA took steps to encourage whistleblowers to raise the alarm. The approach to whistleblowing prior to the introduction of the new regime was largely policy orientated and concentrated on gathering intelligence from whistleblowing.[12]

9.3.1 FCA and PRA Rules

In October 2015, the PRA issued a Supervisory Statement[13] and the FCA and PRA issued a Policy Statement[14] on Whistleblowing in deposit–takers, PRA-designated investment firms and insurers, containing a package of measures to formalise firms' whistleblowing procedures. These rules go further than the requirements of PIDA and ERA 1996. These proposals arose as a response to the PCBS recommendations that banks put in place a mechanism to allow their employees to raise concerns internally. The Policy Statement PS15/24 attaches new rules to be included in the Senior Management Arrangements Systems and Controls Sourcebook (SYSC) and the Prudential Source-book for Investment firms (IFPRU). Relevant firms have until 7 September 2016 to comply with the requirements. The requirements to assign responsibilities to a whistleblowers champion will take effect on 7 March 2016, together with the Senior Manager's Regime. Between 7 March 2016 and 7 September

---

[12] For the FCA, Chapter 18 Senior Management Arrangments, Systems and Controls Sourcebook (SYFC), section 2.4 Investment Firms Prudential source-book, section 2.5 Recognised Investment Exchange Sourcebook. For the PRA section 4.1.15 Senior Management Arrangements, Systems and Controls Source-book which forms part of its Handbook.

[13] Supervisory Statement SS39/15 Whistleblowing in deposit-takers, PRA designated investment firms and insurers (October 2015).

[14] Policy Statement PS15/24 Whistleblowing in deposit-takers, PRA designated investment firms and insurers (October 2015).

2016 the whistleblower's champion will be responsible for overseeing the steps the firm takes to implement the new regime.

In summary the new rules propose that relevant firms (see below) should:

- put internal whistleblowing arrangements in place (if they are not already) that are able to handle all types of disclosure from all types of person;
- inform their UK based employees that they can blow the whistle to the FCA or the PRA regardless of whether they have made an internal report;
- require its appointed representatives and tied agents to tell their UK based employees about the FCA whistleblowing service;
- include a specified passage in settlement agreements clarifying that nothing in the agreement prevents an employee or ex-employee from making a protected disclosure;
- allocate responsibility for whistleblowing under the Senior Managers Regime to a "whistleblowers' champion";
- inform the FCA if it loses an employment tribunal case with a whistleblower; and
- present a report on whistleblowing to its board at least annually.

9.3.1.1   Who do the new rules apply to?

The FCA and PRA propose that the new rules will apply at first to:

- UK deposit taking firms (meaning UK regulated banks, building societies and credit unions) with total gross assets exceeding £250 million;
- PRA designated investment firms; and
- Insurance and re-insurance firms regulated by the PRA.

The requirements will not apply to UK branches of overseas banks, although the FCA will explore this further in a future consultation. In addition, firms which do not fall within the rules may adopt the rules and guidance as best practice, and may tailor its approach taking into account its size, structure and headcount. Although this would mean that small credit unions would be exempted from these requirements because of their limited resources, it may be best practice to require the arrangements to be in place for good corporate governance.

9.3.1.2 *Disclosures to the regulators*

The FCA and the PRA both run dedicated whistleblowing services which can be used to report a concern. The new rules will require that all employees of relevant firms who are based in the UK should be informed about the whistleblowing services provided by the PRA and the FCA including how to contact them, the protections they offer and the kinds of disclosures it would be appropriate to make. The regulators will also require relevant firms to tell employees that they can blow the whistle to them at any stage regardless of whether they have raised the concern internally first. The communication making it clear that reporting to the PRA or the FCA is not conditional on a report first being made using the firm's internal arrangements must be included in the employee handbook or other equivalent document.

Despite the new rule, employees should be reminded, that in order to be protected under ERA 1996 if they choose to inform the regulator instead of their employer they have the added burden of showing that they believe the allegation forming the protected disclosure to be substantially true.

9.3.1.3 *Offer whistleblowing protection*

There is currently no requirement for an employer to have whistleblowing arrangements in place. However, the FCA and the PRA want relevant firms to have internal procedures in place that would reassure all employees that they can raise concerns and will be listened to. The proposals of the FCA and the PRA are that in adopting internal procedures, firms should:

- respect the confidentiality of whistleblowers who raise concerns;
- be able to deal with anonymous disclosures. Whilst Government guidance and the Whistleblowing charity Public Concern at Work encourage whistleblowers to raise concerns openly, there is no specific provision on confidentiality in PIDA. Whistleblowers can be reminded that it may be more difficult to take action in certain circumstances without the open testimony of the whistleblower, but firms should be able to deal with a situation where the whistleblower wishes to remain anonymous;
- allow for concerns to be made through a range of communication methods, for example, a dedicated phone line or email address;
- assess and escalate concerns raised by whistleblowers within the firm or, where justified to an external organisation;
- track the "outcome" of disclosures and provide feedback to whistleblowers where appropriate;
- track what happens to an internal whistleblower to determine whether they are subsequently disadvantaged as a result of speaking out;
- prepare and maintain records of reportable concerns made and the firm's treatment of those reports including the outcome;
- prepare written procedures (e.g. employee handbooks etc.); and
- take all reasonable steps to ensure that no person under the firm's control engages in victimising whistleblowers and take appropriate measures against those responsible for such victimisation.

9.3.1.4   *The extent of the whistleblowing protection*

As set out above, a disclosure of information will only be a qualifying disclosure if it is in relation to one of the matters listed in s.43 ERA 1996. The new rules extend the topics which could be covered by a firm's internal whistleblowing arrangements. This could cover any type of concern including those not related to breaches of the FCA and/or PRA rules and which do not qualify as protected disclosures under PIDA. The reason for this proposal is that it would encourage individuals to "speak up". This has to be balanced against the firms and regulators receiving a vast number of disclosures that are unrelated to regulatory issues and may be purely personal to the employee with no wider public interest implication. The regulators believe that firms should be able to filter out genuine whistleblowing cases from those that can be dealt with by alternative routes such as customer complaints or individual human resources grievance procedures. Written procedures containing these rules may set out that the whistleblowing arrangements can be used to blow the whistle after alternative routes have been exhausted. It is also clear that if an employee knowingly makes a false disclosure with a malicious intent then the proposals should not prevent the firm from taking appropriate action against that employee. The employee will not be protected by PIDA or by the ERA 1996 if they do not satisfy the requirements set out in that legislation.

In addition the new rules require that the arrangements should cover protected disclosures by employees, non-executive directors, former employers, secondees, interns and work experience placements, volunteers, agency workers, contractors, agents and employees of subsidiaries, competitors, appointed representatives and suppliers. These include people who would not fall within the definition of "worker" in ERA 1996 referred to above. As such these people would not have the protection of PIDA. The consultation paper in February 2015[15] explained that although an internal arrangement could set out that these people will have the same protections, the employer would have to explain to people who are not covered by PIDA the limits of their legal protections and the implications for them. Although the disclosures can be made from any person, the regulators do not expect the arrangements to be promoted to anyone other than the firm's UK based employees. The regulators also suggest that firms should be prepared to receive anonymous disclosures, although whistleblowers may want to be notified of the advantages of disclosing their identity.

---

[15] Consultation Paper FCA CP15/4, PRA CP6/15 Whistleblowing in deposit-takers, PRA designated investment firms and insurers (February 2015).

The amendments to SYSC Chapter 18 refer to a "reportable concern" being:

- anything that would be the subject matter of a protected disclosure, including breaches of the PRA and/or FCA rules;
- a breach of the firm's policies and procedures; and
- behaviour that harms or is likely to harm the reputation or financial well-being of the firm.

The definition of whistleblower extends to any *person* that has disclosed, or intends to disclose, a reportable concern to a firm, or to the regulators or in accordance with PIDA.

A firm must establish, implement and maintain appropriate and effective arrangements for the disclosure of reportable concerns by whistleblowers. This means that firms may have to deal with disclosures from third parties, for example, customers as part of the whistleblowing procedure. These concerns may more appropriately be addressed through the customer complaints procedure, and firms should have processes in place which can direct such concerns to the appropriate route. However, the guidance makes it clear that if mainstream escalation routes have been exhausted or ineffective, the whistleblowing arrangements will remain as a last resort.

9.3.1.5   *The requirement in settlement agreements*

Generally, all settlement agreements which are legally binding contracts in which an individual waives their rights to statutory employment claims, will also include a confidentiality clause which prevents a worker from disclosing confidential information. In general settlement agreements should also include the following paragraph:

> "For the avoidance of doubt, nothing should preclude the employee from making a protected disclosure within the meaning of the Employment Rights Act 1996".

The provision simply reflects the existing position under s.43J ERA 1996 which renders void any provision in an agreement between a worker and his employer which purports to prevent a worker from making a protected disclosure. The regulators are concerned to ensure that this is well known amongst employers of relevant firms and therefore want the more substantial wording provided in guidance to be included (although use of alternative wording which has the same meaning would be equally acceptable). This would read:

> "For the avoidance of doubt, nothing shall preclude [name of worker] from making a "protected disclosure" within the meaning of Part 4A (Protected Disclosures) of the Employment Rights Act 1996. This includes protected disclosures about topics previously disclosed to another recipient."

The regulators have said that the practice of requiring individuals to give a warranty that they have not made a protected disclosure and know of no information that could form the basis of a protected disclosure will be prohibited. Employees should not be at risk of being sued for breach of warranty.

The original consultation proposal was that the wording should also be included in employment contracts, but the regulators have clarified that firms will have discretion as to whether to include such text in employment contracts and also whether to request that employment agencies used by the firm include such text in settlement agreements entered into between the employment agency and its workers.

9.3.1.6 *Staff of appointed representatives and agents*

The final FCA rules set out that relevant firms must ensure that their appointed representatives and tied agents inform any of their UK based employees who are workers about the FCA whistleblowing services. It is not proposed that principal firms would be required to request that the appointed representatives and tied agents put whistleblowing arrangements in place. Many representatives or agents may be small operations and such a requirement may not be practicable. By requiring appointed representatives and tied agents to inform their staff about the FCA whistleblowing service, principal firms will ensure that intelligence from whistleblowers is not lost.

9.3.1.7   The duty to blow the whistle

The PCBS recommendations called for employment contracts, codes of conduct and employee handbooks to include clear references to the "duty" to blow the whistle internally. The regulators have not placed a regulatory requirement on individuals to blow the whistle on wrongdoing in the final rules. The FCA and the PRA are concerned that a requirement on employees to speak up may place individuals in a position where they feel they face being penalised for whatever course of action they take and also lead employees to make defensive reports of little value that overwhelm whistleblowing services. However, even though a duty to blow the whistle has not been recommended the regulators make it clear that this does not affect the long-standing obligation on approved persons to be open and transparent with the regulator. In addition, some of the conduct rules under the SMR require the individual to disclose wrongdoing, for example Statement of Principle 4 and SM4 that "you must disclose appropriately any information of which the FCA or PRA would reasonably expect notice". Firms may therefore choose to require certain employees to come forward if they are aware of any wrong doing.

9.3.1.8   The whistleblowers' champion

The proposals in the Consultation Paper in February 2015[16] recommended that the prescribed responsibility for whistle-blowing under the Senior Managers' Regime should be given to an individual (referred to as the whistleblowers champion). The new rules state this person will have responsibility for "ensuring and overseeing the integrity, independence and

---

[16] Consultation Paper FCA CP15/4, PRA CP6/15 Whistleblowing in deposit-takers, PRA designated investment firms and insurers (February 2015).

effectiveness of the firm's policies and procedures on whistleblowing arrangements", including arrangements for protecting
whistleblowers against detrimental treatment.[17]

The new rules confirm that the whistleblowers' champion will
be a non-executive director who is a Senior Manager subject to
the Senior Managers' Regime or the Senior Insurance Managers' Regime. It is clear, however, that if a firm doesn't have any
non-executive directors, it would not be expected to create the
position specifically to perform the role. In order to ensure that
the non-executive director role is appropriate the new rules
make it clear that the role will be to "oversee" the arrangements: the whistleblowers' champion need not have a day-to-
day operational role handling disclosures. In addition, whilst
the consultation paper had recommended that the champion is
expected to be open to direct approaches, that is no longer
necessary. Relevant firms have until 7 September 2016 to
comply with the new requirements in SYSC 18. The requirement to assign responsibilities to a whistleblowers' champion
takes effect on the same date as the rest of the Senior Managers'
Regime, 7 March 2016. Between 7 March and 7 September 2016,
the whistleblowers' champion will be responsible for overseeing the steps the firm takes to prepare for the new regime.

The whistleblowers' champion should have authority and
independence within the firm. The rules also make it clear that
they should have access to resources including access to
independent legal advice and training and information sufficient to enable the individual to carry out the role.

The PCBS recommendations were that firms should include
whistleblowing in their annual reports and suggested that the
FCA and the PRA should set out which data should be
included. In the February 2015 Consultation Paper the regulators suggested that a new regulatory return could be made
public. Alternatively the whistleblowers' champion could
present a report to their firm's senior management at least
annually. It would then be for the firm to decide whether such
a report could be made public. However, concern was

---

[17] 18.4.4 SYSC.

expressed that if a report were made public it may contain information which the whistleblower would prefer should not be made public (particularly information about the whistle-blower) and this would discourage individuals from coming forward to make disclosures. The final rules include a provision that relevant firms should prepare a report for the board made at least annually. This report would be available to the regulators but would not be made public. The whistleblow-ers' champion would not need to prepare the report, but should oversee its preparation as part of his or her oversight role. The actual content of the report is not set out in the final rules, allowing firms to tailor the report as appropriate. The rules simply specify that the report should cover the operation and effectiveness of its systems and that it must maintain the confidentiality of individual whistleblowers.[18]

The FCA guidance also notes that financial groups should have flexibility about how to allocate the prescribed responsibility of the whistleblowers' champion. Under the Senior Managers Regime, there is to be a Group Entity Senior Manager Function. This may mean that a ring fenced group could use this function to appoint one whistleblowers' champion for multiple ring-fenced entities. It may also be that if a firm has its headquarters outside the UK then the whistleblowers' champion could be based overseas to tie in with any existing group wide whistleblowing arrangements. The firm would need to be satisfied that the individual could perform the role effectively.

9.3.1.9   Informing the regulators

The PCBS recommended that the FCA require firms to inform it of any employment tribunal cases brought by workers relying on PIDA where the tribunal finds in the worker's favour. The FCA agrees that this would encourage the whistleblowers' champion to take an interest in cases where the worker had suffered a disadvantage and to ensure that lessons were learned. The final rules clarify that a relevant firm must report promptly to the FCA about each case the firm

---

[18]   18.3.1(2)(f)(i) SYSC.

contested but lost at tribunal where the claimant successfully based all or part of their claim on the basis that they had suffered a detriment as a result of making a protected disclosure or was unfairly dismissed under section 103A ERA 1996. The reporting requirements are not a task for the whistleblowers' champion, although it will be something for which he or she has oversight as part of the role.

9.3.1.10 Link to fitness and propriety

Prior to the new rules it is clear that the adoption of internal procedures to deal with whistleblowing disclosures should be part of a firm's effective risk management system. The FCA make it clear in the new rules that it would regard as a serious matter any evidence that a firm had acted to the detriment of a whistleblower.

A failure to respond in relation to a protected disclosure could call into question the fitness and propriety of the firm or relevant members or its staff and therefore could affect not only the firm's reputation, but also the individual's continued certification of fitness and propriety. In other words, if there is victimisation of a whistleblower then the effect on both the firm and any individual's involved may be substantial.

9.3.1.11 No financial incentives

In July 2014 the FCA published a summary of its research into the effectiveness of offering financial incentives to whistle-blowers (a mechanism used in some whistleblowing regimes in the United States), which concluded that financial incentives would be unlikely to improve the quality of disclosures and that such incentives could lead to, among other issues, opportunism. In addition, the FCA recognised that the often highly remunerated workers in the financial services sector would most likely require significant financial incentives to encourage whistleblowing (given the perceived potential harm to their careers which could result), and that such incentives could appear inappropriate to the public at large, particularly in the current economic climate and given perceived animosity towards bankers held by the general public.

9.4   Other Changes

9.4.1   Prescribed persons disclosure publication

Section 148 of the Small Business Enterprise and Employment Act 2015 (SBEEA) inserts a new s.43FA into the ERA 1996. This provision allows the Secretary of State of the Department of Business, Innovation & Skills to make regulations requiring "prescribed persons" to produce and publish annual reports on disclosures of information made to the prescribed person by workers. An employment tribunal may, pursuant to reg.14 of The Employment Tribunals (Constitution and Rules of Procedure) Regulations 2013, send details of a whistleblowing claim to a "prescribed person" where the claimant has given their express consent. The new s.43FA is intended to improve transparency and consistency in the process of handling disclosures by prescribed persons and give reassurance to whistleblowers that action is being taken. The regulations under the SBEEA will include details of what information should be included in the report, where the report must be published and at what time intervals. Details which could identify the worker who has made the disclosure or the employer or other person in respect of whom a disclosure has been made must not, however, be included. The Government has published draft regulations (the draft Prescribed Persons (Report on Disclosures of Information) Regulations 2015), but these regulations have not yet been brought into force.

9.5   Practical steps

The introduction of a whistleblowing policy in accordance with the new rules will require the following practical considerations:

(a) New systems and controls should be subject to oversight by the audit and compliance functions.

(b) Record keeping may need to be introduced. Any records kept will need to be held in a secure environment so secure information technology will be required to support the procedures.

(c) The functions which monitor the whistleblowing need to be established. The relevant firm needs to consider which part of the organisation should include the whistleblowing function. The Consultation Paper in February 2015 points out that the Human Resources department is unlikely to be appropriate as whistleblowers may be concerned that an HR team will automatically treat their disclosure as a grievance claim, or that by reporting they may prejudice their employment record in some way. No specific guidance is given in the final rules although it may be that the whistleblowing function should fall within the internal audit function.

(d) Do the firms want to introduce a third party whistleblowing hotline? The firm can operate its arrangements internally, within a group or through a third party. The third party provider provides information to the firm. For employees the third party provider may be considered to be offering anonymity, confidentiality and independence and so may be more willing to disclose their information. There are issues in appointing third party providers since the firm will still be primarily responsible to the FCA and will need to ensure that the third party meets the regulators' expectations. In addition, firms need to be aware of the data protection issues if the information is sensitive data. Also if the hotline is a global hotline available across all companies within an organisation, firms will need to be aware of the legal issues that may apply in different jurisdictions.

(e) Communication methods need to be considered. The rules allow for disclosures to be made through a range of communication methods. Firms should consider how the disclosures are to be made e.g. by telephone, email or post. Also are anonymous disclosures to be allowed? Again, some jurisdictions may not allow anonymous disclosures.

(f) The firm needs to consider what topics the disclosures might cover. As mentioned above, the FCA and PRA recommended that the topics should extend further than that listed under PIDA and firms need to consider how this will work in practice. For example, will those to whom the disclosure is made be responsible for directing the workers to the most appropriate process whether it is the whistleblowing process or grievance procedure or discrimination and harassment procedure?

(g) The firm needs to consider which individuals can use the whistleblowing mechanism. The FCA and PRA have established that the firms should allow the procedure to apply to those beyond the "worker" under PIDA?

(h) Provide feedback to a whistleblower about a reportable concern, where this is feasible, firms need to consider the manner of providing feedback.

(i) The nature and content of the report to the board.

(j) How information is to be reported to the FCA and PRA.

(k) Training: the implementation or amendment of a relevant firm's whistleblowing policy will require training for UK based employees, and managers of UK based employees wherever the manager is based, and other employees responsible for operating the internal arrangements. Guidance for the content of the training is included in the new rules.[19] It includes:

- examples of events that might prompt the making of a reportable concern;
- examples of action that might be taken by the firm after receiving a reportable concern by a whistleblower;
- how to protect the whistleblower and ensure their confidentiality and how to provide feedback where appropriate;
- steps to ensure that no person is subjected to a detriment or victimisation; and
- sources of internal and external advice and support on the matters.

---

[19] 18.3.4 SYSC.

9.5.1 Whistleblowing policy

Many firms already have in place a whistleblowing policy. The new rules require that up to date written procedures are readily available to the firm's UK based employees outlining the firm's processes for complying with the new rules. Having a well-drafted and well-publicised policy will ensure that workers are informed about their rights and obligations and will encourage them to blow the whistle internally. Effective whistleblowing procedures are also strongly advisable in order to prevent and identify bribery. Whistleblowing arrangements also form part of the sound system of internal control set out for listed companies under the UK Corporate Governance Code.

Where a policy is put in place relevant firms should also ensure that it is brought to the attention of their workers, for example through workshops or training sessions with the aim of promoting an atmosphere in which workers are not afraid to blow the whistle internally.

In addition to the points already raised in 5.1 above the policy should also include:

- a clear statement that the firm takes any wrongdoing, malpractice or risk seriously;
- an indication of what is regarded as a wrongdoing, malpractice or risk and what may be regarded as a reportable concern;
- an assurance that, where a protected disclosure has been made, the firm will take all reasonable steps to ensure that no person under its control engages in victimisation;
- penalties for making false and malicious allegations, for example that they will be considered a disciplinary offence;
- providing access to an external body such as an independent charity for advice;
- telling workers how they can properly blow the whistle outside the firm if necessary; and
- encouraging managers to be open to concerns.

Chapter 10

Individual Accountability and Enforcement

Katie Stephen
Partner
Norton Rose Fulbright

Elisabeth Bremner
Partner
Norton Rose Fulbright

10.1   Introduction

The Individual Accountability Regime has required firms to formalise and bring clarity to areas of individual senior management responsibility. It has also encouraged a move away from the matrix management structures which have in the past hindered the regulators in seeking to hold individuals to account in the event of firm failings.

The government's proposal in October 2015 to remove the reverse burden of proof legislated for banking sector firms will mean that Senior Managers will feel better able to focus on the needs of their business and customers, rather than on protecting their own positions.[1] In practice, however, there will remain much pressure on the regulators to hold senior individuals to account and make the new regime be seen to be working. The authorities have been careful to emphasise that they do not see this shift as a significant one.

---

[1]   Bank of England and Financial Services Bill (HL Bill G5) (the "2015 Bill"). The 2015 Bill received Royal Assent as of 4 May 2016.

10.2   Background

Under the previous regulatory regime Approved Persons in the banking sector could be sanctioned by the FCA and/or the PRA where:

(a)   they were found to have been "knowingly concerned" in a firm breach; and/or

(b)   they were found to have breached one or more of the Statements of Principle for Approved Persons (s.66 of the Financial Services and Markets Act 2000 ("FSMA")).

The Financial Services (Banking Reform) Act 2013 ("FS(BR)A") extended the regime in a number of respects for banking sector firms:

(a)   First, it enabled the authorities to make rules applicable to a wider population of individuals (beyond Approved Persons). These rules are now set out in the Code of Conduct for Staff sourcebook ("COCON/Conduct Rules"). From March 2016, the authorities will be able to bring disciplinary action against any member of staff falling within the scope of the Individual Conduct Rules where they are found to be in breach. The FCA will apply its Individual Conduct Rules to the large majority of those working in relevant firms. Meanwhile, the PRA proposes to apply its Individual Conduct Rules to those Senior Managers approved by the PRA or FCA and members of staff who fall within the PRA's Certification Regime.[2] The Senior Manager Conduct Rules will apply to all those who perform a Senior Management Function as specified under FSMA.

(b)   Secondly, it introduced a new basis upon which Senior Managers in banks could be sanctioned. Where a Senior Manager was, at the relevant time, responsible for the management of those activities in relation to which the firm's contravention occurred, a Senior Manager would be

---

[2]   Under the Bank of England and Financial Services Bill published on October 15, 2015, the PRA and FCA will be able to make Rules of Conduct applicable to non-executive directors who are not otherwise Senior Managers.

guilty of misconduct unless he could show that he took reasonable steps to prevent the breach occurring (the "Presumption of Responsibility").[3]

(c) Thirdly, it enabled the authorities to bring enforcement actions against a broader set of persons where they are found to be "knowingly concerned" in a firm breach, extending it to employees of banking sector firms (i.e. not just Approved Persons).

10.3 Presumption of Responsibility becomes Duty of Responsibility and the extension of the Individual Accountability Regime

On October 15, 2015, the Bank of England and Financial Services Bill was published (the "2015 Bill"). The 2015 Bill extends aspects of the Individual Accountability Regime to all firms authorised to provide financial services under FSMA. It also introduces a statutory "Duty of Responsbility" to be applied consistently to all Senior Managers across the financial services industry, superseding the Presumption of Responsibility which would have applied to all banking sector firms from March 2016. Where there has been a regulatory breach in an area for which they are responsible, the burden will now not be on Senior Managers of firms in the banking sector to prove that they have taken reasonable steps to prevent the breach occurring. Instead, before they can bring disciplinary proceedings on this ground, the burden will be on the regulators to prove that a Senior Manager failed to take such steps.

Commenting at the time on the publication of the 2015 Bill, Tracey McDermott, acting chief executive of the FCA, said:

> "Extending the Senior Managers' and Certification Regime is an important step in embedding a culture of personal responsibility throughout the financial services industry.

---

[3] Now amended by the 2015 Bill and the Financial Services (Banking Reform) Act 2013 (Commencement No.9) (Amendment) Order 2015.

While the presumption of responsibility could have been helpful, it was never a panacea. There has been significant industry focus on this one, small element of the reforms, which risked distracting senior management within firms from implementing both the letter and spirit of the regime. The Senior Managers' and Certification Regime is intended to deliver better decisions to help avoid problems arising. We remain committed to holding individuals to account where they fail to meet our standards."

At the same time, Andrew Bailey, chief executive of the PRA, said:

"The introduction of the 'duty of responsibility' in place of the 'presumption' makes little difference to the substance of the new regime. Once introduced, it will be for the regulators (rather than the Senior Manager) to prove that reasonable steps to prevent regulatory breaches were not taken. This change is one of process, not substance."

The Presumption of Responsibility had reflected the recommendations of the Parliamentary Commission on Banking Standards ("PCBS"). In her evidence to the PCBS, Tracey McDermott had spoken of the difficulties in meeting the evidential standards required by the present regime and the need to show that an Approved Person had been personally culpable:

"The test for taking enforcement action is that we have to be able to establish personal culpability on the part of the individual, which means falling below the standard of reasonableness for someone in their position. The way in which our guidance is drafted makes it very clear that we will not hold somebody to account simply because there is a failure on their watch, particularly if they have properly delegated and so on."

Proposals for introducing a rebuttable presumption were met with a number of objections and questions were raised about the potential scope. Andrew Bailey proposed reversing the burden of proof in cases where a significant failing had been identified and where an Approved Person had responsibility for the particular area in question. It was thought this would make clear to Approved Persons that delegation of authority did not equate to delegation of responsibility or allow the person concerned to avoid accountability if something went wrong.

Tracy McDermott also made the case for linking a rebuttable presumption to a concept of responsibility, saying that it would be helpful for the regulator if the starting point was for senior management to have to establish why the steps taken met the relevant standard and respond to any areas of challenge where the regulator identified that other steps could have been taken. She noted that this would shift, "in a significant way", the nature of the investigation and have an important "signalling effect", while recognising that it should not "short-circuit" the requirements of a full investigation.

Andrew Tyrie, Chair of the Treasury Select Committee and PCBS, said that he hoped the 2015 Bill and reversal of the presumption had not been a response to industry lobbying and that he would have preferred that more time had been taken to enable the new system to bed down.

Speaking before the Treasury Select Committee on October 20, 2015 in defence of the changes, Andrew Bailey suggested that the Presumption of Responsibility could have breached European human rights legislation:

"I am worried this piece of the regime might not work … I don't want a regime which has a flaw in it which they [banks and lawyers] can exploit … there are signs of developments in the way people are approaching this regime which introduces unhelpful behaviour."

In his Mansion House speech a few days later, on October 22, 2015, Andrew Bailey stressed that the move to the Duty of Responsibility would not affect the substance of the new regime:

477

"Let me be very clear, substituting 'duty' for 'presumption' changes the mechanism of enforcement not the substance of the requirement on senior managers, and I would not support changing the latter. There has been a lot of noise around the new regime in recent months, and I have asked people involved whether their problem was with the 'presumption', or with the regime more broadly. The universal answer has been that the difficulty was with the 'presumption' not the regime which appears to have broad support."

10.4 Where to now?

In 2015, the PRA and the FCA consulted on draft guidance on the application of the earlier intended Presumption of Responsibility and "reasonable steps" (PRA Draft Supervisory Statement—February 2015[4] ("PRA Draft Supervisory Statement") and FCA Draft Guidance—March 2015[5] ("FCA Draft Guidance")). In July 2015, the PRA published the final version of its Supervisory Statement[6] ("PRA Supervisory Statement").

The concept of "reasonable steps" is well used in the existing Statements of Principle for Approved Persons and accompanying Code of Practice which sets out the evidential factors which the PRA and FCA will take into account in determining whether an Approved Person is in breach. Much of the guidance provided is consistent with that found in the existing Code of Practice.

While the PRA and FCA are yet to confirm precisely how the 2015 Bill might impact their approach to the revised Duty of Responsibility, given that much of the proposed guidance on the application of the Presumption of Responsibility has its roots in the current Approved Persons regime, it seems unlikely that there will be significant change. What we may expect is further direction on when the authorities might elect

---

[4] Consultation Paper PRA CP7/17, February 2015, Appendix 2.
[5] Consultation Paper FCA15/9, March 2015, Appendix 2.
[6] PRA Supervisory Statement SS28/15, July 2015.

to commence an investigation for a breach of the Duty of Responsibility, as opposed to the Conduct Rules, although in practice, and given the significant overlap, in many cases action may be brought in respect of both in combination.

Whether a Senior Manager is or is not responsible for managing any of the firm's relevant activities will be a question of fact. While the Statements of Responsibility and Responsibilities Maps will provide the primary evidence of the Senior Manager's responsibilities, the authorities may look beyond these in appropriate circumstances. More than one Senior Manager may be held responsible for misconduct, depending on the nature and extent of the firm's breach and the scope of individual Senior Managers' responsibilities.

The authorities will consider the steps that a competent Senior Manager would have taken at that time; in the specific individual's position; with that individual's role and responsibilities; and in all the existing circumstances.

They will look for Senior Managers to demonstrate that they have established adequate governance arrangements and established and tested appropriate control frameworks. They will consider whether Senior Managers can demonstrate that they have implemented adequate training; clearly communicated to staff their roles and responsibilities; and whether systems and controls have been improved based on lessons learned. Senior Managers will be expected to delegate tasks appropriately while maintaining adequate oversight and retaining ultimate responsibility.

10.5   Conduct Rules

As noted above, in banking sector firms the Conduct Rules have replaced the existing Statements of Principle for Approved Persons. The PCBS recommended that the regulators develop a new set of standards, drawing on the existing Approved Persons regime, which would then apply to a wider group of individuals.

The PRA applies its Individual Conduct Rules to all individuals who are approved by the PRA or FCA as Senior Managers or who fall within the PRA's Certification Regime. The FCA applies its Individual Conduct Rules to almost all staff, supporting its broad statutory objectives to protect consumers and market integrity. Under both the PRA and FCA regimes, the Senior Manager Conduct Rules apply to Senior Managers only.

The regulators have taken different approaches to guidance on the Conduct Rules, reflecting their different approaches to guidance generally and the proposed difference in scope of the regimes. In both cases, the authorities have again drawn on the existing Code of Practice within APER although additional text has been added where there is no direct parallel.

Broadly, the Conduct Rules will apply only to an individual's employment and not to their private life, unless an individual's wider behaviour could affect his or her ability to comply with the rules. The way in which a person behaves in their private life may also be relevant to any fit and proper assessment under the FIT sourcebook.

A person will only be in breach of the Conduct Rules where they are personally culpable. This will arise where:

(a) their conduct was deliberate; or
(b) their standard of conduct was below that which would be reasonable in all the circumstances.

10.6   The FCA Enforcement Process

10.6.1   Introduction

This Part focusses on the part of the FCA enforcement process which is most likely to be relevant to individual conduct issues. Enforcement action can also be taken by the PRA which has adopted an enforcement process which tends to mirror that of the FCA. However, the PRA process is largely untested and it has yet to take disciplinary action against individuals.

The DEPP chapter of the FCA's Handbook sets out the FCA's decision-making procedures, including in relation to issuing statutory notices. The FCA's approach to enforcement is set out in the Enforcement Guide ("EG") which does not form part of the FCA Handbook but is intended as general guidance pursuant to s.139B FSMA.

10.6.2   *Referral to Enforcement*

Matters are often referred to Enforcement by Supervision as giving rise to concern. Issues regarding the conduct of Senior Management may also come to light during a firm investigation as individual failings emerge. In light of the expensive and resource-intensive nature of enforcement action, the FCA has a wide discretion to determine whether enforcement action is appropriate in all the circumstances and represents the best use of its resources.

Whereas, in the case of a firm, the FCA may have alternative means of achieving its objectives in an efficient, effective and proportionate way such as through skilled persons reports, requiring firms to pay redress or restricting certain activities or products, that may not be so for Senior Management. It is clear that, in accordance with the FCA's "credible deterrence" strategy, the FCA will continue to take action where it is likely to send a clear message that wrongdoers in the financial services industry will be held to account and that meaningful sanctions will apply.

Speaking in April 2016, Mark Steward, director of enforcement and market oversight at the FCA, stated:

> "It should go without saying that we will not take a punctillius approach in enforcing this new regime. We'll

only be looking at cases that involve real fault elements, real culpability by senior managers."[7]

Although the FCA is mindful that an individual will generally face greater risks from enforcement action in terms of financial implications, reputation and livelihood, than a corporate entity and that such cases are harder prove and take longer to resolve, the FCA is committed to pursuing such cases robustly (EG 2.11.2).

Following a review of the enforcement decision-making process in 2014, a final report published in December 2014 recommended that the FCA should publish a clear expression of the key criteria which influence the decision of whether enforcement action, as opposed to supervisory intervention, is appropriate. In July 2015, FCA published its new referral criteria: Enforcement Referral Criteria to provide a clearer understanding of the questions that the FCA asks before convening a formal investigation.

The primary driver of the enforcement referral decision remains whether an investigation is likely to further the FCA's aims and statutory objectives; however, the new criteria introduces two overarching questions which the FCA will consider in making this decision:

(a) What is the strength of the evidence and is an enforcement investigation likely to be proportionate?; and

(b) What purpose or goal would be served if the FCA were to take enforcement action in this case?

The criteria also remain under review at subsequent stages of the investigation, such as where failings come to light which differ from those suspected at the outset.

Although the new criteria do not suggest a change of approach in the FCA's enforcement referral decision-making process, they do provide a helpful summary of the key drivers and

---

[7] Mark Steward, director of enforcement and market oversight at the FCA, speaking to Thomson Reuters Compliance and Risk Forum in London.

relevant factors taken into account when the enforcement referral decision is made and highlight the high level of discretion exercised by the FCA in selecting which enforcement cases to pursue, which renders any challenge to a referral decision more difficult.

In April 2016, the FCA and PRA published a joint consultation paper (FCA CP 16/10; PRA CP 14/16) ("CP 16/10") on proposals to implement some of the recommendations arising from the December 2014 HM Treasury report on its review of enforcement decision-making (the "HMT Review") and from the report by Andrew Green QC on enforcement action following the failure of HSBOS plc. The proposals include amendments to the EG to reflect the referral criteria and case selection approach. The FCA's proposals also include making reference in an "Enforcement Referral Document" to all potential subjects and a summary of the circumstances and reasons why a firm or individual is or is not being referred, to be signed by a Head of Department.

10.6.3 Firm enforcement action and consequences for Senior Managers (including third party rights)

Senior Managers may also be impacted by enforcement action taken against other parties including their employer firm and any published outcomes relating to matters in which they have been involved.

10.6.3.1 Settlement

Where a firm settles enforcement action with the FCA, admissions may be made which impact on any ongoing contested proceedings between a member of the firm's Senior Management team and the FCA. It can prove challenging for an individual to re-open findings set out in the firm's Final Notice.

The Upper Tribunal has recognised that the FCA cannot pursue a case against an individual which is inconsistent with a case concerning the same facts including where that case has been settled.[8]

10.6.3.2   *Third Party Rights*

Where a Warning Notice or Decision Notice is issued to a firm in respect of a proposed financial penalty or censure, a copy of the notice must also be given to any third person who is identified in the reasons contained in the notice if, in the opinion of the FCA, any of those reasons is prejudicial to the third party unless this is impractical or a notice is also given to the third party in relation to the same matter (section 393 FSMA). The third party must also be given at least 14 days to make representations and copies of any subsequent notices. The third party also has the right to refer to the Upper Tribunal the decision (to the extent that it is based on reason which identifies him and is prejudicial) or any opinion expressed in relation to the third party. Any person who alleges that a copy of the notice should have been given to him but was not may also make a reference to the Upper Tribunal.

The extent of third party rights and the circumstances in which they apply have been considered in a number of cases. The Upper Tribunal has taken the view that section 393(4) FSMA affords third party rights only to a person who is identified in the relevant notice, not to a person who is identified in the "matter" to which the reasons in the decision notice relate as ascertained by looking at external sources[9]. However, the Tribunal did not accept the FSA's argument that section 393(4) does not apply unless the individual is identified in the notice either by name or by job description. Identification may be by express naming, by job description, or by some collective reference to particular officers of the company, but it does not

---

[8]   See Tariq Carrimjee v FCA [2015] UKUT 0079 (TCC): "it would be a breach of the Authority's public law duty to act rationally were it to seek to advance a position which is factually inconsistent with the conclusions it had reached with regard to the behaviour of the subject of a Final Notice on the same evidence in respect of the same subject in that Final Notice".

[9]   See Sir Philip Watts v FSA 13 September 2005.

necessarily have to be[10]. The question in each case will simply be whether the person concerned is identified in the relevant notice. If so, the question will then be whether that person is prejudiced.

The Upper Tribunal has confirmed that third party rights should be given to individuals who have been "singled out" in the notice such that their identity is apparent, even if they are not named and even where it is necessary to refer to other sources (such as press reports) to identify them[11].

10.6.4 Overview of FSMA powers and conduct of investigation

10.6.4.1 Penalties

Under FSMA, the FCA has a range of powers to take action pursuant to an administrative process against individuals who have failed to meet the required standards. These include:

(a) prohibiting an individual from undertaking specific regulated activities;
(b) suspending an individual for up to two years from undertaking specific controlled functions;
(c) censuring an individual by means of a public statement;
(d) imposing a financial penalty.

A prohibition may be made in respect of both approved and non-approved persons where it appears that the person is not fit and proper to carry out functions in relation to regulated activities. Sometimes a prohibition will be imposed in respect of certain functions only. On occasion, an indication will be given as to the time after which an application might be made to vary or revoke the prohibition.[12] When considering an application to vary or revoke a prohibition order, the FCA will

---

[10] See also the decision in Jan Laury v FSA 12 September 2007.
[11] See Achilles Macris v FCA 10 April 2014 and Christian Bittar v FCA [2015] UKUT 0602 (TCC) in which reference was made to the knowledge of a well-informed participant of information contained not only in the Final Notice but also in the public domain.
[12] EG 9.6.

take into account a number of factors[13] but an application is unlikely to be granted unless the individual has taken substantive steps to remedy his misconduct and to demonstrate his fitness and propriety; recognition of the misconduct is also a relevant factor.[14] Breach of the order is a criminal offence.

The FCA has provided guidance in relation to the factors to be taken into account when making decisions in relation to the imposition of penalties:

(a) the factors to be taken into account when considering whether or not to impose a sanction are set out in DEPP 6.2[15];

(b) the criteria for determining whether it is appropriate to issue a public censure rather than a financial penalty are set out at DEPP 6.4;

(c) the factors to be considered in determining the appropriate level of a financial penalty are set out at DEPP 6.5.

Financial penalties are determined by reference to a five stage process which, in non-market abuse cases, involves a calculation by reference to the individual's relevant income. Relevant income is the gross amount of all benefits received by the individual from the employment in connection with which the breach occurred and for the period of the breach.[16] Where the breach was a one-off or lasted for less than 12 months, the relevant income will be that for the 12 months prior to the breach. Aggravating and mitigating factors can also give rise to an increase or decrease in the amount of the penalty.[17] Financial penalties cannot be insured against or paid by the individual's employer.[18]

---

[13] EG 9.6.

[14] See, for example, the cases of Jonathan Townrow and Mark Thorogood.

[15] The FCA Draft Guidance referred to above at para.10.4 published amendments to DEPP 6.2. These proposed amendments are not yet in force and may be subject to revision following Royal Assent of the 2015 Bill.

[16] DEPP 6.5B.2G.

[17] See, for example, Anthony Wills who achieved a 10% reduction having requested an exit interview and volunteered information relating to the findings which were the subject of the notice.

[18] GEN 6.1.

One of the factors to be taken into account when deciding between a censure and a financial penalty is the financial impact on the person concerned. The FCA will also consider whether a financial penalty should be reduced if the penalty would cause serious financial hardship (DEPP 6.5D). An individual will be required to provide full, frank and timely disclosure of verifiable evidence that such hardship would be caused and to cooperate and answer any questions the FCA may have. The threshold is that a person's net annual income will fall below £14,000 and capital below £16,000. However, where funds may become available in the future, this may be taken into account.[19]

The FCA also has other powers including to apply to the court to obtain injunctions and to apply to the court or order restitution.[20]

In addition, the FCA can prosecute some criminal offences in the criminal courts (such as insider dealing). A decision to commence criminal proceedings is made by the RDC (or where the matter is exceptionally urgent by a senior FCA employee).[21]

The FCA can also decide to issue a private warning rather than proceed with formal disciplinary action. This may be considered appropriate for minor breaches or where full and immediate remedial action has been taken and can be issued to both approved and non-approved persons. The FCA will first issue a "minded to" letter. The intended recipient can respond with any comments which will be considered before a decision is made. A private warning does not signify that any adverse findings have been made, rather it is a record of regulatory concerns which forms part of an individual's compliance record and may be taken into account in the context of any future issues arising. As the name implies, a private warning is not published and no announcement is made by the FCA. However, in the case of an approved person, the FCA will

---

[19] Terence Andrew Joint v FCA [2015] UKUT 0636 (TCC).
[20] See EG10 and EG11.
[21] The FCA's approach to the prosecution of criminal offences is set out at EG12.

consider whether the individual's employer should be informed. It may also be necessary to make disclosure to a future employer.

10.6.4.2   Process

The FCA has published a leaflet setting out an overview of the enforcement process including a flowchart illustrating the progress of a typical enforcement case where the matter is dealt with under its administrative powers under FSMA (which can be found here).[22]

By way of overview, the key stages of the process (with reference to individuals), following a referral to Enforcement are set out below.

10.6.4.3   Appointment of investigators

Following a referral to enforcement, investigators are appointed and a notice of investigation is provided to the individual subject of the investigation. The notice includes a 'memorandum of appointment' which sets out the provisions of FSMA under which the investigators have been appointed; outlines the reasons for the investigation (including any rules which the FCA believes may have been breached) and gives the names of the individual investigators. An amended notice should be provided whenever there is a change in the composition of the enforcement team or to reflect a change in the scope of the investigation.

Once an individual is notified of an investigation into his conduct, he should consider whether any further notifications need to be made such as:

(a)   to any other regulatory or professional body;
(b)   to an employer;

---

[22] http://www.fca.org.uk/static/documents/enforcement-information-guide.pdf.

(c) to D&O or other insurers, if they have not already been notified (or whether another form of indemnity is available).

Consideration should also be given to the potential for a conflict of interest between the individual and his employer firm. Individuals may need separate legal representation and issues such as any indemnity provided by the firm will need to be addressed. A firm may require an individual to undertake to repay fees in the event of a disciplinary sanction being imposed. Although there is no bar to payment of legal costs and expenses, a firm cannot make payment of an individual's fine nor can such fines be covered by insurance (GEN 6.1).

Individuals should take care to secure any existing material that may be relevant to the investigation (in order to avoid the possibility of a criminal offence arising under s177 FSMA) but should take advice before creating any new material (see further in relation to confidentiality below). A record of steps taken to gather and secure documents should be kept.

10.6.4.4 Scoping

The individual is invited to attend a scoping discussion at which the FCA aims to explain the scope of the investigation and the next steps in the process, including the gathering of information. In practice, where the scoping meeting is held at a very early stage, particularly where legally represented, the individual may derive little additional valuable information from the meeting.

CP 16/10 indicates that the FCA proposes to adopt the recommendation from the HMT Review that scoping meetings should usually take place once investigators are in a position to share their indicative plans on the direction of the investigation and timetabling of key milestones. However, the need to retain flexibility on timing is also recognised, as some individuals and firms prefer to meet as soon as possible after the investigators have been appointed and it may be difficult to give much information if the meeting is held so early. The FCA will also explore, as part of the forthcoming review of its penalty policy, the HMT Review recommendation that subjects be expressly invited to indicate whether they accept the suspected misconduct or specific aspects of it.

10.6.4.5 *Investigation*

The enforcement team embarks on the gathering of information which may include interviews with the individual subject and also other relevant persons. EG4 provides guidance on the FCA's conduct of investigations.

The FCA has a wide range of powers to gather information depending on the nature and subject of the investigation. Information regarding the FCA's approach to the use of these powers is set out in EG3. Guidance is also provided in relation to investigations commissioned by firms and the circumstances where the FCA may prefer that a firm does not investigate. Where a firm investigation is conducted, the FCA may require production of underlying material including any notes of interviews with individuals (EG 3.11.10).[23]

As set out below, "protected items" can be withheld. Legal advice should be sought when responding to information requests and when considering the creation of any new materials.[24]

It is possible that both the FCA and PRA may be investigating different aspects of the same matter. In these circumstances, the FCA will try to ensure that the individual is not prejudiced or unduly inconvenienced. The FCA and PRA have entered into a high-level framework for cooperation which is set out in a Memorandum of Understanding ("MoU"). The section of the MoU entitled 'Formal regulatory processes and enforcement' provides guidance on how the authorities will consult with

---

[23] See also a speech given by Jamie Symington on 5 November 2015 on internal investigations by firms in which he referred to unhelpful "gaming" of the process in relation to interview notes and indicated that the FCA's starting point is that it expects firms conducting internal investigations to share with it the evidence obtained.

[24] Section 413 FSMA.

each other in relation to investigations, enforcement action and other regulatory action. Annex 1 to the MoU provides further detail.

The FCA's standard practice is to use its statutory powers to compel individuals to provide documents, information or answers to questions at interview. Failure to comply or failure to attend a compelled interview without reasonable excuse, or unreasonably failing to answer questions, may be treated as contempt of court. Such non-cooperation may also give rise to a breach of Statement of Principle 4 or COCON 2.1.3R (2.1.3). A person required to attend a compelled interview has no entitlement to insist that the interview takes place voluntarily.

Statements made at a compelled interview can be used:

(a) as evidence against the individual except in market abuse or criminal proceedings;
(b) to obtain evidence for use in criminal or market abuse proceedings; or
(c) as evidence that the FCA has been misled.

However, the Upper Tribunal has recognised that evidence obtained at interview may not be entirely reliable in certain circumstances (the Upper Tribunal preferred to base its decision in the case of Norman McIntosh and LA Mortgage Services on the evidence before it rather than on the interview transcript commenting that the interview was long, having lasted for three and a half hours, and Mr McIntosh was not accompanied by any legal representative).

In some circumstances, such as where individuals are suspects in criminal or market abuse investigations, the FCA may prefer to question an individual on a voluntary basis, possibly under caution.[25] The FCA has confirmed that choosing not to attend or answer questions at a voluntary interview will not give rise to disciplinary proceedings against an approved person for breach of Statement of Principle 4 or COCON 2.1.3R but an

---

[25] EG 4.7.1.

adverse inference may be drawn from a reluctance to partici-pate in a voluntary interview.[26] Evidence obtained may be used in any subsequent proceedings.

The FCA also has powers to require other individuals (who are not subject to investigation) to provide information and attend interviews. Legal advice should be sought regarding the extent of the power and compliance with the request. Interviewees should be aware that the transcripts of their interviews may be provided to the subject of the investigation and also that issues may arise from the interview which give rise to a broadening of the investigation or to their inclusion as a subject of the investigation.

Compliance with Statement of Principle 4 and COCON 2.1.3R should be maintained throughout the investigation. Positive co-operation may provide mitigation in terms of the considera-tion of any penalty whereas any omissions or the provision of potentially misleading information may not only be an aggravating factor but may of itself also give rise to further grounds for disciplinary action or prosecution.[27] It is also possible that a lack of acceptance in the face of obvious wrongdoing may impact on the FCA's view of an individual's fitness and propriety.

Where the investigation relates to the individual's employ-ment, the employer may also want to attend the interview. However, the FCA may be reluctant to allow this, particularly where there are concerns that this might prejudice the investigation, such as where the individual may be less forthcoming when in the presence of the employer's repre-sentatives. The FCA may also ask an individual whether he or she is comfortable with the attendance of an employer representative.

---

[26] EG 4.7.3.

[27] See the case involving David Hobbs who was prohibited as a result of having misled the FCA despite being cleared of market abuse and also the decision in Stephen Robert Allen.

In advance of an interview, the FCA will usually provide an individual with relevant documents to which reference may be made at the interview. Preparation should include careful review of these materials as well as explanations of any relevant background such as career history, current role, controlled functions and reporting lines.

The interview will be recorded. The individual will be provided with a copy of the recording and the transcript and invited to provide any corrections to the transcript. The interview documents and interview transcript may contain information which is protected from onward disclosure by s.348 FSMA in which case it should not be shared with third parties including the employee's employer (see further in relation to confidentiality below). In any event, permission to share should be sought from the FCA.

The FCA also has the power to seek a search warrant under s.176 FSMA in certain circumstances. The exercise of a warrant will be supervised by the police.

Consideration should be given as to whether to gather further material from third party sources such as potential witnesses (who may not be interviewed by the FCA) or expert evidence. Individuals may be dependent on their employers for assistance with accessing relevant material and should take care to preserve a right of access following departure from their firms or any internal reorganisation.

10.6.4.6   Preliminary Investigation Report

Following completion of the investigative steps, the case will be reviewed by the enforcement team and by a legal adviser who has not been involved in gathering the evidence. It is usual practice for the FCA to provide an individual with a preliminary findings letter and/or Preliminary Investigation Report (PIR). Supporting documents may include the transcripts of interviews with other individuals. The PIR will not include details of the proposed penalty but does indicate the enforcement team's views on the matters under investigation.

An individual will normally be given 28 days to respond to the PIR (although, as set out below, the statutory period for responding to the Warning Notice and Decision Notice is only 14 days). Requests for more time can be made and will be considered on a case by case basis.

When responding to the PIR, individuals should bear in mind that a further opportunity to respond will be afforded if a Warning Notice is issued. The advantage of a full response to the PIR is that it may deter the enforcement team from proceeding to the Warning Notice stage and avoids the impression of arguments being made at a later stage as an afterthought (allowing the FCA to seek to undermine the credibility of a point by arguing that it should have been raised earlier[28]). However, a potential disadvantage may be that the response to the PIR effectively gives the enforcement team advance notice of the individual's case and provides the enforcement team with an opportunity to address any issues or make changes to its case prior to the matter being considered by the RDC.

10.6.4.7   Warning Notice

If the enforcement team decides that formal disciplinary action should be taken, a draft Warning Notice will be prepared and submitted by the enforcement team to an RDC panel. The RDC is a committee of the FCA Board and its members include practitioners and non-practitioners, none of whom is an FCA employee (further information about the RDC and some FAQs have been published on the FCA's website[29]). The purpose of the RDC is to meet the requirement to ensure that penalty decisions are not made by those who have been involved in the investigation (as set out in section 395(2) FSMA). The draft notice sets out the proposed penalty and the reasons for it. The RDC will also be provided with an Investigation Report (which takes into account any response to the PIR made by the individual).

---

[28] See by way of example Arch Financial Products LLP and others v FCA [2015] UKUT 0013 (TCC).

[29] http://www.fca.org.uk/about/structure/committees/rdc-faqs.

Following review of the papers by the RDC a meeting may be held between the enforcement team and the RDC panel at which the enforcement team will present the case and the RDC can raise queries. The RDC can decide to issue the Warning Notice as requested, can make changes to the Warning Notice or can decide that no disciplinary action is merited and that no Warning Notice should be issued.

If the RDC agrees that a Warning Notice should be issued, a copy is sent to the individual together with the material on which the RDC relied in taking the decision (such as the Investigation Report and supporting documents) as well as secondary material which might undermine that decision (under section 394 FSMA). This material may include a note of discussions between the RDC and the enforcement team at the Warning Notice meeting. However, there are some exceptions to the requirement to provide material such as where it constitutes a protected item (under section 413 FSMA), where the material relates to another person and was taken into account for comparison purposes or where access would not be in the public interest (see section 394 FSMA).

The FCA may also publish certain information about some Warning Notices (see section 10.6.7.2 below).

A Warning Notice may also give rise to third party rights (see para.10.6.3.2).

10.6.4.8   Oral and Written Representations

Following receipt of a Warning Notice, the individual will normally be given 14 days to make representations, although requests can be made for more time (s.387 FSMA). Representations can be written and/or oral.

If no representations are made, a Decision Notice may be issued in the same terms as the Warning Notice. The fact that no representations have been made does not impact on the ability to refer the Decision Notice to the Upper Tribunal. In some circumstances, an individual may consider it would be preferable not to make representations with a view to expediting a reference to the Upper Tribunal.

If the individual wishes to make oral representations, a meeting will be arranged so that the RDC panel (including the Chairman or Deputy Chairman) can hear these (which is not likely to be possible within the prescribed 14 day period). An oral representations meeting is held at the FCA. It is not a formal judicial hearing and does not involve the calling or cross-examination of witnesses, although an individual may wish to consider whether to take third parties such as an expert or character referee. An individual does not have to be legally represented.

A key feature of the oral representations meeting is that it allows an individual to address the RDC directly, to emphasise key points that may be best conveyed in person and to answer any queries arising from the case. The RDC panel may also, at the outset, give an indication of those issues with which they are particularly concerned which provides a further opportunity to focus on and deal with any particularly difficult aspects of the case and to highlight points which may not be easily understood from the relevant documents. The individual's approach to this meeting, demeanour and credibility will be under significant scrutiny and care should be devoted to the impression given.

The focus of representations should usually be on the substance of the case and not on extraneous matters such as the way in which the investigation has been conducted or procedural issues.

The enforcement team also attends the oral representations meeting and may be asked questions by the RDC. All discussion at the meeting should take place through the RDC rather than directly between the enforcement team and the individual.

The RDC panel may ask for further information to be provided after the meeting.

10.6.4.9   Decision Notice

Following consideration of any written and oral representations, the RDC will make a decision as to whether a Decision
Notice should be issued and, if so, whether any changes should
be made to the penalty or reasons set out in the Warning
Notice. If no Decision Notice is to be issued, a Notice of
Discontinuance will be provided to the individual unless the
discontinuance results in the granting of an application made
by the recipient of the notice (s.389(2) FSMA).

10.6.4.10   Upper Tribunal and Beyond

If a Decision Notice is issued, the individual has 28 days to
make a reference to the Upper Tribunal. The Decision Notice
must give "sufficient reasons to enable the person to whom it is
addressed to understand why it has been given" but need not
deal with every submission made. The Court of Appeal has
held that a challenge to a Decision Notice must not be made by
way of judicial review when an alternative remedy in the form
of a reference to the Upper Tribunal is available.[30] A Decision
Notice may also give rise to third party rights (see below).

Of the relatively few cases referred to the Tribunal, a higher
proportion relate to individuals rather than firms. The Upper
Tribunal proceedings allow the case to start again and be
considered afresh. Consideration of whether to make a referral
must take into account previous case decisions which confirm
that the FCA can seek an alternative or increased penalty. In the
Jabre case, the RDC concluded that there had been a breach of
Statements of Principle 2 and 3 (but not 1) and that a fine
should be imposed. When Jabre made a reference to the
Tribunal, the Tribunal considered that it was the allegations
made in the decision notice and the circumstances on which
these were based that fell to be considered and evaluated by
the Tribunal and that these comprise the matter referred under
s.133 FSMA. Accordingly, the FCA was entitled to reintroduce
a breach of Statement of Principle 1 and seek a prohibition.

---

[30]   R. on the application of C v FSA [2013] EWCA Civ 677.

It is also possible that challenging the decision of the RDC may be viewed in a negative light by the Upper Tribunal, particularly when considering fitness and propriety of an individual and so prove counterproductive in circumstances where evidence of acceptance and remorse might achieve a more sympathetic hearing and a more lenient outcome.[31]

However, as set out above, the Upper Tribunal has recognised that the FCA cannot pursue a case against an individual which is inconsistent with another case concerning the same facts.[32] In addition, some individuals have achieved a markedly different outcome at the Upper Tribunal.[33]

If a reference is made, the FCA may publish the Decision Notice on its website pending the outcome of the reference and the individual's name will appear in the register of current references on the Upper Tribunal's website (see below in relation to Publicity).

Following a reference, the Upper Tribunal proceedings will involve the parties taking certain procedural steps, including the filing of Statements of Case and exchange of witness statements and experts reports, followed by a hearing which is normally held in public. At the hearing, witnesses can give evidence and be cross-examined. The Upper Tribunal decides what action the FCA should take and remits the matter to the FCA for the FCA to give effect to the Upper Tribunal's decision (or, in the case of a prohibition order, remits the case to the FCA with a direction to reconsider its decision)[34] and the FCA will

---

[31] See Milan Vukelic v FSA 6 April 2009: "Mr Vukelic cannot be penalised for exercising his rights to fight this case but neither can he claim the credit due to those who acknowledge their failings. The RDC did not find Mr Vukelic to be dishonest so he did not need to challenge their decision on that ground. Further a persistent failure to recognise shortcomings is a particularly important consideration in a regulatory case where an applicant claims the right to continue to function in a position of trust".

[32] See Tariq Carrimjee v FCA [2015] UKUT 0013 (TCC).

[33] Compare the case of Mr Kerr who was sanctioned by the FSA for assisting Mr Hobbs to commit market abuse with the case of Mr Hobbs who made a reference and persuaded the Upper Tribunal that no market abuse had occurred.

[34] See, for example, the case of Mr Carrimjee, where the decision taken by the FCA following the matter being remitted to it by the Upper Tribunal and set out in a "Further Decision Notice" has itself been referred to the Upper Tribunal.

issue a Final Notice or Notice of Discontinuance, subject to any appeal to the Court of Appeal (see below). A Notice of Discontinuance will not be issued if the discontinuance results in the granting of an application by the recipient of the Decision Notice (section 389(2)).

The Upper Tribunal also has the power to order a party to pay the costs of another party whose conduct has been vexatious or unreasonable, including where the FCA acted unreasonably in making its decision.[35]

If no reference is made (or following a decision by the Upper Tribunal, depending on the outcome), the FCA may issue a Final Notice, together with a press release in which the FCA may seek to draw attention to certain features of the case. An individual may wish to consider seeking some advice on this, including from a public relations perspective.

A Final Notice will usually be published on the FCA's website. The Final Notice must set out the terms of any public censure, order or action to be taken and the amount of any penalty (and the time for payment). As set out above, fines cannot be insured against or paid by the individual's employer.

There are a number of possible avenues for challenging a decision of the Upper Tribunal. In particular, in the event of a procedural irregularity, a decision may be set aside where it is in the interests of justice to do so; an appeal can be made to the Court of Appeal on a point of law or an application may be made for judicial review in certain limited circumstances.

---

[35] See the decision in the case of Davidson and Tatham where the Upper Tribunal held that the FCA's decisions were unreasonable, although it was noted that the matters identified as being unreasonable were unlikely to re-occur in the future given the changes in the decision-making process following the 2005 enforcement process review.

10.6.5 Settlement

Negotiating a settlement with the FCA cannot be approached in the same way as a commercial dispute. The FCA will be taking a regulatory decision and must have regard to its statutory objectives. In addition, some of the factors which may justify a settlement in the case of the firm such as achieving redress for customers or remediation of systems and controls will not be available in individual cases.

In order to incentivise early settlement, the FCA operates a discount scheme for financial penalties (and periods of suspension). This means that an individual can obtain a reduction in the amount of a financial penalty of upto 30%. Under the current process, the following discounts apply:

(a) Stage 1 (up to the point at which the FCA has sufficient understanding to make a reasonable assessment of the penalty, communicated that assessment and allowed a reasonable opportunity to reach agreement): 30%;
(b) Stage 2 (up to the expiry of the period for making written representations to the RDC or the date on which such representations are made): 20%
(c) Stage 3 (up to the issue of the Decision Notice): 10%.[36]

Although it is possible to make a settlement approach to the FCA even after a Decision Notice has been issued, in practice the FCA is unlikely to agree to a compromise which lessens the findings or penalty in the Decision Notice.

With a view to reaching settlement, the FCA and the person subject to enforcement can agree to mediate at any stage of the enforcement process (although the FCA has indicated that mediation is unlikely to be appropriate where it is contemplating a criminal prosecution or where urgent action is required). An independent mediator will be appointed who will facilitate settlement discussions with a view to reaching a mutually acceptable outcome. The mediator does not have the power to

---

[36] The FCA is currently consulting on proposed changes to the settlement discount scheme (see CP16/10 and para.10.6.8 below).

make a binding decision and there is no obligation to agree to a settlement. Mediation may be worth considering where there is chance that involving a neutral party could assist in breaking a deadlock.

Any settlement discussions with the enforcement team are without prejudice to the RDC and Upper Tribunal proceedings which means that any settlement discussions, including any concessions made in the context of these, will not be disclosed. However, the FCA can follow up, through other means, on any new issues of regulatory concern which come to light during settlement discussions (EG5.3).

A proposed settlement, negotiated with the enforcement team, must be agreed by the FCA's Settlement Decision Makers (drawn from a pool of FCA Directors and Heads of Department). This can sometimes render the process somewhat cumbersome as negotiations do not take place directly with the decision makers who will be constrained by the settlement terms previously approved.

Settlement will generally include the negotiation of the wording of a settlement agreement and a Final Notice to be published on the FCA website. The FCA will not normally enter into discussions regarding the wording of any press release to accompany the Final Notice. An individual may wish to consider whether to make his or her own announcement.

As set out below, the CP16/10 proposals include a 28-day notice period prior to the commencement of Stage 1; the abolition of the Stage 2 and Stage 3 discounts and the introduction of a streamlined procedure to narrow the issues between the FCA and the subject by entering into a 'focused resolution agreement' on the facts and liability with the RDC determining only the action to be taken.

10.6.6 *Confidentiality*

Before volunteering to provide information to the FCA, an individual should consider whether the information is protected from disclosure such as by any duty of confidentiality owed to a third party.

Protected items need not be disclosed to the FCA (under s.413 FSMA). Broadly speaking a document which is protected by legal professional privilege, or enclosed with or referred to in such a document, will qualify as a protected item. Legal advice should be sought prior to making any disclosure of material which may be privileged (such as communications with legal advisers). Issues may arise as to whether an individual is entitled to rely on and disclose legal advice where the privilege belongs to another party (including the individual's employer firm). Privileged material may be disclosed to the FCA pursuant to a 'limited waiver' with a view to protecting its subsequent disclosure to other parties. However, the FCA will not consider itself restricted in terms of its use of the information in pursuit of its statutory obligations (EG3.11.13). Legal advice should be sought prior to the creation of any new documents that might fall to be disclosed.

Documents subject to a duty of banking confidentiality may also be withheld but only in certain restricted circumstances (see s.175(5) FSMA).

Information provided to the FCA (whether to Supervision or Enforcement) in the exercise of its duties is generally protected from onward disclosure to others by s.348 FSMA pursuant to which a recipient obtaining confidential information from the FCA may not disclose that information without the consent of both the person who provided the information to the FCA and the person to whom it relates. For these purposes, information is confidential if it relates to the business or other affairs of any person and was received by the FCA in discharge of its function provided it has not been made public or is in the form of a summary or collection so that it is not possible to ascertain information relating to a particular person. Disclosure of information contrary to this provision is an offence (s.352 FSMA). The protection does not apply to information which a person has originally provided to the FCA because the person did not "obtain" this information from the FCA.[37]

The FCA can, however, disclose information under its statutory gateways which allow it to pass information to others such as overseas regulators and prosecuting authorities and also allow disclosure for any purpose which furthers the FCA's objectives.

Third parties may also be able to obtain disclosure of documents from the FCA in limited circumstances, such as in the context of certain proceedings.

10.6.7 Publicity

10.6.7.1 Investigation

The FCA does not normally comment on whether it is investigating an issue and its expectation is that the person under investigation will also treat the matter as confidential (EG 4.6.1). Subject to the restrictions under s.348 FSMA (see below), this does not prevent an individual seeking legal advice or making notifications as required by law or contract.

10.6.7.2 Warning Notice

Once a Warning Notice has been issued, the FCA may publish certain information where the FCA proposes to:

(a) impose a penalty against a person who has performed a controlled function without approval (s.63B FSMA); or
(b) take disciplinary action against an approved person (under s.66 FSMA).

The power to publish does not apply where the FCA proposes to impose a prohibition or withdraw an individual's approval.

---

[37] See Real Estate Opportunities Ltd v Aberdeen Asset Managers Jersey Ltd & others [2006] EWHC 3249 (CH).

The starting point is that it will normally be appropriate to publish a statement containing limited information regarding a Warning Notice but not to identify the individual (in contrast to the position for firms which will normally be identified). However, there are cases in which individuals will be identified (examples provided in the EG include where it would help to protect consumers or investors or it is desirable to quash rumours in the market (EG6.2.6).

The decision on publication will be made by the RDC, taking into account any representations from the recipient of the Warning Notice. Publication may not be made if the FCA considers that this would be unfair to the subject of the action, prejudicial to the interests of consumers or detrimental to the stability of the UK financial system (s.391(6) FSMA). In considering whether publication would be unfair, the FCA will take into account whether the FCA is proposing to take action against an individual and the extent to which the person has been made aware of the case against him. A person seeking to demonstrate potential unfairness must provide "clear and convincing evidence" of how unfairness may arise and how he could suffer a "disproportionate level of damage". A material effect on health, bankruptcy, loss of livelihood or a significant loss of income or prejudice to criminal proceedings are given as examples. Arguments related to reputational damage alone or media intrusion are unlikely to be sufficient but, are more likely to carry weight where evidence of the harm that will be caused as a result is also provided. Arguments on the merits will not be viewed as material to publication decisions.

Where information is published, a statement will usually appear on the FCA's website and consideration will be given as to what information should be placed on the Financial Services Register but details of the proposed sanction will not normally be given.

10.6.7.3 Decision Notice

The FCA is required to make information public when a Decision Notice or Final Notice is issued. The FCA expects normally to publish a Decision Notice where the recipient has made a reference to the Upper Tribunal but publication may also occur before any reference is made if the FCA considers there is a compelling reason to do so (such as where necessary for market confidence or to protect consumers).

The FCA will give notice of the proposal to publish and consider any representations made but will not normally deicide against publication solely on the basis that it would have a negative impact on reputation (EG6.2.13). A decision not to publish may be made where the FCA considers that it would be unfair, prejudicial to investors or consumers or detrimental to the stability of the UK financial system (such as where it may damage market confidence or undermine market integrity in a way which could be damaging to consumers). However, satisfying the Upper Tribunal on these grounds is unlikely to be straightforward.

In the case of Arch Financial Products LLP, Farrell & Addison, an application was made to the Tribunal for an order preventing the publication of the Decision Notices and to remove names from the register of references. In summary, the grounds for the application were that publication would cause serious reputational harm; a real risk that the individuals' lives (and those of their families) would be adversely affected by the actions of disgruntled investors and might also adversely affect the various civil proceedings in which they were defendants. The Upper Tribunal commented that no evidence had been provided that fears concerning the personal safety of the individuals and their families were well founded; reports had appeared in the press mentioning the case in which the individuals presented their own side of the story and court papers regarding the civil proceedings were publicly available. In these circumstances the Tribunal considered that there may be merit in the publication of the Decision Notices so that the individuals could be free to explain the position; publication of the notices would not make the situation materially worse and "cogent evidence of disproportionate damage" arising from publication had not been provided. The possibility of prejudice to the civil proceedings and to settlement was dismissed as pure speculation.

The Decision Notice will normally be published in full on the FCA's website together with a statement that a reference has been made to the Upper Tribunal. Information may also be included in the Financial Services Register.

Once the FCA has published information, the protection afforded by s.348 FSMA no longer applies to that information.

The FCA will, on request, consider whether information should be removed from its website and will take into account a number of factors (including whether the person is a firm or an individual, the educational value, the public interest, and the length of time since publication) (EG6.2.17). The FCA's expectation is that material will not be removed until six years have passed since publication.

A notice of discontinuance may be published when the FCA decides not to take action following publication in relation to a Warning Notice or Decision Notice.

10.6.7.4 Upper Tribunal and the Court

When a reference is made to the Upper Tribunal the case will also be listed on the register of current references which is published on the Upper Tribunal's website. The register provides dates of upcoming hearings as well as an indication of the decision made.

Proceedings before the Upper Tribunal are generally public and members of the public can attend hearings.

In the context of judicial review proceedings, the Court of Appeal has declined to hold a hearing in private and to preserve the anonymity of the applicant, instead affirming the principle of open justice (R. on the application of C) v Financial Services Authority [2013] EWCA Civ 677).

10.6.8 *Treasury review of FCA/PRA enforcement process*

As noted above, in 2014, HM Treasury conducted a review of enforcement decision-making by the PRA and the FCA. A final report, the HMT Review, was published in December 2014 which included a number of recommendations. Since then the following documents have been published:

(a) in July 2015, the FCA published details of its enforcement referral criteria (as set out above); and

(b) in April 2016, the FCA and PRA published a joint consultation paper (FCA CP 16/10; PRA CP 14/16) on proposals to implement more of the HMT Review recommendations as well as the recommendations made in the report by Andrew Green QC on enforcement action following the failure of HSBOS plc which was published in November 2015.

The FCA proposals include:

— enhanced record-keeping in relation to referral decision-making to include all potential subjects and reasons for referring or not referring individuals;

— quarterly update meetings between supervision and enforcement with scope and potential addition of new subjects to be a standing item on the agenda to be minuted;

— subjects of investigations to be provided, at the same time as the "memorandum of appointment", with a summary of potential breaches, the matters which are said to give rise to breaches and an explanation of the criteria applied in reaching a decision to refer;

— periodic updates, on at least a quarterly basis, to cover the steps taken in the investigation, next steps and indicative guidelines;

— further guidance to be provided on factors taken into account when considering a request to extend time for responding to a PIR or Warning Notice;

— 28 days' notice to be given of the commencement of the Stage 1 early settlement window and key evidence to be identified by the FCA at the commencement of Stage 1 where necessary to help resolve factual disputes or to assist the individual to make an informed decision about whether to resolve the dispute;

— a streamlined procedure to narrow the issues between the FCA and the subject by entering into a 'focused resolution agreement' on the facts and liability with the RDC determining only the action to be taken. The subject would have to accept all facts and issues of whether the facts amount to a breach and a 30% discount would be applied where agreement was reached during Stage 1 and the only contested issue was the penalty. Comments are also invited on alternative proposals involving: (1) acceptance by the subject of all facts but disagreement as to whether those facts amount to breaches; or (2) acceptance by the subject of some issues but not all; and

— the abolition of the Stage 2 and 3 discounts.

The FCA's forthcoming review of its penalty policy will include consideration of whether it may be appropriate to expressly incentivise admissions at scoping meetings.

10.7 Enforcement Themes

10.7.1 *Learning lessons from enforcement cases—key themes*

This part of the Chapter focuses on some of the key themes emerging from FCA enforcement cases and lessons that may be learned in determining the likely expectations of the authorities under the new regime. This will have application to Senior Managers both in relation to the application of the Duty of Responsibility and the Conduct Rules. While the focus is on FCA enforcement actions[38], no analysis of individual accountability would be complete without an assessment of the issues which arose in the cases of Peter Cummings, the former chief executive officer of the corporate division of Bank of Scotland Plc ("HBOS") and John Pottage, the former chief executive officer of UBS Wealth Management (UK) Ltd and UBS AG (the

---

[38] As opposed to FSA cases.

"UBS Wealth Management Business"). Frequently cases centre on whether an individual understood the business for which they were responsible; whether they understood the applicable regulatory expectations; and whether they had maintained adequate oversight of their business area.

The key themes considered below are:

(a) understanding the business and potential risks;
(b) governance, controls and procedures;
(c) knowledge of regulatory concerns;
(d) delegation;
(e) management Information; and
(f) timely and appropriate action.

10.7.2 *Understanding the business and potential risks*

Individual Conduct Rule 2

You must act with due skill, care and diligence.

Presumption of Responsibility/"Duty of Responsibility"

PRA Supervisory Statement

The PRA will consider:

1. what the Senior Manager actually knew, or a Senior Manager in that position ought to have known (taking into account, among other factors, the length of time they have been in the role and handover arrangements to those new in a role); and

2. what expertise and competence the Senior Manager had, or ought to have possessed, at the time to perform his/her specific Senior Management Function.

Examples of steps that might be considered to be reasonable actions could include:

1. investigations or reviews of the Senior Manager's areas of responsibility;

2. seeking and obtaining appropriate expert advice or assurance (whether internal or external);

Presumption of Responsibility/"Duty of Responsibility"

3. awareness of relevant external developments, including key risks; and

4. pre-emptive actions to prevent a breach occurring, including any initial reviews of the business or business area on taking up a Senior Manager Function.

FCA Draft Guidance

The FCA will have regard to whether the Senior Manager took reasonable steps to understand and inform themselves about the firm's activities in relation to which they were responsible, including, but not limited to, whether they:

1. permitted the expansion or restructuring of the business without reasonably assessing the potential risks;

2. inadequately monitored highly profitable/unusual transactions or business practices or individuals who contributed significantly to the profitability of a business area or who had significant influence over the operation of a business area;

3. failed to obtain an independent expert opinion where appropriate;

4. failed to seek an adequate explanation of issues within a business area, whether from people within that business area, or elsewhere within or outside the firm, if they were not an expert in that area; and

5. failed to maintain an appropriate level of understanding about an issue or a responsibility that they delegated to an individual or individuals.

Key Themes

1. Understand the business for which you are responsible.

2. Understand and inform yourself of and investigate the associated risks.

3. Require explanation of unusual/highly profitable business or individuals who contribute significantly to the profitability and verify these explanations.

4. Seek an independent expert opinion where appropriate.

> **Key Themes**
>
> 5. Maintain an appropriate level of understanding even where a matter has been delegated.
> 6. Understand and assess the risks of expanding business into new areas.

Senior Managers are expected to understand the business for which they are responsible and ensure that they are sufficiently well informed of the associated risks. Although they are unlikely to be an expert in all aspects of a complex financial services business, Senior Managers should understand and inform themselves about the business sufficiently to understand the risks.

In particular, Senior Managers ought properly to assess the risks of expanding the business into new areas and ensure that before approving any expansion plans, they give due consideration to the risks involved. Further, where unusually profitable business is undertaken, or where the profits are particularly volatile, or the business involves funding requirements on the firm beyond those reasonably anticipated, Senior Managers should require explanations from those who report to them. Where those explanations are implausible or unsatisfactory, steps should be taken to test the veracity of those explanations.

Where a Senior Manager does not himself have the necessary expertise, he ought to seek an independent opinion (internal or external as appropriate) and where a matter has been delegated, he ought to maintain an appropriate level of understanding of that matter.

10.7.2.1 Enforcement cases: John Pottage

The case of Pottage remains one of the most helpful insights into the steps that Senior Managers will be expected to take to understand their business and identify potential risks. The case was the first attempt by the FSA to bring an action against a senior individual for a supervisory failing.

In April 2012, the Upper Tribunal dismissed the FSA's allegations of misconduct against Pottage, the chief executive officer of the UBS Wealth Management Business between September 2006 and July 2007.

The bank had been fined £8 million in 2009 in relation to systems and controls failings at the London branch of its international wealth management business. The FSA found that Pottage had breached Statement of Principle 7,[39] in failing to take reasonable steps to ensure that the UBS Wealth Management Business complied with the relevant requirements and standards of the regulatory system. Specifically, the FSA considered that, on assuming the chief executive role, Pottage had failed to carry out an adequate initial assessment or sufficient continuous monitoring of the business.

While the Tribunal considered that there were serious flaws in the compliance and risk functions within the wealth management business, it concluded that the FSA had failed to establish that Pottage had not exercised reasonable care in meeting his regulatory obligations. To be held accountable, Pottage needed to be personally culpable, "and not simply because a regulatory failure [had] occurred in an area of business for which he [was] responsible". As a result, the Tribunal directed that the FSA take no further action against him.

10.7.2.2 *Pottage: Initial assessment on taking up a role and continuous monitoring*

Pottage took up the role of chief executive officer in September 2006, having previously been head of wealth planning, deputy head of the UK domestic business and head of products and services at the UBS Wealth Management Business. The thrust of the FSA's case was that while Pottage had taken steps to undertake an operational risk review, namely the London Operational Risk Review ("LORR") (a "drains-up" review)

---

[39] An Approved Person performing an accountable Significant Influence Function must take reasonable steps to ensure that the business of the firm for which he is responsible in his accountable function complies with the relevant requirements and standards of the regulatory system.

commenced in July 2007, he should have appreciated sooner the serious flaws in the design and operation of the governance and risk management framework of the business and should have acted more quickly in undertaking the review and taking corrective action.

Although the FSA accepted that Pottage had taken various steps upon taking up his role and had addressed problems as they emerged, it considered that those steps had not been sufficiently detailed and that he had been too accepting of the assurances that he had received that there were no fundamental deficiencies with the design and operational effectiveness of the governance and risk framework. According to the FSA, Pottage should have undertaken an initial assessment and adequate continuous monitoring, focusing on certain aspects of the business.

The FSA said that, at the time of taking up his appointment, there were various matters that should have increased Pottage's awareness of the need to spend substantial time ensuring that the governance and risk management frameworks operated effectively. These were said to be: the existence of a number of inherent risks in the business; the absence of an independent middle office; the operation of a global matrix management structure; cultural issues concerning responsibility for risk management; and the fact that Pottage had approved a significant expansion of the business at a time when there were "known operational issues which had arisen prior to his appointment".

Shortly after starting his new role, Pottage held a series of meetings with senior management, most of them Approved Persons (and Significant Influence Function holders) in their own right, including those concerned with "risk management", "legal, risk and compliance" and group internal audit.[40] Pottage also met with the chief operating officer, the business unit head and Pottage's predecessor. It was accepted that none

---

[40] Specifically, Pottage met with the head of the risk and compliance functions in the business, the heads of legal, risk and compliance for the region and the relevant global heads.

of the individuals with whom Pottage had met—each specialists in their own right—had expressed any concern as to the effectiveness of the risk control framework and had not raised any of the matters relied upon by the FSA in its Statement of Case against Pottage.

Pottage said that he had not reached the "tipping point" at which a systematic overhaul (as undertaken in the LORR) became an imperative until July 2007 when an incident of unauthorised trading exposed front-office failings. Until then he had understood the failings to be confined to the back office (i.e. operations) and believed that these were covered by a change programme which was already in progress.

The Tribunal found that Pottage could not reasonably be expected to have reacted any earlier to any deficiencies, or to have proactively identified weaknesses, when the bank's own senior risk and compliance specialists had not done so themselves and had also not considered that certain warning signals merited a wider systems and controls review. The Tribunal concluded that the LORR was reasonable in its timing and that there was insufficient evidence that Pottage had needed to "dig deeper" in challenging his team.

While Senior Managers cannot blindly trust the information received from those responsible for risk and compliance, they are entitled to rely on it provided reasonable steps are taken to probe and verify such information. Senior Managers will need to satisfy themselves that key risks have been identified and are subject to continuous monitoring.

10.7.2.3   Enforcement Cases: Peter Cummings

In making submissions to the FSA's Regulatory Decisions Committee ("RDC"), Peter Cummings (former chief executive officer of the corporate division of HBOS) raised a number of (ultimately unsuccessful) arguments based on the Tribunal's decision in Pottage. While the FSA acknowledged that Cummings had taken a number of steps during the relevant period to address identified issues with the corporate division and that he had not acted deliberately or recklessly, it nevertheless considered, and the RDC agreed, that he had failed to meet his regulatory obligations.

Unlike Pottage, Cummings decided not to refer his case to the Upper Tribunal. Reports at the time indicated that although Cummings disagreed with the FSA's findings, he did not wish to incur the additional costs and stress of taking his case further.

Cummings was chief executive officer of the corporate division of HBOS from January 2007 up to the time of its acquisition by Lloyds Banking Group. The group ultimately required a multi-billion pound re-capitalisation during the financial crisis. In September 2012, the FSA found that Cummings had breached Statement of Principle 6[41] by failing to exercise due skill, care and diligence, and in particular, by pursuing an aggressive expansion strategy without suitable controls in place. The FSA also found that Cummings was "knowingly concerned" in HBOS's failure to take reasonable care to organise and control its affairs responsibly and effectively with adequate risk management systems. In addition to being fined £500,000, Cummings was prohibited from performing any Significant Influence Function in any authorised firm or bank.

In his submissions to the RDC, Cummings characterised the test to be applied when assessing his conduct as comprising three conditions, which had to be satisfied before action could be taken against a member of the senior management at a bank which had encountered financial difficulties such as HBOS. He relied on the Tribunal's decision in Pottage in support of his submissions.

(a) First, Cummings submitted that he could not be found to have committed regulatory breaches on a strict liability basis, as confirmed by Pottage. He further submitted that it was not sufficient to say that, regardless of whether or

---

[41] An Approved Person performing an accountable Significant Influence Function must exercise due skill, care and diligence in managing the business of the firm for which he is responsible in his accountable function.

not he had engaged in any misconduct, he was personally liable for the failure of HBOS simply because of the positions he had held. In this regard, he stated that it was important to draw a distinction between responsibility and fault.

(b) Secondly, Cummings submitted that in order to demonstrate that he had committed regulatory breaches it had to be shown that his conduct had been unreasonable. He suggested that this test of unreasonableness was "set at a very high level" and that it would be necessary to show that his decisions were "beyond the range of plausible judgement". He further submitted that the appropriate level of reasonableness should be equated with conduct that could be defined as irrational or evidently irresponsible.

(c) Thirdly, Cummings submitted that there should be very clear evidence to support the allegations against him.

In response to these submissions, the FSA accepted that action could not be taken against Cummings on a strict liability basis. However, the FSA found that Cummings was personally responsible for the matters that it had highlighted. In reaching its decision, the FSA noted that it had taken into account and applied the test outlined in Pottage.

10.7.2.4 *Cummings: Knowledge of the business*

When considering Cummings' actions, the FSA noted that he had specific responsibility for the corporate division's strategy and performance, for its overall framework and for managing risks. Until November 2007, Cummings was the chair of the corporate credit risk committee, which was responsible for considering and developing credit risk strategies and policies, levels of portfolio exposure and parameters for sector limits to be adopted within all areas of the division. Further, Cummings was also the chair of the executive credit committee, which was responsible for sanctioning lending decisions on high value or complex credit transactions.

The FSA found that, at Cummings' instigation, the corporate division had pursued an aggressive growth strategy, entering into many transactions with weak lending criteria or aggressive lending structures. The corporate division was the highest risk part of HBOS's business with a vulnerable level of exposure to the economic cycle, meaning that effective assessment, management and mitigation of credit risk in the corporate division was all the more important. The FSA considered that there were significant failings in both the sanctioning and subsequent monitoring of transactions entered into by the division.

Cummings had relied on the effectiveness of the credit sanctioning process to mitigate the high-risk profile of the portfolio. The FSA noted that Cummings considered this to be a key mitigant of the risks associated with increasing the portfolio's exposure to commercial property at a time when he recognised or should have recognised that the market seemed to be reaching its peak.

In addition, the FSA considered that the low credit quality of the transactions which made up the portfolio meant that there was a relatively high risk of default. It therefore found that effective monitoring of individual transactions and the portfolio as a whole was of particular significance.

However, the FSA found that during the relevant period Cummings was aware or should have been aware that:

(a) there were continuing and significant weaknesses in credit skills and processes at all stages of the transaction cycle;
(b) there were continuing, significant and widespread weaknesses in the effectiveness of management supervision and oversight of relationship managers;
(c) the substantial increase in the volume and complexity of new transactions meant that the key sanctioning committees had less time to scrutinise individual transactions, which impacted on the effectiveness of those committees;
(d) the increasing pressure to increase growth and the significant amount of time and resource which was taken

up by a wide range of change management projects meant that less attention would necessarily be paid to risk management; and

(e) as a consequence of these serious deficiencies, the controls framework failed to provide robust oversight and challenge to the business.

The FSA found that Cummings was aware, or should have been aware, that there were repeated failings of key controls across all areas of the business and considered that these controls were crucial to the effective sanctioning and monitoring of individual transactions.

10.7.2.5 Cummings: Understanding the impact of external events: Foreseeability

Cummings submitted that when assessing the reasonableness of his conduct it was also important to consider his conduct in the context of what had been predicted for the economy and what he could reasonably be expected to have foreseen. He explained that throughout much of the relevant period it was commonplace, and thus not unreasonable, to hold an optimistic view of the economic outlook and that internal and external advice at HBOS also supported this positive assessment of the economy. Cummings disputed the suggestion that a downturn had been foreseeable from the start of the relevant period. He also submitted that the financial crisis was so severe and worsened with such speed that it was not realistic to have expected him to have planned for such an event. He asserted that the problems within the division only arose because of the speed and severity of the financial crisis.

The FSA accepted that the full severity of the financial crisis was not reasonably foreseeable during the early part of the relevant period. It noted that the severity of the financial crisis caused many of the transactions to become stressed. However, the FSA did not criticise Cummings simply because in light of the financial crisis it questioned whether those transactions should have been entered into. Instead the FSA considered that

Cummings had committed a regulatory breach because corporate, under his direction, had entered into these high-risk transactions as part of its growth strategy, at a time when it did not have the systems and controls in place to be able to manage such business.

The FSA considered that his conduct would have amounted to a regulatory falling at any time in the economic cycle and that the severity of the financial crisis merely served to highlight the potentially disastrous consequences of such conduct.

10.7.2.6 *Cummings: Acting prudently while deficiencies are being addressed*

The FSA accepted that a number of the deficiencies in the control framework pre-dated the appointment of Cummings as chief executive officer and that during the relevant period Cummings had initiated a number of change projects which were designed to improve the control framework and the approach to risk management. However, it rejected the suggestion by Cummings that it was wrong to bring disciplinary action against him personally, even though he had initiated a number of projects to rectify the problems within the corporate division. The FSA held Cummings out as an example to those holding Significant Influence Functions of the importance of acting prudently while they are attempting to rectify deficient systems and controls.

10.7.2.7 *Cummings: Role in collective decision making*

Cummings submitted that his responsibility had to be considered in the context of the involvement of others in decisions which were central to the allegations against him. He submitted that it was clear from Pottage that his role was one of oversight. He was not personally responsible for the design, creation or implementation of controls nor was he to do the job of an appropriately appointed delegate. Instead, the obligation was on him to take reasonable steps to ensure that the business had compliant systems and controls.

He submitted that throughout the relevant period he had reasonably placed reliance upon others such as group risk and the corporate risk function. He also noted that decisions, such as those concerning significant transactions, were made by committee. He stated that all decisions had been taken in a "proper collegiate way" and in accordance with appropriate governance arrangements. In making his submissions, Cummings accepted that the fact that he was not solely responsible for various aspects of the management of corporate did not mean that he could not be found to be culpable for any of the alleged failings within the division.

In relation to the aggressive growth targets that had been set during the relevant period, Cummings maintained that the targets were reached following extensive and appropriate discussions by the group board. He submitted that it was wrong to suggest that he had personally directed the growth strategy and suggested that instead, the proper way to characterise his conduct would be to say that he had implemented a plan agreed upon by the group board. While the FSA accepted that the growth targets were agreed with the group board, it considered that as chief executive officer of corporate, Cummings was personally responsible for the setting and achievement of these targets. This responsibility had been made clear in Cummings' job description.

The FSA did accept that the fact that others were involved in making some of the relevant decisions provided some mitigation for Cummings' misconduct. Nevertheless, the FSA considered that this must be balanced with the fact that a significant degree of reliance had been placed upon Cummings' judgement and experience. Moreover, in his role, he was obliged to have oversight of the systems and controls of the firm and he was required to take reasonable steps to ensure that corporate's systems and controls were compliant with regulatory standards. The FSA considered that Cummings had failed to discharge his regulatory obligations in this regard.

10.7.3 Governance, controls and procedures

Individual Conduct Rule 2

You must act with due skill, care and diligence.

Senior Manager Conduct Rule 1

You must take reasonable steps to ensure that the business of the firm for which you are responsible is controlled effectively.

Senior Manager Conduct Rule 2

You must take reasonable steps to ensure that the business of the firm for which you are responsible complies with the relevant requirements and standards of the regulatory system.

Presumption of Responsibility/Duty of Responsibility

PRA Supervisory Statement

The PRA will consider the actual responsibilities of the Senior Manager and the relationship between those responsibilities and the responsibilities of other Senior Managers in the firm (including in relation to any joint- responsibilities or matrix-management structures).

Examples of steps that might be considered to be reasonable actions could include:

1. implementing, policing and reviewing appropriate policies and procedures;

2. structuring and control of day-to-day operations, including ensuring any delegations are managed and reviewed appropriately. This includes in relation to any 'matrix-management' arrangements;

3. ensuring that the firm and/or relevant area has adequate resources, and that these are appropriately deployed, including for risk and control functions; and

4. pre-emptive actions to prevent a breach occurring, including any initial reviews of the business or business area on taking up a Senior Manager function.

Presumption of Responsibility/Duty of Responsibility

FCA Draft Guidance

The FCA will have regard to:

1. whether the Senior Manager took reasonable steps to ensure that the reporting lines, whether in the UK or overseas, in relation to the firm's activities for which they were responsible, were clear to staff and operated effectively;

2. whether the Senior Manager took reasonable steps to satisfy himself, on reasonable grounds, that, for the activities for which they were responsible, the firm had appropriate policies and procedures for reviewing the competence, knowledge, skills and performance of each individual member of staff, to assess their suitability to fulfil their duties; and

3. whether the Senior Manager took reasonable steps to assess, on taking up each of their responsibilities, and monitor, where this was reasonable, the governance, operational and risk management arrangements in place for the firm's activities for which they were responsible (including, where appropriate, corroborating, challenging, and considering the wider implications of the information available to them), and whether they took reasonable steps to deal with any actual or suspected issues identified as a result in a timely and appropriate manner.

Key Themes

1. Establish risk appetite/tolerance.
2. Ensure risk appetite/tolerance widely understood—implement an appropriate communication policy.
3. Understand impact of strategic initiatives on operational risk profile.
4. Ensure adequate resourcing of risk management function.
5. Ensure independence of risk management function.
6. Ensure clarity of roles, apportionment of responsibilities and reporting lines.
7. Ensure no gaps in assignment of responsibilities.

Key Themes

8. Regularly review apportionment of responsibilities.

9. Take action where responsibilities not clearly apportioned.

10. Establish effective processes to identify, manage, monitor and report risks.

11. Implement, police and review appropriate policies and procedures.

12. Ensure appropriate and consistent staff communications on acceptable behaviours across all channels.

13. Review on an ongoing basis competence, knowledge, skills and performance of individual staff members and suitability to roles.

14. Do not give undue weight to financial performance when considering suitability to role.

15. Ensure vacancies do not put regulatory compliance at risk.

16. Consider strength of ongoing monitoring with regulatory compliance.

17. Undertake periodic reviews of key risks and operational risk management framework.

18. Challenge effectively.

10.7.3.1   *Identification of risks*

The degree of control and strength of monitoring reasonably required will depend to a large extent on the risk appetite of the business, which itself is determined by the strategy and plans of the business. Senior Managers with responsibility for establishing the risk appetite of the firm will be expected to exert greater control and monitoring over the business if the risk appetite of the business is high. They must ensure that the firm's risk appetite is widely understood within the business for which they are responsible and that there are effective processes to identify, manage, monitor and report risks.

It is particularly important for Senior Managers to understand the risks associated with expanding the business or entering a new business area. Before any such expansion or new business is undertaken, Senior Managers should investigate and satisfy themselves about the associated risks.

10.7.3.2 *Enforcement cases*

A number of recent enforcement cases have highlighted the importance of maintaining adequate systems and controls to identify and manage a firm's exposure to risks within their business.

In December 2013, Lloyds TSB Bank Plc ("Lloyds TSB") and Bank of Scotland ("BOS") were fined £28 million as a result of failures regarding systems and controls governing financial incentives given to sales staff in Lloyds TSB, Halifax and BOS branches who sold protection and investment products to customers on an advised basis ("Lloyds Incentive Schemes"). In sanctioning the firms, the FCA stressed the important role which remuneration schemes play in setting the sales culture of a firm and the risk that they may undermine a firm's positive efforts to treat customers fairly. Firms must ensure that their systems and controls are sufficiently robust to mitigate the risk of any adverse impact the incentives may have on staff behaviours. This should include appropriately focused risk-based monitoring. In the period between 2010 and 2015, Lloyds Banking Group was expected to double its customer base, focusing on sales of protection products over investment products. Various financial incentive schemes, which were designed to encourage advisers to maximise their sales volumes, were implemented. These schemes included a number of high-risk features, for example the firms' information systems allowed advisers to see on a daily basis the number of sales that they had made and on at least a weekly basis their performance against their sales point targets. Advisers were also provided with information that enabled them to calculate their potential bonuses. There was therefore a significant risk that advisers would be improperly motivated by their own personal financial circumstances. The FCA found that there were serious deficiencies in the firms' governance over the incentive schemes and noted that the root cause of these deficiencies was the collective failure by senior management to identify remuneration and incentives for advisers as a key area of risk requiring specific and robust oversight. A report produced by group internal audit in November 2011 noted that: "Management does not have an effective governance framework for its remuneration and incentive schemes. Management has not fully assessed the risks or performed effective oversight of the schemes." Although the firms had various systems and controls in place to monitor the quality of the sales made by advisers, they did not ensure that these controls were appropriately focused on the specific higher risk features of advisers' incentives.

In November 2014, the Royal Bank of Scotland Plc ("RBS"), National Westminster Bank Plc and Ulster Bank Plc were fined £42 million by the FCA and £14 million by the PRA for failing to have adequate systems and controls to identify and manage their exposure to operational IT risk. The breaches resulted in an IT incident triggered by incompatibilities between existing and new batching software, which is used to update customer accounts overnight. The authorities concluded that the firms had not sufficiently recognised and addressed the strategic IT risks, noting that their IT risk appetite (and so relevant policy standard) focused on low probability but high-impact business continuity events. The authorities considered that the firms' risk appetite and policy standard ought to have focused on more probable events of disruption, such as batching failures. The FCA noted that the firms did not ensure that technology services—the function with the broadest view of IT risk—had a sufficient business profile or direct involvement in business prioritisation and decision making.

In November 2014, Chase de Vere Independent Financial Advisers Limited ("Chase de Vere") was fined £560,000 for failures surrounding the sale of Keydata traded life settlement products to 2,806 customers who had invested approximately £50 million. The FCA considered that the process underlying the research, assessment and approval of the Keydata products was insufficiently rigorous. Chase de Vere did not generally risk rate individual products or set limits on sales of individual products. Once a product had been accepted it was left to the individual adviser's judgement to decide to whom to sell the product and in what amounts, based on each customer's individual circumstances. The FCA found that Chase de Vere failed to put in place adequate systems and controls to ensure that the features of the Keydata products were sufficiently well researched to understand the risks posed to investors and ensure those risks were properly understood by the advisers. In addition, the FCA commented that Chase de Vere failed to implement adequate risk management systems to mitigate the risk that its advisers would fail to disclose appropriately the distinctive features and risks of the Keydata products. During some of the relevant period, instead of relying on product descriptions that had been approved by compliance, advisers were free to compose their own product descriptions and risk disclosures when describing structured products to customers. This meant that some of the suitability letters sent to customers contained inaccurate or incorrect information. The FCA found that had Chase de Vere adequately researched the Keydata products from the outset, it would have realised that additional controls and restrictions on sales were required, particularly in relation to customers with a cautious attitude to risk.

10.7.3.3 *Governance arrangements and reporting lines*

Effective governance arrangements should be adopted to manage the risk relating to the firm's activities, processes and systems. A firm's organisational structure should encompass clear reporting lines and routes of escalation to ensure there are processes in place to identify, manage, monitor and report any actual or potential risks.

Senior Managers should ensure that:

(a) the organisation of the business and the responsibilities of those within it are clearly defined, communicated and formally documented (this is particularly important where staff have dual reporting lines);
(b) each area of the business for which they are responsible is clearly assigned to an individual; and

(c) they establish, implement and maintain effective internal reporting and communication of information at all relevant levels of the firm.

10.7.3.4 *Enforcement cases*

The absence of clear reporting lines, where individuals do not know who they report to, and Senior Managers do not know who they are responsible for, can potentially lead to serious governance failings. Cases have also emphasised the importance of establishing and maintaining an appropriate independent risk management function.

In May 2014, Martin Brokers (UK) Ltd ("Martins") was fined £630,000 for misconduct relating to the London Interbank Offered Rate ("LIBOR"). The FCA commented that Martins' reporting lines and responsibilities were unclear at every level, including among senior managers, meaning that responsibility for compliance oversight of individual brokers was unclear and effectively uncontrolled as a result. Each desk operated as its own independent business, few formal controls were imposed and while brokers had an informal reporting line to the chief executive officer, in practice this was not used and oversight of brokers was left entirely to managers. However, this structure took no account of the risk that managers would engage, and indeed were themselves complicit, in the misconduct that took place. In circumstances where managerial performance was judged primarily on their success in maximising desk revenue and in the absence of any oversight or formal controls, the FCA found that a very weak compliance culture developed on Martins' broking desks which allowed broker misconduct to flourish and go undetected for a number of years.

In August 2014, RBS and National Westminster Bank Plc were fined £14.5 million for failing to conduct their advised mortgage business with due skill, care and diligence ("RBS Mortgages"). The FCA found that the firms did not take reasonable care to ensure the suitability of mortgage advice to customers and adequately remedy the failings once identified.

527

The FCA also considered that the firms did not take reasonable care to ensure that an individual or team was properly responsible or accountable for the advised mortgage sales process, including checking whether the process was updated and compliant with regulatory requirements. In particular, the FCA noted that the project management and governance of a working group, put together to resolve issues raised by the FSA following its review of mortgage sales in September/October 2011, had no executive members and managers would in some cases delegate attendance to someone more junior. The FCA considered that the governance surrounding the working group was inadequate in that there were no terms of reference, it was not required to report to any individual or committee, there was no agenda and most of its meetings were not minuted, nor was a record of decisions taken or comprehensive list of action points, responsibilities or deadlines maintained.

The FCA concluded that there was "no executive in charge who was in practice taking responsibility" to resolve the issues raised and "without meaningful executive challenge or guidance ... many of those involved ... were not clear which executive had been made accountable".

10.7.3.5   Policies and procedures

Senior Managers are responsible for ensuring their firms' compliance with the relevant regulatory requirements and must ensure that all staff are aware of the need for compliance. In particular, steps should be taken to ensure that the business has clearly defined operating procedures and systems which enable staff to identify how they can comply with the relevant requirements. Implementing and maintaining adequate internal control mechanisms will assist Senior Managers to secure their firms' compliance with decisions and procedures.

In addition, Senior Managers should ensure that appropriate policies and procedures are in place to review the competence, knowledge, skills and performance of each member of staff under their control. If any concerns are raised regarding an individual's performance, an assessment of the individual's suitability should be undertaken by the Senior Manager. Where an individual ceases to perform a function, Senior Managers must ensure that there is an orderly transition where that individual is replaced and, in the event of any temporary vacancies, take reasonable steps to ensure that suitable cover is arranged.

10.7.3.6 Enforcement cases

As demonstrated in the recent LIBOR and FOREX cases, Senior Managers with responsibility for compliance oversight should have particular regard to the application and specificity of their policies and procedures.

In November 2014, the FCA fined Citibank NA ("Citi"), HSBC Bank Plc ("HSBC"), JPMorgan Chase Bank NA, RBS and UBS AG, and in May 2015, fined Barclays Bank Plc ("Barclays") a total of approximately £1.4 billion. The FCA found that the banks failed to exercise adequate and effective control over their G10 spot FX trading businesses which resulted in widespread trader misconduct. While the banks were found to have policies in place, they were high level in nature and applied generally across a number of the banks' respective business divisions. There were no policies specific to FX and any guidance provided in the group-wide policies contained limited practical examples regarding the types of issues that the FX traders faced daily and what amounted to unacceptable behaviour. In addition, the FCA found that the banks failed to take adequate steps to ensure that general policies regarding confidentiality, conflicts of interest and trading conduct were effectively implemented in each of their FX trading businesses and there was insufficient training and guidance on how those policies applied. To the extent that training was provided/introduced, often this was not mandatory and was therefore poorly attended. The FCA held that the absence of such adequate training and guidance resulted in an increased risk that trader misconduct would occur.

The FCA made a number of similar findings in relation to Deutsche Bank. In April 2015, Deutsche Bank AG ("Deutsche") was fined £226,800,000 for misconduct in relation to LIBOR and EURIBOR (together, "IBOR") and for failing to deal with the FCA in an open and cooperative way ("Deutsche IBOR"). Although Deutsche had in place general policies and procedures concerning compliance standards, it had no IBOR-specific systems and controls. In particular, the FCA noted that Deutsche had inadequate systems and controls in place to support audit and investigation of trader misconduct more generally and as a result misconduct went unchecked. Deutsche's systems for identifying and recording traders' telephone calls and tracing trading books to individual traders were inadequate which directly impeded the FCA's investigation, causing significant delays and difficulties.

In October 2014, Yorkshire Building Society was fined £4.1 million for failings in relation to its handling of mortgage customers in payment difficulties and arrears ("Yorkshire Building Society Mortgages"). The FCA considered that Yorkshire Building Society's arrears policy, which was approved by a senior risk committee, did not contain sufficient detail to provide meaningful guidance to call handlers as to how they should approach holistically the consideration of customers' specific circumstances. Call handlers often sought ad hoc payments without sufficiently considering how the payments may have affected a customer's overall debt burden. They also failed to consider all payment options which, in cases of long-term unaffordability, may have included a voluntary sale by the customer or even repossession by Yorkshire Building Society. The FCA considered that while repossession was properly viewed as a last resort for customers in payment difficulties, management did not take account of the fact that where repossession is appropriate, delays in repossession cause further significant detriment for customers because arrears build up and increased fees and associated interest are incurred.

10.7.3.7   Initial assessment following commencement of a new role

Senior Managers will be expected to conduct an initial assessment when commencing a new role in order to satisfy themselves that the operational and risk management arrangements in place within their area of responsibility are effective. Where issues are identified during this initial assessment, Senior Managers will need to take steps to address them.

10.7.3.8   Enforcement cases

It was recognised by the Tribunal in Pottage that Senior Managers are under an obligation to conduct a detailed initial assessment when taking up a new role. Pottage demonstrates that while Senior Managers cannot blindly trust the information received from those responsible for risk and compliance, they are entitled to rely on it provided reasonable steps are taken to probe and verify that information.

In January 2015, Jeremy Kraft (former compliance officer at Martins) was fined £105,000 for compliance and cultural failings at his firm. Kraft, who had no extensive compliance experience prior to commencing his role as compliance officer at Martins, relied on discussions with various senior executives to determine the compliance risk profile of the firm as low. Kraft formed this view despite knowing that the FSA had previously expressed concerns regarding the resourcing of Martins' compliance department. Kraft trusted the senior executives' assessment that the business was low risk on the basis that those executives had a sufficient understanding of the related compliance issues, without undertaking any independent assessment to validate such a view.

In March 2015, John Allin (internal auditor of the Bank of Beirut) and Anthony Wills (former compliance officer of the Bank of Beirut) were fined £9,900 and £19,600 respectively for failing to deal with the regulator in an open and cooperative way when responding to queries about the implementation of various remediation action points taken to mitigate financial crime risk. In particular, the FCA noted that Allin only became aware of the Bank of Beirut's remediation plan action points some five months after his arrival and only as a result of a reminder from the FSA regarding its implementation rather than making any enquiries or undertaking an internal audit upon joining the firm.

10.7.3.9   *Monitoring of governance arrangements*

Senior Managers are expected, on a regular basis, to monitor the effectiveness and adequacy of the internal control framework, including the firm's risk management policies and procedures, and to take steps to resolve any deficiencies identified.

Firms and senior managers have, in the past, been fined for failing to undertake continuous monitoring duties to ensure that the firm's governance and compliance arrangements, in respect of activities for which they are responsible, are adequate and meet regulatory requirements.

10.7.3.10   *Enforcement cases*

In the recent FOREX cases, the FCA identified that day-to-day oversight of the spot FX traders' conduct was insufficient. There was inadequate supervision by the front office, who had primary responsibility for identifying, assessing and managing the risks associated with the FX spot trading business, and limited monitoring of the traders' communications took place. In addition, the second and third lines of defence failed to challenge the management of these risks by the front office. The failure to identify, assess and manage these risks was especially serious given that a number of those who were responsible for managing the front office were aware of, and/or at times involved in, the misconduct. These failings resulted in the failure to sufficiently embed the right values and culture and identify and prevent the widespread trader misconduct which went undetected for a number of years.

In June 2014, Credit Suisse International ("Credit Suisse") was fined over £2 million for failing to pay due regard to the information needs of its customers and communicate with them in a way which was clear, fair and not misleading. The

FCA found that brochures relating to Credit Suisse's Cliquet Product (a fixed-term capital protected structured product) gave undue prominence to the product's maximum return when the firm was aware that the chance of receiving the maximum return was close to zero and that the brochures did not adequately explain the product's early exit fees. Yorkshire Building Society, a third-party distributor of the Cliquet Product, was fined £1.4 million for similar failings.

In respect of Credit Suisse, the FCA noted that its financial promotions procedures did not provide for any holistic periodic review of the materials' compliance with regulatory requirements. In reviewing product brochures and terms and conditions, Credit Suisse's compliance, legal and sales departments focused on approval of individual changes in isolation, rather than undertaking any periodic review of the documents as a whole. The FCA considered that if Credit Suisse's processes had included such a review, this may have led to the proactive identification of such issues.

As noted above, in the RBS Mortgages case, the FCA found that the monitoring of the advised sales process was ineffective. The firms' principal monitoring function, the mortgage business quality unit, tested only against compliance with the sales process as set out in the mortgage sales guide, rather than assessing the quality of advice and checking whether sales were being made in compliance with regulatory requirements. The FCA identified that this had a knock-on effect on the quality of information available to the firms and their ability properly to identify risks relating to poor customer outcomes.

10.7.3.11   *Effective challenge*

The FCA has made it clear in a number of recent enforcement cases that it expects Senior Managers to independently verify and challenge information available to them. Where a Senior Manager needs to demonstrate that they took reasonable steps to secure regulatory compliance, they will generally be in a stronger position to do so where there is documentary evidence to demonstrate the steps they have taken.

10.7.3.12 *Enforcement cases*

In Kraft, the FCA commented that Kraft, as the compliance officer, had failed to challenge the chief executive officer's insistence on taking responsibility for broker supervision and his resistance to Kraft's efforts to involve himself directly in communicating with the brokers. The FCA found that Kraft wrongly deferred in his judgement to the chief executive officer, trusting that he was sufficiently close to the brokers to detect any misconduct. The FCA found that "this approach and attitude led to Mr Kraft's improper abdication of his responsibility to monitor Brokers". Responsibility for ensuring that an effective compliance framework is in place rests ultimately with the individual occupying the CF10 role. Compliance officers must therefore be prepared to challenge senior executives (and where possible evidence such challenge) where they have any concerns regarding the firm's compliance objectives.

10.7.4 *Knowledge of regulatory concerns*

Senior Manager Conduct Rule 2 You must take reasonable steps to ensure that the business of the firm for which you are responsible complies with the relevant requirements and standards of the regulatory system.

Presumption of Responsibility/Duty of Responsibility *PRA Supervisory Statement* The PRA will consider: 1. what steps the Senior Manager could have taken, considering what alternative actions might have been open to the Senior Manager at the time and the timelines within which he could have acted; and

Presumption of Responsibility/Duty of Responsibility

2. the overall circumstances and environment at the firm and more widely, in which the Senior Manager was operating at the time. For example, where a Senior Manager was subject to competing priorities, the PRA may consider whether the way in which he or she prioritised them was informed by an appropriate risk assessment.

Examples of steps that might be considered to be reasonable actions could include:

1. pre-emptive actions to prevent a breach occurring, including any initial reviews of the business or business area on taking up a Senior Manager Function;
2. awareness of relevant requirements and standards of the regulatory system;
3. raising issues, reviewing issues and following them up with relevant staff, committees and boards; and
4. awareness of relevant external developments, including key risks.

FCA Draft Guidance

The FCA will have regard to:

1. whether the Senior Manager reached a reasonable conclusion on which to act; and
2. the knowledge the Senior Manager had, or should have had, of regulatory concerns, if any, relating to their roles and responsibilities.

Key Themes

1. Take reasonable steps to implement appropriate systems and controls to comply with regulatory requirements.
2. Monitor compliance with relevant requirements.
3. Inform yourself adequately about the reasons for significant breaches (suspected or actual) taking into account the systems and procedures in place.
4. Investigate whether systems or procedures may have failed and extrapolate across other relevant areas of the business lessons learned.

Key Themes

5. Obtain expert opinions on the adequacy of systems and controls where appropriate.

6. Ensure procedures and systems and controls are reviewed and improved following the identification of significant breaches (suspected or actual).

7. Learn lessons from regulator guidance and enforcement actions.

Senior Managers must take reasonable steps to ensure the firm's compliance with regulatory requirements. The nature and extent of the systems of control that are required will depend upon the relevant regulatory requirements and the nature, scale and complexity of the business.

Senior Managers will be expected to investigate whether systems or procedures may have failed and extrapolate their findings across to other relevant areas of the business. Importantly, Senior Managers will be expected to learn lessons from regulator guidance (formal and informal); enforcement actions; thematic reviews; mystery shops; complaints; FOS decisions; supervisory visits and internal investigations. Senior Managers will be expected to apply to their businesses the messages conveyed and consider the wider implications at all times.

10.7.4.1   Enforcement cases

Recent enforcement cases have highlighted the need for Senior Managers to keep up to date with regulator expectations, conduct reviews of their areas of the business as risks change and consider the wider implications of their findings from those reviews.

10.7.4.2   Extrapolation of lessons learned

The FOREX cases in particular highlight that firms that do not learn from the publicised failures of others, and their own internal enquiries, will be penalised more harshly by the regulator. Following the FCA's well-publicised action in relation to LIBOR, the banks had engaged in remediation programmes across their businesses and had taken steps to promote changes to culture and values. However, the FCA found that, despite these improvements, the steps taken in the banks' G10 spot FX businesses had not adequately addressed the underlying root causes of the failings. Tracey McDermott, then the FCA's director of enforcement and financial crime, stated that: "[f]irms could have been in no doubt, especially after Libor, that failing to take steps to tackle the consequences of a free for all culture on their trading floors was unacceptable ... [w]here problems are identified we expect firms to deal with those quickly, decisively and effectively and to make sure they apply the lessons across their business. If they fail to do so they will continue to face significant regulatory and reputational costs." As a consequence of their failure to respond adequately to the misconduct identified in relation to LIBOR, each bank's fine was increased by £225 million (save for Barclays, where its fine was increased by £125 million).

In Barclays' Forex Final Notice, in addition to LIBOR, the FCA also referred to the Final Notice it issued against Barclays in May 2014 in respect of the gold fix. The subject matter of the Notice concerned an attempt by a Barclays' gold trader on June 28, 2012 to manipulate the gold fix on that day in order to benefit the bank's position in an option product referencing the fix. The Final Notice identified, among other things, significant failings around Barclays' systems and controls in relation to its participation in the gold fix in 2012.

The FCA noted that after the FCA had published its Final Notice on the gold fix in May 2014, Barclays undertook a significant amount of work to review its systems and controls in relation to the gold fix and other reference rates in precious metals. This resulted in the implementation of policies and procedures related specifically to the gold fix, and a subsequent update to its systems to specifically record the gold fix trades.

The FCA found that despite being on notice of the gold fix issue since 2012, Barclays did not make similar improvements to its FX options business until the introduction of guidance in early March 2013, adherence to which could not be monitored by Barclays due to a lack of controls.

10.7.5 Delegation

Senior Manager Conduct Rule 3

You must take reasonable steps to ensure that any delegation of your responsibilities is to an appropriate person and that you oversee the discharge of the delegated responsibility effectively.

Presumption of Responsibility/Duty of Responsibility

PRA Supervisory Statement

The PRA will consider whether the Senior Manager delegated any functions, taking into account that any such delegation should be appropriately arranged, managed and monitored.

Examples of steps that might be considered to be reasonable actions could include structuring and control of day-to-day operations, including ensuring any delegations are managed and reviewed appropriately. This includes in relation to any 'matrix-management' arrangements.

FCA Draft Guidance

The FCA will have regard to whether the Senior Manager took reasonable steps to ensure that any delegation of their responsibilities, where this was itself reasonable, was to an appropriate person, with the necessary capacity, competence, knowledge, seniority or skill, and whether they took reasonable steps to oversee the discharge of the delegated responsibility effectively.

Key Themes

1. Delegation should be appropriate.
2. Consider the competence, knowledge and seniority of delegates and their past performance and record.

> **Key Themes**
>
> 3. While the resolution of an issue, or authority for dealing with a part of the business can be delegated, it is not possible to delegate responsibility.
> 4. Supervise and appropriately monitor delegates.
> 5. Maintain a satisfactory understanding of any delegated issues.
> 6. Take personal action where progress is unreasonably slow or where unsatisfactory explanations are provided.
> 7. Require adequate reports once the resolution of an issue has been delegated.
> 8. Test the veracity of explanations provided by delegates.

The extent to which Senior Managers personally manage the business for which they are responsible on a day-to-day basis will depend, among other things, on the nature, scale and complexity of the business and the specific role undertaken by the Senior Manager. The larger and more complex the business, the greater the need for clear and effective delegation. While Senior Managers may delegate the management of an issue, or authority for dealing with a part of the business, to individuals who report to them, they must have reasonable grounds for believing that the delegate has the competence, resources, knowledge, seniority and skill to deal with it. The FCA has said that it will not hold somebody to account simply because there is a failure on their watch, provided any delegation was appropriate.

Although the performance of specific parts of a responsibility can be delegated, Senior Managers retain overall accountability and cannot delegate their personal responsibility. Senior Managers should therefore ensure they:

(a) receive reports on matters that are delegated;
(b) monitor the delegate; and
(c) interrogate and challenge information provided by the delegate.

In particular, where issues raise significant concerns, Senior Managers should take reasonable steps to ensure that systems are in place which result in issues being escalated and addressed in a timely manner, and at the appropriate level. Where necessary, clear and decisive personal action should be taken by the Senior Manager to resolve any issues. This may include: suspending the individual or relieving them of all or part of their responsibilities; increasing the resource allocated to the issue; reassigning the resolution internally; or obtaining external advice or assistance. If Senior Managers have any doubts regarding how to address an issue, they should raise these concerns with the FCA

10.7.5.1 *Enforcement cases*

FCA enforcement cases highlight the importance of Senior Managers taking steps to ensure that the individual to whom the Senior Manager delegates responsibility has the requisite skills, experience and qualifications.

10.7.5.2 *Delegation to an appropriate person*

In the case of Kraft (former compliance officer at Martins), the FCA found that Kraft had delegated his compliance responsibilities to junior colleagues who lacked compliance experience. He failed to give these individuals adequate training to ensure that they had the necessary competence, knowledge or skill to deal with these responsibilities. Specifically, Kraft delegated the creation of Martins' compliance manual to a junior colleague with no regulatory qualifications or experience. The junior prepared the compliance manual using a bank's compliance manual as a template and no advice was sought from any compliance consultant or external lawyer. The compliance manual failed to mention key industry guidance and did not address key issues for brokers such as inducements.

10.7.5.3   *Effective oversight of the delegate*

In the Deutsche IBOR case, the FCA identified instances where Deutsche provided inaccurate or misleading information, including in relation to a number of failures arising during the course of its investigation, such as the provision of a formal attestation which was known to be untrue by the person who drafted it at the time it was sent to the FCA. In light of the widespread concerns regarding LIBOR, the FSA wrote to Deutsche, and a number of other banks, requesting an attestation as to the adequacy of the systems and controls in place for its LIBOR submissions. A senior manager had delegated responsibility for a review of Deutsche's LIBOR systems and controls, and the preparation of the attestation, to the compliance officer and, in turn, a junior member of staff. Following a review, the compliance officer identified that there were no specific systems and controls to ensure the integrity of Deutsche's LIBOR submissions. Notwithstanding these findings, the compliance officer prepared an attestation stating, "DB currently has adequate systems and controls in place for the determination and submission of DB's LIBOR fixings". The senior manager subsequently approved the attestation but did not independently verify the accuracy of the information provided, even though the attestation expressly relied on the senior manager's personal approval of the systems and controls.

While the FCA and PRA will expect Senior Managers to challenge and interrogate information received from delegates, the case of Pottage demonstrates that in some circumstances it may be reasonable for Senior Managers to rely on appropriately appointed delegates. In Pottage, the Tribunal found that while the chief executive officer's role is one of oversight, a chief executive officer may rely on appropriately appointed delegates to implement compliant systems and controls. On taking up his role, Pottage met with various members of senior management within risk, legal, compliance and internal audit, most of whom were Approved Persons and Significant Influence Function holders themselves. The Tribunal found that if senior individuals, who are each specialists in their areas, do not have material concerns about compliance monitoring and operational risk management, then a chief executive officer in Pottage's position will more likely have no, or insufficient, information on which to base his own challenge or with which to make his own corroborative tests.

In December 2013, Christopher Willford (group finance director at Bradford & Bingley Plc (Bradford & Bingley)) received a £30,000 fine in relation to his failure to have proper regard to available financial information and its relevance to a rights issue. The FCA also found that Willford had failed appropriately to advise the board of Bradford & Bingley and had failed to provide the board with appropriate documents and information. In Willford, when deciding the level of sanction to impose, the FCA took into account, as a mitigating factor, the breadth of Willford's role as the group finance director and his consequent reliance on the experienced group financial controller. Willford's responsibilities went beyond purely a financial role and included legal, group risk and compliance. While Willford accepted that he was ultimately responsible for the financial information produced by the finance team and reporting to the board, including in relation to any material changes, responsibility for financial reporting to Willford himself was held by the group financial controller. The FCA accepted that Willford regarded the group financial controller as "wholly trustworthy and reliable and as such Mr Willford felt he could rely on his recommendations to him without further detailed enquiry".

10.7.6 *Management information*

Individual Conduct Rule 2
You must act with due skill, care and diligence.

Presumption of Responsibility/Duty of Responsibility

PRA Supervisory Statement

Examples of steps that might be considered to be reasonable actions could include obtaining appropriate internal management information and critically interrogating and monitoring that information.

FCA Draft Guidance

The FCA will have regard to:

whether the Senior Manager exercised reasonable care when considering the information available to them

---

Key Themes

1. Ensure management information is relevant and focused.
2. Critically analyse and challenge management information to identify potential risks.
3. Where issues are identified, act appropriately and promptly to address them.
4. Evidence actions taken to resolve issues.

In summary, good management information should enable management to make good decisions and enable firms to comply with their regulatory obligations. The FCA has made it clear that management information should be both qualitative and quantitative. It is not just about numbers; commentary and opinions can also help provide a comprehensive and balanced view.

Management information should be:

(a) Relevant to the business: Firms need processes and controls to make sure they obtain the right management information. Firms should consider adopting a risk-based approach, so that an area of the business is monitored more closely where it involves higher levels of risk.
(b) Accurate: To make the right decisions, the information needs to be accurate.

(c) Timely: The information is unlikely to be effective if it does not get to the right people at the right time.

(d) Seen: An appropriate level of management should receive, understand and review the information to identify issues and trends in any given area. Firms should also consider bringing together all their management information to measure performance and identify risks on an aggregated basis.

(e) Challenged: Such challenge should involve not only considering the reasonableness of the results, but also considering the substance and the quality of the management information itself.

(f) Analysed and monitored: So that the right messages and conclusions are drawn from the information. In general, firms should aim to avoid using the absence of poor results as a sign that the firm is achieving its objectives. Further, there are situations where the information may not give management any indication of the root cause of the results they are seeing. In those situations, the FCA expects management to perform a more detailed analysis.

(g) Acted upon: Findings, trends and issues should be acted upon appropriately and promptly by the relevant area of the firm. Different areas of the firm may need to work together to resolve identified issues. Firms will also need to be able to demonstrate the effectiveness of their actions.

(h) Consistent: On a period-to-period basis to allow managers to spot trends and make sound decisions.

(i) Recorded: Not only should the management information be recorded, but also the circulation of, and action taken following, that management information.

10.7.6.1 *Enforcement cases*

Recent enforcement cases serve to highlight the need for management information to be sufficiently detailed and, where appropriate, aggregated. Firms have also been criticised for failing adequately to challenge and analyse the management information provided.

10.7.6.2   Detail and focus

In the Lloyds Incentive Schemes case, the FCA noted that the firms produced monthly reports from their risk gateways to enable management to oversee, at a high level, the sales performance of advisers and their risk-ratings. However, the FCA considered that there were significant deficiencies in the selection of sales for verification and the risk gateways themselves. As a result, the FCA found that the management information produced by the firms may have presented advisers who were responsible for a number of unsuitable or potentially unsuitable sales and/or complaints as rated green or amber, rather than red.

In the Yorkshire Building Society Mortgages case, the FCA found that weaknesses in Yorkshire Building Society's quality assurance monitoring and the provision of management information meant that unfair customer outcomes were not properly identified. Quality assurance was conducted by team managers, but no formal training was provided to the managers as to how they should judge the call handlers' assessment of either the customers' specific circumstances or advice on the available options. The FCA noted that expressions of dissatisfaction were made during the course of arrears-handling telephone calls, yet often call handlers did not identify or acknowledge that a complaint had been made. Consequently, such complaints were neither recorded nor investigated. On other occasions, the FCA considered that although call handlers acknowledged the customers' dissatisfaction, they nonetheless failed to log or record it as a complaint and consequently it was not investigated. The FCA found that this meant that Yorkshire Building Society management was deprived of information which may have revealed underlying problems in the handling process. The FCA noted that the analysis of the information collated as a result of the quality assurance process was directed towards identifying the performance of each call handler, rather than identifying common issues or problems which may have led to unfair customer outcomes. This meant that no common issues were reported to senior management.

The FCA concluded that because no end-to-end assessment of arrears cases was carried out, little information was available to enable management effectively to assess the fairness of outcomes over time and to take action to remedy the problems. While Yorkshire Building Society collated and reported data on the numbers of customers entering various payment solutions, it did not report the numbers remaining within each solution and did not carry out customer-level monitoring to assess the length of time customers remained within a particular solution. Consequently, the ability of management to identify delays in the system and trends in the use or success of various payment solutions was limited.

10.7.6.3   Aggregation

In March 2014, Santander UK Plc ("Santander") was fined approximately £12.4 million by the FCA, after the regulator found that during the period April 2004 to December 2012, there had been a significant risk of Santander giving unsuitable investment advice to its customers. When considering management information, the FCA recognised that Santander had obtained management information from a number of sources. However, it noted that Santander had not aggregated that information. For example, the FCA found that Santander did not aggregate the results of its mystery shopping exercises and, in doing so, had not provided senior management with a holistic view of the issues identified. Had the results been aggregated, management would have found that, among other matters, over 60 per cent of advisers who were subject to the mystery shopping exercises had failed the assessment.

10.7.6.4   Trends and root cause analysis

The Lloyds Incentive Schemes case looked at the importance of obtaining trend-based management information. The FCA noted that Lloyds/BoS did not produce management information that was sufficient to identify spikes or trends in advisers' sales, which might have indicated areas that warranted more appropriately risk-based monitoring and verification. The FCA has also highlighted similar issues in Final Notices for other firms that did not include commentary on trends and root causes in their management information.

10.7.6.5   *Challenge*

In August 2014, the FCA fined Stonebridge International Insurance Ltd ("Stonebridge") over £8 million in relation to sales of accident insurance products that were underwritten by Stonebridge and sold to customers by various outsourcing companies. The FCA found that Stonebridge had poor systems and controls, and inadequate oversight of its outsourcing companies. In particular, the FCA found that Stonebridge's audit and risk committee should not have accepted verbal assurances that a lack of compliance reviews or outcome testing as to sales made through outsourcing companies was being addressed. The FCA considered that the committee should have called for specific management information to establish whether any customer detriment was arising.

In addition, the FCA commented that a committee tasked with assisting Stonebridge's audit and risk committee had failed to address or challenge the accuracy of Stonebridge's management information dashboard or deficiencies in the underlying metrics used to produce it. The FCA noted that the dashboard regularly produced a RAG rating that was obviously incorrect and the result was simply overridden to reflect the correct position. However, the underlying deficiencies in the metrics used in the dashboard were not addressed within a reasonable time.

10.7.6.6   *Analysis*

In Willford, the FCA found that Willford (group finance director at Bradford & Bingley) had failed to appreciate that the draft group results and a mortgage impairment paper, when taken together, indicated a "possible material change in the financial outlook of [Bradford & Bingley]". The FCA also noted that Willford had failed "to take a sufficiently pro-active approach in relation to the emerging information throughout the relevant period".

10.7.7   *Timely and appropriate action*

Senior Manager Conduct Rule 2

You must take reasonable steps to ensure that the business of the firm for which you are responsible complies with the relevant requirements and standards of the regulatory system.

Presumption of Responsibility/"Duty of Responsibility"

PRA Supervisory Statement

The PRA will consider what steps the Senior Manager could have taken, what alternative actions might have been open to the Senior Manager at the time and the timeliness within which he or she could have acted.

Examples of steps that might be considered to be reasonable actions could include where a breach is continuing, any response taken to that breach.

FCA Draft Guidance

The FCA will have regard to whether the Senior Manager, where they were aware of, or should have been aware of actual, or suspected issues, where these involved possible breaches by their firm of relevant requirements relating to their role and responsibilities, took reasonable steps to ensure that they were dealt with in a timely and appropriate manner.

Key Themes

1. Ensure that any actual or suspected problems/regulatory breaches are dealt with in a timely and appropriate manner and are adequately investigated.
2. Inform yourself adequately about the reasons for significant breaches (suspected or actual) taking into account the systems and procedures in place.
3. Implement recommendations for improvements to systems and procedures in a timely manner.

Where a Senior Manager becomes aware of actual or suspected problems that involve possible breaches of relevant require-ments and standards falling within their area of responsibility, that Senior Manager should take reasonable steps to ensure those problems are dealt with in a timely and appropriate manner.

By way of example, such steps may include conducting an adequate investigation to find out whether any systems or procedures may have failed and why and/or obtaining expert opinion on the adequacy and efficacy of existing systems and procedures.

Where independent reviews of systems and procedures are undertaken which result in recommendations for improvement, the Senior Manager responsible for that business area should ensure that, unless there are good reasons not to, any reasonable recommendations are implemented in a timely manner. In circumstances where recommendations are not followed, Senior Managers should be able to evidence why not.

10.7.7.1 *Enforcement cases*

At the point at which a regulator has become involved and enforcement action is in prospect, firms and individuals regularly take clear and decisive action to address concerns raised, for example, by withdrawing sales forces, ceasing to carry out a particular activity and/or offering to carry out extensive past business reviews and customer contact exercises. However, as can be seen from recent Final Notices, by the time these actions are taken it is often too late to avoid the onset of enforcement. The key is to take action before issues become so serious that regulator involvement/enforcement becomes warranted.

10.7.7.2 *Acting on recommendations*

In addition to Kraft (former compliance officer of Martins), David Caplin (former chief executive officer of Martins), was fined by the FCA in January 2015 in relation to failings that contributed to Martins' misconduct in respect of LIBOR. The FCA found that both Kraft and Caplin had failed to act on recommendations during the relevant period.

In relation to Caplin, the FCA noted that in 2005, Martins had instructed external compliance consultants to review the compliance arrangements at Martins in order to assess gaps in its compliance systems and controls. The review found a number of deficiencies and concluded that: "Management should be setting out to put in place a risk review and the processes necessary to demonstrate compliance with the SYSC rules as a matter of urgency." The FCA found that Caplin, as chief executive officer of Martins, had failed to act on the recommendation or apportion responsibilities, even though the 2005 Review had expressly stated that it was his responsibility to ensure this was completed. The FCA found that this pattern continued when a later 2006 review was undertaken by the same compliance consultants and Caplin failed to ensure that the compliance officer addressed the serious deficiencies identified.

In respect of Kraft, the FCA found that despite the findings of two separate compliance reviews which revealed serious systems and controls deficiencies and subsequent assurances provided by Kraft in response to these criticisms, Kraft introduced no significant improvements to Martins' systems and controls in the relevant period.

10.7.7.3   Acting when issues are raised

As discussed above, in June 2014, Credit Suisse and Yorkshire Building Society were fined by the FCA because the FCA found that brochures relating to Credit Suisse's Cliquet Product gave undue prominence to the product's maximum return and did not adequately explain the product's early exit fees.

The issues concerning the prominence of maximum returns, the likelihood of achieving the maximum returns and the early exit fees had been brought to both entities' attentions by the FSA and the publication, Which? (in September 2010), and (in the case of Credit Suisse) distributors of the product.

Following the comments of Which?, Credit Suisse had conducted a customer experience survey which found that around

18 per cent of customers expected to achieve the maximum return compared to about 8 per cent who expected to receive the minimum return. Credit Suisse knew from its own separate analysis that there was close to a 0 per cent probability of achieving the maximum return and a 40–50 per cent chance of receiving the minimum return.

Various distributors of the Cliquet Product also conducted customer surveys during the relevant period, including Yorkshire Building Society. Those surveys similarly found that a high proportion of customers expected to attain the maximum return. The FCA considered that the results of these customer experience surveys should have prompted the firms to "challenge whether the content of the financial promotions satisfied the clear, fair and not misleading criteria and whether the [financial promotions] contained a balanced presentation of the potential returns". However, the FCA found that Credit Suisse and Yorkshire Building Society did not make any material amendments to the financial promotions following the customer survey results.

10.7.7.4   Action must be timely

Even where recommendations are followed, it is important to ensure that actions are progressed to closure within a reasonable time frame. As discussed above, in Stonebridge, the FCA found that Stonebridge had poor systems and controls, and inadequate oversight of its outsourcing companies that sold accident insurance products on its behalf. In particular, the FCA considered that Stonebridge's operating board failed to ensure that the systems and controls weaknesses affecting customers, which were raised at board level, were remedied on a timely basis and that requested actions were progressed to closure. In September 2011, the board called for a paper to confirm that all the actions requested by the regulator in a 2009 review had been completed, however, this was still outstanding in March 2012.

While Santander took steps in 2011 to: (i) conduct a gap analysis of its investment advice business in line with March

2011 FSA Final Guidance on Assessing Suitability; and (ii) remedy deficiencies identified by that gap analysis, the FCA noted that it was not until June 2012, over a year after Santander's gap analysis, that certain key steps to remedy the deficiencies were rolled out to advisers.

In the case of Wills (a former compliance officer at Bank of Beirut), the FCA found that Wills had failed to develop, implement and conduct the Bank of Beirut's compliance monitoring plan adequately over a year after the required deadline. The FCA also noted that throughout the relevant period, Wills had failed to inform the regulator about delays in the Bank of Beirut's implementation of the compliance monitoring plan and the lack of compliance monitoring.

In respect of the RBS Mortgages case, the FCA noted that issues were identified by the FSA's review of mortgage sales in September/October 2011, details of which were recorded in a letter to the bank, and a September 2012 group internal audit report. The FCA considered that the issues raised had not been addressed in a timely manner. It noted that it was only in September 2012, once the group internal audit report was circulated and nine months after the FSA's initial letter, that the firms began to properly coordinate and resource the steps necessary to effectively remedy the issues.

10.7.8 Conclusion

As noted above, there is a significant degree of overlap between the Conduct Rules and the Duty of Responsibility. Statements of Responsibility will concentrate minds on the scope of responsibility of particular individuals and so while the reverse burden of proof of the Presumption of Responsibility has now been dropped, in practice, Senior Managers will need to remain focused on whether they can demonstrate that they have taken reasonable steps and that they have properly discharged their duties.

Chapter 11

Senior Responsibility—the Future Regime for Managers in Insurance Companies

Laura Hodgson
Senior Knowledge Lawyer
Norton Rose Fulbright

11.1   Introduction

The introduction of Solvency II on 1 January 2016, alongside changes to the Senior Managers Regime for banks, building societies and credit institutions (following the review into individual accountability in banking by the Parliamentary Committee on Banking Standards [see Chapter 1]) will change the requirements applied to senior managers in both insurance and reinsurance undertakings in the UK.

The proposals effectively end the familiar system which operated under the Financial Services Authority and its successors under s.59 of FSMA. Although s.59 remains in place requiring individuals in controlled functions to be approved, the list of controlled functions and the obligations upon individuals in those functions will change under proposals put forward by both the Prudential Regulation Authority (PRA) and Financial Conduct Authority (FCA).

The decision by the PRA to amend the requirements applied to insurers along the lines of the Senior Managers Regime for banks was taken on the basis that operating two distinct regimes would be "complex and inefficient" (CP26/14). However, given the different business model upon which insurers operate, the regime for banks and that for insurers will not be identical. The different approach to be taken to insurers is also the consequence of distinct legislation at both a UK and European level which constrains the manner in which the PRA and FCA may regulate individuals in firms.

The majority of the proposed regime will only apply to "Solvency II Firms" i.e. insurance and reinsurance undertakings that fall within the Solvency II regime (broadly, undertakings with gross premium income over €5 million per annum). Insurance intermediaries and appointed representatives will be required to follow a similar regime when proposals being brought in as a result of the Bank of England and Financial Services Bill 2015–16 are enacted.

Importantly, Solvency II requirements and the revised senior insurance managers regime (SIMR) being introduced by the UK regulators co-exist but are essentially different. Section 59 of FSMA requires that individuals performing certain pre-determined controlled functions must be *pre-approved* for suitability for their role by the regulators. Solvency II, however, requires that as part of its risk-management, a firm must itself determine whether individuals in key functions are fit and proper. Apart from four functions specified by Solvency II, the firm must determine for itself which functions are "key" to its business. Notification to inform the regulator about individuals in those key functions is made *after* the individual has been vetted by the firm.

For non-Solvency II Firms (there are around 100 UK firms that will fall under the Directive's threshold), the PRA proposes a simplified regime that defines the roles of individuals who need to be approved by the PRA to a single small insurer senior management function (SIMF25).

The new regime applicable to Solvency II Firms must be effective by 1 January 2016 when the Solvency II Directive[1]

---

[1] Directive 2009/138/EC of the European Parliament and of the Council of 25 November 2009 on the taking up and pursuit of the business of Insurance and Reinsurance (Solvency II).

comes into force. The changes to controlled functions being introduced by both the PRA and FCA under FSMA will be applicable from 7 March 2016 to coincide with the measures being introduced for banks, building societies and credit institutions. Grandfathering of roles will be available within a limited period.

Both the PRA and FCA published consultation papers (some jointly) on the amendments to the supervision of senior insurance managers before publishing final proposals in August 2015. Consultation papers, policy statements and supervisory statements published are as follows:

PRA papers

- CP26/14 – Senior insurance managers regime: a new regulatory framework for individuals (November 2014).
- PS3/15 – Strengthening individual accountability in banking and insurance – responses to CP14/14 and CP26/14 (March 2015).
- CP12/15 – Senior Insurance Managers Regime: a streamlined approach for non-Solvency II Firms (March 2015).
- PS22/15 – Strengthening individual accountability in insurance: responses to CP26/14, CP7/15 and CP13/15 (August 2015).
- SS35/15 – Strengthening individual accountability in insurance (August 2015).

FCA papers

- CP14/25 – Changes to the Approved Persons Regime for Solvency II Firms (November 2014).
- CP15/15 – Changes to the Approved Persons Regime for insurers not subject to Solvency II (March 2015).
- PS15/21 – Changes to the Approved Persons Regime for Solvency II firms: Final rules (including feedback

on CP14/25, CP15/5 and CP15/16) and consequentials relating to CP22/15 on strengthening accountability in banking.

Joint PRA/FCA papers

- FCA CP15/5, PRA CP7/15 – Approach to non-executive directors in banking and Solvency II Firms & Application of the presumption of responsibility to senior managers in banking firms (February 2015).
- FCA CP15/16, PRA CP13/15 – FCA and PRA: Changes to the Approved Persons Regime for Solvency II Firms: forms, consequential changes and transitional arrangements & FCA only: governance proposals and feedback to CP14/25 (March 2015).

11.2 Implementing Solvency II governance requirements

Solvency II introduces a risk-based solvency regime applicable to insurance and reinsurance undertakings across the EU (and also applied to EEA states). Under Solvency II, existing European legislation is amended and re-cast in order to introduce a consistent, risk-based regime that better reflects modern solvency and reporting techniques. Importantly, Solvency II requires firms to capture all their risks in order to understand better how much capital they need to hold in order to meet their liabilities.

In order for firms to manage their risk exposure better, Solvency II introduces various governance requirements for firms. Firms must ensure that:

"all persons who effectively run the undertaking or have other key functions fulfil the following requirements:

(a) their professional qualifications, knowledge and experience are adequate to enable sound and prudent management (fit); and

(b) they are of good repute and integrity (proper). "
(Article 42(1) Solvency II Directive)

Solvency II therefore identifies two types of person that should meet the requirements to be both fit and proper: those who "effectively run the firm" and those who "have other key functions". Guidance written by the European Insurance and Occupational Pensions Authority (EIOPA)[2] clarifies that those effectively running the firm covers the board and senior management. Those who have other functions will include both: individuals who lead areas of the firm that are considered to be of suitable significance to the stability of the business or to the protection of policyholders (defined as "Key Function Holders" alongside those individuals who effectively run the firm); and also those individuals who "perform" a key function.

Solvency II identifies four specific, but non-exhaustive, key functions in insurance firms that must meet the fit and proper criteria. These are the:

- risk management function (art.44(4) of Solvency II);
- compliance function (art.46(2) of Solvency II);
- internal audit function (art.47(1) of Solvency II); and,
- actuarial function (art.48(1) of Solvency II).

As a minimum, these functions should be identified in the firm. Alongside those individuals that are identified as effectively running the firm, the identity of those in charge of the above functions must be notified *ex poste* to the national competent authority with supporting evidence that these individuals are both fit and proper (these persons will be included in the list of Key Function Holders). The requirement to be both fit and proper is ongoing and Solvency II requires that firms notify their national supervisors of any changes to the identity of Key Function Holders and also when a person is no longer considered to be fit and proper for their role (art.42(2) and (3) of Solvency II).

---

[2] EIOPA Guidelines on systems of governance (14 September 2015).

Both those notified to national supervisors as Key Function Holders and those who *perform* key functions must be fit and proper. The EIOPA Guidelines state that those "performing" a key function will cover all those people who perform tasks related to a key function; whereas a Key Function Holder is someone with responsibility for that key function.[3] The only requirement for those who perform a key function is to adhere to a limited number of conduct requirements (considered below).

Details of what is required by Solvency II is fleshed out in both the Commission Delegated Regulation 2015/35[4] (which implements much of the detail of Solvency II) and the EIOPA Guidelines on systems of governance.

Article 273(1) of Regulation 2015/35 requires firms:

> "establish, implement and maintain documented policies and adequate procedures to ensure that all persons who effectively run the undertaking or have other key functions are at all times fit and proper within the meaning of Article 42 of Directive 2009/138/EC".

The assessment of whether a person is fit will include an assessment of the person's professional and formal qualifications, knowledge and relevant experience within the insurance sector, other financial sectors or other businesses and shall take into account the respective duties allocated to that person and, where relevant, the insurance, financial, accounting, actuarial and management skills of the person (Regulation 2015/35 art.273(2)).

Regulation 2015/35 also considers how the board should be considered to meet the fit criteria. The firm should assess the board collectively to take into account the respective duties

---

[3] EIOPA Guidelines on systems of governance (14 September 2015) para.1.21.
[4] Commission Delegated Regulation (EU) 2015/35 supplementing Directive 2009/138/EC of the European Parliament and of the Council on the taking-up and pursuit of the business of Insurance and Reinsurance (Solvency II).

allocated to individual members to ensure appropriate diversity of qualifications, knowledge and relevant experience and to ensure that the firm is managed and overseen in a professional manner (art.273(3)). In particular, there should be a collective knowledge of insurance and financial markets, business strategy and business models, systems of governance, financial and actuarial analysis and an understanding of the regulatory framework and its requirements. It is not expected that each member of the board is suitably expert in all of these areas so long as the collective knowledge is present.[5]

Assessing whether an individual is proper will require that their criminal records are checked and a review is undertaken of any disciplinary matters in their employment history. The assessment of propriety will take into account a person's honesty and financial soundness based on evidence regarding their character, personal behaviour and business conduct including any criminal, financial and supervisory aspects relevant for the purposes of the assessment (Regulation 2015/35 art.273(4)).

The EIOPA Guidelines on systems of governance require that firms have their own policies and procedures to assess fitness and propriety[6]. This policy should set out a procedure for the identification of key functions for which a notification should be sent to the national supervisor, a procedure to ensure that those in key functions are fit and proper, a description of situations that give rise to a reassessment of the requirements and a description of the procedure for assessing the skills, knowledge and expertise and personal integrity of personnel not subject to Solvency II requirements. In short, EIOPA expects national competent authorities to ensure that firms establish rigorous internal policies so that all those in key functions within firms are subject to extensive suitability and competence requirements.

---

[5] Guideline 11 of the EIOPA Guidelines on systems of governance (14 September 2015).
[6] Guideline 13 of the EIOPA Guidelines on systems of governance (14 September 2015).

Solvency II requires firms to identify individuals who "effectively run the undertaking". The EIOPA Guidelines of systems of governance specify that this phrase will cover

> "members of the administrative, management or supervisory body taking into account national law, as well as members of the senior management. The latter includes persons employed by the undertaking who are responsible for high level decision making and for implementing the strategies devised and the policies approved by the administrative, management or supervisory body".[7]

PRA policy statement 3/15[8] recommends that firms might consider whether certain specific roles would fall within the criteria of being of specific importance to the sound and prudent management of the firm. Given their mention in the policy statement, in practice where firms have people in these roles, the PRA is likely to expect those individuals to be considered to fall within the group of people who "effectively run the undertaking". Those roles are:

- the investment function (accordingly, investment managers will be Key Function Holders[9]);
- the claims management function (especially in general or health insurance firms);
- the IT function; and
- the reinsurance function (where this role is different to other key functions such as risk management).

In addition, firms should consider whether there are any other key decision-makers apart from those specifically identified by Solvency II or the PRA who might need to be vetted as Key Function Holders. When assessing whether an aspect of the business is a key function, PRA SS35/15 states that firms will be expected to take into consideration whether:

---

[7]   EIOPA Guidelines on systems of governance (14 September 2015) para.1.21.
[8]   PS3/15:Strengthening individual accountability in banking and insurance—responses to CP14/14 and CP26/14 (March 2015).
[9]   SS35/15: Strengthening individual accountability in insurance (August 2015) para.2.27.

- the function is essential for the proper functioning of the firm or group considering its risk profile and business;
- the function assumes material or complex financial market risks as part of its activities, or assumes material credit risks through the activity of providing loans;
- the function needs a competence that is difficult to replace; or
- any failure in the operation or effectiveness of the function may seriously threaten the interests of the insurance firm or group or its policyholders.[10]

Where a key function is outsourced, firms must apply a fit and proper assessment to any person employed by the outsourced service provider. The firm must also designate an internal person who meets fit and proper requirements and has knowledge of the outsourced service to have overall responsibility for the relevant outsourcing.

11.3   The PRA Senior Insurance Managers Regime

The scope of the SIMR will extend to those individuals within a firm that require pre-approval to carry on a controlled function as defined by s.59 FSMA (as amended by the Financial Services (Banking Reform) Act 2013 in order to introduce the concept of "senior management functions") together with all those who are Key Function Holders under Solvency II. In CP26/14,[11] the PRA proposed replacing the current list of Approved Persons in SUP10B of the PRA Handbook with a more limited number of Senior Insurance Management Functions ("SIMFs") to be included in the new PRA Rulebook. The PRA proposed to focus only on those roles that are most relevant to its statutory objectives: to promote the safety and soundness of the firms it regulates and to contribute to securing an appropriate degree of protection for those who are or may become policyholders. Those individuals identified as SIMFs and approved for their

---

[10] SS35/15: Strengthening individual accountability in insurance (August 2015) para.2.24.
[11] CP26/14: Senior insurance managers regime: a new regulatory framework for individuals (November 2014).

roles will be held accountable for the ongoing safety and soundness of their firm and the appropriate protection of policyholders. The PRA expects firms to put forward individuals for approval even where they are located outside the UK.

The PRA will replace its existing Approved Persons regime with the SIMR in order to delineate responsibilities more clearly within firms and to ensure greater personal accountability in management. The PRA maintains that having a more focused list of people subject to regulatory pre-approval reinforces the critical role that such people play within firms. With a closer alignment between specific roles and responsibilities, the PRA hopes to make lines of accountability clearer and to be able to hold individuals to account more easily when needed. The requirements for each SIMF will be more closely tailored to the specific roles in insurance undertakings, enabling the regulator to assess whether the person to be appointed is suitable for that role. In this respect, the approach taken to insurance and reinsurance firms resembles that being introduced for bankers. However, the PRA regime for insurers does not introduce any criminal sanction for causing the failure of a firm (s.36 of the Financial Services (Banking Reform) Act 2013), nor does it apply extensive rules of conduct to nearly all staff in the firm. (For further information on these requirements for banks see Chapter 4).

The SIMR regime comprises:

- new s.59 FSMA controlled functions in the form of the SIMFs;
- the allocation of prescribed responsibilities to SIMFs in order to increase personal accountability;
- the requirement for Governance Maps and Scope of Responsibility documents;
- the requirement to identify Solvency II key functions and ensure that Key Function Holders are fit and proper; and
- a requirement that all SIMFs adhere to certain new Conduct Standards to be included in the PRA Rulebook (and Conduct Rules to be introduced by the FCA).

11.3.1 *Senior Insurance Management Functions (SIMFs)*

The list of PRA SIMFs for Solvency II Firms (contained in the PRA Rulebook: SII Firms, Insurance – Senior Insurance Management Functions, 3-10) is set out in Table 1:

Table 1

Function	Description
SIMF1 – Chief Executive	The Chief Executive function is the function of having responsibility under the immediate authority of the governing body, alone or jointly with others, for carrying out the management of the conduct of the whole of the business (or relevant activities) of the firm.
SIMF2 – Chief Finance	The Chief Finance function is the function of having responsibility for the management of the financial resources of a firm and reporting to the governing body of a firm in relation to its financial affairs.
SIMF4 – Chief Risk	The Chief Risk function is the function of having responsibility for overall management of the risk management system of the firm.
SIMF5 – Head of Internal Audit	The Head of Internal Audit function is the function of having responsibility for management of the internal audit function of the firm.

Function	Description
SIMF7 – Group Entity Senior Insurance Manager	The Group Entity Senior Insurance Manager function is the function of having a significant influence on the management or conduct of one or more aspects of the affairs of the firm in relation to its regulated activities (other than in the course of the performance of another SIMF) and which is performed by a person employed by, or an officer (other than a non-executive director) of: (1) a parent undertaking or holding company of a firm; or (2) another undertaking which is a member of the firm's group.
SIMF9 – Chairman (NED)	The Chairman function is the function of having responsibility for chairing, and overseeing the performance of the governing body of the firm.
SIMF10 – Chair of Audit Committee (NED)	Chair of the Audit Committee function is the function of having responsibility for chairing, and overseeing the performance of any committee responsible for the oversight of the internal audit system of the firm.
SIMF11 – Chair of Risk Committee (NED)	The Chair of the Risk Committee function is the function of having responsibility for chairing and overseeing the performance of any committee responsible for the oversight of the risk management system of the firm.
SIMF12 – Chair of Remuneration Committee (NED)	The Chair of the Remuneration Committee function is the function of having responsibility for chairing, and overseeing the performance of any committee responsible for the oversight of the design or implementation of the remuneration policy of the firm.

Function	Description
SIMF14 – Senior Independent Director (NED)	The Senior Independent Director function is the function of performing the role of a senior independent director, and having particular responsibility for leading the assessment of performance of the person performing the Chairman function.
SIMF19 – Third Country Branch Manager	The Third Country Branch Manager function is the function of having responsibility for the conduct of all activities of a third country branch undertaking that are subject to the UK regulatory system.
SIMF20 – Chief Actuary	The Chief Actuary function is the function of having responsibility for the actuarial function of the firm. The PRA has commented that it may be possible to have an external actuary in this function, subject to that individual having sufficient time and resources to carry out their responsibilities adequately. Conflicts of interest should also be appropriately managed to ensure that the person can carry out their duties in a sound, honest and objective manner (PS3/15).
SIMF21 – With-profits Actuary	The With-Profits Actuary function is the function of having responsibility for advising the governing body of a firm transacting with-profits insurance business on the exercise of discretion affecting part, or all, of that business.
SIMF22 – Chief Underwriting Officer (applicable to general insurance firms and Lloyd's managing agents)	The Chief Underwriting Officer function is the function of having responsibility for the underwriting decisions in respect of material insurance risks that: (1) in relation to firms that carry on general insurance business, are borne by the firm; or (2) in relation to managing agents, are borne by the members.

Function	Description
SIMF23 – Underwriting Risk Oversight (only applied to the Society of Lloyd's)	The Underwriting Risk Oversight function is the function of overseeing and influencing underwriting plans by managing agents in respect of risks borne by members.

The existing model of approval and consent set out in FSMA will operate to ensure that the FCA is content about any PRA approved SIMF from a conduct perspective.

11.3.2 Implementing Solvency II fit and proper requirements into PRA rules

Solvency II requires that both Key Function Holders and individuals performing key functions must meet the requirements to be both fit (i.e. possess the appropriate skills, qualifications and experience) and proper (be of good repute). (As mentioned above, those *performing* a key function will be staff working within the function rather than those in charge of that function.)

In PS3/15[12], the PRA responded to concerns that the determination of who should fall into the category of a Key Function Holder was not sufficiently clear. The PRA stated that Key Function Holder is not intended to be a closed category but should cover those functions whose operation, if not properly managed, could lead to significant losses being incurred or to a failure in the ongoing ability of the firm to meet its obligations towards policyholders. The firm itself must make a judgement as to which functions this will cover.

---

[12] PS3/15: Strengthening individual accountability in banking and insurance—responses to CP14/14 and CP26/14 (March 2015).

In CP7/15[13] the PRA proposed that in deciding whether a person is both fit and proper, the firm must be satisfied that the person:

- has the personal characteristics (including being of good repute and integrity);
- possesses the level of competence, knowledge and experience;
- has the qualifications; and
- has undergone or is undergoing all training,

required to enable that person to perform their function effectively and in accordance with any relevant regulatory requirements.

The firm should consider past business conduct and be satisfied that the person discharges their functions in accordance with regulatory conduct standards. The determination of whether a person is fit and proper will take into account criminal records and references from the applicant's previous employers (covering at least the past six years). Regulatory references must include details of any breaches of regulatory conduct requirements that have taken place within the past six years.

When considering whether an individual is fit and proper to be performing a key function, PRA PS3/15 suggests that firms may wish to consider internal recruitment requirements such as pre-employment questionnaires in order to elicit information about past conduct. Where information comes to light that might raise concerns about a candidate, the firm should make reasonable enquiries to ensure that the candidate is fit and proper for the role.

Unless Solvency II or a PRA rule requires a role to be performed independently (as is the case with the Internal Audit Function), roles may be combined. SS35/15 states that

---

[13] FCA CP15/5, PRA CP7/15: Approach to non-executive directors in banking and Solvency II Firms & Application of the presumption of responsibility to Senior Managers in banking firms (February 2015).

"the PRA expects SIMFs to be shared between individuals only where appropriate and justified". The PRA can decide not to approve duplication of roles where:

- there could be a significant conflict of interest from combining the functions that would be difficult to manage satisfactorily (such as Chairman and CEO); or
- the individual's qualifications or competencies render them fit only for one of the proposed roles.

In limited circumstances, firms may be able to have more than one individual performing a SIMF. However, the PRA will expect to see clear justification of how the relevant responsibilities are apportioned between the individuals along with details of each person's reporting line. In accordance with the principle of proportionality, the PRA expects that smaller firms may be able to combine responsibilities for different SIMFs with a single candidate. Whether such an arrangement is approved will depend upon the need for appropriate management of any conflicts of interest and accountability and the requirement that at least two individuals should run the firm.

The PRA will only review the fitness and propriety of SIMF NEDs in respect of the competence relevant to the remit of their committee or board role. This will not necessarily result in the PRA requiring such individuals to have greater knowledge or skills than other NEDs not taking up a role on the board that will require regulatory pre-approval (for example, NEDs not in one of the PRA or FCA controlled functions).

Smaller insurers will not be expected by the PRA to have the full range of board committees. However, where boards elect to include such committees, PRA approval must be granted for the relevant chairs.

11.3.3 Prescribed responsibilities

PS26/14 requires that persons performing either a PRA or FCA controlled function within the firm are allocated responsibilities that are additional to the day-to-day duties of their role.

These prescribed responsibilities are designed to enable sound management and ensure that aspects of effective governance are assigned to named individuals.

The prescribed responsibilities (to be set out in the PRA Rulebook: SII Firms, Insurance—Allocation of Responsibilities Rulebook, 3) are set out in Table 2:

Table 2

1.	ensuring that the firm has complied with the obligation to satisfy itself that persons performing a key function are fit and proper;
2.	leading the development of the firm's culture and standards;
3.	embedding the firm's culture and standards in its day-to-day management;
4.	production and integrity of the firm's financial information and regulatory reporting;
5.	allocation and maintenance of the firm's capital and liquidity;
6.	development and maintenance of the firm's business model;
7.	performance of the firm's Own Risk and Solvency Assessment (ORSA);
8.	induction, training and professional development for all the firm's Key Function Holders;
9.	maintenance of the independence, integrity and effectiveness of the whistleblowing procedures, and the protection of staff raising concerns; and
10.	oversight of the firm's remuneration policies and practices.

The PRA proposes that responsibilities (9) and (10) should be allocated to a NED within the SIMR (i.e. one of the SIMF NEDs).

The PRA may challenge the allocation of prescribed responsibilities where the responsibility is inconsistent with the overall nature and responsibilities of the SIMF held by an individual.

It is important to remember that the allocation of governance and management responsibilities to individuals will not alter the fiduciary responsibilities of the board which should at all times retain ultimate responsibility for the firm's affairs. The individual accountability imposed by the SIMR is additional to the collective accountability of the board under the Companies Act 2006. In PS22/15,[14] the PRA emphasised that having both PRA-approved and non-approved NEDs does not create a two-tier board with greater accountability amongst the NED SIMFs.

11.3.4 Governance Maps

Firms will be required to have and to maintain a document or a coherent collection of documents that can be used as a Governance Map. The Governance Map must set out the scope of individual responsibilities, show who effectively runs the firm and set out the key functions and Key Function Holders. The map also needs to record the allocation of significant management responsibilities and reporting lines for each of the senior persons within the firm. Where a firm is a member of a group the map should show how the firm's governance and management arrangements work within the group structure. The document should be updated at least quarterly and whenever there is a significant change to the governance structure or to the allocation of responsibilities. It should also show to whom prescribed responsibilities have been allocated within the business. Where prescribed responsibilities are shared, the map should provide details of how the responsibilities are to be effectively allocated to each person.

The PRA anticipates that supervisors will refer to firms' Governance Maps during the supervisory lifecycle. For example, during an initial assessment for PRA approval to perform a SIMF, the scope of responsibilities will be taken into consideration in view of the candidate's ability to perform the role. The PRA also expects to use the Governance Map in order to identify to whom they should address specific questions, and

---

[14] PS22/15: Strengthening individual accountability in insurance: responses to CP26/14, CP7/15 and CP13/15 (August 2015).

to understand how the allocation of responsibilities reflects changes to the firm's business model or external changes.

A record of individual responsibilities should be kept for at least ten years. Following a significant change, a revised version of the Governance Map should be sent to the PRA.

11.4 The FCA Approved Person Regime for Solvency II Firms

To complement the SIMR, the FCA will amend the current Approved Persons Regime to avoid unnecessary duplication of controlled functions. The revised FCA regime comprises:

- a revised list of FCA Approved Persons for Solvency II Firms; and
- Conduct Rules to replace the existing Statement of Principles for Approved Persons (APER).

The FCA will not make such sweeping changes as the PRA in its approach towards approving senior managers. However, all those individuals who perform a controlled function with a significant influence on how the firm is run must be approved in the designated FCA senior management functions. Following consultation, the FCA decided to continue the application of FCA governing functions to Solvency II Firms (CP14/25 had proposed that where someone in a senior management function had PRA approval, any FCA function would fall away). PS15/21[15] and PS22/15 confirmed that FCA governing functions will continue but that approval for the relevant function will be granted alongside PRA approval. The individual will need to provide information on the FCA function which they will be undertaking in their Statement of Responsibilities document, submitted alongside their application for regulatory pre-approval.

---

[15] PS15/21—changes to the Approved Persons Regime for Solvency II firms: Final Rules (including feedback on CP14/25, CP15/5 and CP15/16) and consequentials relating to CP22/15 on strengthening accountability in banking.

The FCA has determined that two NED positions should require pre-approval as governing functions, the Chair of the Nominations Committee (CF2a) and Chair of the With-Profits Committee (CF2b), where such committees exist.

The FCA senior management functions identified for Solvency II Firms are set out in Table 3:

Table 3

Function	Description
CF1: Director	Where relevant subsumed into PRA approval in Solvency II Firm (see SUP 10A.11.12R).
CF2a: Chair of the Nomination Committee	The chair of the nomination committee function is the function of acting in the capacity of chairman of that committee.
CF2b: Chair of the With-Profits Committee	The chair of the With-Profits committee function is the function of acting in the capacity of chairman of that committee.
CF10: Compliance	The function of having responsibility for the oversight of compliance as required by SYSC. (This function does not cover the meaning of compliance included within Solvency II which is primarily focused on compliance with prudential requirements.)
CF11: Money Laundering Reporting Officer	The function of acting in the capacity of a money laundering reporting officer in a firm.
CF28: Systems and controls	FCA approval for CF28 may be required for a third-country branch or Insurance Special Purpose Vehicle (ISPV) but only to the extent that the activities are not already covered by a PRA controlled function that applies to the firm or are not activities already carried on by a person who has been approved by the PRA. CF28 is expressly limited to that part of the function that relates to compliance with FCA requirements and standards.

Function	Description
CF29: Significant management	The function of acting as a senior manager with responsibility for a significant business unit.
CF30: Customer function	The function of providing advice on particular insurance investment products.
CF51: Actuarial conduct function holder in third country branch	The actuarial conduct function in Solvency II third country undertakings is that part of the function of acting in the capacity of an actuary appointed under the requirements for third country branches in the PRA Rulebook. This function should be allocated when there is no Chief Actuary (SIMF20) in a branch.

The FCA has taken the decision not to alter significantly its controlled functions for the purposes of Solvency II. However, the Fit and Proper Test for Approved Persons (FIT) will be amended in order to reflect the fact that firms will have undertaken their own consideration of the suitability of candidates for Solvency II functions.

11.5   New codes of conduct

Both the PRA and FCA will introduce new conduct requirements: the PRA will have "Conduct Standards", while the FCA will have "Conduct Rules". These will be based upon the existing Statements of Principle currently in APER 2.1A (see Table 4 below). Both the PRA and FCA conduct requirements can only be applied to those in s.59 FSMA controlled functions. The PRA Conduct Standards closely reflect the standards applied in banks, although notably with the introduction of a requirement to have regard to the interests of policyholders (and future policyholders) as required under Solvency II and the PRA's statutory objectives. The FCA Conduct Rules and PRA Conduct Standards are largely identical.

11.5.1 *PRA Conduct Standards*

The PRA Conduct Standards that will be applied to insurers will not be applied to nearly all staff members as will be the case within banks as there is no legislative ability to require this. However, there will be three generic standards (or "individual standards") relevant to any individual performing a key function (i.e. not limited to Key Function Holders). These three individual standards should appear in the firm's staff handbook and should be taken into account when setting an individual's personal objectives.[16] The remaining standards required of all the Key Function Holders should be included in individual's terms and conditions of employment. "Notified" NEDs (i.e. NEDs not requiring approval as either a PRA SIMF or FCA controlled function) need only comply with the generic standards and two additional standards.

The Conduct Standards will apply to all PRA SIMFs and also to those in the CF1, CF7, CF10, CF28 and CF51 function (i.e. those who have some responsibility for the prudential management of the firm).

The PRA will be unable directly to require that Notified NEDs and non-SIMF Key Function Holders comply with the Conduct Standards but the regulator will expect firms to take into account compliance with the Conduct Standards when reviewing the individuals as fit and proper.

11.5.2 *FCA Conduct Rules*

The FCA will introduce Conduct Rules for Approved Persons with the aim of introducing greater consistency in the rules applied across the banking and insurance sectors. The FCA Conduct Rules are based on the existing Statements of Principle in APER but have two additions: to pay due regard to the interests of customers and to ensure that any delegation of responsibilities is effectively overseen. As with the PRA Conduct Standards, the application of the Conduct Rules for

---

[16] PS22/15, 2.6.

insurers will be limited to those in controlled functions or Solvency II Key Function Holders.

Unlike the PRA Conduct Standards, the FCA has adopted a two-tiered approach to its Rules. The first tier (rules 1–5) are applicable to all those who perform a controlled function under FSMA (i.e. both PRA SIMFs and FCA Approved Persons). The second tier (SI1–SI4) apply only to PRA SIMFs and FCA Significant Influence Functions (SIFs). The second tier Conduct Rules, for example, will not be applied to those in the customer function (CF30).

In addition to the PRA and FCA conduct requirements, the PRA proposes that firms should require all individuals performing key functions to observe any additional conduct requirements applied by the business. This means that the PRA and FCA conduct requirements should form the core of wider standards, suited to the individual firm and its risks.

Table 4: The application of the PRA and FCA conduct requirements

PRA Conduct Standard	Applies to			Applies to	FCA Conduct Rule
Act with integrity.	PRA SIMF, FCA SIFs, Key Function Holders and those performing a key function.	3.1	Rule 1	Anyone performing a Controlled Function in a Solvency II Firm.	Act with integrity.
Act with due skill, care and diligence.	PRA SIMF, and FCA SIFs, Key Function Holders and those performing a key function.	3.2	Rule 2	Anyone performing a Controlled Function in a Solvency II Firm.	Act with due skill, care and diligence.
Be open and co-operative with the FCA, PRA and other regulators.	PRA SIMF, and FCA SIFs, Key Function Holders and those performing a key function.	3.3	Rule 3	Anyone performing a Controlled Function in a Solvency II Firm.	Be open and co-operative with the FCA, PRA and other regulators.

PRA Conduct Standard	Applies to			Applies to	FCA Conduct Rule
			Rule 4	Anyone performing a Controlled Function in a Solvency II Firm.	Pay due regard to customers and treat them fairly.
			Rule 5	Anyone performing a Controlled Function in a Solvency II Firm.	Observe proper standards of market conduct.
Take reasonable steps to ensure that the business of the firm for which you are responsible is controlled effectively.	PRA SIMF and FCA SIFs.	3.4	SI1	Anyone holding a Significant Influence Function (includes both FCA and PRA CFs) in a Solvency II Firm.	Take reasonable steps to ensure that the business of the firm for which you are responsible is controlled effectively.

PRA Conduct Standard	Applies to			Applies to	FCA Conduct Rule
Take reasonable steps to ensure that the business of the firm for which you are responsible complies with the relevant requirements and standards of the regulatory system.	PRA SIMF and FCA SIFs.	3.5	SI2	Anyone holding a Significant Influence Function (includes both FCA and PRA CFs) in a Solvency II Firm.	Take reasonable steps to ensure that the business of the firm for which you are responsible complies with the relevant requirements and standards of the regulatory system.
Take reasonable steps to ensure that any delegation of responsibilities is to an appropriate person and that the person oversees the discharge of the delegated responsibility effectively.	PRA SIMF and FCA SIFs.	3.6	SI3	Anyone holding a Significant Influence Function (includes both FCA and PRA CFs) in a Solvency II Firm.	Take reasonable steps to ensure that any delegation of responsibilities is to an appropriate person and that the person oversees the discharge of the delegated responsibility effectively.

PRA Conduct Standard	Applies to			Applies to	FCA Conduct Rule
Must disclose appropriately any information of which the FCA or PRA would reasonably expect to have notice.	PRA SIMF and FCA SIFs.	3.7	SI4	Anyone holding a Significant Influence Function (includes both FCA and PRA CFs) in a Solvency II Firm.	Must disclose appropriately any information of which the FCA or PRA would reasonably expect to have notice.
When exercising responsibilities, must pay due regard to the interests of current and potential future policyholders in ensuring the provision by the firm of an appropriate degree of protection for their insured benefits.	PRA SIMF and FCA SIFs.	3.8			

11.6 Areas of overlap between Solvency II and the SIMR

There will inevitably be overlaps between the Solvency II Key Function Holders and those in PRA SIMFs or FCA controlled functions. First of all, all PRA SIMFs will also be considered to be Key Function Holders. Accordingly, the Solvency II Actuarial Function is likely to be held by the Chief Actuary (SIMF20), the Risk Management Function by the Chief Risk Officer (SIMF4), etc. The key functions will not only overlap with PRA functions but also with FCA SIFs in some instances. For example, the Compliance Function will in some respects overlap with the FCA Compliance Officer function (CF10), although the compliance key function will be focused upon compliance with the Solvency II Directive. Where an individual will be undertaking a controlled function and is also a Key Function Holder, they must be subject to both regulatory pre-approval and firm assessment as fit and proper.

11.7 Third Country Branches

The principle of proportionality will apply to the application of the new SIMR regime to third country branches in the UK. Accordingly, branches will have far greater flexibility to combine different functions allocated to one individual. In PS26/14 the PRA put forward the proposal that only one individual in a UK branch of a third country firm (overseas firms not authorised in the EEA) will require pre-approval: the Third Country Branch Manager (SIMF19). This person should have responsibility for the conduct of all actions subject to the regulatory system applied to the branch. If the branch conducts with-profits business, however, the PRA will also require that someone fulfils the SIMF21 function. Where the branch has individuals appointed as Chief Finance Officer, Chief Risk Officer, Chief Actuary, Chief Underwriting Officer or Head of Internal Audit who provide dedicated support to branch operations, approval for these respective SIMFs must be sought from the PRA.

A limited number of the PRA prescribed responsibilities (namely (1),(4),(5),(6) and (7)—see Table 2, above) should be allocated to one or more of the branch SIMFs. Furthermore, the prescribed responsibilities need only take into account the activities effected by the branch with the exception of (4) which should take into account whether the branch has adequate worldwide financial resources for PRA purposes. The branch Governance Map should cover the operations effected by the branch.

The PRA has proposed that the following are key functions in third country branches for Solvency II purposes and individuals in these roles should accordingly be included in a notification:

- the Risk-management function;
- the Compliance function;
- the Internal audit function;
- the Actuarial function;
- the function of effectively running the operations of the branch;
- the function of being the authorised UK representative; and
- any other function which is of specific important to the sound and prudent management of the branch.

Third country branches must identify key functions relevant to branch operations but should include at least the four functions required by Solvency II (see above in 11.2). The PRA will require branch SIMFs to comply with Conduct Standards 1–3 (i.e. the individual standards) and the remaining standards only to the extent that they are relevant to the activities of the branch.

The FCA proposes that any current controlled function (whether or not one of the FCA SIFs) will remain a requirement for third country branches. For example, the Director (CF1) Compliance (CF10), CASS operational oversight (CF10a), Money Laundering Reporting Officer (CF11), Systems and

Controls (CF28), Significant Management (CF29) and Customer Function (CF30) might all fall within scope for FCA-approval.

If the branch does not have anyone approved as a Chief Actuary (SIMF20), it will need to ensure that someone is approved from a conduct perspective for the FCA Actuarial conduct function (CF51) holder in a third country branch role.

11.8 UK Insurance Special Purpose Vehicles (ISPVs)

Like third country branches, a more limited range of SIMFs will be required by the PRA for ISPVs. Accordingly, only the Chief Executive (SIMF1), Chief Finance (SIMF2) and Chief Actuary (SIMF20) function will require approval. Other roles in the ISPV (for example, risk and internal audit) will be considered a conduct function under the existing CF28 (systems and controls) function.

All the PRA prescribed responsibilities should be allocated amongst the SIMFs.

FCA controlled functions will apply to ISPVs as to other Solvency II Firms.

11.9 Non-executive Directors

The PRA and FCA published a joint approach to non-executive directors in both banking and Solvency II Firms in February 2015 (FCA CP1/5, PRA CP7/15). The roles of Chairman (SIMF9), Senior Independent Director (SIMF14) and Chairs of the Audit (SIMF10), Remuneration (SIMF12) and Risk Committees (SIMF11) will require pre-approval from the PRA as SIMFs (see Table 1 above). The FCA proposes that the chairs of the Nomination Committee (CF2a) and With-Profits Committee (CF2b) should require pre-approval as a SIF. Importantly, standard NEDs (i.e. those not in one of the PRA SIMFs or in either of the FCA approved NED roles) will not require pre-approval. Instead, these NEDs (known as "Notified" NEDs) should be considered to be Solvency II Key Function Holders and subject to *ex-poste* notification requirements only. As Key Function Holders, the firm will need to ensure that all Notified NEDs meet the requirements to be fit and proper.

Guidance on the expected responsibilities of NEDs for Solvency II Firms has been set out in the Appendix of PRA SS35/15.

All firms, with the exception of third country branches, will be required by the PRA to have someone in the role of Chairman (SIMF9). Other NED SIMFs will only be required where either UK or EU law or guidelines require the firm to establish certain board committees.

Section 59ZA(2) FSMA (introduced by the Financial Services (Banking Reform) Act 2013) defines "managing" to include participating in the taking of decisions about how one or more aspects of a firm's affairs should be carried on. The concept of a senior manager can therefore extend to NEDs who "manage" a significant aspect of the firm's affairs and might make decisions about the safety and soundness of the firm. Although there is no presumption of responsibility, NEDs performing a SIMF or SIF role can be held individually accountable where they have failed to meet the applicable conduct requirements or been knowingly concerned in a contravention of a regulatory requirement.

CP7/15 states that the PRA proposes to require that firms ensure that their assessment of NEDs is as rigorous as the assessment undertaken of any other Key Function Holder.

11.10 Group Entity Senior Insurance Manager

Individuals in a group who fall within the FSMA definition of being in a senior management function and who are also considered to be in a key function may need to be approved as

Group Entity Senior Insurance Manager (SIMF7). Accordingly, senior executives in a parent, holding or other group company that have a significant influence on the management or conduct of the affairs of the Solvency II Firm must seek PRA approval as a SIMF7. The firm should also ensure that those individuals are fit and proper as Key Function Holders. The PRA expects firms to put forward for approval individuals employed by a parent or group entity for SIMF7 where those individuals are involved in decisions affecting the firm's UK business. This is likely to include a CEO, group Chairman or the chair of a key group board committee where that committee has direct oversight of the affairs of the Solvency II Firm. The PRA also expects that the SIMF7 role should be allocated to senior insurance managers or executive directors with responsibility for the safety and soundness of the group or PRA Solvency II Firms within the group. PRA SS35/15[17] states that approval as a SIMF7 should not normally be required of individuals with primary responsibility for conduct matters or NEDs in another group company. The PRA will expect those approved as SIMF7 to have regard for the duties of NEDs in subsidiary boards and to acknowledge that the board should provide oversight of the subsidiary in accordance with the Companies Act 2006. The SIMF7 may therefore only direct business in the subsidiary to the extent that the board consents.[18]

11.11   How will the changes apply to an incoming EEA branch?

The PRA does not have any jurisdiction over an EEA incoming branch. The FCA has supervisory powers in only limited areas. Accordingly, it is expected that the FCA will require that the Money Laundering Function (CF11), the Significant Management Function (CF29) and the Customer Function (CF30) will be required to be approved in incoming EEA branches.

---

[17] PRA SS35/15: strengthening individual accountability in insurance (August 2015).
[18] PRA SS35/15 para.2.8.

11.12 Grandfathering provisions for the new regime?

The changes to supervising senior insurance managers will take place in two stages. The Solvency II requirements (i.e. the requirements imposed on Key Function Holders and on all those performing a key function) must take effect from 1 January 2016. The changes to the various controlled functions under s.59 of FSMA will take effect from 7 March 2016 (when the changes introduced by the Banking Reform Act come into effect).

From 7 March 2016 a new Form A will be in operation. Anyone who takes up a post as a Solvency II Key Function Holder but who is not already in, and is not applying to be in, either a PRA or FCA existing controlled function after 1 January 2016 must meet the fit and proper requirements and complete a new notification form (Form K). This form will be accompanied by a "Scope of Responsibilities" document. Importantly, anyone already in post in one of the Solvency II key functions must also submit this notification form alongside the Scope of Responsibilities.

In PS22/15, the PRA responded to concerns about the timeframe for completing the Scope of Responsibilities part of the application form and notification of those key function holders who do not need to be pre-approved. Acknowledging these concerns, the PRA allowed firms until 7 September 2016 to prepare and complete this information, although a summary version must be included in the Governance Maps available from 1 January 2016.

On 7 March 2016 those currently performing a PRA or FCA controlled function who will be taking up a substantially corresponding PRA SIMF or FCA SIF will be grandfathered into the new post (FCA CP15/16, PRA CP13/15)—provided that a notification is submitted by 8 February 2016. Otherwise, approvals will lapse on 7 March and new applications using the new Form A must be made.

Where a firm does not know whether an application for one of the new functions will be approved before the commencement of the new regime, the PRA and FCA propose that a combined application for the new regime and for grandfathering an existing position should be submitted in order to cover both eventualities.

Table 5: Grandfathering of equivalent functions (Reproduced from PS22/15)

Pre-implementation PRA or FCA controlled function	PRA Senior Insurance Management Function	FCA Function
UK Solvency II Firm		
Directors (CF1)	Chief Finance function (SIMF2) Chief Risk function (SIMF4) Head of Internal Audit function (SIMF5) Group Entity Senior Insurance Manager function (SIMF7) Chief Actuary function (SIMF20) Chief Underwriting Officer function (SIMF22) Underwriting Risk Oversight function (Lloyd's) (SIMF23)	FCA Director (CF1)

Pre-implementation PRA or FCA controlled function	PRA Senior Insurance Management Function	FCA Function
Non-executive director (CF2)	Group Entity Senior Insurance Manager function (SIMF7) Chairman (SIMF9) Chair of the Risk Committee (SIMF10) Chair of the Audit Committee (SIMF11) Chair of the Remuneration Committee (SIMF12)	Chair of the Nomination Committee (CF2a) Chair of the With-Profits Committee (CF2b)
Chief executive (CF3)	Chief Executive Function (SIMF1)	

Pre-implementation PRA or FCA controlled function	PRA Senior Insurance Management Function	FCA Function
Director of unincorporated association (CF5)	Chief Finance function (SIMF2) Chief Risk function (SIMF4) Head of Internal Audit function (SIMF5) Group Entity Senior Insurance Manager function (SIMF7) Chief Actuary function (SIMF20) Chief Underwriting Officer function (SIMF22) Chairman (SIMF9) Chair of the Risk Committee (SIMF10) Chair of the Audit Committee (SIMF11) Chair of the Remuneration Committee (SIMF12) Senior Independent Director (SIMF14)	FCA Director of unincorporated association function (CF5) Chair of the Nomination Committee (CF2a) Chair of the With-Profits Committee (CF2b)
FCA Apportionment and oversight (CF8)	To be dis-applied.	
FCA Compliance (CF10)		Compliance (CF10)

Pre-implementation PRA or FCA controlled function	PRA Senior Insurance Management Function	FCA Function
FCA Money Laundering Reporting (CF11)		FCA Money Laundering Reporting (CF11)
PRA Actuarial function holders (CF12)	Chief Actuary function (SIMF20)	
PRA With-Profits Actuary (CF12A)	With-Profits Actuary function (SIMF21)	
PRA Lloyd's Actuary (CF12B)	Chief Actuary function (SIMF20) Underwriting Risk Oversight function (Lloyd's) (SIMF23)	
PRA Systems and Controls (CF28)	Chief Finance function (SIMF2) Chief Risk function (SIMF4) Head of Internal Audit (SIMF5)	FCA Director (CF1)
FCA Significant Management (CF29)	Chief Underwriting Officer function (SIMF22) Group Entity Senior Insurance Manager function (SIMF7) Chief Actuary function (General Insurance firms) SIMF20 Underwriting Risk Oversight function (Lloyd's) SIMF23	
FCA Customer function (CF30)		Customer function (CF30)

Pre-implementation PRA or FCA controlled function	PRA Senior Insurance Management Function	FCA Function
UK ISPV		
Director (CF1)	Chief Finance function (SIMF2) Chief Actuary function (SIMF20) Group Entity Senior Insurance Manager function (SIMF7)	FCA Director (CF1)
Non-executive director (CF2)	Chairman (SIMF9)	Chair of the Nomination Committee (CF2a) Chair of the With-Profits Committee (CF2b)
Chief executive (CF3)	Chief Executive Function (SIMF1)	
FCA Apportionment and oversight (CF8)	To be dis-applied.	
FCA Compliance (CF10)		Compliance (CF10)
FCA Cass Operational Oversight (CF10a)		Cass Operational Oversight (CF10a)
FCA Money Laundering Reporting (CF11)		FCA Money Laundering Reporting (CF11)
PRA Actuarial function holder (CF12)	Chief Actuary function (SIMF20)	
PRA Systems and controls	Chief Finance function (SIMF2)	FCA Systems and Controls function (CF28)

Pre-implementation PRA or FCA controlled function	PRA Senior Insurance Management Function	FCA Function
PRA Significant Management (CF29)	Group Entity Senior Insurance Manager function (SIMF7) Chief Actuary function (SIMF20)	All CF29s not otherwise approved by the PRA
FCA Customer function (cf30)		Customer function (CF30)
Third country branch		
Director (CF1)	Head of Third Country Branch function (SIMF19) Chief Finance finction (SIMF2) Chief Risk function (SIMF4) Head of Internal Audit function (SIMF5) Chief Actuary function (SIMF20) Chief Underwriting Officer function (SIMF22) Group Entity Senior Insurance Manager function (SIMF7)	FCA Director function (CF1)

Pre-implementation PRA or FCA controlled function	PRA Senior Insurance Management Function	FCA Function
Non-Executive Director (CF2)	Chairman (SIMF9) Senior Independent Director (SIMF14) Chair of the Risk Committee (SIMF10) Chair of the Audit Committee (SIMF11) Chair of the Remuneration Committee (SIMF12) Group Entity Senior Insurance Manager function (SIMF7)	
Chief Executive (CF3)	Head of Third Country Branch function (SIMF19)	
FCA Apportionment and oversight (CF8)	To be dis-applied.	
FCA Compliance (CF10)		Compliance (CF10)
FCA Money Laundering Reporting (CF11)		Money Laundering Reporting Officer (CF11)
PRA With-Profits Actuary (CF12A)	With-Profits Actuary function (SIMF21)	

Pre-implementation PRA or FCA controlled function	PRA Senior Insurance Management Function	FCA Function
PRA Systems and Controls (CF28)	Chief Finance function (SIMF2) Chief Risk function (SIMF4) Head of Internal Audit function (SIMF5)	Systems and controls (CF28)
PRA Significant Management (CF29)	Chief Underwriting Officer (SIMF22) Group Entity Senior Insurance Manager function (SIMF7)	Significant Management (CF29)
FCA Customer function (CF30)		Customer function (CF30)

11.13 Senior management requirements for insurance firms not subject to Solvency II

In accordance with the principle of proportionality, insurance firms that fall outside the scope of Solvency II (non-Directive firms) will be subject to a more limited regime for the approval of senior managers. "Small" non-Directive firms will include firms that have assets relating to regulated activities of less than £25m. A "Large" non-Directive firm will include firms with assets of more than £25m over two consecutive annual accounts. The PRA proposed in CP12/15[19] that small non-Directive firms will require at least one person to be approved in the single small insurer senior management function

---

[19] CP12/15—Senior Insurance Managers Regime: a streamlined approach for non-Solvency II Firms (March 2015).

(SIMF25). The SIMF25 role would be applied to any individuals with responsibility for the conduct of the regulated activities of the firm and for chairing the board or management committee.

Small non-Directive firms should still comply with the requirements to ensure that individuals are fit and proper (even though this is a Solvency II obligation) and will be expected to consider whether roles are carried out in accordance with the various conduct requirements.

The following prescribed responsibilities should be allocated to one or more individuals acting as SIMF25 (in PRA Rulebook, Non-Solvency II Firms, Insurance—Allocation of Responsibilities Instrument, 3). Allocation, however, need not take place until 7 March 2017.

- Business plan and management information;
- Financial resources;
- Legal and regulatory obligations; and
- Oversight of proportionate systems and controls, and risk management.

The PRA has proposed that Large non-Directive firms would be expected to apply a regime closer to the full SIMR. Accordingly, these firms must obtain approval for those individuals in the Chief Executive (SIMF1), Chief Finance (SIMF2), Chief Risk (SIMF4), Head of Internal Audit (SIMF5), Chief Actuary (SIMF20), Chief Underwriting (SIMF22), (and Group Entity and with-profits,) where appropriate.

In CP15/15[20] the FCA proposed that all individuals in executive or governing functions not approved as SIMF25 should be FCA SIF holders (including CF1 Director and CF3 Chief Executive). Where non-Directive firms have people in the role of Chairman (CF7), Senior Independent Director (CF7B) and Chairs of the Audit (CF7E), Remuneration (CF7C), Risk

---

[20] CP15/15: Changes to the Approved Persons Regime for insurers not subject to Solvency II (March 2015).

(CF7D) and Nominations or With-Profits Committees (CF2a or CF2B), FCA approval as SIFs must be sought and granted.

Furthermore, CP15/15 proposes that all non-Directive firms retain a document setting out the responsibilities of each approved person in a SIF for at least 10 years (mirroring the requirement for Solvency II Firms to maintain Governance Maps).

In CP12/15 the PRA proposes that individuals in non-Directive firms already in a controlled function will be grandfathered into the new regime without requiring further assessment.

Chapter 12

Conduct Rules for Financial Services Firms Not in Scope

Jane Walshe
Barrister

Many firms will not be subject to the Senior Managers and Certified Persons regime until around 2018, which is the approximate date by which the UK government would like one regime to apply to individual behaviour in financial service firms. Until that time, staff in investment management firms and independent financial advisory firms, as well as appointed representatives among others, must abide by the existing rules. This Chapter provides an overview of these rules.

12.1 Approved Persons not within the SMR

The list of FCA approved persons subject to the rules in the Statements and Principle and Code of Practice for Approved Persons (APER) section of the FCA handbook is shown in the following table[1].

Part 1 (FCA controlled functions for FCA-authorised persons and appointed representatives)		
Type	CF	Description of FCA controlled function
FCA governing functions*	1	Director function
	2	Non-executive director function
	3	Chief executive function

---

[1] SUP10A.4.4

Part 1 (FCA controlled functions for FCA-authorised persons and appointed representatives)		
	4	Partner function
	5	Director of unincorporated association function
	6	Small friendly society function
FCA required functions*	8	Apportionment and oversight function
	10	Compliance oversight function
	10A	CASS operational oversight function
	11	Money laundering reporting function
	40	Benchmark submission function
	50	Benchmark administration function
Systems and controls function*	28	Systems and controls function
Significant management function*	29	Significant management function
Customer-dealing function	30	Customer function
*FCA significant-influence functions		

Part 2 (FCA controlled functions for PRA-authorised persons) (See Note 1)		
Type	CF	Description of FCA controlled function
FCA governing functions*	1	Director function (see Note 2)
	2a	Chair of the nomination committee function (See Notes 2 and 3)
	2b	Chair of the with-profits committee function (see Notes 2 and 3)

Part 2 (FCA controlled functions for PRA-authorised persons) (See Note 1)		
	3	Chief executive function (see Note 3A)
	5	Director of an unincorporated association function (see Notes 2 and 3B)
	6	Small friendly society function (see Note 3C)
	10	Compliance oversight function
	10A	CASS operational oversight function
	11	Money laundering reporting function
	40	Benchmark submission function
	50	Benchmark administration function
	51	Actuarial conduct function (third country) (see Note 4)
Systems and controls function*	28	Systems and control function (see Note 5)
Significant management function*	29	Significant management function
Customer-dealing function	30	Customer function
*FCA significant-influence functions		
Note 1: Part 2 of this table does not apply to appointed representatives of PRA-authorised persons, Part 1 applies instead. (See SUP 10A.4.2R.)		
Note 2: Solvency II firms (including large non-directive insurers) and small non-directive insurers.		
Note 3: Solvency II firms (including large non-directive insurers) only.		
Note 3A: small non-directive insurers only.		
Note 3B: Solvency II firms (including large non-directive insurers) and small non-directive insurers.		
Note 4: Third country insurance or reinsurance undertakings which are Solvency II firms only.		

Part 2 (FCA controlled functions for PRA-authorised persons) (See Note 1)
Note 5: Only Solvency II firms that are: (a) third-country insurance or reinsurance undertakings; or (b) ISPVs.

The FCA functions are split into two categories; those that are significant influence functions (marked by a star on the table), and the customer function (CF30). A significant influence function is defined (in relation to the carrying on of a regulated activity by a firm) as a function that is likely to enable the person responsible for its performance to exercise a significant influence on the conduct of the firm's affairs, so far as relating to the activity.

12.1.1   Governing Functions

Various duties and responsibilities fall on the shoulders of those that govern a firm. At the purest level, these are found in the FCA Handbook, and in primary legislation and related material dealing with director's duties, and the Code of Corporate Governance that applies to Directors of UK listed firms. Beyond the letter of the law and the rules, however, lies a large body of material including speeches, policy documents and statements from UK and international standard setting bodies such as the Financial Stability Board, focused on governance that also needs to be given due consideration. The Chapter on Directors' Duties provides further detail, as does Chapter 3. Concepts such as tone from the top and conduct and culture are as applicable to those governing investment management and other firms as they are to those running banks.

12.1.2   Required Functions

The required functions are so called because all regulated firms must have them – if applicable (i.e. only non-MiFID firms need a CF8 and only insurers will have the actuarial required functions).

12.1.2.1 CF8—Apportionment and Oversight function

The requirement to have a formal CF8 function holder, responsible for apportionment and oversight duties, applies only to non Solvency II insurance firms and firms conducting non-MiFID business. A firm is required to allocate to one or more individuals the function of:

- dealing with the apportionment of responsibilities, and
- overseeing the establishment and maintenance of systems and controls.

Responsibilities must be apportioned so that it is clear which directors and senior managers hold which duties, and also so that the business and affairs of the firm can be adequately monitored and controlled.

Generally, the CF8 will be a firm's chief executive, unless the firm is a member of a group in which case it will be the director or senior manager who is responsible for the overall management of the group, or a group division within which the regulatory activities are conducted.

12.1.2.2 Apportionment and oversight duties in MiFID firms

Although MiFID firms do not need a formal CF8, they are still bound by SYSC 4.3 obligations and are under a duty, when allocating functions internally, to ensure that senior personnel (i.e. those persons who effectively direct the business of the firm, which could include a firm's governing body and others) and the supervisory function (i.e. any function within a common platform firm that is responsible for the supervision of its senior personnel) are responsible for ensuring that the firm complies with its obligations under the regulatory system.

Specifically, senior personnel (and where appropriate the supervisory function, e.g. the audit committee), must "assess and periodically review the effectiveness of the policies, arrangements and procedures put in place to comply with the firm's obligations under the regulatory system and take appropriate measures to address any deficiencies".

Since approved persons can be held to account for behaviour that extends beyond the specific remit of their controlled function, those who are approved in a firm (even where a CF8 is not required) and who engage in apportionment and oversight, are liable to be held responsible under the approved persons regime for any failures in relation to this, should they occur.

The Statements of Principle also make this clear, in that Principle 5 requires that:

> "an approved person performing an accountable significant influence function must take reasonable steps to ensure that the business of the firm for which he is responsible in his accountable function is organised so that it can be controlled effectively".

Examples of a failure to comply with this, provided in the Code of Practice, includes a failure to take reasonable steps to apportion responsibilities, or to apportion responsibilities sufficiently clearly, for all areas of the business under the approved persons control, by, for example:

- implementing confusing or uncertain reporting lines;
- implementing confusing or uncertain authorisation levels; or
- implementing confusion or uncertain job descriptions and responsibilities.

12.1.2.3 *CF10 Compliance oversight function*

All regulated firms not within the SMR must have a CF10 compliance oversight function (firms in the SMR also have this function under a different name—the SMF 16). This is the function of acting in the capacity of a director or senior manager as detailed in SYSC 3.2.8 (insurers) and SYSC 6.1.4 (all other firms). Rules contained in SYSC 6.1.3 apply to common platform firms and management companies (and apply as "guidance" to other firms), and state the firms must (or should if not a common platform firm) maintain a permanent and effective compliance function which operates independently and which has the following responsibilities:

- to monitor and, on a regular basis, to assess the adequacy and effectiveness of the measures and procedures put in place in accordance with SYSC, and the actions taken to address any deficiencies in the firm's compliance with its obligations; and
- to advise and assist the relevant persons responsible for carrying out regulated activities to comply with the firm's obligations under the regulatory system.

"Relevant person" is widely defined as anyone employed by the firm, its tied agents or appointed representatives or who is engaged by the firm in an outsourcing arrangement.

SYSC 6.1.4 further provides that the compliance function must have (or should have):

- the necessary authority, resources, expertise and access to all relevant information;
- the people involved in the compliance functions must not be involved in the performance of services or activities they monitor;
- the method of determining the remuneration of the relevant persons involved in the compliance function must not compromise their objectivity and must not be likely to do so.

There are a number of points to note contained within these rules.

12.1.2.3.1 The duty of the compliance function is to monitor, and to advise and assist

The SYSC rules make it explicit that the duty of the compliance function is on the one hand to monitor compliance with requirements, and on the other to advise and assist the business. This indicates that it is the business itself which owns the risk of non-compliance, which it should seek to mitigate with the assistance of the compliance function. The compliance function is an advisory function, that occupies a supporting role.

Compliance needs to work closely with internal audit and risk if it is to ensure it has the requisite line of sight into all areas of the business.

12.1.2.3.2   Independence of the compliance function

The obligation on a firm to appoint a CF10 of sufficient standing and seniority needs to be balanced with the duty to have an independent compliance function. Although SYSC itself says that the CF10 function can be held by a director as well as a senior manager, it is questionable whether the CF10 should also be a CF1 Director who sits on the Board. This is because one of the most important and evolving functions of a firm's compliance team is to look at how well a firm's governing body executes its duties – from a number of different perspectives. For example, compliance may wish to advise and monitor how well a board challenge executive decisions, and other issues around the strength of corporate governance. It might be more difficult for a CF10 Compliance Officer to do this if he also occupied a seat at the Board table. There is of course the option of the CF10 reporting directly to the Board, and perhaps attending Board meetings as a non-voting member.

12.1.2.3.3   A non-independent compliance function in small firms

The requirement contained in SYSC 6.1.4(3) (that compliance staff must not be involved in the performance of services or activities they monitor), and in SYSC 6.1.4(4) (that the method of determining compliance staff's remuneration must not compromise their objectivity and must not be likely to do) are subject to a qualification, that means that common platform firms and management companies need not comply with them. If the firm is able to demonstrate that in the view of the nature, scale and complexity of its business, and the nature and range of financial services and activities it is engaged in, the requirements under those rules are not proportionate and that its compliance function continues to be effective, it need not comply (SYSC 6.1.5).

This rule enables small firms engaged in straightforward work to perhaps have a CF1 Director as the CF10 Compliance Oversight person too. If such a firm operates with a handful of staff if may not be practical to require it to employ dedicated compliance staff who do not do anything else. However, given the current regulatory environment, it is likely that very few firms will avail themselves of this qualification; the risk to a firm's business of not employing a dedicated compliance expert—either as the CF10 or to advise the CF10, may be viewed as greater than any potential saving to be gained from not employing such a person.

12.1.2.4   CF10a—CASS operational oversight function

Following on from a number of scandals involving the poor handling of client assets that came to light in 2010 and 2011 (the JP Morgan fine of £33 million being just one), the FSA created the CF10a function with effect from October 2011.

All CASS medium and large firms (see CASS 1A.2.7 for definitions) must have an individual approved for the CASS operational oversight function (CF10a), who will be a director or senior manager within the firm.

The CF10a role has responsibility for:

- overseeing the operational effectiveness of that firm's systems and controls that are designed to achieve compliance with CASS;
- reporting to the firm's governing body in respect of that oversight; and

- completing and submitting the Client Money and Asset Return (CMAR) to the FCA in accordance with the requirements contained in SUP 16.14.

CASS small firms do not need to apply for a CF10a but they must allocate a director or a senior manager performing a significant influence function the role of CASS operational oversight, who must:

- have oversight of the firm's operational compliance with CASS;
- report to the firm's governing body in respect of that oversight; and
- ensure their firm complies with its notification requirements under CASS 1A.

12.1.2.5 *CF11—Money Laundering Reporting Function*

All firms must appoint a CF11, who is responsible for the oversight of the firm's compliance with the FCA's rules on systems and controls against money laundering. The MLRO must have a level of authority and independence within the firm, and access to resources and information sufficient to enable him to carry out his responsibilities.

The duties of the MLRO are extensive and go beyond what is contained in the FCA handbook to other bits of legislation and guidance, including the Terrorism Act 2000, the Proceeds of Crime Act 2002 and the Money Laundering Regulations. Detailed requirements are found in the guidelines produced by the Joint Money Laundering Steering Group (JMLSG). Depending on the nature, scale and complexity of a firm's business, it might be appropriate for the CF10 also to perform the role of the CF11, although the more complex a firm the less likely this is to be a workable formula.

12.1.2.6   *The Systems and Controls Function (CF28)*

This function is that of acting in the capacity of an employee of the firm with responsibility for reporting to the governing body, or the audit committee (or its equivalent) in relation to the firm's:

- financial affairs (i.e. the chief financial officer)
- setting and controlling its risk exposure (i.e. the head of risk, head of operational risk, head of market risk etc)
- adherence to internal systems and controls, procedures and policies (i.e. the internal audit function).

The rules (found in SUP10A.8.1) do not state that the CF28 should be someone acting in the capacity of a director or senior manager, as they do for many of the required functions. Rather the CF28 can be an employee and therefore not necessarily as senior as some of the other significant influence function holders (although in practice such function holders are invariably senior people).

However, firms are expected to ensure that the employee has sufficient expertise and authority to perform the function effectively. FCA guidance in SUP provides that 'a director or senior manager would meet this expectation', whereupon the rules become somewhat circular; the regulators do not assume that the CF28 will be acting in the capacity of a director or senior manager but by the same token operate a presumption of competence where a director or senior manager is appointed. What this means is that firms who appoint a CF28 who is not a director or senior manager will have to take steps to assure themselves, and by extension the regulators, that the appointee has the requisite skills, experience and seniority.

12.1.2.6.1   Job roles likely to require approval as CF28

The CF28 function is not a required function and so is not mandatory. Some larger and more complex firms may have a number of individuals, performing different roles, approved as CF28 given that the description of this function is made up of three distinct strands. However many firms, at the smaller end of the spectrum, may not have anyone approved as CF28, because the staff who perform the equivalent functions are already approved as CF1 Directors, and dual approval would serve little additional purpose. How many approved persons to have, and the functions they ought to be approved for, will differ from firm to firm, and beyond the need to have a CF10 and at least two CF1s, firms can decide for themselves how to organise their governance taking into account its nature, scale and complexity.

12.1.2.7   *The Significant Management Function (CF29)*

Whether or not a firm has any people occupying the significant management function will depend on their nature, scale and complexity, and guidance in the Supervision Manual states that the FCA does not anticipate many firms requiring approval for this function. This is because in most firms those holding governing functions, required functions or the systems and controls function are likely to exercise all the significant influence at senior management level (SUP 10A.9.2). Therefore the head of a significant business unit who is already approved under one of the other controlled functions, is not also expected to be approved as a CF29. In reality only the largest, most complex firms will have CF29s. Many of these firms are also now likely to fall within the new SMR.

The significant management function is described as that of acting as a senior manager with significant responsibility for a significant business unit that, amongst other things, carries on designated investment business, effects contracts of insurance, makes material decisions on the commitment of a firm's financial resources and processes payments (SUP 10A.9.9).

Firms who engage in proprietary trading (and are still outside the SMR) are expected to assess all their proprietary traders in order to decide who should be approved as CF29. This is because proprietary traders have the ability to commit the firm and therefore have the potential to be able to exercise significant influence on the firm.

12.1.2.8   When is approval required to perform CF28 or CF29?

Where an individual is approved to perform a governing function (other than that of non- executive director) they will not require additional approval to perform the systems and controls function. This is because the FCA will already have approved the individual as a CF1 or CF3, for example, and thus will be satisfied as to their competence and capabilities.

Where an individual does not already hold governing function approval, an application must be made to become a CF28. However, where someone who holds a governing function wishes also to hold a required function (CF10 compliance oversight for example) specific additional approval must be obtained, in all cases from the FCA, as the FCA has jurisdiction over CF8, CF10, CF10a and CF11 for all firms.

Those in single regulated firms who wish to hold a significant management function, and who hold an FCA governing function, do not require specific additional approval to perform the significant management function (SUP10A.6.4). However, this does not apply to non executive directors, and directors of a corporate who are from a parent undertaking or holding company and their role is limited to this, which is logical given that it'd be unlikely for an NED to be appointed as a CF28 or CF29—ditto an employee of a parent—and if such a person were fielded the relevant regulator would wish to probe the matter further (SUP10A.6.4(2)).

12.2   The Customer Function

The customer function is the only one of the controlled functions that is not a "significant influence function" and therefore only Statements of Principle 1 to 4 apply. Many thousands of individuals are approved as CF30s since all those who deal with customers—both retail and professional—or their property in a way that is "regulated", need to hold this approval. The function does not apply to general insurance business.

The CF30 function is that of dealing with the customers of a regulated firm, or dealing with the property of the customers of a regulated firm, in a manner substantially connected with the carrying on of the regulated activity. Administrative and back office staff who deal with customers in a way that is not "substantially connected" with a regulated activity do not need to be approved as CF30s. Neither is approval required for staff who merely input customer instructions into an automatic execution system where no discretion is or may be exercised by that staff member. The activities of introducing a customer to a firm, and of distributing advertisements do not require approval as a CF30 (although the advertisements themselves will need to comply with the financial promotion rules).

Specifically, the function comprises:

- advising on investments (other than a non-investment insurance contract) and performing other functions related to this e.g. dealing and arranging deals, for both retail and professional clients;
- giving advice to clients (both retail and professional) solely in connection with corporate finance business (and performing other functions relating to this);
- giving advice to a person on becoming, continuing or ceasing to be a member of a Lloyd's syndicate;
- dealing as principal or agent, and arranging deals in investments (other than a non-investment insurance contract) with, for, or in connection with customers where the dealing or arranging deals is governed by COBS 11;
- acting as an investment manager and carrying on functions connected to this, for both retail and professional clients;
- acting as a "bidder's representative" in relation to bidding in emissions auctions (see the Auction Regulation).

12.2.1 Geographical scope of the function

Only business carried on by a firm from a UK office (or by a UK appointed representative) is covered by the requirement to ensure that those dealing with customers are approved to do so.

Where the person who is giving advice or dealing in investments on behalf of a UK customer is based overseas, he need not be approved as long as he spends no more than 30 days in the UK in any 12-month period, and he must be supervised by someone who holds the requisite approval (SUP 10A.10.8). FCA guidance states that where this individual visits a UK customer he should be accompanied. Various other provisions deal with the application of the training and competence requirements to staff based oversees—see SUP10A.10.9.

12.2.2 The competent employees rule

The competent employees rule is found in SYSC 3.1.6 (non common platform firms) and SYSC 5.1.1 (common platform firms) and states that "A firm must employ personnel with the skills, knowledge and expertise necessary for the discharge of the responsibilities allocated to them."

For those CF30s working with retail clients or customers, the competent employees rule is supplemented by the requirements contained in the Training and Competence Sourcebook (TC).

TC does not apply to CF30s working with professional clients. However, those working in the wholesale rather than the retail sphere are still obliged to meet the competent employees rule, although they have more flexibility in how they do this compared to those working with retail clients. SYSC states that firms which are carrying on activities that are not subject to TC may nevertheless wish to take TC into account in complying with the training and competence requirements in SYSC.

In practice, many CF30s working with professional clients and in a non-retail environment will have passed recognised industry exams; this is because the passing of such an exam is the most straightforward way for the firm to assure both itself, and the regulator, that the employees who are approved to deal with customer or firm property are competent to do so. However, a firm is at liberty to devise other methods of ensuring and then assessing competence where retail clients are not being dealt with.

It should also be remembered that all CF30s need to be compliant on a continuing basis with the Statements of Principle, one of which is observing a proper standard of market conduct. Staff, both in the retail and wholesale spheres, will need training on what a proper standard of market conduct is, and on becoming familiar with the provisions in the Code of Market Conduct (MAR). The risk to a firm and to CF30s individually from failing to understand and appreciate the need to comply with MAR are great and may include criminal sanctions where manipulation, insider dealing or money laundering occur.

12.2.3 *Training and competence Requirements for the Customer Function engaged in retail activities*

As stated above, TC only applies to individuals who engage in retail activities (see TC App 1.1 for full details of application)— i.e. carry on designated investment business for a retail client, or non-investment insurance business carried on for a consumer, regulated mortgage activity and reversion activity carried on for a customer. It should be noted that not everyone who falls within the remit of the requirements contained in TC needs to be approved as a CF30 (for example TC applies to those advising on non investment insurance contracts, but these staff do not need to be approved as CF30s).

Twenty activities fall within the scope of TC (TC App 1.1), of which 18 have specific appropriate qualification requirements, a list of which can be found in TC App 4.1.

12.2.4 Retail investment advisors and the Retail Distribution Review

New qualification requirements for those CF 30s wishing to give retail investment advice came into force on 31st December 2012, as a result of a wide ranging review of standards conducted as part of the FSA's Retail Distribution Review. Advisers who already hold qualifications that fall within TC App 4 have to engage in a gap fill analysis to ensure that they have the requisite level of skill required by the FSA (now FCA), rather than sitting additional exams. More about these 'professionalism requirements' can be read in TC App 7.

The attempt to increase the professionalism of those working in retail investment advice is part of the overall drive by the conduct regulator to put the fair treatment of the consumer, and consumer protection, at the heart of its work. More can be read about the RDR on the FCA website.

12.2.5 Ethics as a component of competence in both a retail and wholesale environment

In TC, it is stated that competence means having the skills, knowledge and expertise needed to discharge the responsibilities of an employee's role, and that this includes achieving a good standard of ethical behaviour. Although TC doesn't apply to non retail CF30s, firms employing these staff would be well advised to follow the course set by it. High ethical standards are part and parcel of the competent employees rule.

For retail investment advisors falling within the remit of the RDR, there is a requirement to join a recognised professional body and to obtain from them a 'Statement of Professional Standing'; a component of this is an agreement to adhere to that body's ethical code of conduct, as well as certifying adherence to the Statements of Principle and Code of Practice for Approved Persons (APER). These requirements will help the CF30s to understand and take seriously their ethical responsibilities, and that is part of their intention.

However, for CF30s not caught by the RDR, and CF30s not working in retail, the firm itself needs to work out how to ensure appropriate ethical standards are met. At the most basic level, a firm will need to ensure that the CF30s are familiar with APER and understand its ramifications. Beyond this, most firms will have some sort of code of conduct that staff must follow, but the relevance of this to specific job roles may not be clear, and firms may wish to consider drafting clear ethical standards for different populations.

Ethics is high up on the agenda for the regulators, and forms part of the culture of an organisation. The culture in financial services firms is something the regulators are constantly emphasising as being critical to compliant operations. The catalogue of unethical behaviour seen in recent years means that the regulatory beam is focused on ethical and cultural issues, and firms need to respond accordingly.

12.2.6 *Assessment of competence*

TC 2.1 provides that a firm must assess the competence of its staff but that this need not be done prior to them taking up their post. However, where a role has a qualification requirement attached to it, the staff member is not permitted to start in post until he has passed the regulatory module (although he can pass the other module(s) at a later date). The exception to this is where the activity is one of the following – all of which are complex in nature – in which case all parts of the appropriate qualification must have been passed prior to the employee starting that job:

1) Advising on and dealing in securities which are not stakeholder pension schemes, personal pension schemes or broker funds;
2) Advising on and dealing in derivatives;
3) The activity of a broker fund adviser;
4) Advising on syndicate participation at Lloyd's; or
5) The activity of a pension transfer specialist.

An exception exists to the examination requirements for someone who is advising retail clients on retail investment products, or engaging in activities 3, 4 and 5 above, whereby only the regulatory module needs to be passed prior to the activity being done. This is where the staff member has at least three years' up-to-date relevant experience in the activity in question obtained while employed outside the UK and has not previously been required to comply fully with the relevant qualification requirements. The exception enables appropriately skilled foreign workers to work in the UK without having to take additional exams, apart from a regulatory exam.

For CF30s who are not caught by TC—i.e. those not working in a retail environment, it is for the firm to decide how and when to assess their competence. In order to avoid too much people risk, many wholesale firms may require their CF30s to at the very least pass a test on the UK regulatory environment before being let loose on the property of the firm or its clients. The FCA itself suggests that these firms may wish to adopt the model that is mandatory for retail firms as outlined in TC. The benefit of this is that the firm need not reinvent the wheel and can utilise the numerous professional courses and qualifications that are available in the marketplace. The benefit for CF30 staff themselves in sitting recognised exams is that it may make it easier for them to move from firm to firm, and to evidence their level of skill and competence. On the flip side, some wholesale firms may wish to run their own qualification and assessment programmes, and they are at liberty to do this, resource permitting. This might be an attractive model for an international firm that wishes to have uniform global standards of competence and therefore devises its own training and assessment programmes.

12.2.7 Supervision of CF30s in the retail sphere

A firm must ensure that all staff carrying out activities outlined in TC App 1.1 are appropriately supervised by someone who has the necessary coaching and assessment skills as well as technical knowledge and experience to act as a competent supervisor and assessor. There is no formal requirement that the supervisor has passed the exams that the staff member will need to pass in order to be adjudged competent; but a firm ought to consider the degree to which they can act as a supervisor without having passed the requisite exam.

The amount and type of supervision required will depend on the experience and skills of the employee, and whether they have been signed off as 'competent'. The FCA requires a firm to have clear criteria and procedures relating to the specific point at which the employee is assessed as competent in order to be able to demonstrate when and why a reduced level of supervision may be considered appropriate.

12.3 Statements of Principle and Code of Practice for Approved Persons (APER)

The Statements of Principle and Code of Practice section of the FCA handbook (APER) applies to approved persons who are not within 'relevant authorised persons' (i.e. banks within the SMR), or Solvency II insurance firms, and appointed representatives. APER applies to appointed representatives (rather than COCON) even where their principal is a relevant authorised person or Solvency II firm.

The Statements of Principle are as follows:

1) An approved person must act with integrity in carrying out his accountable functions
2) An approved person must act with due skill, care and diligence in carrying out his accountable functions
3) An approved person must observe proper standards of market conduct in carrying out his accountable functions
4) An approved person must deal with the FCA, the PRA and other regulators in an open and cooperative way and must disclose appropriately any information of which the FCA or the PRA would reasonably expect notice.
5) An approved person performing an accountable significant-influence function must take reasonable steps to ensure that the business of the firm for which he is

responsible in his accountable function is organised so that it can be controlled effectively

6) An approved person performing an accountable significant-influence function must exercise due skill, care and diligence in managing the business of the firm for which he is responsible in his accountable function.

7) An approved person performing an accountable significant-influence function must take reasonable steps to ensure that the business of the firm for which he is responsible in his accountable function complies with the relevant requirements and standards of the regulatory system.

Statements of Principle 1 to 4 apply to all approved persons; Statements of Principle 5 to 7 apply only to approved persons performing a significant influence function, who have additional obligations and responsibilities under the system.

12.3.1 What can Approved Persons be held responsible for?

The Statements of Principle and Code of Practice use the phrase "accountable function". An accountable function encompasses the controlled functions, and in addition encompasses "any other functions in relation to the carrying on of a regulated activity" (in the FCA definition). So an approved person can be held responsible by the FCA not only for activities within their strict remit as a controlled function holder, but for any other function they perform in the firm, that's connected to the carrying on of a regulated activity. Arguably the majority of activities in a regulated firm can be said to be "connected" to that carrying on.

The duties of those performing governing functions are substantial. The FCA has stated that it intends to hold more individuals to account where firms fail to meet their regulatory obligations. Liability of an approved person will only arise where they have failed to take "reasonable steps" to execute their duties as described in the Statements of Principle above. What is "reasonable" in a particular case will depend on the circumstances. Guidance at APER 3.1.4.4A (G) (1) builds upon this, and provides that an approved person will only be in breach of a Statement of Principle where he is personally culpable. Personal culpability arises where an approved person's conduct was deliberate or where the approved person's standard of conduct was below that which would be reasonable in all the circumstances. Two contrasting enforcement actions taken by the FSA in 2012 against those holding governing functions illustrate that what is reasonable will depend on the matter in hand.

The facts of Pottage (Chief Executive at UBS at the relevant time) and Kumagai (former Chief Executive of Mitsui Sumitomo Insurance Company (Europe) Ltd), are well known. In both cases, with varying degrees of success, the FSA sought to argue that the duties and responsibilities of the Chief Executives were wide ranging and that they should be held to account for failings discovered in their respective firms. Pottage beat the FSA at Tribunal, whereas Kumagai accepted his fine. The main difference between the actions of the men appears to have been one of timing; Pottage acted in a timely fashion to address failure when it was identified (and so took "reasonable steps"), whereas Kumagai did not.

In an ideal world, chief executives and directors will identify risks and take steps to mitigate them well in advance of them coming to fruition. However, where this has not been possible, it is important that timely action is taken following the identification of an issue. Further, waiting for a colleague to take action in the belief that it is within their area of remit, may not suffice as a defence for a chief executive or director, given the fact that they can be held responsible for failure to act in relation to almost any matter connected to the carrying on of a regulated activity. Arguably, those holding governing functions could be held responsible for all instances of non compliance within their firm, where they were in a position to identify and mitigate these, because the buck stops with them.

APER (3.3.1 and 3.3.2) provides then when considering compliance with Statements of Principle 5 to 7, the FCA will consider whether the approved person:

- exercised reasonable care when considering the information available to him;
- reached a reasonable conclusion which he acted on;
- the nature, scale and complexity of the firm's business;
- his role and responsibility as an approved person performing an accountable significant-influence function;
- the knowledge he had, or should have had, of regulatory concerns, if any, arising in the business under his control.

These are questions that those holding significant influence functions could be asking themselves in relation to their job performance on a regular basis. They also highlight how important it is for decision makers to record the rationale behind the decisions that they make. An approach to an area of the business which subsequently goes awry may not lead to regulatory sanction where the responsible approved person can provide evidence of his careful consideration of all relevant matters that led him to making that decision, and that it was reasonable in all the circumstances at that time.

12.3.1.1 *Knowledge of the Business and Delegation*

Statement of Principle 6 of the Statements of Principle for Approved Persons deals with knowledge of the business and delegation. Although a chief executive or director bears a large amount of responsibility for what goes on within a firm, they must be able to effectively delegate if they are to perform their job efficiently and effectively and the regulators allow for this.

Guidance at APER 4.6.11 provides that the extent to which an approved person performing a significant influence function will manage the business on a day to day basis himself will depend on its nature, scale and complexity, and his position within it. In a large, complex firm, the approved person must take reasonable steps to ensure that systems are in place which result in issues being addressed at the appropriate level. When issues come to his attention, he should deal with them in an appropriate way. The approved person must be satisfied that he will be informed when issues that ought to require his attention come about; key to this will be having trusted and skilled staff among whom the approved person can delegate various tasks.

The Code of Practice for Approved Persons provides examples of the sorts of behaviour that the regulator would regard as falling foul of the statements of principle. Examples of poor behaviour in relation to Principle 6 and more specifically, delegation, are where the approved person:

- fails to take reasonable steps to maintain an appropriate level of understanding about an issue or part of the business that he has delegated to an individual or individuals (whether in-house or outside contractors) falls within;
- delegates the authority for dealing with an issue or a part of the business to an individual or individuals (whether in-house or outside contractors) without reasonable grounds for believing that the delegate had the necessary capacity, competence, knowledge, seniority or skill to deal with the issue or to take authority for dealing; or
- disregards an issue or part of the business once it has been delegated, and fails to get reports on the delegation.

Examples of an approved person not knowing enough about the business are given as when he:

- fails to take reasonable steps to adequately inform himself about the affairs of the business for which he is responsible
- permits transactions without a sufficient understanding of the risks involved;
- permits expansion of the business without reasonably assessing the potential risks of that expansion;
- inadequately monitors highly profitable transactions or business practices or unusual transactions or business practices;
- accepts implausible or unsatisfactory explanations from subordinates without testing the veracity of those explanations;

- fails to obtain independent, expert opinion where appropriate.

12.3.1.2 *Ensuring the business complies with the relevant requirements and standards of the regulatory system –Statement of Principle 7*

Statement of Principle 7 is wide ranging, mainly because the regulatory requirements themselves are now so extensive. Not only do approved persons need to ensure that the letter of the law is complied with, but also that more subjective and difficult to measure matters are effectively handled, for example, establishing that the firm treats its customers fairly, or has a business model that does not pose a threat to the sound functioning of the markets. These high level objectives are the responsibility of the governing functions, rather than those lower down the chain of command.

Examples of non compliance with this principle given in the Code of Practice are where the approved person:

- fails to take reasonable steps adequately to inform himself about the reason why significant breaches have happened
- fails to take reasonable steps to monitor (either personally or through a compliance department or other departments) compliance with the relevant requirements and standards of the regulatory system
- fails to take reasonable steps to implement (either personally or through a compliance department or other departments) adequate and appropriate systems of control to comply with the relevant requirements and standards

Further guidance provides that when the approved person becomes aware of breaches they should be dealt with in a timely and appropriate manner. Also, the approved person is not expect to personally put in place the systems and controls the business requires, but rather to ensure that areas he is responsible for have operating procedures and systems which include well defined steps for complying with the detail of relevant requirements, and for ensuring that the business is run prudently. (APER 4.7.4). Where expert external advice has been given and recommendations made, these should be implemented unless there are good reasons not to do so.

Index

This index has been prepared using Sweet and Maxwell's Legal Taxonomy. Main index entries conform to keywords provided by the Legal Taxonomy except where references to specific documents or non-standard terms (denoted by quotation marks) have been included. These keywords provide a means of identifying similar concepts in other Sweet and Maxwell publications and online services to which keywords from the Legal Taxonomy have been applied. Readers may find some minor differences between terms used in the text and those which appear in the index. Suggestions to *sweetandmaxwell.taxonomy@thomson.com*.